Ethnic Issues in Adolescent Mental Health

Ethnic Issues in Adolescent Mental Health

EDITED BY

Arlene Rubin Stiffman
Larry E. Davis

SAGE PUBLICATIONS
The International Professional Publishers
Newbury Park London New Delhi

For information address:

SAGE Publications, Inc.
2455 Teller Road
Newbury Park, California 91320

SAGE Publications Ltd.
6 Bonhill Street
London EC2A 4PU
United Kingdom

SAGE Publications India Pvt. Ltd.
M-32 Market
Greater Kailash I
New Delhi 110 048 India

Printed in the United States of America

Library of Congress Cataloging-in-Publication Data

Main entry under title:

Ethnic issues in adolescent mental health / Arlene Rubin Stiffman and
  Larry E. Davis, editors.
     p. cm.
  Includes bibliographical references.
  ISBN 0-8039-3984-1. — ISBN 0-8039-3985-X (pbk.)
  1. Minority teenagers—Mental health—United States. 2. Minority
teenagers—United States—Sexual behavior. I. Stiffman, Arlene
Rubin, 1941-   . II. Davis, Larry E.
RJ503.E84   1990
362.2'0835—dc20   90-8735
                                                                       CIP

FIRST PRINTING, 1990

Sage Production Editor: Diane S. Foster

Contents

Preface

ARLENE RUBIN STIFFMAN
LARRY E. DAVIS

The chapters in this volume attempt to illuminate the effects of ethnicity on adolescent mental health. The volume is divided into five sections. Each section covers a specific mental health problem, and the chapters within each section focus on different ethnic groups.

A dual set of issues drives this volume: the importance of adolescent mental health in contributing to adult well-being, and the necessity of understanding ethnicity in studying and treating mental health problems. The first issue is based on an awareness that untreated adolescent mental health problems may be placing an entire segment of our population at risk during the rest of their lives. Our knowledge of adolescence has led us to understand that adolescence is not a discontinuous part of the life cycle. Problems during adolescence may often continue into adulthood, keeping the adults from finding personal satisfaction and contributing as productive citizens, and keeping them from effectively rearing the next generation. The continuity in problems from adolescence to adulthood raises particular concerns about the future of minority youths. We know that certain mental health problems disproportionately affect minority youths. Therefore the future functioning of individuals from various ethnic minorities may depend on successful intervention for mental health problems experienced during adolescence.

The second issue arises from the need for effective intervention to ensure the future welfare of minorities. Specifically, it concerns the provision of services to various ethnic groups. For years, service providers have noticed and reported varying effects from similar services provided to different ethnic groups. Yet the study of ethnic effects on mental health is a relatively new field. Sometimes the design of the service was not acceptable to all groups, sometimes it was the service provider, sometimes the method of treatment, sometimes the definition of what constituted a problem, and sometimes even what constituted improvement. However, providing a service that will be effective in helping populations from all strata is a necessity. To do that we must understand the ethnic differences that determine the incidence and prevalence of problems, help seeking, and reaction to services. This volume attempts to gather and present the most current information about ethnic issues in adolescent mental health. This accumulation of knowledge can then serve as a first step toward developing effective interventions that will help adolescents grow into healthy and productive adults.

General Mental Health Issues

The first section of this volume presents four chapters that explore ethnic issues in broad ranges of mental health problems. Jewelle Taylor Gibbs, in "Mental Health of Black Adolescents" focuses on one of the most vulnerable and victimized groups in American society. This chapter describes their mental health issues and problems, and discusses sociocultural factors that influence assessment, diagnosis, and treatment. As such, this article provides a starting point for the other chapters in this book, which also discuss aspects of mental health, psychosocial problems, and assessment of individuals.

The second chapter in this section, by Jean S. Phinney, Bruce Lochner, and Rodolfo Murphy, entitled "Ethnic Identity Development and Psychological Adjustment in Adolescence" discusses the contribution of minority group membership to the identity formation of American Indian youths.

John M. Chavez and Collette E. Roney, in the third chapter, "Psychocultural Factors Affecting the Mental Health Status of Mexican American Adolescents," discuss the effect of acculturation on a variety of mental health problems. The authors present two contrasting concepts: cultural integration and deculturation.

In contrast to the preceding chapters that focus on negative stereotypes, William T. Liu, Elena Yu, Ching-Fu Chang, and Marilyn Fernandez, in "The Mental Health of Asian American Teenagers: A Research Challenge," highlight the consequences of positive stereotyping. Such positive stereotyping makes Asian youths conclude they are scapegoats, trivializes their problems, enhances blaming of less successful groups rather than society, and overlooks the diversity of Asian American demographics.

Antisocial Behavior/Violence/Delinquency

The second section of this volume concerns the issues of violence within the lives of youths and their antisocial behavior. The first chapter of this section focuses on environmental violence. Nora Gustavsson and Pallassana R. Balgopal, in "Violence and Minority Youth: An Ecological Perspective," illustrate the impact of racism and capitalism on minority youths. Minority youths, these authors argue, experience daily violence ranging on a continuum from physical blows to psychological attacks on their self-esteem at home, in their neighborhood, and in school.

The second chapter in this section explores causes and correlates of minority youths' antisocial behavior. Cheryl L. Thompson asserts convincingly, in her article "In Pursuit of Affirmation: The Antisocial Inner-City Adolescent," that juvenile crime results from a coalescence of discrimination, poverty, and wounded narcissism.

The last chapter in this section concentrates on Hispanic youths. Orlando Rodriquez and Luis Zayez, in "Hispanic Adolescents and Antisocial Behavior: Sociocultural Factors and Treatment Implications," contrasts our knowledge of Hispanic adolescents' high risk for many problems with our paucity of data, correlates, causes, or cures.

Sexuality

The chapters in this section focus on ethnic issues in adolescent sexual behavior, pregnancy, and parenting. The disproportionate focus on the black community in the news, politics, research, and literature is reflected by these chapters in their focus on black youths. The chapters move in chronological progression from sexual behavior through parenting and from microsystem to macrosystem.

The first chapter, by Algea Harrison, entitled "High Risk Sexual Behavior Among Black Adolescents," presents demographic information indicative of the involvement of black adolescents in high risk sexual behavior; conceptual explanations for that behavior, and a review of society's response to the social problems that emerge from that behavior.

In the next chapter, "Social Support and Teen Pregnancy in the Inner City," Brenda G. McGowan and Amy Kohn highlight the discussion of conceptual explanations for sexual behavior by contrasting the decline in teen births with the rise in unwed pregnancy. They concentrate on the role of social support in mediating the negative consequences of teen parenting.

Sandra Y. Lewis, in "Black Teens Parenting in the Inner City: Problems and Recommendations," forcefully moves us to a discussion of teen parenting and its effects on the parent and child who live in an inner city. The point is poignantly made that the harsh realities of life for black teen mothers in the inner city dim their hopes and dreams for marriage, stability, and health.

This section's final chapter concludes with policy implications. William Marsiglio and John H. Scanzoni, in "Pregnant and Parenting Black Adolescents: Theoretical and Policy Perspectives," review and assess recent research, social interventions, theory, and policy that deal with repeat pregnancies among black adolescents.

Substances: Use and Abuse

The section on substance use and abuse contains chapters that discuss both licit and illicit substance use. The first chapter concerns alcohol use in terms of broad ethnic issues. Edith M. Freeman, in "Social Competence as a Framework for Addressing

Ethnicity and Teenage Alcohol Problems," discusses social competence and alcohol use. The chapter concludes with an exploratory study of the treatment of adolescent substance abusers, and a discussion of the implications for further treatment and evaluation of competence in clients.

The remaining three chapters in this section concern illicit drug use. The first of the three covers minority issues in general, the second and third specifically address American Indians and Hispanics, respectively.

Ura Jean Oyemade and Valora Washington, in their chapter entitled "The Role of Family Factors in the Primary Prevention of Substance Abuse Among High Risk Black Youth," discuss physiological, psychodynamic, and environmental factors that affect drug abuse. They argue for an ecological approach to developing models for preventive intervention.

E. Daniel Edwards and Margie Egbert-Edwards, in "American Indian Adolescents: Combating Problems of Substance Use and Abuse Through a Community Model," discuss substance use problems and the need for community-based prevention programs. This chapter presents examples of present programs that fit this model, and discusses some of the difficulties in launching such programs.

The final chapter of this section focuses on Hispanics' illicit substance usage, and highlights problems inherent in preventing and treating drug abuse. Melvin Delgado, in his thoughtful discussion "Hispanic Adolescents and Substance Abuse: Implications for Research, Treatment, and Prevention," presents a demographic profile of Hispanics. He reviews the literature on Hispanic teen substance abuse, discusses the emerging characteristics of high risk Hispanic youths and presents research, treatment methods, and recommendations for prevention.

Suicide

The final section of this volume presents two chapters: one contrasting suicidal behavior in several different minority groups and one focusing on black youths. Karen F. Wyche and Mary Jane Rotheram-Borus, in "Suicidal Behavior Among Minority Youth in the United States," discuss suicide rates for several ethnic groups in relationship to the possible effects of different cultural norms. They close by offering suggestions for ways in which a white therapist might acquire increased sensitivity.

The final chapter of this volume includes a discussion of economics, urbanization, drug abuse, and family problems with a special concern for how those factors explain the rise in youths' suicide rates. Essie Manuel Rutledge, in "Suicide Among Black Adolescents and Youth Adults: A Rising Problem," does an excellent job examining and analyzing suicide trends among black adolescents and young adults.

Conclusion

The collection of chapters presented in this volume is designed to raise the reader's awareness of the extent of problems in various ethnic groups, ethnic-related causes of problems and barriers to treatment, and possible interventions. The two repeated themes are the effect of social and environmental conditions as causes of mental health problems and the necessity for understanding ethnic values and attitudes in developing appropriate helping strategies. It is the editors' hope that the content of these chapters will stimulate further discussion, thought, interventions, research, and understanding.

Introduction

LARRY E. DAVIS
ARLENE RUBIN STIFFMAN

For minority youths of color, the 1990s have the potential to be both the best and worst of times. It can be a time of tremendous growth and advancement. Many will have the chance to benefit from the civil, social, economic, and political opportunities created in the 1960s, 1970s, and 1980s. And, because their numbers have increased relative to that of white youth, their labor and societal contributions will be sorely needed. Indeed, in the immediate years to come many minority youth will be afforded opportunities not only to participate in America's future but to be leaders and architects of that future.

Despite these positive signs for the future opportunities of many minority youths, many others are clearly in danger of experiencing mental health problems and being left without a future. They are faced with being classified as mentally disabled and relegated to a future devoid of an opportunity to participate as productive citizens in our society. They subsequently risk being part of a generation of lost youth for whom society will have little need, and for whom little will be done.

America's minority youth are clearly a population at risk, as is apparent from the titles of the chapters in this volume. The problems of identity formation, acculturation, education, antisocial behavior, sexuality, substance abuse, and suicide are afflicting disproportionately the mental health, and hence the life chances, of minority youth.

So What?

Why should our society concern itself with the mental health status of these youths of color? Why should mental health professionals be encouraged to pay attention to these youth who often seem so unimportant to the overall well-being of the country? Indeed minority youths are most often portrayed in our news media as more of a national liability than a national resource. Why devote an entire volume to problems pertinent to their mental health? Why invest our time and energies working with these youth who seem to have so little to contribute to society?

It is estimated that by the middle 1990s, 30% of all American youths will be minority youths. Specifically it is estimated that by then 4.5% of youth will be Native American and Asian and Pacific Islander, 12% will be Hispanic, and 15% will be African American (Wetzel, 1989). In a number of our major cities minority youth already comprise the majority of the youth population. And by the end of this century their numbers will have increased further still. Hence, in the future, when we speak of youths we will be increasingly referring to minority youths of color.

In light of our society's changing racial demographics, minority adolescents will increasingly become those whom our society must teach, train, and employ. And, in turn, they will soon be those to whom we, as a society, will look to provide services, employment, and future leadership.

In fact, due to the changing racial demographics of minority youth, the Department of Labor has stated that minority youth will have to fill 56% of the new jobs that will become available between now and the year 2000 (New York Times, September 25, 1989). However, the employment picture of black and Hispanic male youths (the two largest groups of minority youth) has become bleak, resulting in a drop in their earnings of 30% to 50% since 1973 (Children's Defense Fund, 1987). The absence of employment for minority youths is particularly damaging to their development of productive skills and work habits and to their subsequent positive self-conceptions as workers.

College enrollments, as well as employment, for minority youth have steadily decreased since the 1970's (Jaynes & Williams, 1989). This is at a time when most jobs in the future, even more so than in the past, will require at least some college or technical training. Minority males, in particular, are rapidly joining the ranks of what it is now in vogue to refer to as America's "underclass."

Clearly a crisis exists for minority youth. They are, however, unlikely to experience this crisis alone. Indeed, if a large segment of our youthful population becomes socially and economically disenfranchised, it is bound to have onerous implications for all of society. And yet, only rarely have those other than social scientists recognized the seriousness of our current situation. One such exception was a recent statement made in the New York Times (September 25, 1989) by the former chairman of Proctor and Gamble, Mr. Brad Butler: "If we continue to let children who are born into poverty fail to get the kind of education that will allow them to participate in our economy productively . . . [t]hen some time in the 21st century this nation will cease to be a peaceful prosperous democracy." Mr. Butler did not provide us with any particular scenario outlining the end of our society as we know it. However, he is forewarning us that those who are "left out" of our society are unlikely to sit by and let the rest of use peacefully enjoy it.

Many Americans already harbor images of minority youth that are quite negative. Both art and literature are beginning to reflect this image. Of note, Tom Wolfe, author of the best selling book *The Bonfire of the Vanities*, asserts in his novel that the greatest fear for many of us is to be met on the street at night by a black youth wearing tennis shoes (Wolfe, 1987). This fearful image of minority youth is not held solely by whites, as some might be inclined to believe, but by other members of the minority groups as well. In fact, because of their close proximity, members of the minority community are apt to experience the greatest fear of these youths, many of whom have come to perceive themselves as the larger society often perceives them: mentally and socially inferior with little to offer, and nothing to lose.

Making the Connection

As mental health professionals we must make the connection between what we so often view as the absence of mental health for minority youth and the social perils that so often characterize these youth. We must more clearly point out the impossibility of sustaining mental health in environments that promote and sustain pathology. In short, we must begin to make the connection between the myriad of social problems experienced by youths of color and the frequently deleterious effects to their mental health.

What We Must Know

It should by now be painfully clear to everyone, that seeking to improve the mental health of minority youths requires an ecological perspective. As one of the contributors to this volume has noted elsewhere, "Life does not take place in a vacuum" (Balgopal & Vassil, 1983, p. 19). In short, if we as mental health professionals are to have any meaningful effect on the mental health of minority youths we must include in our conceptualization not just their intrapsychic dynamics. Instead we must also consider, as part of our preventative and remediation efforts, their racial and cultural contexts. In other words, we must become more cognizant of the connection between the state of their mental health and the harsh social realities to which they are frequently exposed.

As is suggested by the authors in the pages to follow, the life experiences of minority youth often differ dramatically from those of most white youth. Unquestionably, those who will be effective in their attempts to help minority youth establish and sustain positive mental health must first acknowledge the significance that color, culture, and race play in the lives of these young people. More often than not, these factors place them at an extreme disadvantage to other youth in our society. Failure to recognize this most basic fact all but assures the failure of workers' interventive efforts. Minority youth often see and experience realities that are so disparate from those of white middle-class youth as to make comparisons between the two spurious at best and invidious at worst. Significant numbers of minority youth are experiencing not the American dream, but an American nightmare. Such realities as drug wars, drive-by shooting, gang violence, and street murders point out most dramatically the validity of this fact. Actually many of these youths have been witness to extreme deprivation and violence with its accompanying psychological distress. Having undergone such experiences should automatically warrant many of these youths being classified as victims of post-traumatic stress.

What We Must Do

We must intervene in the social and environmental networks that affect these youths of color. If our professional interventions are to be effective they must assist minority youths in answering a few very basic questions: Why? Why, do I need concern myself with obtaining or sustaining my mental health? Will I need it to perform some job? Will I need it in my role as a parent? Will I need it to assist my community to be a place where I or others like me want to live? Failing in our interventive efforts to offer assistance at answering questions such as these speaks poorly of our efforts, and of our probabilities of being successful with these youths.

Thus in addition to our normal therapeutic efforts, we must take other steps. In short, our efforts to adequately address the mental health problems of minority youth must acknowledge that these youth, because of their color and culture, will need interventions that are sensitive to their social realities and to the lower quality of life experiences so frequently afforded them. This volume strives toward this goal. The reader will find that most chapters in this volume address only one minority group and one form of social problem. Even so, because of the variety of minority groups and nature of topics addressed, the volume as a whole offers those who are concerned with the mental health of minority youth a wealth of useful suggestions, strategies, and insights.

References

Balgopal, P., & Vassil, T. (1983). *Groups in social work: An ecological perspective.* New York: Macmillan.

Children's Defense Funds (May, 1987). *Declining earnings of young men: Their relation to poverty, teen pregnancy, and family formation.* Washington, DC: Children's Defense Fund Adolescent Pregnancy Prevention Clearing House.

Jaynes, G., & Williams, R. (Eds.). (1989). *A common destiny: Blacks and American society.* Washington, DC: National Academy Press.

New York Times. (1989, September 25). Impending U.S. jobs disaster: Work force unqualified to work. (Article written by Edward B. Fiske.)

Wetzel, J. (1989). *American youth: A statistical snapshot.* Washington, DC: Youth and America's Future: The William T. Grant Commission on Work, Family, and Citizenship.

Wolfe, T. (1987). *The bonfires of the vanities.* New York: Farrar, Straus.

PART 1

General Mental Health Issues

1

Mental Health Issues of Black Adolescents: Implications for Policy and Practice

JEWELLE TAYLOR GIBBS

Mental Health of Black Adolescents

Black adolescents occupy an unenviable position as one of the most vulnerable and victimized groups in American society. As the largest group of minority youth, they frequently have been misdiagnosed by the mental health system, mislabeled by the educational system, mishandled by the juvenile justice system, and mistreated by the social welfare system. As we enter the last decade of the 20th century, the problems of black youth have become so severe that they have been called an "endangered species" (Gibbs, 1984, 1988b) and a population "at risk" for social and psychological dysfunction (Children's Defense Fund, 1987; Myers & King, 1983;).

Generations of discrimination, prejudice, and economic deprivation have contributed to high rates of psychological and behavioral disorders as well as a number of problematic psychosocial behaviors among black youth, with a disproportionate impact on those from low-income families. It is a tribute to the resiliency and adaptability of the black family that the majority of these youth develop

21

into competent and well-functioning adults (Looney & Lewis, 1983).

This chapter has the following goals: (a) to describe the mental health issues and problems of black adolescents, (b) to discuss the sociocultural factors that influence the assessment, diagnosis, and treatment of these youth, and (c) to discuss the implications for policies of prevention and strategies of intervention to promote positive mental health for these youth. This chapter will focus on black youth in the 13-21 year age group, viewing adolescence as a stage extending from the entry into junior high school through the end of the college years.[1] For the purpose of this chapter, "black" will refer primarily to non-Hispanic blacks who are also identified as African-American or Afro-American.

The mental health issues of black youth must be viewed in the context of the historical, social, economic, and political factors that have shaped their experiences in American society. Knowledge of these factors will facilitate an understanding of the values, attitudes, and behaviors that black youth have developed as adaptive responses to their social environment. Moreover, "mental health" is defined in its broadest sense to encompass psychosocial, behavioral, and intrapsychic dimensions as measures of adaptation and dysfunction for black youth.

Demographic Information

In 1986, there were approximately 5 million black youth in the 13- to 21-year-old age range, with 2,591,000 in the 10-14 year old age range, 2,785,000 in the 15- to 19-year-old category, and 2,813,000 in the 20- to 24-year-old category (U.S. Census Bureau, 1987b). In this age range the ratio of males to females is about equal, although females begin to outnumber males in the 20-24 age group. With a median age of 26.9 compared to a white median age of 32.7, blacks are a relatively youthful population, a fact that has significant implications for mental health problems, programs, and services in the black community (U.S. Census Bureau, 1987b).

In 1987, nearly one third of all black families were classified below the poverty line (U.S. Census Bureau, 1987a). However, over half of black families with children under 18 were female-headed and two thirds of these families had incomes below the official poverty line. Thus nearly half of all black youth under the age of 18 are born into poverty and will spend up to 20 years of their lives in poverty (American Public Welfare Association, 1986). Black youth in female-headed families were five times more likely to be welfare-dependent than those in intact families.

Even when these youth are reared in stable two-parent families, their fathers are twice as likely to be unemployed than adult white males. In 1986, the median income for black families was $17,604, only 57% of white median family income, a decreasing ratio since 1970 when it was 61%. However, when both parents were employed, median family income of blacks was $26,583 (U.S. Census Bureau, 1987a).

In terms of education, the average educational level of black adults is 12.2 years of school completed. While this educational level has improved substantially since the end of World War II, it is still much lower than the comparable figure for white adults.

The majority of blacks live in urban rather than rural areas, yet these areas are precisely those that have experienced the greatest loss of industrial and manufacturing jobs, resulting in declining employment opportunities and high unemployment rates for black males (Kasarda, 1985; Larson, 1988; Schorr, 1986). These high rates of unemployment have contributed to family dissolutions and the increasing phenomenon of female-headed households in the black community (Wilson, 1987). Moreover, as a consequence of family instability, black youth have higher rates than white youth of out-of-home placements in foster homes and institutions due to neglect, abuse, or abandonment and they stay in these placements longer because of the lack of appropriate long-term adoptive or permanent foster homes (Children's Defense Fund, 1987).

The low socioeconomic status of many black families is reflected in their residential concentration in central-city areas that are characterized by substandard housing, inferior schools, inadequate health care facilities, high crime rates, economic dislocation, and social isolation. There is abundant clinical and ethnographic evidence that such living conditions create a stressful and unpredictable environment that adversely affects the mental health and social development of children and adolescents (Grier & Cobbs, 1968; Myers, 1989; Pierce, 1974;).

Due to their lack of access to health care facilities and health insurance coverage, black youth suffer from disproportionately high rates of health and psychosomatic problems, including high rates of asthma, diabetes, vision and hearing problems, iron-deficiency anemia, lead poisoning, hypertension, and sexually-transmitted diseases (Carter, 1983; Gibbs, 1988b). The combination of a stressful environment and chronic health problems increases their vulnerability to psychological and behavioral disorders, as will be described in the following sections.

Epidemiology of Mental Health Problems

In the absence of large-scale epidemiological surveys of black adolescent mental health problems, it is necessary to rely on a variety of clinical studies and community surveys to provide estimates of the incidence of psychological and behavioral disorders among black youth. These studies can be divided into two broad categories (i.e., data on psychological disorders and data on behavioral disorders and psychosocial problems).

Psychological Disorders

Several studies have found a significant relationship between low socioeconomic status (SES) and stressful life events for adolescents, yet the investigators have not always been able to isolate the separate effects of race and SES as moderators of stress (Gad & Johnson, 1980; Lewis, Siegel, & Lewis, 1984; Newcomb, Huba, & Butler, 1981; Pryor Brown, Cohen, Hightower, & Lotyczewski, 1986;). In a more recent study of 1,347 black female adolescent medical patients, Pryor Brown, Powell, and Earls (1989) found a significant association between stress and psychiatric symptomatology. Those subjects who had experienced a higher number of stressful events in the preceding 12 months reported significantly higher rates of depression and conduct disorder, as well as a higher number of symptoms of post-traumatic stress disorder, somatic complaints, and substance use. The results of this study lend strong support to the frequently hypothesized relationship between stressful life events, low socioeconomic status, and psychological maladjustment in black youth (Franklin, 1982; Gibbs, 1984; Myers, 1989; Tolmach, 1985).

Most of the studies of psychological disorders in black adolescents have been conducted on urban, low-income samples and the generalizability of their findings is limited by methodological problems in sampling, differences in research design, and the use of different research instruments. Given these limitations, research on the following psychological disorders will be summarized: depression, conduct disorders, eating disorders, psychosomatic disorders, and suicidal behaviors. In addition, there is some data available on utilization rates of psychiatric facilities by black youth.

Depression. The incidence of depression among black youth has been investigated in various nonclinical school and community samples by researchers using a range of instruments, sampling methods and designs. They have found rates of mild to moderate depression from 20% to 40% and rates of severe depression from 5% to 15% in these samples. Higher rates of depression have generally been found among black adolescents and lower income youth, but no significant racial differences are found when age, SES, and sex are controlled (Gibbs, 1985b; Kaplan, Hong, & Weinhold, 1984; Schoenbach, Kaplan, Wagner, Grimson, & Miller, 1983).

Eating Disorders. The incidence of eating disorders is very low among black youth, as only 16 cases of anorexia nervosa or bulimia were reported in the literature through 1985 (Pumariega, Edwards, & Mitchell, 1984; Robinson & Andersen, 1985). Most of these cases, including 14 females and 2 males, were diagnosed as anorexia nervosa, but several cases were described as "atypical." Although self-starvation is rare in this group, a fairly high proportion of black adolescents are overweight due to a combination of poor nutrition and lack of exercise. Yet, it is unclear how many of these overweight teenagers may overeat in order to ward off feelings of depression, anxiety, or inadequacy.

Conduct Disorders. In estimating the incidence of conduct disorders among black youth, it is important to distinguish the clinical diagnosis from the disposition and labeling by the juvenile court. In clinic samples, black teens are more likely than white teens to be diagnosed as "conduct disordered" or labeled as "antisocial" (Dembo, 1988). Black males, particularly, are more likely than whites to be disciplined, suspended, or expelled in junior high and high school (Children's Defense Fund, 1985; Committee for Economic Development, 1987).

Psychosomatic Disorders. Psychosomatic disorders, which have traditionally been linked to stress and tension, occur with high frequency among black youth. Asthma is the most common chronic childhood illness among black children. Morbidity and mortality rates from asthma are higher among black children, ages 1-19, who have an annual age-adjusted death rate nearly six times higher than the rate for whites (National Center for Health Statistics, 1986). In their study of discharge rates for children hospitalized for asthma in the state of Maryland, Wissow and his colleagues (1988) found that the overall discharge rate for black youth, ages 1-19, was three times higher than for white youth, but the rate was five times higher for black youth in the 15-19 year age group. However, the authors concluded that poverty accounted for 30% of the variation in asthma rates for both races and that there were very similar discharge rates for black and white children of comparable poverty levels. Thus black children may be at increased risk for severe asthma because of their disproportionate poverty status, a socioeconomic factor that is associated with increased levels of stress, environmental pollution, and inadequate access to health care (Children's Defense Fund, 1986; Egbuono & Starfield, 1982; Wise, Kotalchuck, & Mills, 1985).

Hypertension is another stress-related chronic illness that has a higher prevalence rate among blacks than whites at every age level (Cruickshank & Beevers, 1982). Hypertension is one of the five leading causes of mortality among black youth (U.S. Department of Health and Human Services, 1986), yet very little research has been conducted to isolate the etiological causes and psychosocial correlates of the disease. A few studies have demonstrated a relationship between suppressed anger and essential hypertension in blacks, but most of these used adult male samples (Gentry, Chesney, Gary, Hall, & Harburg, 1982; Harburg, Erfurt, & Havenstein, 1973). In their recent study of a sample of black and white male high school sophomores, Johnson and his colleagues (1987) found that higher systolic blood pressure was related to suppres sion of anger in both black and white males. However, for black males the "anger-in" variable accounted for nearly 68% of the variance of the 4-variable regression equation, and the diastolic blood pressure of this group was consistently higher than for white males at every level of the "anger-in" variable.

Psychiatric Treatment Rates. Recent data from the National Institute of Mental Health (NIMH) indicates that the utilization rates and patterns of psychiatric services for black adolescents have changed rather significantly since 1975. In 1986, a total of 12,803 non-Hispanic black adolescents were hospitalized for psychiatric treatment, constituting 11.1% of all hospitalized youth in the 10-18 age bracket. However, they were overrepresented in state and county mental hospitals (15.3%) and general hospitals (13.5%), and underrepresented in private psychiatric hospitals (6.0%). The percentage of non-white adolescents admitted to inpatient psychiatric facilities has decreased since 1975, yet their proportion of the youth population has increased, suggesting that some black youth with psychological and behavioral problems may have been routed through the juvenile justice system, where their numbers have increased in that same period (National Institute of Mental Health, 1986).

Black youth, 10-18 years of age, constituted 19.7% of all adolescents who received partial psychiatric services in day treatment services (National Institute of Mental Health, 1986). They also accounted for 38,562 or 10.4% of all youth, 10-18 years of age, who obtained psychiatric services in outpatient facilities. Although the proportion of nonwhite adolescents who received outpatient psychiatric treatment in 1975 and 1986 was nearly identical, the *rate* per 100,000 did increase from 719.5 in 1975 to 773.9 per 100,000 in 1986. Black adolescents were less likely than their white peers to have private insurance to cover the costs of psychiatric treatment and more likely to pay for their care through Medicaid or other sources of funds, suggesting a primary cause of the major disparity in their access to private psychiatric treatment facilities.

Suicide. Suicidal behavior among black youth is increasing, although suicide rates are much lower for blacks than for white youths. Since 1960, suicide rates have nearly tripled for young black males from 4.1 to 11.2 per 100,000 in 1984 and doubled for black females from 1.3 to 2.4 per 100,000 so that it is currently the third leading cause of death in this age group (U.S. Department of Health and Human Services, 1986). Several clinicians have noted that the symptoms of suicidal behavior in black youth are often masked by acting-out and high risk behaviors, thus it is more difficult to assess suicidal intent in this group. Moreover, the incidence of suicide may be underestimated for black youth due to problems of lack of validity in determining the cause of "undetermined deaths" and lack of reliability in reporting suicide statistics across jurisdictions (Gibbs, 1988a; Shaffer & Fisher, 1981; Warshauer & Monk, 1978).

Psychosocial Problems

An evaluation of the mental health status of black adolescents would not be complete without a discussion of psychosocial problems experienced by these youth. It has been proposed that low-income blacks, in general, have a tendency to externalize their psychological distress and to transmit these patterns to children through socialization strategies that reinforce acting-out rather than acting-in as appropriate ways to handle conflicts (Clark, 1965; Schulz, 1969). These behaviors are presumably reflected in the statistics on social indicators, such as school drop-out rates, delinquency rates, alcohol and drug use rates, unwed teenage pregnancy rates, and homicide rates.

On the other hand, in response to self-report surveys, black adolescents consistently report lower rates than white adolescents on the use of alcohol and most illicit drugs, as well as very similar rates of delinquent behaviors. In their recent longitudinal study of at-risk behaviors of a national representative sample of high school seniors, Benson and Donahue (1989) found that black males and females reported lower rates than their white peers of regular cigarette and alcohol use, decreasing lifetime use of cocaine, and slightly lower use of marijuana over a 10-year period, as well as lower rates of recent truancy. While most results of this survey have been replicated in other studies, the authors point out that higher drop-out rates and higher nonresponse rates among the black seniors may account for some of the racial differences in at-risk behaviors. Caution is certainly necessary in interpreting these results, as well as in evaluating the statistics on social indi-

:ators that represent fewer than one fourth of all black youth, many of whom are counted in several categories and thus inflate the total number of those involved in antisocial or self-destructive activities (Gibbs, 1984, 1988b).

School drop-out rates.   Overall, school drop-out rates among black youth, 18-19 years old, have actually decreased from 31.2% in 1970 o 17.3 in 1985, approaching parity with their white peers whose drop-out rates decreased slightly from 14.1% to 13.8% in the same period (U.S. Census Bureau, 1987). However, drop-out rates for inner-city black youth range from 40% to 60%, with higher rates for males than females. Higher rates of functional illiteracy also have been found among black male youth (College Entrance Examination Board, 1985; Reed, 1988). These educational deficiencies, combined with poor job skills, lead to high rates of unemployment and few opportunities for legitimate income for inner-city black youth.

Juvenile delinquency.   In 1985, black youth accounted for 23.2% of all juvenile arrests in the United States, yet they were less than one fifth of the total youth population under the jurisdiction of the juvenile court (Krisberg, Schwartz, Fishman, Eiskovits, & Guttman, 1986). They were also more likely than white youth to be arrested, convicted, and incarcerated for the same category of offenses. Although black youth were more likely to be arrested for serious felony offenses than any other race or sex category of juveniles, a recent investigation concluded that there were no significant differences between black and white youth in their rates of self-reported delinquency in a variety of surveys of diverse samples (Krisberg, et al., 1986).

Several studies have found that black juvenile delinquents have high rates of depression, psychological, and neurological symptoms that are frequently undetected, undiagnosed, and untreated Dembo, 1988; Gibbs, 1982; Lewis & Balla, 1976). As these authors have pointed out, the juvenile justice system has increasingly served as the channel for "handling" black youth with behavioral disorders, while white youth with similar behaviors are more likely to be referred for treatment in the mental health system.

Substance abuse.   In community surveys of adolescent drinking patterns, black youth have consistently reported lower rates of lifetime as well as current alcohol use than white youth (Bachman, Johnston, & O'Malley, 1981; Barnes & Welte, 1986; Blane & Hewitt, 1977; Fishburne, Abelson, & Cisin, 1979; Rachal et al., 1980). In a 1974 cross-sectional survey of a nationwide probability sample of all junior and senior high students in grades 7-12, 62% of black students versus 73% of white students reported that they drank more than once a year (Harford, 1986). Black drinkers in this sample were significantly more likely than nondrinkers to be male, older in age, to have fewer older siblings and to associate with older peers. Drinkers also were more likely than nondrinkers to report more parental models for drinking, to place more emphasis on the social effects of drinking, to have greater access to alcohol, to be more involved in other forms of deviant behavior, to use marijuana, to be less involved in religion, and to perform less well in school (Harford, 1986).

Surveys of adolescent drug use have reported mixed results. While there is no significant difference in marijuana use between black and white youth, the pattern of drug use varies considerably by ethnicity. Lower overall drug usage rates were reported by black teenagers in large samples of junior high and high school students in New York and California (Gibbs, 1985a; Kandel, 1978; Skager, 1986). Rates of cocaine and heroin use are generally reported to be higher among older black youth than among their white counterparts (Brunswick, 1979).

The findings of school-based surveys are limited in their generalizability because they do not include out-of-school youth, probably resulting in an underestimation of substance use. This methodological issue is particularly relevant to samples of urban black youth, which are not representative of the large numbers of school drop-outs who are more likely to be involved in a range of deviant activities associated with drug and alcohol use (Halikas, Darvish, & Rimmer, 1976).

For black adolescents, drug use is particularly troublesome because it is frequently linked to a delinquent and dysfunctional lifestyle (Brunswick & Messeri, 1986). If and when these youth are referred for treatment, they usually present with multiple psychological, physical, and social problems (Beschner & Friedman, 1986).

One of the major unintended effects of drug use among black youth is the current epidemic of AIDS (acquired immunodeficiency syndrome) that has rapidly increased in this group, primarily due to the sharing of unsterilized needles. As of September 1988, the Centers for Disease Control reported that there were 300 cases of AIDS among 13-19 year old black youth. While they represented only 33% of the total population of adolescents with AIDS, experts have predicted that AIDS will increase in this group due to their high-risk drug and sexual behaviors, while it appears to be leveling off among white male homosexuals (Children's Defense Fund, 1988). As the incidence of AIDS increases among black youth, it will inevitably be accompanied by major psychological problems in patients and their families as they cope with the disabling effects of the illness and the threat of impending death and loss.

Teenage Pregnancy and Parenthood. Teen pregnancy is one of the major psychosocial problems for black adolescents, who often experience multiple negative social, economic, and psychological outcomes (Children's Defense Fund, 1988; Chilman, 1983). In 1986, the birth rate for unwed black females, ages 15-19, was 86.4 per 1,000 compared to 18.5 per 1,000 for white females in this age group. Although birth rates to black teenage females actually have dropped since 1960, they are still nearly five times as likely as white females to have a child out of wedlock.

Adolescent childbearing among black females is associated with higher rates of school drop-outs, welfare dependency, and unemployment (Children's Defense Fund, 1988). These teenage mothers also were more likely than girls who delayed their first pregnancy to experience a range of physical, psychological, and family problems (Chilman, 1983; Furstenberg, Lincoln, & Menken, 1981). Since most of these youthful mothers are still coping with adolescent identity issues, their own developmental tasks frequently are in conflict with the developmental needs of their children.

Very little attention has been paid to the impact of parenthood on teenage males. Recent studies suggest that for young black males, early fatherhood is associated with high rates of psychological symptoms, dropping out of school, and economic and marital instability (Connor, 1988; Robinson, 1988). However, recent studies have indicated that family support and living with their parents helps to moderate the negative consequences of adolescent childbearing (Colletta & Lee, 1983; Furstenberg & Crawford, 1978; Marsiglio, 1989; Mayfield-Brown, 1989).

Homicide. In 1986, homicide was the leading cause of death among black males, ages 15-19. The increasing phenomenon of black youth killing other black youth parallels the rise of the drug trade in the black community and reflects the easy availability of handguns (Gibbs, 1988a). Homicide is not only a constant threat to black youth involved in the drug trade, but it has also contributed to higher levels of fear and anxiety in inner-city neighborhoods where innocent victims are often caught in the cross fire. This level of violence can be viewed as a public health problem that should be addressed by epidemiological strategies to identify those at risk and to reduce the risk of homicide for specific population groups. It also can be viewed as a community mental health problem that should be addressed by general programs of prevention and early intervention to alleviate the underlying causes of the violence, which is symptomatic of the poverty, discrimination, community disorganization, and social isolation that characterize the inner cities (Rose, 1986).

Sociocultural Issues in Assessment

Psychological assessment of black youth can be viewed from three different perspectives: (a) theoretical, (b) sociocultural, and (c) multidimensional levels of functioning. First, a combination of two theoretical perspectives that are particularly relevant in illuminating the mental health issues of black youth are the ego-oriented developmental theory of Erik Erikson (1950; 1959) and the ecological theory of Urie Bronfenbrenner (1979).

Since minority youth are more likely than white youth to experience socioeconomic disadvantages, discriminatory treatment, and barriers to educational and occupational mobility in American society, these theories would predict more negative outcomes for black youth. For example, Erikson (1959) suggests that these adolescents are at risk for the development of "negative" identities and dysfunctional behaviors. According to Bronfenbrenner (1979) youth who grow up in noxious and unsupportive social environments are exposed to greater risks and fewer opportunities to develop a healthy sense of competence. Although these two theories are useful in understanding many of the psychological and behavioral problems of black youth, clinicians must be cautious about overpathologizing and stereotyping all black youth as victims of their racial identity and/or their socioeconomic status. It is important to emphasize that the *majority* of black youth are not referred for psychological or behavioral problems and appear to be coping effectively with their ethnicity and their economic resources.

Second, sociocultural factors should be evaluated in assessing black youth, with particular attention to their degree of school and neighborhood integration, religiosity, family structure, social support systems, and social isolation. Such factors have been found to predict differences between blacks and whites in definitions of mental health, attitudes toward mental disorders, help-seeking behaviors, symptomatology, distribution of psychiatric disorders, and response to treatment (Gardner, 1972; Griffith & Jones, 1978; Hall & Tucker, 1985; Jones & Korchin, 1982; Neighbors, 1985).

Third, black youth should be assessed in terms of multidimensional levels of functioning, for example: (a) individual, (b) family, (c) school, and (d) community, all of which are consistent with the dual individual and ecological theoretical perspectives (Gibbs, 1989).

Individual Assessment

The long-held view that black adolescents have greater difficulty in forming a positive identity due to the stigma of their minority status has been challenged by Chestang (1984), who proposed a dichotomy between "personal identity" and "racial identity" among blacks. This dichotomy has been supported in several studies that indicate blacks are able to separate their personal self-evaluations from society's evaluation of their racial identity (Foster & Perry, 1982; Spencer, 1982). In evaluating identity development in black adolescents, the clinician should assess those aspects of identity formation such as the self-concept, sense of competence, management of sexual and aggressive feelings, degree of autonomy from parents, and educational-vocational aspirations.

Attitudes toward self. Black youth develop their feelings of self-concept and self-esteem from the reflected appraisals of their families, peers, and role models in their own communities (Spencer, 1982). In contrast to several earlier clinical and empirical studies that found that black youth had negative self-concepts and low self-esteem (Clark & Clark, 1940; Goodman, 1952), the results of more recent studies of large nonclinical samples of black youth indicate that their self-concepts and self-esteem are as positive or more positive than comparative samples of white youth (Gibbs, 1985a; Powell, 1985; Rosenberg & Simmons, 1971; Taylor, 1976). Moreover, a few studies have shown that black youth in segregated schools express higher levels of self-esteem than those in integrated schools, suggesting the importance of a supportive homogeneous social environment (Nobles, 1973; Powell, 1985)

Black youth who are referred for treatment may report negative self-evaluations because of their physical appearance, their low-income family status, their lack of competence in culturally-valued skills, or their feelings of racial victimization (Franklin, 1982; Grier & Cobbs, 1968; Mayo, 1974). Significant sources of esteem may vary for black adolescents, as well as parental and peer reinforcements for valued behaviors and environmental supports for social competence. For example, a variety of studies suggest that black youth place a high value on verbal skills (e.g., "rapping"), assertiveness, physical attractiveness (especially for females), and athletic ability (especially for males) (Cauce, 1986; Jenkins, 1982; Mancini, 1980; Schulz, 1969).

Academically oriented black students frequently complain that they are negatively labeled as "braniacs," particularly in predominantly black high schools. Although intellectual achievement is valued by most black parents, high-achieving adolescents often feel caught between the low expectations of their white teachers and the anti-intellectual attitudes of their peers (Harrington, 1989).

Physical characteristics such as height and weight can also be sources of anxiety for males who are small in stature and girls who are precociously mature, exposing them to sarcasm, humor, and aggressive or sexual behaviors. Skin color and socioeconomic status can lead to invidious social distinctions that damage the adolescent's self-esteem. In assessing the self-esteem of black adolescents, the clinician needs to be aware of the impact of these specific sociocultural factors on the adolescent's self-evaluation and how this is mediated in a culturally-consonant or dissonant social context (Rosenberg, 1979).

Affect. Black adolescents typically are described as expressive, lively, and extroverted (Gibbs, 1985a; Ladner, 1971; Mancini, 1980). However, they often are portrayed as angry and hostile or sullen and withdrawn in treatment situations (Franklin, 1982; Ridley, 1984). While these teenagers may appear uncommunicative and uncooperative, their unresponsive demeanor is often a facade masking underlying depression and feelings of helplessness over multiple personal and family problems (Franklin, 1982; Gibbs, 1982, 1986a).

Speech and language. Contrary to popular stereotypes, black adolescents usually have good verbal skills even if they express themselves primarily in "black English" (Kernan, 1971; Kochman, 1972; Labov, 1972). Many teenagers can switch easily from "black English" to standard English, enabling a flexible clinician to communicate effectively. Clinicians can facilitate communication if they understand that language not only serves symbolic functions for black youth (e.g., the use of "rapping" as a form of artistic expression and "playing the dozens" as a form of confrontation), but it can also represent a source of conflict in schools and in the workplace where their linguistic style is not viewed as appropriate or adaptive (Kochman, 1972; Labov, 1972; Mancini, 1980).

Interpersonal relations. Social and cultural factors also shape the nature of relationships among black adolescents, who often form same-sex peer groups with strong bonds and group norms that provide a sense of social identity and social cohesion (Mancini, 1980; Schulz, 1969). In inner-city areas with high rates of female-headed families, studies have found strong social support networks among adolescent and young adult mothers (Belle, 1982; Ladner, 1971; Stack, 1974). Conversely, these strong bonds can also foster group conflicts, gang rivalries, and pressures to participate in antisocial activities. For example, one study found that low academic achievement and premarital sexual activity were significantly related to high participation of low-income black teenagers in certain types of cohesive peer networks (Felner, Aber, Primavera, & Cauce, 1985). In some neighborhoods, males who are not gang members are at risk for frequent verbal and physical harassment.

Sexuality.   Sexual relationships and their consequences are major issues for black adolescents, who initiate sexual activity about one year earlier than white adolescents (Children's Defense Fund, 1988; Chilman, 1983). Since black teenagers tend to be less effective than whites as users of contraception, black females have higher rates of unintended pregnancy and higher birth rates than white females (Children's Defense Fund, 1988).

Black adolescent females are often referred for issues of sexuality, pregnancy and parenting, so clinicians should be familiar with their attitudes concerning premarital sexual activity, contraception, childbearing and childrearing (Gibbs, 1986b). Many authors have suggested that for many low-income black teenagers, early parenthood is viewed as a rite of passage to adulthood and is not fraught with the degree of anxiety, shame, and social stigma experienced by middle-class white adolescents (Franklin, 1988; Ladner, 1971; Stack, 1974).

Anxiety and patterns of defense.   Black youth may experience anxiety because of a number of factors, including school, family, work, and community issues. Thus it is essential for the clinician to evaluate the level of anxiety, the mode of expression, and the typical situations evoking it. As a result of childrearing patterns that often reinforce the externalization of anxiety, black youth may be more likely to deny, displace, or project anxiety rather than expressing it directly (Schulz, 1969). In younger adolescents, patterns of hyperactivity, acting-out, and aggression are frequently indicative of anxiety, while delinquency, substance abuse, and sexual promiscuity can be indicators of anxiety or depression in older youth (Gibbs, 1982; Franklin, 1982). Clinicians should also recognize that somatic symptoms can be clues to anxiety in black youth.

Coping and adaptive behaviors.   To compensate for their marginality in American society, black youth have developed a repertoire of adaptive behavioral patterns. For example, many black males have focused on developing athletic abilities, one of the limited number of routes to mobility for low-income youth. Black females have been rewarded for developing their social and interpersonal skills, yet they have not always been able to translate these skills into educational and career opportunities (Gibbs, 1985a; Ladner, 1971; Powell, 1985; Smith, 1982). Several studies have identified specific patterns such as "playing it cool" or "getting over" employed by black youth to respond to the uncertainties of their environment (Kochman, 1972; Mancini, 1980; Schulz, 1969). Despite the fact that these patterns are usually inappropriate or maladaptive for success in the dominant society, they reflect the resilience and creativity of black youth in responding to their social environment.

The Family System

Assessment of the family system of the black adolescent should focus on the following areas: the structure and roles of the family, socioeconomic status and living arrangements, degree of integration/acculturation, communication patterns, support system, and help-seeking patterns.

Family structure and roles. The structure of the family (i.e., intact, single-parent or extended) is an important force in shaping the adolescent's socialization and identity, as well as placing constraints on his social role development. Teenage females in single-parent families may become parent-substitutes with detrimental effects on their educational and occupational outcomes. Alternately, teenagers in extended families are more likely to experience conflicts over discipline and autonomy in relating to several adult caretakers. Those youth from nontraditional family structures may express shame or embarrassment about their home environments to middle-class clinicians.

Socioeconomic status and living arrangements. Parental occupations and family income are important predictors of the adolescent's lifestyle, material resources, and educational opportunities. In many low-income families, black youth live in overcrowded households that lack basic amenities, adequate study facilities, and personal privacy. They are often exposed at early ages to family violence or abuse, unsafe neighborhoods, and antisocial activities, all of which are negative influences on their health and mental health.

Degree of integration/acculturation. The level of integration of the black youth's neighborhood and school, as well as the degree of his family's acculturation to the mainstream society, are relevant to the assessment phase. Studies suggest that variations in the experiences of black youth in integrated settings are related to different patterns of symptomatology, problem behaviors, and their adaptation to the community (Gibbs, 1975; 1985a; Powell, 1985).

Social support system. Kinship relationships and social support networks of the youth and his family should be evaluated. If a family is actively involved in church, their minister can be an important source of support and an ally in treatment. Extended families and fictive kin can also provide useful information and multiple sources of support for troubled youth. Traditionally, black families have sent troubled teenagers to live temporarily with other relatives, exchanging goods and services, and strengthening family bonds through mutual aid (McAdoo, 1981; Stack, 1974).

Communication patterns. Ethnographic and experimental studies suggest that interaction in black families is shaped by socioeconomic factors and level of acculturation. Parent-child communication in low-income families tends to be more authoritarian, critical, unidirectional, and confrontational (Bartz & Levine, 1978; Cahill, 1966; Peters, 1981). Mutual teasing, sarcasm, and denigrating comments are more frequently observed than overt expressions of affection, nurturance, support, and praise among these families (Ladner, 1971; Schulz, 1969). In order to preserve their self-esteem in these situations, black youth learn to use self-deprecating humor and stereotypes. Middle-class black families are more likely than low-income families to engage in communication patterns that are bidirectional, authoritative, and mutually supportive (Bartz & Levine, 1978; Durrett, O'Bryant, & Pennebaker, 1975; Peters, 1981).

Help-seeking patterns. Since black families do not usually seek psychiatric treatment as the initial source of help for their troubled children, these youth are more likely to be referred by schools, the juvenile court, and the social welfare system. Due to a variety of social and cultural factors, black families are generally more likely to seek help for a troubled member from the family doctor, minister, relatives, and friends than from a mental health professional (Neighbors, 1985). This help-seeking pattern may result in delaying effective treatment for youth whose symptoms will increase in severity and ultimately require more intensive intervention.

School Assessment

Black youth have long had a problematic relationship with the public school system, the major source of their referrals for academic and behavioral problems. Clinicians face the challenge of separating out the youth's presenting problems from factors in the school setting that may have contributed to them.

School environment. Schools in low-income black neighborhoods can be generally described as having less adequate facilities, lower teacher morale, greater disciplinary problems, and lower achievement scores than schools in middle-income areas (Reed, 1988; Rivers, Henderson, Jones, Ladner, & Williams, 1975). Responses of black youth to these school environments range from apathy and alienation, anger, and hostility to fear and anxiety, leading to high rates of truancy, vandalism, and dropping out.

Educational issues. Black students are more likely than any other group to be mislabeled as learning-disabled or emotionally handicapped and placed in special education programs or nonacademic tracks (Committee for Economic Development, 1987; Reed, 1988; Rivers, Henderson, Jones, Ladner, & Williams, 1975). After years of experiencing low teacher expectations, unchallenging classes, and chaotic school environments, black youth are also more likely to be suspended, expelled, or "pushed out" of school even before they reach the age of 16. If clinicians are evaluating the general ability of black youth, they should use a culturally sensitive measure such as the System of Multicultural Pluralistic Assessment (SOMPA) battery (Mercer, 1975; Samuda, 1975; Snowden & Todman, 1982). If there is a discrepancy between the test results and the client's educational program, the most effective intervention might be a recommendation for a more appropriate academic placement.

Peer relationships. The school achievement and experiences of black adolescents are strongly influenced by the attitudes and behaviors of their peers (Cauce, Felner, & Primavera, 1982; Gibbs, 1985a; Ogbu, 1985). High-achieving youth often are ridiculed and excluded socially in inner-city schools (Hare, 1988). Permissive attitudes toward early experimentation with drugs and sexual activity create strong pressures toward conformity (Anderson, 1989;

Ladner, 1971). The clinician will find it useful not only to assess the adolescent's ability to cope with peer pressures but also to help him to identify environmental and social supports for pro-social behaviors.

Community Assessment

Adolescence may signal the first introduction to overt racial discrimination and prejudice for black youth who enter an integrated high school, seek employment, or participate in community-wide sports and recreational activities. As they perceive barriers to their full participation in American society, they simultaneously are gaining greater exposure to the effects of poverty, drugs, and crime in their neighborhoods. These experiences foster feelings of cynicism, anger, alienation, and despair in many youth, increasing their risk for involvement in antisocial or self-destructive activities such as drug abuse, unwed teenage pregnancy, homicide, and suicide (Gibbs, 1988b; Hare, 1988).

Clinicians evaluating these youth need to assess their underlying feelings of depression, anger, and alienation in order to develop appropriate treatment recommendations (Franklin, 1982; Grier & Cobbs, 1968). In the following section the implications for practice with troubled black youth will be discussed in terms of a range of intervention options.

Implications for Clinical Practice

Four modalities of treatment for black adolescents will be briefly described: individual, family, group, and crisis intervention.

Individual Treatment

The treatment of choice for black youth with nonpsychotic behavioral and emotional problems is short-term, ego-oriented treatment as described by Norman (1980). Since this approach is time-limited and focuses on problem-solving and strengthening adaptive skills, it is useful for a wide range of adolescent psychosocial problems.

Clinicians should be aware of special issues in beginning treatment with black adolescents, who are especially attentive to signs of prejudice, superiority, disapproval, or rejection from therapists (Franklin, 1982; Gibbs, 1985c; Ridley, 1984). Black youth initially tend to judge clinicians on their interpersonal skills and attitudes rather than their instrumental skills and they approach treatment with a great deal of anxiety, distrust, and misapprehension. Clinicians can minimize these feelings by demystifying psychotherapy through a brief verbal or videotaped description of the therapeutic process (Acosta, Yamamoto, & Evans, 1982; Frank, Hoehn-Saric, Imber, Liberman, & Stone, 1978).

In order to establish rapport, the clinician should use active, expressive directive strategies with black youth, who are more likely than whites to be more reluctant to self-disclose, and more likely to seem resistant and hostile at the outset of treatment. The limits of confidentiality should be clarified, particularly since most of these youth probably are not voluntary self-referrals.

In order to establish a working alliance with the black adolescent, the clinician must anticipate a period of "testing" behaviors during which the client will challenge the therapist's authority and control (Franklin, 1982). These testing behaviors can range from uncooperative attitudes to hostile or seductive behaviors, all of which are defensive strategies to protect the adolescent's fragile sense of self-esteem.

Humor is an effective tool in facilitating a relationship with the black adolescent, who is from a culture with an oral tradition in which humor plays a prominent role (Kochman, 1972; Labov, 1972). Humor also can be used to foster insight in clients, who are otherwise not responsive to dynamic interpretations of their intrapsychic conflicts.

In the treatment of black youth, clinicians must be attuned to the social and political realities of their environment and to their culturally-patterned behavior patterns, as well as to their individual variations in response to stress and intrapsychic conflict.

Family Treatment

Clinical and cultural issues in working with black youth and their families have been carefully delineated by several authors (Boyd-Franklin, 1989; Harris & Balgopal, 1980; Sager, Brayboy, &

Waxenberg, 1970). Family therapy is especially appropriate where the adolescent's problems are viewed as symptomatic of a dysfunctional family system, a breakdown in family communication, or a family scapegoating process.

An eclectic approach that combines structural and strategic techniques is appropriate for these families, which can benefit from a dual focus on restructuring family roles and modifying family communication patterns (Minuchin, 1974). These techniques can be effective for a range of presenting problems such as teenage pregnancy, school failure, substance abuse, delinquency, and suicidal behavior, all of which are ways black adolescents may act out the negative expectations and hostile affect they receive from parents, who themselves are frequently displacing their anger and frustrations onto their children.

Group Treatment

Group therapy has become a popular and cost-effective treatment modality for adolescents in both outpatient and residential treatment settings. In forming groups for black adolescents, clinicians should consider several factors, such as balancing the group by gender, race, and social class; racial and sexual balance of the cotherapists; homogeneity or heterogeneity of diagnostic categories or presenting problems.

Psychoeducational groups may be most effective for delinquents, school drop-outs, and troubled youth who are in need of a comprehensive treatment program that includes counseling as well as educational and vocational services (Franklin, 1982).

Group leaders should be carefully selected for their ability to serve as role models as well as their skills in group process, since many black youth lack positive adult role models who can assist them with problem-solving, conflict resolution, identity issues, and realistic career planning.

Crisis Intervention

Black youth who are victims of abuse, suffering from drug overdoses, suicidal, psychotic, or extremely violent are increasingly referred to crisis intervention services. They may become more paranoid under stress, thus exacerbating their symptoms and appearing very fearful and suspicious. The emergency room can be a frightening experience for black adolescents, who may respond by withdrawing, verbally abusing the staff, or refusing medication.

Due to the increasing epidemic of "crack" in inner-city areas, emergency services are strained by victims of drug-related trauma and violence. Clinicians need to be familiar with community mental health services and drug treatment programs in order to refer these youth for follow-up counseling and treatment.

In responding to the urgency of the situation, clinicians should not only focus on the immediate relief of symptoms and the restoration of effective functioning, but they should also evaluate the teenager's family environment and social support system. The clinician may find that effective treatment of black adolescents requires active intervention in multiple systems impinging on their lives, such as the family, the school, the workplace, the juvenile justice system, and the social welfare system.

To summarize, these four modalities of treatment are appropriate for youth whose psychological or behavioral symptoms have already resulted in individual, family, or community problems. Yet there are numerous black youth at risk for psychosocial dysfunction whose potential problems can be prevented or minimized through policies and programs of prevention and early intervention, as proposed below.

Implications for Policies and Programs of Prevention

Policies of prevention must be rooted in increasing resources and promoting the stability of low-income black families through a comprehensive set of family assistance policies that would focus on three major social goals: to improve income supports for poor families and children, to increase the self-sufficiency of current welfare recipients through education and employment training programs, and to provide adequate levels of social services, health care, and low-income housing, all of which would improve the socioeconomic status and strengthen the functioning of these families (Edelman, 1987; Schorr, 1986; Solomon, 1988).

The educational system needs increased levels of federal and state support to expand programs of early childhood education such as Head Start, compensatory educational programs in the elementary and secondary schools such as Chapter I programs, and innovative drop-out prevention programs in inner-city schools (Committee for Economic Development, 1987).

School-based health clinics have been successful at improving the health status of black youth, reducing their pregnancy rates, and educating them about drug abuse, sexually transmitted diseases, and suicide prevention (Children's Defense Fund, 1986).

Employment and training programs are necessary for older black youth who have dropped out of school without marketable skills. Successful programs such as the Job Corps, the Youth Conservation Corps, and JOB START, are characterized by comprehensive services including remedial education, basic skills instruction, counseling, and health care (Children's Defense Fund, 1989).

Finally, increased funding for innovative prevention and early intervention projects authorized by the Juvenile Justice and Delinquency Act would strengthen community resources for at risk black youth, as would improved coordination of programs currently existing in the child welfare, juvenile justice, mental health, and special education systems (Children's Defense Fund, 1989). Ultimately, however, there is a consensus among public policy specialists that the most effective strategy for preventing crime and drug abuse is increasing educational and employment opportunities for black youth and improving the socioeconomic status of their families (Edelman, 1987; Schorr, 1986; Wilson, 1987).

Summary and Conclusions

Black youth in American society are at risk for multiple psychosocial and psychological problems, as documented in the preceding pages. Since they are more likely than white youth to be initially referred to the juvenile justice system, they also are less likely to receive a comprehensive psychological assessment, diagnosis, and treatment for any underlying psychological problems.

The multiple risk factors for black youth have been described, as well as the social and cultural milieu that shapes their values, norms, and behaviors. In order for clinicians to serve these clients effectively, they must be sensitive to their attitudes and beliefs about mental health and mental illness, their choice of symptoms, their adaptive patterns and defensive behaviors, their patterns of help-seeking and service utilization, and their responsiveness to different modalities of psychotherapeutic treatment.

Four modalities of treatment for black youth have been briefly described: individual, family, group, and crisis intervention. Special issues in initiating treatment and establishing a working alliance with black adolescents were also discussed. Policies and programs of prevention and early intervention to reduce the incidence of psychological or behavioral problems also were proposed.

In summary, the mental health status of black youth in America has actually deteriorated in the past 30 years. As economic, social, and political changes have eroded the progress of the black family, their children have been the innocent victims of persistent poverty, discrimination, and economic dislocation. In the face of a growing political conservatism and a reduction in social welfare programs in the past decade, black youth and their families will continue to need a wide range of social and mental health services to address the psychological and behavioral problems that are symptomatic of a hostile social environment.

Since black youth will constitute one fifth of the nation's youth at the beginning of the 21st century, it is not only important to provide expanded and culturally appropriate treatment services for them, but it is also essential to develop a comprehensive coordinated set of government policies and programs that will improve the socioeconomic status of their families, increase their educational and economic opportunities, and enhance their options for meaningful and productive lives in American society.

Note

1. Government statistics do not usually break down into this age category, but are usually reported in 10-14, 15-19, or 15-24 age ranges.

References

Acosta, F. X., Yamamoto, J., & Evans, L. A. (1982). *Effective psychotherapy for low-income and minority patients.* New York: Plenum.

American Public Welfare Association. (1986). *One child in four.* New York: Author.

Anderson, E. (1989). Sex codes and family life among poor inner-city youths. In W. J. Wilson (Ed.), The ghetto underclass: Social science perspectives. *The Annals of the American Academy of Political and Social Science.* Newbury Park, CA: Sage.

Bachman, J. T., Johnston, L. D., & O'Malley, P. M. (1981). Smoking, drinking and drug use among American high school students: Correlates and trends, 1975-1979. *American Journal of Public Health, 71,* 59-69.

Barnes, G. M., & Welte, J. W. (1986). *Journal of Studies on Alcohol, 47,* 53-61.

Bartz, K. W., & Levine, E. S. (1978). Childrearing by black parents: A description and comparison to Anglo and Chicano parents. *Journal of Marriage and the Family, 40,* 709-719.

Belle, D. (Ed.). (1982). *Lives in stress: Women and depression.* Beverly Hills, CA: Sage.

Benson, P. L., & Donahue, M. J. (1989). Ten-year trends in at-risk behaviors: A national study of black adolescents. *Journal of Adolescent Research, 4,* 125-139.

Beschner, G., & Friedman, A. (Eds.). (1986). *Teen drug use.* Lexington, MA: Lexington Books.

Blane, H. T., & Hewitt, L. E. (1977). *Alcohol and youth: An analysis of the literature, 1960-1975* (Report no. PB-268-698). Springfield, VA: U.S. National Technical Information Service.

Boyd-Franklin, N. (1989). *Black families in therapy.* New York: Guilford.

Bronfenbrenner, U. (1979). *The ecology of human development: Experiments by nature and design.* Cambridge, MA: Harvard University Press.

Brunswick, A. F. (1979). Black youths and drug-use behavior. In G. Beschner & A. Friedman (Eds.), *Youth and drug abuse: Problems, issues and treatment.* Lexington, MA: Lexington Books.

Brunswick, A. F., & Messeri, P. (1986). Drugs, life style and health. *American Journal of Public Health, 76,* 52-57.

Cahill, I. D. (1966). Child-rearing practices in lower socio-economic ethnic groups. *Dissertation Abstracts, 27,* 31-39.

Carter, J. H. (1983). Vision or sight: Health concerns for Afro-American children. In G. Powell, J. Yamamoto, A. Romero, & A. Morales (Eds.), *The psychosocial development of minority group children.* New York: Brunner/Mazel.

Cauce, A. M. (1986). Social networks and social competence: Exploring the effects of early adolescent friendships. *American Journal of Community Psychology, 14,* 607-629.

Cauce, A. M., Felner, R., & Primavera, J. (1982). Social support in high-risk adolescents: Structural components and adaptive impact. *American Journal of Community Psychology, 10,* 417-428.

Chestang, L. (1984). Racial and personal identity in the black experience. In B. White (Ed.). *Color in a white society.* Silver Spring, MD: NASW Publications.

Children's Defense Fund. (1985). *Black and white children in America.* Washington, DC: Author.

Children's Defense Fund. (1986). *Welfare and teen pregnancy: What do we know? What do we do?* Washington, DC: Author.

Children's Defense Fund. (1987). *A children's defense budget.* Washington, DC: Author.

Children's Defense Fund. (1988). *Teens and AIDS: Opportunities for prevention.* Washington, DC: Author.

Children's Defense Fund. (1989). *The lessons of multi-site initiatives serving high-risk youths.* Washington, DC: Author.

Chilman, C. (1983). *Adolescent sexuality in a changing American society.* New York: John Wiley.

Clark, K. (1965). *Dark ghetto: Dilemmas of social power.* New York: Harper & Row.

Clark, K., & Clark, M. (1940). Skin color as a factor in racial identification of Negro pre-school children. *Journal of Social Psychology, 2,* 154-167.

College Entrance Examination Board. (1985). *Equality and excellence: The educational status of black Americans.* New York: The College Board.

Colletta, N., & Lee, D. (1983). The impact of support for black adolescent mothers. *Journal of Family Issues, 4,* 127-143.

Committee for Economic Development. (1987). *Children in need: Investment strategies for the educationally disadvantaged.* New York: Author.

Connor, M. (1988). Teenage fatherhood: Issues confronting young black males. In J. T. Gibbs (Ed.). *Young, black and male in America: An endangered species.* Dover, MA: Auburn House.

Cruickshank, J. K., & Beevers, D. G. (1982). Epidemiology of hypertension: Blood pressure in blacks and whites. *Clinical Science, 62,* 1-6.

Dembo, R. (1988). Delinquency among black male youth. In J. T. Gibbs (Ed.). *Young, black and male in America: An endangered species.* Dover, MA: Auburn House Publishing Company.

Durrett, M. D., O'Bryant, S., & Pennebaker, J. W. (1975). Child-rearing reports of white, Black, and Mexican-American Families. *Developmental Psychology, 11,* 871-878.

Edelman, M. W. (1987). *Families in peril: An agenda for social change.* Cambridge, MA: Harvard University Press.

Egbuono, L., & Starfield, G. (1982). Child health and social status. *Pediatrics, 698,* 550-556.

Erikson, E. H. (1950). *Childhood and society.* New York: Norton.

Erikson, E. H. (1959). Identity and the life cycle. *Psychological Issues, 1,* Monograph 1. New York: International Universities Press.

Felner, R. D., Aber, M. S., Primavera, J., & Cauce, A. (1985). Adaptation and vulnerability in high-risk adolescents: An examination of environmental mediators. *American Journal of Community Psychology, 13,* 365-379.

Fishburne, P. M., Abelson, H. I., & Cisin, I. (1979). *National survey on drug abuse: Main findings: 1979.* Rockville, MD: National Institute on Drug Abuse (NIDA).

Foster, M., & Perry, L. R. (1982). Self-evaluation among Blacks. *Social Work, 27,* 60-66.

Frank, J. D., Hoehn-Saric, R., Imber, S., Liberman, B., & Stone, A. (1978). *Effective ingredients of successful psychotherapy.* New York: Brunner/Mazel.

Franklin, A. J. (1982). Therapeutic interventions with urban black adolescents. In
    E. E. Jones & S. J. Korchin (Eds.). *Minority mental health*. New York: Praeger.
Franklin, D. L. (1988). Race, class, and adolescent pregnancy: An ecological analy-
    sis. *American Journal of Orthopsychiatry, 58*, 339-354.
Furstenberg, F., Jr., & Crawford, A. G. (1978). Family support: Helping teenage
    mothers to cope. *Family Planning Perspectives, 10*, 322-333.
Furstenberg, F., Jr., Lincoln, R., & Menken, J. (1981). *Teenage sexuality, pregnancy, and
    childbearing*. Philadelphia: University of Pennsylvania Press.
Gad, M., & Johnson, J. (1980). Correlates of adolescent life stress as related to race,
    SES, and levels of perceived social support. *Journal of Clinical Psychology, 9*, 13-16.
Gardner, L. (1972). The therapeutic relationship under varying conditions of race.
    Psychotherapy: Theory, research and practice, 8, 78-87.
Gentry, W. D., Chesney, A. P., Gary, H. G., Hall, R. P. & Harburg, E. (1982). Habitual
    anger-coping styles-I. Effect on mean blood pressure and risk for essential hyper-
    tension. *Psychosomatic Medicine, 44*, 273-281.
Gibbs, J. T. (1975). Use of mental health services by black students at a predomi-
    nantly white university: A three-year study. *American Journal of Orthopsychiatry,
    45*, 430-445.
Gibbs, J. T. (1982). Personality patterns of delinquent females: Ethnic and sociocul-
    tural variations. *Journal of Clinical Psychology, 38*, 198-206.
Gibbs, J. T. (1984). Black adolescents and youth: An endangered species. *American
    Journal of Orthopsychiatry, 54*, 6-21.
Gibbs, J. T. (1985a). City girls: Psychosocial adjustment of urban black adolescent
    females. *SAGE: A Scholarly Journal of Black Women, 2*, 28-36.
Gibbs, J. T. (1985b). Psychosocial factors associated with depression in urban ado-
    lescent females: Implications for assessment. *Journal of Youth and Adolescence, 14*,
    47-60.
Gibbs, J. T. (1985c). Treatment relationships with black clients: Interpersonal vs.
    instrumental strategies. In C. Germain (Ed.). *Advances in clinical social work prac-
    tice*. Silver Spring, MD: NASW Publications.
Gibbs, J. T. (1986a). Assessment of depression in urban adolescent females: Implica-
    tions for early intervention strategies. *American Journal of Social Psychiatry, 6*,
    50-56.
Gibbs, J. T. (1986b). Psychosocial correlates of sexual attitudes and behaviors in
    urban early adolescent females: Implications for intervention. *Journal of Social
    Work and Human Sexuality, 5*, 81-97.
Gibbs, J. T. (1988a). Conceptual, methodological, and sociocultural issues in black
    youth suicide: Implications for assessment and early intervention. *Suicide and
    Life-Threatening Behavior, 18*, 73-89.
Gibbs, J. T. (Ed.). (1988b). *Young, black, and male in America: An endangered species*.
    Dover, MA: Auburn House.
Gibbs, J. T. (1989). Assessment and treatment of black adolescents. In J. T. Gibbs
    and L. N. Huang (Eds.). *Children of color: Psychological interventions with minority
    youth*. San Francisco: Jossey-Bass.
Goodman, M. E. (1952). *Race awareness in young children*. Reading, MA: Addison-
    Wesley.
Grier, W., & Cobbs, P. (1968). *Black rage*. New York: Basic Books.

Griffith, M., & Jones, E. (1978). Race and psychotherapy: Changing perspectives. *Current Psychiatric Therapies, 18,* 225-235.

Halikas, J. A., Darvish, H. S., & Rimmer, J. D. (1976). The black addict: I. Methodology, chronology of addiction, and overview of population. *American Journal of Drug and Alcohol Abuse, 3,* 529-543.

Hall, L. E., & Tucker, C. M. (1985). Relationships between ethnicity, conceptions of mental illness and attitudes associated with seeking psychological help. *Psychological Reports, 57,* 907-916.

Harburg, E., Erfurt, J. C. & Havenstein, L. S. (1973). Sociological stress, suppressed hostility, skin color, and black or white male blood pressure: Detroit. *Psychosomatic Medicine, 35,* 276-296.

Hare, B. R. (1988). Black youth at risk. *The state of black America 1988.* New York: National Urban League, Inc.

Harford, T. C. (1986). Drinking patterns among black and non-black adolescents: Results of a national survey. *Annals of the New York Academy of Sciences, 472,* 130-141.

Harrington, W. (August 27, 1989). Hoops and dreams. *Washington Post Sunday Magazine,* pp. 17-39.

Harris, D. C., & Balgopal, P. R. (1980). Intervening with the black family. In C. Janzen & O. Harris (Eds.). *Family treatment in social work practice.* Itasca, IL: F. E. Peacock.

Hines, P. M., & Boyd-Franklin, N. (1982). Black families. In M. McGoldrick, J. K. Pearce, & J. Giordano (Eds.). *Ethnicity and family therapy.* New York: Guilford.

Jenkins, A. (1982). *The psychology of the Afro-American.* New York: Pergamon.

Johnson, E. H., Spielberger, C. D., Worden, T. J., & Jacobs, G. A. (1987). Emotional and familial determinants of elevated blood pressure in black and white adolescent males. *Journal of Psychosomatic Research, 31,* 287-300.

Jones, E. E., & Korchin, S. J. (Eds.). (1982). *Minority mental health.* New York: Praeger.

Kandel, D. B. (1978). Convergences in prospective longitudinal surveys of drug use in normal populations. In D. B. Kandel (Ed.). *Longitudinal research on drug use.* Washington, DC: Hemisphere.

Kaplan, S. L., Hong, G. K., & Weinhold, C. (1984). Epidemiology of depressive symptomatology in adolescents. *Journal of the American Academy of Child Psychiatry, 23,* 91-98.

Kasarda, J. (1985). Urban change and minority opportunities. In P. E. Peterson (Ed.). *The new urban reality.* Washington, DC: The Brookings Institution.

Kernan, C. (1971). Language behavior in a black urban community. *Monograph of the language behavior research laboratory, 2.* Berkeley: University of California.

Kochman, T. E. (1972). *Rappin' and stylin' out.* Urbana: University of Illinois Press.

Krisberg, B., Schwartz, I., Fishman, G., Eiskovits, Z., & Guttman, E. (1986). *The incarceration of minority youth.* Minneapolis: H. H. Humphrey Institute of Public Affairs, University of Minnesota.

Labov, W. (1972). *Language in the inner city: Studies in the black English vernacular.* Philadelphia: University of Pennsylvania Press.

Ladner, J. (1971). *Tomorrow's tomorrow.* Garden City, New York: Doubleday.

Larson, T. E. (1988). Employment and unemployment of young black males. In J. T. Gibbs (Ed.). *Young, black and male in America: An endangered species.* Dover, MA: Auburn House.

Lewis, C. E., Siegel, J. M., & Lewis, M. A. (1984). Feeling bad: Exploring sources of distress among pre-adolescent children. *American Journal of Public Health, 74,* 117-122.

Lewis, D., & Balla, D. (1976). *Delinquency and psychopathology.* New York: Grune & Stratton.

Looney, J. G., & Lewis, J. M. (1983). Competent adolescents from different socioeconomic and ethnic contexts. In M. Sugar (Ed.). *Adolescent psychiatry* (Vol. 11), pp. 64-74. Chicago, IL: University of Chicago Press.

Mancini, J. K. (1980). *Strategic styles: Coping in the inner city.* Hanover, NH: University Press of New England.

Marsiglio, W. (1989). Adolescent males' pregnancy resolution preferences and family formation intentions. *Journal of Adolescent Research, 4,* 214-237.

Mayfield-Brown, L. (1989). Family status of low-income adolescent mothers. *Journal of Adolescent Research, 4,* 202-213.

Mayo, J. (1974). The significance of sociocultural variables in the psychiatric treatment of black outpatients. *Comprehensive Psychiatry, 15,* 471-482.

McAdoo, H. (1981). *Black families.* Beverly Hills, CA: Sage.

Mercer, J. (1975). Psychological assessment and the rights of children. In N. Hobbs (Ed.). *Issues in the classification of children* (Vol. 1). San Francisco: Jossey-Bass.

Minuchin, S. (1975). *Families and family therapy.* Cambridge, MA: Harvard University Press.

Myers, H. F. (1989). Urban stress and mental health of Afro-American youth: An epidemiologic and conceptual update. In R. L. Jones (Ed.). *Black adolescents.* Berkeley, CA: Cobbs & Henry.

Myers, H. F., & King, L. M. (1983). Mental health issues in the development of the black American child. In G. Powell, J. Yamamoto, A. Roberto, & A. Morales (Eds.). *The psychosocial development of minority group children.* New York: Brunner/Mazel.

National Center for Health Statistics (N.C.H.S.). (1986). *Health—United States, 1986.* Washington, DC: U.S. Department of Health, Education, and Welfare.

National Institute of Mental Health. (1986). *Preliminary sample survey data.* Rockville, MD: Author.

Neighbors, H. W. (1985). Seeking professional help for personal problems: Black Americans' use of health and mental health services, *Community Mental Health Journal, 21,* 156-166.

Newcomb, M., Huba, G., & Butler, P. (1981). A multidimensional assessment of stressful life events among adolescents: Derivation and correlates. *Journal of Health and Social Behavior, 22,* 400-414.

Nobles, W. (1973). Psychological research and the black self-concept: A critical review. *Journal of Social Issues, 29,* 11-31.

Norman, J. S. (1980). Short-term treatment with the adolescent client. *Social Casework, 61,* 74-82.

Ogbu, J. U. (1985). A cultural ecology of competence among inner-city blacks. In M. Spencer, G. Brookins, & W. Allen (Eds.). *Beginnings: The social and affective development of black children.* Hillsdale, NJ: Lawrence Erlbaum.

Peters, M. F. (1981). Parenting in black families with young children: A historical perspective. In H. McAdoo (Ed.). *Black families.* Beverly Hills, CA: Sage.

Pierce, C. M (1974). Psychiatric problems of the black minority. In S. Arieti & G. Caplan (Eds.). *American handbook of psychiatry, Vol. 2* (2nd ed.). New York: Basic Books.

Powell, G. J. (1985). Self-concepts among Afro-American students in racially isolated minority schools: Some regional differences. *Journal of the American Academy of Child Psychiatry, 24,* 142-149.

Pryor Brown, L. J., Cowen, E. L., Hightower, A. D., & Lotyczewski, B. S. (1986). Demographic differences among children in judging and experiencing specific stressful life events. *Journal of Special Education, 20,* 339-346.

Pryor Brown, L. J., Powell, J. & Earls, F. (1989). Stressful life events and psychiatric symptoms in black adolescent females. *Journal of Adolescent Research, 4,* 140-151.

Pumariega, A., Edwards, P., & Mitchell, C. Anorexia nervosa in black adolescents. (1984). *Journal of the American Academy of Child Psychiatry, 23,* 111-114.

Rachal, J. V., Guess, L. L., Hubbard, R. L., Maisto, S. A., Cavanaugh, E. R., Waddell, R. & Benrud, C. D. (1980). *Adolescent drinking behavior. Vol. I: The extent and nature of adolescent alcohol and drug use: The 1974 and 1978 national sample studies.* Research Triangle Park, NC: Research Triangle Institute.

Reed, R. (1988). Education and achievement of young black males. In J. T. Gibbs (Ed.). *Young, black and male in America: An endangered species.* Dover, MA: Auburn House.

Ridley, C. R. (1984). Clinical treatment of the nondisclosing black client: A therapeutic paradox. *American Psychologist, 39,* 1234-1244.

Rivers, L. W., Henderson, D. M., Jones, R. L., Ladner, J. A., Williams, R. L. (1975). Mosaic of labels for black children. In N. Hobbs (Ed.). *Issues in the classification of children* (Vol. 2). San Francisco: Jossey-Bass.

Robinson, B. (1988). *Teenage fathers.* Lexington, MA: Lexington Books.

Robinson, P., & Andersen, A. (1985). Anorexia Nervosa in American blacks. *Journal of Psychiatric Research, 19,* 183-188.

Rose, H. M. (1986). Can we substantially lower homicide risk in the nation's larger black communities? In *Report of the secretary's task force on black and minority health* (Vol. 5). Washington, DC: U.S. Department of Health and Human Services.

Rosenberg, M. (1979). *Conceiving the self.* New York: Basic Books.

Rosenberg, M., & Simmons, R. (1971). *Black and white self-esteem: The urban school child.* Rose Monograph Series. Washington, DC: American Sociological Association.

Sager, C., Brayboy, T., & Waxenberg, B. (1970). *Black ghetto family in therapy.* New York: Grove.

Samuda, R. (1975). *Psychological testing of American minorities: Issues and consequences.* New York: Dodd, Mead.

Schoenbach, V., Kaplan, B., Wagner, E., Grimson, R., & Miller, F. (1983). Prevalence of self-reported depressive symptoms in young adolescents. *American Journal of Public Health, 73,* 1281-1287.

Schorr, A. (1986). *Common decency: Domestic policies after Reagan.* New Haven, CT: Yale University Press.

Schulz, D. A. (1969). *Coming up black: Patterns of ghetto socialization.* Englewood Cliffs, NJ: Prentice-Hall.

Shaffer, D., & Fisher, P. (1981). The epidemiology of suicide in children and young adolescents. *Journal of the American Academy of Child Psychiatry, 20,* 545-565.

Skager, R. (1986). *A statewide survey of drug and alcohol use among California students in grades 7, 9, and 11*. Sacramento, CA: Office of the Attorney General.

Smith, E. (1982). The black female adolescent: A review of the educational, career and psychological literature. *Psychology of Women Quarterly, 6*, 261-288.

Snowden, L., & Todman, P. A. (1982). The psychological assessment of blacks: New and needed developments. In E. E. Jones & S. J. Korchin (Eds.). *Minority mental health*. New York: Praeger.

Solomon, B. (1988). The impact of public policy on the status of young black males. In J. T. Gibbs (Ed.)., *Young, black and male in America: An endangered species*. Dover, MA: Auburn House.

Spencer, M. B. (1982). Personal and group identity of black children: An alternative synthesis. *Genetic Psychology Monographs, 106*, 59-84.

Stack, C. (1974). *All our kin*. New York: Harper & Row.

Taylor, R. L. (1976). Psychosocial development among black children and youth: A reexamination. *American Journal of Orthopsychiatry, 46*, 4-19.

Tolmach, J. (1985). "There ain't nobody on my side": A new day treatment program for black urban youth. *Journal of Clinical Child Psychology, 14*, 214-219.

U.S. Bureau of the Census. (1987a). Money, income and poverty status of families and persons in the United States: 1986. *Current Population Reports*, Series P-60, 157. Washington, DC: Author.

U.S. Bureau of the Census. (1987b). *Statistical Abstract of the United States, 1987. (107th Ed.)*. Washington, DC: U.S. Department of Commerce.

U.S. Department of Health and Human Services (DHHS). (1986). *Report of the secretary's task force on black and minority health* (Vol. 5). Washington, DC: Author.

Warshauer, M., & Monk, M. (1978). Problems in suicide statistics for whites and blacks. *American Journal of Public Health, 68*, 383-388.

Wilson, W. J. (1987). *The truly disadvantaged*. Chicago: The University of Chicago Press.

Wise, P. H., Kotalchuck, M., & Mills, M. (1985). Racial and socioeconomic disparities in childhood mortality in Boston. *New England Journal of Medicine, 313*, 360-366.

Wissow, L. S., Gittelsohn, A. M., Szklo, M., Starfield, B., & Mussman, M. (1988). Poverty, race, and hospitalization for childhood asthma. *American Journal of Public Health, 78*, 777-781.

2

Ethnic Identity Development and Psychological Adjustment in Adolescence

JEAN S. PHINNEY
BRUCE T. LOCHNER
RODOLFO MURPHY

Numerous writers from diverse fields have suggested that minority status in society entails risk for a variety of psychological disorders, such as identity confusion (Erikson, 1968), poor self-image (Tajfel, 1978), and feelings of alienation (Blackwell & Hart, 1982) or marginality (Stonequist, 1964). However, in spite of these views of risks faced by minorities, research has yielded conflicting results regarding the contention that minority individuals necessarily suffer lower self-esteem or more adjustment problems than other members of society (Baldwin, 1979; Cross, 1987; Gordon, 1976, 1980; McShane, 1988; Rosenberg & Simmons, 1970). Much of the research and controversy in this area has focused on children, and recent reviews of the literature suggest a variety of factors that

authors' note: Preparation of this chapter was supported in part by PHS Grant R-08101 from the MBRS Program Division of the National Institutes of Health and by Grant 1 R15 HD23349-01A1 from the National Institute of Child Health and Human Development. Address of the first author: Department of Family Studies, California State University, Los Angeles, CA 90032.

explain conflicting findings, including methodological shortcomings (Banks, 1976), confusion between personal and group identity (Cross, 1987), and sociological changes in the status of minorities (Vaughan, 1987).

There has been far less attention paid to the psychological stresses experienced by minority adolescents, in spite of widespread recognition of sociological problems, such as poverty, inferior education, and unemployment (e.g., Blackwell & Hart, 1982; Gibbs, 1988) faced by many of these youth. Adolescents, because of their developmental level and wider experience in school and the community, face more complex psychological issues related to ethnicity than do children.

Central to adolescent development is the task of achieving an identity, a subjective sense of sameness and continuity that serves as a guide for one's life; failure to achieve an identity can lead to confusion and despair (Erikson, 1968). For minority youth, ethnicity is an essential component of the identity process, and the development of an ethnic identity is essential to a healthy personality (Arce, 1981; Baldwin, 1979; Gurin & Epps, 1975; Maldonado, 1975). It is our thesis that *a commitment to an ethnic identity is an important component of the self-concept of minority youth and a factor that mediates the relation between minority status and adjustment.* That is, adolescents who do not explore and take a stand on issues regarding their status as minority group members, nor develop a secure ethnic identity with which to obtain meaning and self-direction in an ethnically heterogeneous society, may be at risk for poor self concept or identity disorders. While we recognize that for many minorities external circumstances are limiting factors in the development of self-concept, our concern here is with how commitment to ethnic identity contributes to psychological adjustment. The discrepant findings in previous research may have resulted in part from a failure to take into account the way individuals respond to and deal with their ethnicity.

We suggest that minority individuals need to resolve two primary issues or conflicts that stem from their status as members of non-dominant group in society. These issues are: (a) the existence of what is at best ignorance, and at worst stereotyping and prejudice towards themselves and their group, and (b) the existence of two different sets of norms and values, those of their own culture and those of the majority, which have varying degrees of impact on their lives. In attempting to respond to these issues and conflicts, minority youth may actively compare options and make decisions on how to deal with them, or ignore and fail to deal consciously with them. Actively exploring and resolving these issues leads to an achieved ethnic identity, while failure to do so leads to a diffused or foreclosed ethnic identity. These approaches are likely to have different mental health outcomes and provide a partial explanation of discrepant findings regarding self-concept in minority youth. Rather than attempt to resolve the question of whether minority adolescents manifest poorer self-esteem or adjustment than white youth, we must determine which youth under what circumstances are most at risk for such problems.

In order to demonstrate the role of ethnic identity in the mental health of minority youth, we describe, in the first section, the two central issues, or sources of stress, that minority group members face. In the second section we discuss the options that have been suggested for dealing with these stresses and the mental health implications of these options. In the final section, we present a model of ethnic identity development that describes the process by which minority individuals come to understand their ethnicity and achieve a positive identity as minority group members. A clarification of these factors can contribute to an understanding of the mental health risks of minority adolescents and provide information useful to mental health workers.

Ethnic Identity Issues and Conflicts

Ignorance, Stereotypes, and Prejudice

According to Tajfel (1978), individuals who belong to a group that is disparaged and treated stereotypically by the majority group face a threat to their self-concept: "As long as the membership of a minority is defined by general consensus as a departure from some ill-defined 'norm' inherent . . . in the majority, the self-image and self-respect problems of minority individuals will continue to be acute" (Tajfel, 1978, p. 9). Evidence for the impact of negative stereotypes on minority youth is widespread, including mental health problems (Gibbs, 1988), poor academic performance

(Howard & Hammond, 1985), and alienation (Blackwell & Hart, 1982).

However, stereotypes lead to a poor self-concept only if they are accepted and believed. Alternatively, minorities may reject the stereotypes and redefine themselves and their group in positive terms (Tajfel, 1978). This may be difficult, in view of the pervasive images of minorities throughout society. Attempts to insulate themselves from the views of the dominant culture may be effective in the short term but are not a permanent solution. More effective are efforts to emphasize the positive elements in one's culture and to develop ethnic pride (for example, promoting the concept, "Black is beautiful").

Conflicts of Norms and Values

Writers from a variety of perspectives have discussed the conflicts that may result from differences in the norms and values of distinct cultural groups. Berry and his colleagues have elucidated the problems associated with attempting to function simultaneously in two cultures that differ in areas such as values, attitudes, customs, and styles of interaction (Berry & Annis, 1974; Berry & Kim, 1988; Berry, Kim, Minde, & Mok, 1987). Four dimensions of cultural differences, based on the writings of a number of psychologists and sociologists, have been suggested as possible sources of conflict among different groups (Rotheram & Phinney, 1987): Individual versus group orientation; active versus passive coping style; authoritarian versus egalitarian interaction style; and expressive versus restrained communication. For example, the white middle-class values of individuality, hard work, frugality, and self-reliance in many instances are in contrast with those of minority groups such as American Indians (Burgess, 1980), lower class blacks (Steele, 1988), and Hispanics (Fitzpatrick & Travieso, 1980). Minority individuals are faced with the necessity of choosing between their own cultural attitudes and behaviors and those of the dominant group, or of attempting to combine them in some way. Ogbu (1987) discusses the extreme form of this conflict among American blacks who, for historical reasons, define what is appropriate or legitimate for them in terms of attitudes, beliefs, and practices *in opposition* to the attitudes and practices of white Americans. These conflicts may be particularly acute for biracial adolescents, as rejection of the values of either group implies a rejection of one parent (Logan, Freeman, & McRoy, 1987). However, similar conflicts are faced by most minority youth.

Ways of Coping with Ethnic Identity Conflicts

In the struggle to deal with the ethnic identity conflicts and issues that have been discussed, a number of possible outcomes or responses have been suggested by Tajfel (1978), Berry and Kim (1988) and others. The possible behavioral and psychological responses to minority group membership can be summarized as follows: (a) alienation or marginalization, (b) separation, (c) assimilation, and (d) integration or biculturalism. Clearly, these responses are not equally available to all minority youth; structural factors such as social boundaries, discrimination, and poverty will affect the outcome for a given individual (Tajfel, 1978). However, each of these is conceptually possible at the individual level. In the following section we discuss these outcomes and their mental health implications.

A. Alienation/Marginalization

Individuals accept the negative self-image presented by society, become alienated from their own culture, and do not adapt to the majority culture.

While there is no normative data to indicate how widespread the phenomenon may be, Tajfel (1978) acknowledges that some individuals accept the majority view of their ethnic group as inferior; such acceptance may lead to a sense of inferiority, and even self-hatred, as has been suggested by Erikson (1968). The clinical and counseling literature documents cases of individuals who are not comfortable with their ethnicity and would prefer to belong to another group (Atkinson, Morten, & Sue, 1983; Mendelberg, 1986; Parham & Helms, 1985a). Several empirical studies similarly provide examples of adolescents who express a current or past preference for the majority group or desire to change their ethnicity

(Kim, 1981; Krate, Leventhal & Silverstein, 1974; Phinney, 1989; Phinney & Tarver, 1988).

Berry and Kim (1988) point out that those who do not value their own culture and cannot participate in the dominant culture experience "feelings of alienation, marginality, and loss of identity . . ." (p. 212). Such marginalization "tends to suspend the individual in a highly stressful crisis" (p. 213) that is predictive of poor mental health. Perhaps the best example of this outcome is among many American Indians whose native traditions have been lost and who have not become part of the mainstream. The dislocation of tribes and alteration of traditions have been tied to hopelessness, alcoholism, and suicide (Berlin, 1987). Suicide rates are higher in tribes whose religious traditions have been disrupted (Berlin, 1986), and Burgess (1980) suggests that disruption of Indian values, particularly in instances where they have not been replaced, has led to helplessness and powerlessness. Lefley (1982) found that among Miccosukee and Seminole tribal groups in Florida low self-esteem was directly related to tribal disintegration and identity conflict resulting from sociocultural change.

The disruption of socialization of American Indians within their culture has had a negative impact on mental health. Studies have documented depression, antisocial behavior, and poor self-image among adolescents sent to boarding school (Berlin, 1986, 1987; Bryde, 1971; McShane, 1988). In many cases adolescents who are forced to leave their tribes and earn a living in the mainstream society find themselves caught between two worlds and accepted by neither. Mindell and Gurwitt (1977) found higher rates of psychotic depression, serious mental illness, and suicide among Indian adolescents adopted by white families than among their counterparts on the reservation.

Studies on alienation among blacks have found a direct link between socioeconomic deprivation and feelings of powerlessness, meaninglessness, and social isolation. In a study with 207 whites and 99 blacks, Middleton (1963) found that alienation was pervasive in the black community and negatively correlated with educational level. Blackwell and Hart (1982) found in a survey conducted in five large cities that 8 in 10 blacks could be classified as somewhat isolated. They also replicated Middleton's finding of a negative correlation between educational level and alienation. In addition, Gordon (1965), and Willie (1965) argue that racial segregation, discrimination, and feelings of dependence constitute the primary sources of alienation in the black community.

B. Assimilation

Individuals attempt to become part of the dominant culture and do not maintain their ties with their ethnic culture.

Minorities may strive to be like the majority group, that is, to take on the values and attitudes of the majority, giving up their own cultural values in the process. For white immigrants from European countries, this may result in complete assimilation in a generation or two, if individuals choose not to maintain their ethnic traditions.

However, for minorities of color, complete assimilation is not possible, as they are immediately identifiable as members of their group. Tajfel (1978) sees their attempt to assimilate as an uneasy compromise that involves rejecting aspects of their own culture and distancing themselves from other members of their own group. Individuals from disparaged groups who attempt to become part of the majority group may still accept the majority's negative view of their group but deal with it by differentiating themselves from their group. In interviews with minority 10th-graders (Phinney, 1989), repeated examples were found of adolescents distancing themselves from aspects of their group; for example, blacks who stated that they were not like the kids who were into gangs and drugs, and Hispanics who said they wanted to do well in school (unlike many of their Hispanic peers). Sazpocznik and Kurtines (1980), from their studies of Cuban Americans, suggest that adolescents who, in their attempts to become American, reject the skills necessary to interact within their own culture are at particular risk for maladjustment.

The issues are particularly complex for middle-class minorities, whose *social class* values are similar to white middle-class values. A middle-class life-style may be seen as a denial or rejection of their ethnic group. The conflict is vividly portrayed by Steele (1988), who states, "My middle-class identity involved a dissociation from the images of lower-class black life" (p. 44). Rodriguez (1982) described the pain of distancing himself from his Mexican-American family as he became successful professionally in the majority culture.

C. Withdrawal or Separation

Individuals emphasize their ethnic culture and withdraw from contact with the dominant group.

According to Tajfel (1978), one of the strategies employed by minority group members to maintain a positive self-concept in the face of negative evaluations by the majority is to embed oneself in one's own ethnic culture, in order to minimize the loss of self-esteem that results from comparisons with the majority group. Through cultural and psychological isolation, minorities can remain encapsulated in ethnic enclaves and thus avoid dealing with negative stereotypes. When comparisons between the ethnic group and the majority culture are minimized, high self-esteem is maintained (Rovner, 1981). According to Tajfel (1978), "One can remain happy and contented inside a ghetto" (p. 13).

Separation may thus provide temporary protection against internalization of negative stereotypes. Powell and Fuller found that black 7th-, 8th-, and 9th-graders in predominantly black schools had higher self-concepts than their peers in integrated schools (Powell & Fuller, 1970, cited in Gordon, 1980). The authors attributed the findings to the influence of black role models and insulation from a devalued view of blacks by the white majority.

However, such segregation may be positive only if it is not seen as imposed separation based on racism (Gordon, 1980; Willie, 1965). Furthermore it leaves the individual unprepared to cope with realities of prejudice and discrimination when they leave their own community. Szapocznik and Kurtines (1980) suggest that individuals in a bicultural context tend to become maladjusted when they remain monocultural and fail to learn how to interact in the mainstream context.

Furthermore the economic and political realities of modern society make it virtually impossible for minority youth to avoid contact with the majority culture, through schools, jobs, and the media. Even on Indian reservations, adolescents are exposed to television with its predominantly white standards of appearance and behavior.

D. Integration/Biculturalism

Individuals retain their ethnic culture and adapt to the dominant culture by learning the necessary skills.

Ethnic minorities may attempt both to retain their own cultural values and to maintain contact with the larger society, a solution that has been called integration (Berry & Kim, 1988), ethnic pluralism, or biculturalism (Szapocznik & Kurtines, 1980). Tajfel (1978) sees this as perhaps the most satisfactory solution for minorities, but it is not without problems. To accomplish this, group members must be able to assert their own ethnic values and traditions without rejecting those of the majority. Aspects of their culture that have been devalued or weakened because they differ from or are disparaged by the majority must be revitalized and strengthened. They can then be affirmed not only within their own group but to the wider society. Specific group characteristics can be reevaluated as positive, for example, by means of assertions that "black is beautiful" and similar statements of ethnic pride.

Evidence for this process can be seen in the trend towards increasingly positive attitudes of blacks toward their own group during and following the Civil Rights movement of the 1960s (Cross, 1987; Gordon, 1980). Blackwell and Hart (1982) found that blacks with a strong sense of group solidarity experienced the lowest feelings of social isolation and the highest degrees of community involvement. Berlin (1987) described efforts of some Indian communities to emphasize teaching of traditional ways while at the same time encouraging the acquisition of academic skills needed in the white culture.

In addition, there is some empirical evidence that maintaining both one's ethnic traditions and contacts with the majority culture affords the best psychological outcomes. In research with a variety of Canadian ethnic groups, Berry, Kim, Mindy, & Mok, (1987) found that those subjects favoring integration experienced the least stress; those preferring separation experienced the most. Among Hispanic subjects, Lang, Munoz, Bernal, and Sorenson (1982) found that those with a bicultural orientation, as opposed to a monocultural Hispanic or Anglo orientation, showed better psychological adjustment. Szapocznik and Kurtines (1980) likewise have shown that bicultural involvement contributes to positive adjustment.

Ideally, the dual focus on both one's own culture and that of the majority culture leads to the ability to see oneself as both ethnic and mainstream (e.g., American), and to accept both aspects of one's identity (Kim, 1981). However, the attempt to be part of two cultures can lead to considerable stress. This stress is likely to be particularly severe within immigrant families, where rapidly acculturating adolescents clash with their more traditional parents over values and behaviors (Arax, 1987; Szapocznik & Kurtines, 1980). Minority youth who are admitted to primarily white schools also experience stress in dealing with two conflicting cultures (Mabry, 1988; Rodriguez, 1982; Rousseve, 1987). In reporting on the case of a Harlem youth who was unable to handle the stress, Rousseve suggests that nonwhite students must not allow their ethnic or racial identity to "intrude destructively on the demanding process of mastering those skills and attitudes that foster . . . success in a modern society" (p. 7). However, there are few models that provide guidance for minority youth as to how to deal with the stress of the duality.

In summary, in order to deal with the reality of being a member of an ethnic group as part of a larger society, individuals are faced with a limited number of options. The four approaches that have been discussed are not mutually exclusive and may not be exhaustive. However, a consideration of these alternatives suggests that minority youth do not necessarily have poor self-concepts or become marginal people in society. There are a variety of outcomes for minority youth, in dealing with their status as minority group members.

In discussing the effects of acculturation, Berry and Kim (1988) state, "It is not the acculturative changes themselves that are important, but how one sees them and what one makes of them" (pp. 217-218). Similarly, for minority youth, an important consideration is how they deal with the issues posed by their ethnicity. Research has recently begun to examine how minority youth develop attitudes and make decisions for themselves with regard to the possible ways of living as an ethnic group member in a pluralistic society. In the final sections we discuss the process by which adolescents examine ethnic identity issues and conflicts as part of the identity formation process.

Identity Development in Adolescence

The key developmental task of adolescence, according to Erikson (1968) is the achievement of a secure identity. Identity is achieved by means of a process of search and commitment outlined by Erikson (1968) and studied empirically by Marcia (1966, 1980), Waterman (1985), Adams (Adams, Bennion, & Huh, 1987), and others. Early empirical work by Marcia (1966), 1980) provided a model for categorizing adolescents in one of four ego identity statuses depending on the extent to which they had explored identity issues and made a decision or commitment regarding them. There are two advanced or mature ego identity statuses: an *achieved identity* characterized by a commitment that has followed an exploration of relevant issues, and *moratorium,* an ongoing search without a commitment; and two less mature statuses: a *foreclosed identity* characterized by commitment without exploration, and *identity diffusion,* the absence of both search and commitment.

Failure to achieve a satisfying identity can have negative psychological implications for all adolescents, not only those from minority groups. Adolescents categorized as relatively low in ego identity, compared to those that are rated as high, have been found to be more susceptible to self-esteem manipulation (Marica, 1967); more apt to accept fake personality sketches of themselves (Gruen, 1960); more likely to think of themselves as misperceived by others (Bunt, 1968); more likely to view chance as a major determinant of events (Adams & Shea, 1978); less likely to be self-accepting (Rasmussen, 1964); more influenced by peer conformity pressure (Adams, Ryan, Hoffman, Dobson, & Nielsen, 1985); and more likely to use cocaine, inhalants, marijuana, and hallucinogens (Jones & Hartman, 1985). An extensive review of research (Waterman, 1984) shows a strong link between ego identity and effective psychological functioning.

The Process of Ethnic Identity Development

The ego identity research has examined the identity domains of occupation, religion, politics, and sex roles, but has not included ethnicity as a dimension of identity formation. There is, however, a separate literature in which minority investigators have described ethnic identity development. Cross (1978) developed a model of the development of black consciousness in college students during the Civil Rights era, and Parham and Helms (1981, 1985a, 1985b) have conducted a series of studies using Cross's model. Kim (1981) developed a model of Asian-American identity development based on interviews with Asian-American young adult females. A model based on clinical experience has been proposed by Atkinson, Morten, and Sue (1983), and Arce (1981) has conceptualized the issues with regard to Chicanos.

Several recent studies (Phinney, 1989; Phinney & Alipuria, 1990; Phinney & Tarver, 1988) present empirical evidence for a model of ethnic identity development that is consistent with Marcia's (1966) model of ego identity and with the ethnic identity models cited. An interview study with Asian American, black, and Mexican American 10th-graders (Phinney, 1989) has provided evidence for three distinct stages of ethnic identity: an initial stage in which ethnicity is not seen an issue and has not been explored (diffusion/foreclosure); a second stage in which there is increasing awareness and concern about ethnicity (moratorium); and a final stage in which the adolescents have come to terms with ethnic issues and accepted themselves as members of a minority group. A description of these stages, with examples from the other ethnic identity models cited, is presented in the following sections, to elucidate the process by which minority youth explore ethnic issues and achieve a positive sense of themselves as minority group members.

Ethnic Identity Diffusion/Foreclosure

The first stage of ethnic identity development is characterized by lack of exploration of ethnic issues. This may be accompanied by lack of interest or concern with the subject (diffusion) or by attitudes about one's ethnicity that are derived from others (foreclosure). Existing models of ethnic identity development suggest that minority subjects in this stage accept the values and attitudes of the majority culture, including, often, internalized negative views of their own group. In this first stage, "the person's world view is dominated by Euro-American determinants" (Cross, 1978; p. 17). Parham and Helms's (1985a) measure of black identity development, which builds on Cross's work, includes items for this stage such as "I believe that the white man is superior intellectually," and "Sometimes I wish I belonged to the white race." Similarly, the model suggested by Atkinson, Morten, and Sue (1983) describes a Conformity Stage, in which individuals show an "unequivocal preference for dominant cultural values over those of their own culture . . . Individuals who acknowledge their distinguishing physical and/or cultural characteristics consciously view them as a source of shame" (pp. 35-36). Kim's (1981) data, based on in-depth interviews with adult Asian American women, gives ample support to this view. She identifies an initial stage in which "subjects . . . internalized the white societal values and standards and saw themselves through the eyes of the white society" (p. 129); in other words, they accepted white values, beliefs, standards, and accepted whites as a reference group.

These descriptions of the first stage of ethnic identity development provide evidence for the internalization of negative stereotypes discussed earlier. However, in interviews with 10th-graders (Phinney, 1989), only limited evidence was found of preference for the majority group. More typically, adolescents in the first stage showed ethnic identity diffusion, in that they had given little thought to ethnicity and seemed unconcerned about it. For example, one black female states, "Why do I need to learn about who was the first black woman to do this or that? I'm just not too interested" (p. 44).

Phinney (1989) found that adolescents at this first stage had consistently lower scores on all four subscales of an independent measure of psychological adjustment (self-evaluation, sense of mastery, social and peer relations, and family relations). A study with Asian American, black, and Mexican American college students reported likewise that students low in ethnic identity search and commitment had lower self-esteem (Phinney & Alipuria, in press). Similarly, a study with black college students, based on the Cross (1978) model, found that low self-esteem was associated with the earliest stage of black identity (Parham & Helms, 1985a). There is thus some evidence that the failure to examine ethnic issues leaves adolescents and young adults at risk for poor self-concept.

Ethnic Identity Search/Moratorium

The initial stage of ethnic identity is thought to continue until individuals have an experience, for example with racism, which forces an awareness of themselves as members of a minority group held in low esteem by the majority. A common experience of Kim's (1981) subjects was that of recognizing that white standards of attractiveness were more valued by society but that one's skin, hair, or features differed from those standards. Mexican American adolescents are faced with a similar conflict, as they become aware of the negative images of their group that are presented to them by society (Mendelberg, 1986). Cross (1978) termed this an encounter experience, which he described as a shocking personal or social event. However, Phinney (1989) found little evidence of a dramatic experience that precipitated a search. Rather, students reported experiences similar to those described by Atkinson, Morton, & Sue, (1983) as "a growing awareness that not all cultural values of the dominant group are beneficial to him/her" (p. 37).

This growing awareness leads to an ethnic identity search, or moratorium. According to Cross (1978), the search or "immersion" stage is characterized by an "intense concern to clarify the personal implications" of ethnicity. For Kim's (1981) subjects, it involved "an effort to better understand themselves and their people," (p. 147); it may include heightened political consciousness, with involvement in social-political movements. In interviews in integrated schools, it was found that about one third of 8th-graders (Phinney & Tarver, 1988) and over half the 10th-graders (Phinney, 1989) had engaged or were currently engaged in some form of exploration regarding their ethnicity. These subjects expressed interest in learning more about their culture and were actively involved in doing so; for example, a Mexican American female stated, "I wanted to know what we do and how our culture is different from others. Going to festivals and cultural events helped me to learn more about my own culture and about myself" (Phinney, 1989, p. 44). These students talked with family or friends about ethnic issues, read books (beyond those required for school courses) and went to ethnic museums. In addition, they had thought about the effects of their ethnicity on their life, in the present and future. They often expressed awareness of prejudice and possible difficulties in attaining their educational or career objectives.

According to some writers, the ethnic identity search, in addition to involving efforts to learn about their culture, is likely to be highly emotional: "Included in this phase is anger and outrage directed toward white society. This occurs when [subjects] discover and allow themselves to feel some of the historical incidents of racism directed against Asian Americans" (Kim, 1981; p. 149). For Cross (1978), the process includes "the tendency to denigrate white people and white culture while simultaneously deifying black people and black culture" and can be accompanied by "euphoria, rage . . . a destructive mood in constant tension with dreams of revitalization, and an intense sense of intimacy toward black life" (p. 17). In writing about black youth, Erikson (1964) acknowledges the intensity of this period and recognizes the role of their anger and destructiveness: "A *transitory* 'negative identity' is often the necessary precondition for a truly positive and truly new one" (p. 37; italics in original). However, in interviews with 8th-graders (Phinney & Tarver, 1988) and 10th-graders (Phinney, 1989), students in this stage showed little of the intense emotion that Cross describes.

The evidence on the psychological adjustment associated with this stage is limited and inconsistent. Parham and Helms (1985a) found that high self-esteem was related to the encounter stage, but low self-esteem to the immersion (moratorium) stage. Phinney (1989) found adjustment scores at this stage slightly but not significantly higher than in the first stage.

Ethnic Identity Achievement

The ideal outcome of the identity process is an achieved identity. Individuals with an achieved ego identity have resolved uncertainties about their future direction and have made commitments that will guide future action (Marcia, 1980). In the area of ethnicity, identity achievement corresponds to acceptance and internalization of one's ethnicity. Writers from diverse ethnic backgrounds have described the sense of ethnic identity achievement as follows: "Following this period of cultural and political consciousness . . .

individuals develop a deeper sense of belonging to the group. . . . When the person finally comes to feel at one with the group, the internalization process has been completed, and ethnic identity established" (Arce, 1981; p. 186). "Tension, emotionality, and defensiveness are replaced by a calm, secure demeanor. Ideological flexibility, psychological openness, and self-confidence about one's blackness are evident" (Cross, 1978; p. 18). According to Kim (1981), "self-concept during this stage is positive. Subjects feel good about who they are and feel proud to be Asian American. They also feel comfortable with both parts of themselves (Asian and American). At last, they feel at home with themselves" (p. 150).

In interviews with 10th-graders (Phinney, 1989), we found that subjects at this stage had come to terms with negative stereotypes and conflicting values. For example, a Mexican American female stated, "People put me down because I'm Mexican, but I don't care any more. I can accept myself more" (p. 44). A black female summarized her development from a foreclosed to achieved ethnic identity as follows:

> I used to want to be white, because I wanted long flowing hair; and I wanted to be real light. I used to think being light was prettier, but now I think there are pretty dark-skinned girls and pretty light-skinned girls. I don't want to be white now. I'm happy being black. (p. 44)

In several studies, we have found that adolescents with an achieved ethnic identity show better psychological adjustment (Phinney, 1989) and higher self-esteem (Phinney & Alipuria, 1990). The implication for those who provide counseling or therapy to minority adolescents is that minority youth should be encouraged to explore their feelings and attitudes regarding their ethnicity. They should learn about the history of their group within a multi-cultural society and discuss the ways of dealing with two cultures. They need to understand and reevaluate negative images of their own group. Although this may invoke a somewhat disturbing exploration or moratorium period, the process can be expected to lead ultimately to a more secure sense of self and more healthy adjustment.

Summary

Youth from minority ethnic groups, especially those from non-white groups, face stresses associated with their membership in a minority group in American society. Two fundamental sources of stress are the pervasive negative stereotypes projected by the majority culture and the conflicts between ethnic and mainstream values and attitudes. Various ways of responding to these stresses have been discussed, including alienation, assimilation, separation, and integration or biculturalism. However, none of these outcomes is completely satisfactory. In order to develop a confident sense of themselves and secure ethnic identity, minority youth need to explore these issues and options and develop their own sense of the meaning of their ethnicity. The stage model that has been presented is useful in mapping out the process by which minority youth achieve an ethnic identity and in demonstrating the importance of this process to the mental health of minority youth.

References

Adams, G., Bennion, L., & Huh, K. (1987). *Objective measure of ego identity status: A reference manual.* Logan, UT: Utah State University.

Adams, G. R., Ryan, J. H., Hoffman, J. J., Dobson, W. R., & Nielsen, E. C. (1985). Ego identity status, conformity behavior, and personality in late adolescence. *Journal of Personality and Social Psychology, 47,* 1091-1104.

Adams, G. R., & Shea, J. H. (1978). The relationship between identity status, locus of control, and ego development. *Journal of Youth and Adolescence, 8,* 81-89.

Arax, M. (1987, April 12). Clash of two worlds leaves many in pain. *Los Angeles Times.*

Arce, C. (1981). A reconsideration of Chicano culture and identity. *Daedalus, 110*(2), 177-192.

Atkinson, D., Morten, G., & Sue, D. (1983). *Counseling American minorities.* Dubuque, IA: William C. Brown.

Baldwin, J. (1979). Theory and research concerning the notion of black self-hatred. *The Journal of Black Psychology, 5,* 51-77.

Banks, W. (1976). White preference in blacks: A paradigm in search of a phenomenon. *Psychological Bulletin, 83,* 1179-1186.

Berlin, I. N. (1986). Psychopathology and its antecedents among American Indian adolescents. In B. B. Lahey & A. E. Kazdin (Eds.), *Advances in Clinical Child Psychology,* (Vol. 9), pp. 125-152).

Berlin, I. N. (1987). Effects of changing native American cultures on child develop-ment. *Journal of Community Psychology, 15*, 299-306.

Berry, J., & Annis, R. (1974). Acculturative stress: The role of ecology, culture, and differentiation. *Journal of Cross-Cultural Psychology, 5*, 382-406.

Berry, J., & Kim, U. (1988). Acculturation and mental health. In P. R. Dasen, J. W. Berry, & N. Sartorius (Eds.), *Health and Cross-Cultural Psychology:* (Vol. 10). Cross-Cultural Research and Methodology Series. Newbury Park, CA: Sage.

Berry, J., Kim, U., Minde, T., & Mok, D. (1987). Comparative studies of acculturative stress. *International Migration Review, 21*, 491-511.

Blackwell, J., & Hart, P. (1982). *Cities, suburbs, and blacks: A study of concerns, distrust, and alienation.* Bayside, NY: General Hall.

Bryde, J. F. (1971). *Indian students and guidance.* Boston: Houghton Mifflin.

Bunt, M. E. (1968). Ego identity: Its relationship to the discrepancy between how an adolescent views himself and how he perceives that others view him. *Psychology, 5*, 14-25.

Burgess, B. J. (1980). Parenting in the Native-American community. In M. D. Fantini & R. Cardenas (Eds.), *Parenting in a multicultural society* (pp. 63-73), New York: Longman.

Cross, W. (1978). The Thomas and Cross models of psychological nigrescence: A literature review. *Journal of Black Psychology, 4*, 13-31.

Cross, W. (1987). A two-factor theory of black identity: Implications for the study of identity development in minority children. In J. Phinney & M. Rotheram (Eds.), *Children's ethnic socialization.* Newbury Park, CA: Sage.

Erikson, E. (1964). A memorandum on identity and Negro youth. *Journal of Social Issues, 20*, 29-42.

Erikson, E. (1968). *Identity: Youth and crisis.* New York: Norton.

Fitzpatrick, J. P., & Travieso, L. (1980). The Puerto Rican family: Its role in cultural transition. In M. D. Fantini & R. Cardenas (Eds.), *Parenting in a multicultural society* (pp. 103-119), New York: Longman.

Gibbs, J. (1988). *Young, black, and male in America: An endangered species.* Dover, MA: Auburn House.

Gordon D. (1965). A note on Negro alienation. *American Journal of Sociology, 70*, 477-478.

Gordon, V. (1976). The methodologies of black self-concept research: A critique. *Journal of Afro-American Issues, 4*, 373-381.

Gordon, V. (1980). *The self-concept of black Americans.* Lanham, MD: University Press of America.

Gruen, W. (1960). Rejection of false information about oneself as an indicator of ego identity. *Journal of Consulting Psychiatry, 24*, 231-233.

Gurin, P., & Epps, E. (1975). *Black consciousness, identity, and achievement.* New York: John Wiley.

Howard, J., & Hammond, R. (1985, September 9). Rumors of inferiority: The hidden obstacles to black success. *The New Republic*, pp. 17-21.

Jones, R., & Hartman, B. (1985). Ego identity, self-esteem, and substance use during adolescence. ERIC Document Reproduction Service No. ED 263 454.

Kim, J. (1981). *The process of Asian-American identity development: A study of Japanese American women's perceptions of their struggle to achieve positive identities.* Unpublished doctoral dissertation, University of Massachusetts.

Krate, R., Leventhal, G., & Silverstein, B. (1974). Self-perceived transformation of negro-to-black identity. *Psychological Reports, 35,* 1071-1075.

Lang, J., Munoz, R., Bernal, G., & Sorenson, J. (1982). Quality of life and psychological well-being in a bicultural Latino community. *Hispanic Journal of Behavioral Sciences, 4,* 433-450.

Lefley, H. (1982). Self-perception and primary prevention for American Indians. In S. Manson (Ed.), *New directions in prevention among American Indian and Alaska Native communities* (pp. 65-88). Portland: Oregon Health Sciences University Press.

Logan, S., Freeman, E., & McRoy, R. (1987). Racial identity problems of bi-racial clients: Implications for social work practice. *Journal of Intergroup Relations, 15,* 11-24.

Mabry, M. (1988, April). Living in two worlds. *Newsweek on Campus,* 52.

Maldonado, D., Jr. (1975). Ethnic self-identity and self-understanding. *Social Casework, 56,* 618-622.

Marcia, J. (1966). Development and validation of ego-identity status. *Journal of Personality and Social Psychology, 3,* 551-558.

Marcia, J. (1967). Ego identity status: relationship to change in self esteem, "general maladjustment," and authoritarianism. *Journal of Personality, 35,* 119-133.

Marcia, J. (1980). Identity in adolescence. In J. Adelson (Ed.), *Handbook of adolescent psychology* (pp. 159-187). New York: John Wiley.

McShane, D. (1988). An analysis of mental health research with American Indian youth. *Journal of Adolescence, 11,* 87-116.

Mendelberg, H. (1986). Identity conflict in Mexican-American adolescents. *Adolescence, 21,* 215-222.

Middleton, R. (1963). Alienation in inner city ghettos. *American Journal of Sociological Review, 28,* 973-977.

Mindell, C., & Gurwitt, A. (1977). The placement of American Indian children: The need for change. In S. Unger (Ed.), *The destruction of the American Indian family* (pp. 61-66). New York: Association on American Indian Affairs.

Ogbu, J. (1987). Opportunity structure, cultural boundaries, and literacy. In J. Langer (Ed.), *Language, literacy, and culture: Issues of society and schooling* (pp. 149-177). Norwood, NJ: Ablex.

Parham, T., & Helms, J. (1981). The influence of black student's racial identity attitudes on preferences for counselor's race. *Journal of Counseling Psychology, 28,* 250-257.

Parham, T., & Helms, J. (1985a). Attitudes of racial identity and self-esteem of black students: An exploratory investigation. *Journal of College Student Personnel, 26,* 143-147.

Parham, T., & Helms, J. (1985b). Relation of racial identity attitudes to self-actualization and affective states of black students. *Journal of Counseling Psychology, 32,* 431-440.

Phinney, J. (1989). Stages of ethnic identity in minority group adolescents. *Journal of Early Adolescence, 9,* 34-49.

Phinney, J., & Alipuria, L. (1990). Ethnic identity in older adolescents from four ethnic groups. *Journal of Adolescence, 13,* 171-183.

Phinney, J., & Tarver, S. (1988) Ethnic identity search and commitment in black and white eighth graders. *Journal of Early Adolescence, 8,* 265-277.

Rasmussen, J. E. (1964). Relationship of ego identity to psychosocial effectiveness. *Psychological Reports, 15,* 815-825.

Rodriguez, R. (1982). *Hunger of memory.* Boston: Godine.

Rosenberg, M., & Simmons, R. (1970). *Black and white self-esteem: The black urban child.* (Rose Monograph Series). Washington, DC: American Sociological Association.

Rotheram, M. J., & Phinney, J. S. (1987). Introduction: Definitions and perspectives in the study of children's ethnic socialization. In J. Phinney & M. Rotheram (Eds.), *Children's ethnic socialization.* Newbury Park, CA: Sage.

Rousseve, R. (1987, March/April). A black American youth torn between cultures. *The Humanist,* 5-8.

Rovner, R. (1981). Ethno-cultural identity and self-esteem: A reapplication of self-attitude formation theories. *Human Relations, 34,* 427-434.

Steele, S. (1988). On being black and middle class. *Commentary, 85,* 42-47.

Stonequist, E. (1964). The marginal man: A study in personality and culture conflict. In E. Burgess & E. Bogue (Eds.), *Contributions to urban sociology.* Chicago: University of Chicago Press.

Szapocznik, J., & Kurtines, W. (1980). Acculturation, biculturalism, and adjustment among Cuban Americans. In A. Padilla, (Ed.), *Acculturation: Theory, models, and some new findings.* Boulder, CO: Westview.

Tajfel, H. (1978). *The social psychology of minorities.* New York: Minority Rights Group.

Vaughan, G. M. (1987). A social psychological model of ethnic identity development. In J. S. Phinney & M. J. Rotheram (Eds.), *Children's Ethnic Socialization.* Newbury Park, CA: Sage.

Waterman, A. (1984). *The psychology of individualism.* New York: Praeger.

Waterman, A. (1985). Identity in the context of adolescent psychology. In A. Waterman (Ed.), *Identity in adolescence: process and contents* (pp. 5-24). San Francisco: Jossey-Bass.

Willie, C. V. (1965). Education, deprivation and alienation. *Journal of Negro Education, 34,* 209-219.

```
┌─────────┐
│         │
│    3    │
│         │
└─────────┘
```

Psychocultural Factors Affecting the Mental Health Status of Mexican American Adolescents

JOHN M. CHAVEZ

COLLETTE E. RONEY

As the Mexican American adolescent population continues to grow, so does the need for more research on this ethnic group, particularly with respect to its mental health. Population statistics indicate that Mexican American families have more children under the age of 18 years than the national average (56% compared to 36% for the rest of the population). Although many of the adolescents are American born, increasing immigration from Mexico also contributes to the overall growth of this group (Hispanic Policy Development Project, 1984; U.S. Census Bureau, 1980). Additionally, many Mexican American families live in high risk environments where opportunities for social, economic, and educational development may be limited. Due to these factors a disproportionately large

Authors' Note: The authors wish to acknowledge Enrique Lopez Carlos for his assistance with the literature collection phase of this chapter. All correspondence should be sent to John M. Chavez, Occidental College, Department of Psychology, 1600 Campus Road, Los Angeles, CA 90041.

number of Mexican American adolescents may be at risk for varying mental health problems.

Unfortunately, very few studies have examined the mental
health status of Mexican American adolescents. Some studies show
poor mental health indicating that Mexican American adolescents
have higher rates of teenage pregnancy, substance abuse, and acquired immunodeficiency syndrome (AIDS) than the general population. Other data indicates that immigrant Mexican American
adolescents demonstrate higher educational achievement than
their U.S. born counterparts (Buriel, 1984). These achievement levels are consistent with those obtained by Euro-American adolescents. As educational achievement generally parallels better
mental health, such data illustrates the complexity of mental health
among Mexican American adolescents and the need to distinguish
between immigrant and U.S. born youth. The higher educational
achievement observed among immigrant Mexican Americans suggests that this group is adjusting well to mainstream society in the
United States despite the stress associated with immigrant status.
This particular finding also suggests that factors other than ethnicity may be related to mental health status.

Other factors, which have not been adequately controlled in
previous studies, include socioeconomic and educational differences. In addition, some studies have equated nativity status with
acculturation and count English-speaking Mexican Americans as
fully integrated into mainstream Euro-American society. Thus,
when comparing Spanish-speaking immigrants to their U.S. born
counterparts, assuming that the latter are more acculturated is
erroneous because they continue, in general, to function at disproportionately lower socioeconomic and educational levels than
those of mainstream Euro-American culture.

Finally, previous studies continue to draw from a theoretical
literature of dubious value. Many studies on Mexican American
adolescents argue that the mental health problems among this
group result from their adherence to Mexican culture. (See Levine
and Padilla, 1980, for a review). This position supports the "cultural damaging" viewpoint, is ethnocentric, and does not consider
the cultural heterogeneity of this ethnic group. A more recent
study, however, found that integration with indigenous Mexican
culture promotes good mental health behavior (Buriel, 1984). The

"cultural-integration" hypothesis posited by Buriel suggests that immigrant Mexican Americans exhibit achievement-oriented values related to a desire for upward mobility and advancement in U.S. mainstream Euro-American culture. This achievement-oriented behavior stems from the idea that immigration to the United States is selective. Fromm and Maccoby (1970) have indicated that these immigrants share personality characteristics including a strong desire for upward mobility and success in a new country. Presumably individuals who immigrate do so out of a common desire for change and, for the most part, share with one another a unique set of behavioral characteristics that distinguish them as one of the most productive segments of the Mexican population.

Fromm and Maccoby (1970) found that productive individuals were more interested in traditional cultural events, and expressed a tendency to identify with the strivings and attitudes of peoples in other parts of the world. Hence, the pride and self-confidence these individuals have in themselves as Mexicans, and their feelings of parity with other peoples, probably allows them to explore other cultural systems without feeling that such actions constitute rejection of their own culture. This implies that the behaviors, dress, skills, and values that immigrants pick and choose from Euro-American culture are viewed simply as added dimensions to their own Mexican culture rather than as a substitute for it. Such an open-minded attitude may account for the relatively rapid acculturation of some immigrants.

In contrast with the cultural-integration hypothesis is the concept of "deculturation." Deculturation, according to Berry (1980) and Buriel (1984), usually occurs among later generation Mexican Americans who lose their original achievement-oriented drives over the passage of successive generations presumably because of lower socioeconomic status, prejudice, and discrimination. Berry (1980) has described deculturation as follows:

> It is characterized by striking out against the larger society and by feelings of alienation, loss of identity, and what has been termed acculturative stress. This . . . is deculturation, in which groups are out of cultural and psychological contact with either their traditional culture or the larger society. (pp. 14-15)

Thus according to Berry, deculturation is a psychological process that occurs when members of an ethnic minority group fail to retain ancestral cultural values and simultaneously do not adopt the cultural values of the mainstream culture. Berry refers to deculturation as being tantamount to ethnocide. Although not always inevitable, deculturation commonly occurs among later generation ethnic minorities who have been the victims of racial discrimination. Victims of long-term discrimination may experience feelings of inadequacy and low self-worth. With the passage of successive generations such individuals are less able to identify with their traditional culture and are hindered from becoming fully integrated into the mainstream culture.

Taken together, the cultural-integration hypothesis and the concept of deculturation constitute important psychological factors that may directly affect the mental health status of Mexican American adolescents.

In light of these considerations, the present chapter examines current research on a number of issues regarding the mental health status of Mexican American adolescents. Specific topics discussed include teenage pregnancy, substance abuse, suicide, AIDS, educational achievement, and the extent to which previous studies support the cultural integration hypothesis and the concept of deculturation. Additionally, this chapter offers recommendations for conducting future research on this ethnic group.

Teenage Pregnancy

While the growing rate of teenage pregnancy confronts all adolescent populations in the United States, the fertility rates among Mexican American adolescents are particularly alarming. To begin with, between 1965 and 1980 the number of premarital births within the adolescent population increased 60% (Becerra & de Anda, 1984). Notably, however, Mexican American teenage pregnancy rates tend to run higher than those among Euro-Americans. For example, in 1981, 19% of the Mexican American adolescent population faced teenage pregnancy compared to only 12% for Euro-Americans (Orozco, 1985). Another study has indicated that Hispanic teenagers are 60% more likely to become pregnant than heir Euro-American counterparts (Garcia, 1981). Despite these ethnic differences, Lindemann and Scott (1982) reported no significant differences among pregnant adolescents in age, age at first menses, age at first intercourse, and number of sex partners between Mexican American and Euro-American adolescent girls. These data suggest that other factors may influence the attitudes of Mexican American adolescents regarding sexual practices.

The few studies that examine possible influence of culture on teenage fertility behavior target acculturation to mainstream American norms as a critical factor in analyzing such behavior among Mexican American adolescents (Becerra & de Anda, 1984; Lindemann & Scott, 1982). Using language status as an index of acculturation, Becerra and de Anda (1984) found that Spanish-speaking Mexican American adolescents differed from English-speaking Mexican American and Euro-American teens in number of pregnancies, availability of support systems, and correct knowledge and use of contraceptives.

Becerra and de Anda compared younger (age 13-17) English-speaking Mexican Americans, Spanish-speaking Mexican Americans, and Euro-Americans to older (age 18-20) English-speaking, Spanish-speaking Mexican Americans, and Euro-Americans. For the first group, younger English-speaking Mexican Americans (13-to 17-year-olds) were more likely to be pregnant with a second child than younger Spanish-speaking Mexican Americans or Euro-Americans. For the second group, older English-speaking Mexican Americans (18-to 20-year-olds) were less likely to have more children before leaving the adolescent phase of development than Spanish-speaking Mexican Americans and Euro-Americans. In other words, Becerra and de Anda's findings suggest that, in the long run, it is the older Spanish-speaking adolescents who continue to have a greater number of pregnancies during this particular phase of development.

With respect to social support, only 21.2% of the Spanish-speaking Mexican American group indicated that they had three or more friends, while 36.4% of the English-speaking Mexican American and 75% of the Euro-American group claimed a similar number. Finally, Euro-American and English-speaking Mexican Americans were found to have greater correct knowledge and use of contraceptives than Spanish-speaking Mexican Americans (Becerra & de Anda, 1984).

Based on these findings, Becerra and de Anda (1984) concluded
that acculturation of Euro-American norms is more likely to lead to
single parenthood; However, those parents have fewer repeat pregnancies during their teenage years—perhaps because their first
pregnancy occurred later. Unfortunately, these authors present no
data on what effect these fertility patterns have on the mental
health status for each of the adolescent groups in their study. The
assessment of the psychosocial stress factors related to fertility
rates would have shed light on this issue. Apart from this omission, Becerra and de Anda also failed to consider the possible
confounding influence of socioeconomic status (SES) and educational status. Finally, since mothers were selected from a nutrition
program that may not represent the general population, the threat
of a selection bias exists.

In summary, Becerra and de Anda concentrated primarily on the
problem of fertility rates (i.e., pregnancies) and did not thoroughly
examine other psychological factors that would assess the extent to
which Mexican American teenage mothers deal with their pregnancies. Thus while Spanish-speaking Mexican American teenage
mothers may have higher fertility rates and fewer support systems
than their Euro-American and English-speaking Mexican American counterparts, no data exists to indicate whether these factors
have long-term negative consequences on their parenting behavior
and overall adjustment to their situation. One might expect that
teen mothers who are integrated into their traditional Mexican
culture and/or mainstream U.S. culture experience less long-term
mental health problems compared to Mexican American teens who
have experienced deculturation and have the additional respons-
bilities of caring and raising their children.

In a similar vein, Lindemann and Scott (1982) examined the
fertility-related behavior of Mexican American and Euro-American
adolescents. The specific independent variables examined were
birthplace, ethnicity, and exposure to U.S. and Mexican culture.
The dependent variables were talking about sex, pregnancy, birth
control, hearing about birth control, and use of birth control.
Lindemann and Scott reported higher rates of pregnancy among
immigrant Mexican American adolescents than U.S. born members. Drawing from the literature on Mexican Americans, these
authors concluded that adherence to indigenous Mexican culture
increases pregnancy rates presumably because of the Mexican

males emphasis on "machismo," and because both immigrant and U.S. born Mexican Americans share the common heritage of historically having been a conquered people. Lindemann and Scott (1982) cite a few studies indicating that Mexican awareness of having once been a conquered people becomes internalized and results in greater passivity and submission among the entire group. With this rationale at hand, the authors then report that their study found no real differences between indigenous Mexican Americans and Mexican immigrants on any of the independent variables, permitting these two groups to be treated as equivalent regardless of differences in birthplace and years of schooling.

More recent research comparing immigrant and U.S. born Mexican Americans suggest that these two groups are not equivalent, but different in several behavioral dimensions (see Buriel, 1984 for a review). Thus the findings by Lindemann and Scott may be accurate with respect to fertility rates, but misleading with respect to the causes behind these differential rates. By distinguishing between immigrant and U.S. born Mexican American adolescents, we can assess the extent to which integration with traditional Mexican American culture and deculturation play a role in the pregnancy rates of this ethnic group. This approach would also make it possible to develop more effective community treatment programs with emphasis on pride towards one's own ancestral culture rather than denial and rejection of it.

Future studies on teenage pregnancy among Mexican Americans need to carefully consider the possible confounding influence of SES, educational status, and levels of deculturation and integration with traditional culture on rates of pregnancy. In addition, researchers need to carefully evaluate the merits of existing data describing the social psychological behavior of Mexican and Mexican American culture.

Substance Abuse

Recent studies indicate an increasing trend of substance abuse among Mexican American youth (Bloom & Padilla, 1979). However, research examining substance abuse rates among adolescent Mexican Americans relative to other youth populations remains contradictory. Some studies report lower drug rates among Mexican Americans than among Euro-Americans (Gossett, Lewis, & Phillips, 1971; Guinn & Hurley, 1976), while others show an opposite trend (Cockerham & Alster 1983; Myers, 1978; Padilla, Padilla, Morales, Olmedo, & Ramirez, 1979).

Gossett, Lewis, and Phillips (1971) found that drug use was reported at higher rates in primarily Euro-American areas than in primarily black or Mexican American sections of the city. Likewise, Guinn and Hurley (1976) reported that substance abuse among Euro-American students was substantially greater than among Mexican American students for all classifications of drugs.

Similarly, studies show that Mexican American youth disapprove of drug use more than blacks and Euro-Americans. Myers (1978) found that 78% of Mexican American youth frown on drug use compared to 72% of blacks and 71% of Euro-Americans.

In contrast, other studies report higher drug use rates among Mexican American youths than among non-Hispanic youths (Cockerham & Alster, 1983). This disparity may be due to the manner in which different ethnic groups define the term "drug." Whether or not different definitions are related to cultural factors is not known. Factors such as lack of drug education cannot be ruled out as another possible explanation for this disparity.

One report claims that Mexican American youth have more favorable attitudes towards marijuana and other drugs, and therefore use it more frequently than other youth groups (Cockerham & Alster, 1983). Similarly, other studies have found rates of marijuana use twice as high for Mexican Americans than for all respondents in a national survey (Rachal et al., 1975). In addition, inhalant abuse was more prevalent among Mexican American adolescents than the national sample of non-Hispanic youth (Padilla, et al., 1979). These findings suggest that Mexican American adolescents may actually use mind-altering substances more frequently than Euro-American adolescents.

Along with the suspected high drug use among Mexican American adolescents are studies identifying specific trends of substance abuse. First, Mexican Americans begin drug use at an earlier age than their Euro-American counterparts: the median age being 15 years for Mexican Americans and 17 years for Euro-Americans (Crowther, 1972). Second, Mexican Americans use a smaller variety of drugs and experiment less with such substances. Crowther (1972) found in a sample of drug users, that 36% of Mexican Americans reported a drug use pattern of marijuana-heroin (M-H), with no other use of opiates. Marijuana, heroin, and then another opiate (M-H-O) were used by 42% of this group. The comparable figures for the Euro-American group were 14% and 30% respectively. On the surface, these figures on age and substance variety suggest significant differences between ethnic groups. However, Morales (1984) suggests that such differences may not be due to cultural factors, but to socioeconomic status instead.

According to Morales (1984), national surveys usually compare middle-class Euro-Americans to lower-class Mexican American adolescents and incorrectly conclude that higher drug use rates observed among the latter group are due to cultural factors rather than to socioeconomic conditions. This finding by Morales would suggest that the different definitions of the term "drug" held by Mexican American youth may be related to socioeconomic factors rather than to cultural ones. That is, less drug education materials may be available in the Mexican American barrios. If cultural factors did account for some of the substance abuse patterns observed among this ethnic group, then it would be important for researchers to distinguish between immigrant and U.S. born Mexican Americans so that within-group differences could be examined. This would also make it possible to examine the extent to which the cultural integration hypothesis and the effects of deculturation apply to this problem. Some investigators have argued that the ability to conduct a thorough study of drug use in the Mexican American barrio is exacerbated by language barriers, youth gangs, fear of police harassment, and illegal immigrant status (Bloom & Padilla, 1979). This suggests that other research avenues should be explored, including the possibility of utilizing community resources to facilitate the data collection process.

As with drug use, a dearth of studies examine alcohol use and abuse among Mexican American adolescents. Research indicates that older Mexican American adolescents have higher rates of alcohol use and abuse than their Euro-American counterparts (U.S. Department of Health, Education, and Welfare (USDHEW), 1978; U.S. Department of Health and Human Services (USDHHS), 1981). However, a USDHEW (1981) study found that Mexican American adolescent females are predominantly abstainers. Other studies have shown that Mexican American youth have lower percentages of drinkers (68.4%) than Euro-Americans (75.2%), when "drinking" is determined by the number of drinks per month. For males, abstinence was reported to be 20.9% for Mexican Americans and only 14.6% for Euro-Americans. For females, abstinence was 27.0% for Mexican Americans and 18.1% for Euro-Americans. However, Mexican American male adolescents had the highest alcohol consumption overall, and Mexican American females the least (Sanchez-Dirks, 1978). Apparently, when Mexican American male adolescents drink, they do so more than Euro-American youth, which would contribute to higher rates of abuse. In contrast, Mexican American female adolescents appear to be at a relatively lower risk for alcohol abuse than their Euro-American female counterparts.

In summary, both drug and alcohol use are suspected to be high among the Mexican American population. Nonetheless, contradictory findings suggest that previous methods for studying substance abuse have been hindered by conditions unique to the Mexican American community. Previous studies also fail to examine possible drug and alcohol consumption differences between immigrant and U.S. born Mexican American adolescents. An examination of within-group differences would make it possible to assess the cultural integration hypothesis and the effects of deculturation. Additionally, future research efforts should consider the utilization of community-based agencies and resources to assist in the assessment of the substance abuse problem in the barrio. This would permit a more thorough examination of the substance abuse problem and would potentially mitigate many of the previously reported difficulties. Consideration of these factors are important in terms of providing effective treatment programs for the Mexican American population.

Suicide

As of 1981, less than a dozen studies examined the problem of suicide among American adolescents (Domino, 1981). The paucity of data on Mexican American adolescent suicide is even more severe. Notably, however, available studies suggest steadily increasing suicide rates for Mexican Americans. For example, Loya (1976) assessed the rate of suicide in Denver for three time periods: 1960-1964, 1965-1969, and 1970-1975, and reported an increase in Mexican American adolescent suicide from 7 to 12.9 per 100,000 over the three periods studied. Similarly, Hatcher and Hatcher (1975) found a seven-fold increase in male Mexican American suicides in El Paso from 1963-1965 to 1970-1972. Both studies also suggest that the incidence of suicide is particularly high among Mexican American males in their twenties. Regarding attitudes held by Mexican American and Euro-American adolescents toward suicide, Domino (1981) noted that Mexican American youth are more likely to ascribe suicide attempts to psychic distress and recommend professional help. Domino (1981) also found that more Mexican Americans perceive anger, an aggressive and destructive nature, impulsivity, and suddenness as being relevant to suicidal behavior. Interestingly, however, fewer Mexican Americans agreed that the suicide rate could be decreased by allowing open expression of such feelings.

While the studies cited above shed light on suicide rates and attitudes among Mexican American adolescents, no concrete indepth investigations on adolescent suicide rates for immigrant and U.S. born Mexican American adolescents exist. Such investigations are important with respect to determining whether integration with traditional Mexican American culture and deculturation result in differential rates and attitudes towards suicide. Consideration of these psychocultural factors would contribute to a better understanding of teenage suicide behavior. One might expect, for instance, that Mexican American teens who are integrated into their traditional culture would be less vulnerable to intrapsychic and extrapsychic stress factors. On the other hand, Mexican American adolescents who are experiencing deculturation might be at greater risk for suicide due to the adjustment difficulties associated with this condition.

Another problem found in previous studies is failure to adequately control for potential SES influence. Thus future studies need to consider not only suicide rates and attitudes, but also the effects SES has on such factors.

Acquired Immunodeficiency Syndrome (AIDS)

Earlier sections of this chapter showed that Mexican American adolescents share unique social demographic characteristics distinguishing them from the rest of the U.S. population. It was found that teenage fertility and substance abuse rates were disproportionately higher for Mexican American adolescents compared to Euro-Americans. These aforementioned findings stress the importance of examining AIDS research on Mexican American youth.

Latinos account for 14% of all diagnosed cases of AIDS while comprising 8% of the population (DiClemente, Boyer, & Morales, 1988). These figures indicate that AIDS cases are occurring nearly three times more frequently among Latinos as measured by reported cases per million population (Rogers & Williams, 1987). Unfortunately, the statistics on AIDS include all Latino populations and do not provide specific breakdowns for Mexican Americans. Among women and children with AIDS, Latinos rank quite high; 73% of women and 79% of children with AIDS are black or Latino. These figures suggest that AIDS cases are occurring 9.1 times as frequently among Latino or black women than among Euro-American women. Cumulative incidence rates in Latino children are 7.4 times the rate of white children (Rogers & Williams, 1987).

The transmission patterns among Euro-American AIDS patients differ markedly from those among Latino patients. Statistics from the Centers for Disease Control (1986) show that homosexual contact between men is the most common route of transmission for all racial and ethnic groups. Transmission of AIDS by way of homosexual contact for Euro-American male patients is 93% compared to 62% for Latino male patients. Further, important differences between Euro-Americans and Latinos also exist. Compared with whites, a higher proportion of Hispanics report that they are bisexual. Among whites transmitting AIDS through homosexual contact, 87% were exclusively homosexual and 13% bisexual. Among Latinos, 80% were exclusively homosexual and 20% bisexual (Rogers & Williams, 1987). Bisexual men may be less likely to consider themselves gay, and thus think they are at less risk for HIV infection. They may be less likely to participate in education and prevention programs designed for homosexuals. Social and sexual practices also may differ among ethnic groups.

A small percentage of Euro-American patients (10%) have acquired the virus through intravenous drug abuse, receipt of blood or blood products, or heterosexual contact with infected persons. Thus the greatest potential for spread among Euro-Americans is through the gay white male population and women having sexual contact with bisexual men. Intravenous drug abuse and heterosexual contact are much more commonly reported as transmission routes among Latinos: 38% of Hispanic adult AIDS patients acquired the infection from intravenous drug abuse and 9% through heterosexual contact, primarily with intravenous drug abusers (Centers for Disease Control, 1986).

While the above data shows an increased rate of infection due to intravenous drug abuse, the explanation for this increased rate remains unclear. Examination of potential cultural as well as socioeconomic and educational factors should be considered. At least one study (DiClemente, Boyer, & Morales, 1988) found important attitudinal differences between Latino and Euro-American adolescents regarding AIDS. DiClemente and colleagues measured the knowledge, attitudes, and misconceptions about AIDS from a sample of Euro-American, black, and Latino (all Spanish surnamed persons) adolescents from the San Francisco Bay area. Latinos and blacks were more than twice as likely as Euro-American adolescents to have misconceptions about AIDS. For example, only 58.3% of the Latinos responded correctly to the statement "using a condom during sex can lower the risk of getting AIDS," whereas 59.9% of blacks and 71.1% of Euro-Americans answered correctly. With respect to the statement "you can get AIDS from kissing," 70.9% of Latinos answered incorrectly while 65.9 and 43.7 percent of blacks and Euro-Americans answered incorrectly, respectively (DiClemente, Boyer, & Morales, 1988).

Unfortunately, a review of the literature did not reveal any other empirical published studies focusing on AIDS among Mexican American adolescents. Despite the paucity of data available, the cultural-integration hypothesis and effects of deculturation appear to be relevant to this problem. It may be that attitudes towards AIDS differ among immigrant and U.S. born Mexican American adolescents. The achievement-oriented values of immigrant members may result in more conservative sexual and drug use practices. Since current statistics do not differentiate AIDS cases on the basis of immigrant versus U.S. born status, the cultural-integration hypothesis cannot be tested with respect to this problem. Nonetheless, an analysis of within-group differences among Mexican American adolescents could reveal important implications for preventing the future spread of this epidemic. For example, in fiscal year 1987, more than 50 million dollars was allocated for programs designed to prevent the spread of AIDS. Yet for these programs to effectively fight AIDS in the Mexican American population, the occurrence of AIDS among immigrant and U.S. born Mexican Americans and the transmission patterns among these groups must be taken into account.

Educational Achievement

Previous studies have generally reported higher educational achievement among Euro-Americans than Mexican American adolescents. However, other investigators have argued that relying on two-group studies (i.e., Euro-American versus Mexican American) falsely assumes cultural homogeneity and gives little or no consideration to within-group differences and the relationship of these differences to educational success (Buriel, 1984).

There appears to be a growing body of data on educational achievement of Mexican American adolescents that supports the implications of the cultural-integration hypothesis and the concept of deculturation. For instance, in a study by Kimball (1968) Mexican American students with Mexican born parents demonstrated higher educational achievement than students with U.S. born parents. A more recent study (Vigil & Long, 1981) of Mexican American high school students in Southern California also found that earlier generation students obtained higher grades than their later generation counterparts.

In another study involving adolescents, Cordova (1970) investigated the relationship of "acculturation" to educational achievement and alienation among 477 6th-grade students in New Mexico. Students were divided into three groups: urban middle-class, urban lower-class, and rural. Analysis of the data failed to show any relationship between acculturation and achievement for either the urban lower-class group or the rural group. However, there was a significant inverse relationship between these two variables for the urban middle-class group. As acculturation increased, the achievement of urban middle-class Mexican American students decreased. Thus the inconsistent relationship between acculturation and achievement when SES is held constant suggests that other factors play a determining role here. Furthermore, for the total sample of students, acculturation in the area of the family was positively correlated with feelings of powerlessness. This suggests that as adolescents moved away from the influence of the traditional Mexican family and presumably closer toward the Euro-American norm, increased feelings of being unable to control rewards sought in educational settings confronted Mexican American adolescents. Cordova's presumably "acculturated" group appears to struggle when functioning in the educational system developed for mainstream U.S. culture. On the basis of these findings, Cordova concluded that "previous assumptions that acculturation is a cure-all for educational problems of Spanish-American students need a new orientation." (Cordova, 1970, p. 180). Furthermore, acculturation appears as a factor that is difficult to define and often is incorrectly used as a marker in distinguishing differences within an ethnic group.

Other studies show that the decision to attend college is also influenced by one's level of cultural integration. For instance, Buriel and Saenz, (1980), found that college-bound adolescents were more bicultural than non-college-bound adolescents. Because one dimension of biculturalism involves a traditional Mexican outlook and set of behaviors, the greater biculturalism of college-bound adolescents challenges the assertion that identification with traditional Mexican American culture depresses higher educational aspirations and achievement motivation (Buriel, 1984).

Even among college-educated Mexican Americans, those who retain an integration with traditional Mexican American culture tend to stay in school longer and to get better grades than later generational members who have presumably acculturated. Long and Padilla (cited in Ramirez, 1971) demonstrated this point in their investigation of bilingual antecedents of academic success among graduates with Spanish surnames at the University of New Mexico. These authors found that 94% of the successful students were raised in bilingual homes compared to 8% of the unsuccessful students. On the basis of this finding, Long and Padilla concluded that bilingual students may have been better able to interact effectively with members of their own group and with Euro-Americans, thus making them better adjusted members of both groups. Similar results are reported in a more recent study by Garcia (1981).

Finally, the High School and Beyond study conducted by the National Opinion Research Center (Nielsen & Fernandez, 1981) provides comprehensive data concerning the relationship of cultural integration to school achievement. In all, 58,728 students were studied, including 1,068 sophomores and 1,204 seniors who were of Mexican descent. Extensive psychological batteries, achievement measures, and background sociodemographic data were collected. Results showed that for both classes Spanish usage was associated with lower scores on achievement measures. However, Spanish proficiency was positively correlated to higher aspirations for both classes and also to greater math and vocabulary achievement for seniors. These findings, along with the findings reported earlier, support the claim that integration with traditional Mexican American culture increases educational achievement. These findings suggest that cultural integration may be an important factor in the mental health status of Mexican American adolescents.

Summary

This chapter presented an overview of the literature describing the mental health status of Mexican American adolescents in the areas of teenage pregnancy, substance abuse, suicide, AIDS, and educational achievement. The cultural-integration hypothesis and concept of deculturation functioned as a conceptual model to examine how factors related to acculturation influence the mental health status of this population. Somewhat paradoxically, previous studies on mental health show that integration with traditional Mexican American culture often promotes good psychosocial adjustment in mainstream U.S. society. In contrast, deculturation appears to interfere with psychosocial adjustment. A fundamental assumption of this chapter is that Mexican American culture arose primarily from the motivations and life-styles of Mexican immigrants. Thus in order to understand why integration with traditional Mexican American culture is conducive to adjustment, the psychocultural characteristics of Mexican immigrants must be analyzed and applied. Future research on the mental health status of Mexican American adolescents must keep these considerations in mind. Furthermore, while the present chapter examined a number of important mental health issues affecting Mexican American adolescents, these do not represent the entire spectrum of problems. Future research also should examine other components of mental health including self-esteem, depression, conduct disorders, and the extent to which these behaviors are influenced by the psychocultural factors of integration with traditional Mexican American culture and the negative conditions of deculturation.

References

Becerra, R. M., & de Anda, D., (1984). Pregnancy and motherhood among Mexican-American adolescents. *Health and Social Work, 9*(2), 106-123.

Berry, J. W. (1980). Acculturation as varieties of adaptation. In A. M. Padilla (Ed.), *Acculturation: Theories, models and some new findings* (pp. 45-56). Boulder, CO: Westview.

Bloom, D., & Padilla, A. M. (1979). A peer interview model in conducting surveys among Mexican American youth. *Journal of Community Psychology, 7*(2), 129-136.

Buriel, R. (1984). Integration with traditional Mexican American culture and socio-cultural adjustment. In J. E. Martinez (Ed.), *Chicano Psychology, Second Edition* (pp. 95-129). Academic Press.

Buriel, R., & Saenz, E. (1980). Psychocultural characteristics of college bound and non-college bound Chicanos. *Journal of Social Psychology, 110,* 245-251.

Centers for Disease Control (1986). Human T-lymphotropic virus type III/lymph-adenopathy-associated virus antibody prevalence in U.S. military recruit applicants. *Morbidity and Mortality Weekly Report, 35,* 421-424.

Cockerham, W., & Alster, J. M. (1983). A comparison of marijuana use among Mexican-American and anglo rural youth utilizing a matched-set analysis. *International Journal of the Addictions, 18*(6), 759-767.

Cordova, I. R. (1970). The relationship of acculturation, achievement, and alienation among Spanish-American sixth grade students. In H. S. Johnson & W. J. Hernandez (Eds.), *Educating the Mexican American* (pp. 252-268). Valley Forge, PA: Judson.

Crowther, B. (1972). Patterns of drug use among Mexican Americans. *International Journal of the Addictions, 7,* 637-647.

DiClemente, R. J., Boyer, C. B., & Morales, E. S. (1988). Minorities and AIDS: Knowledge, attitudes, and misconceptions among black and Latino adolescents. *American Journal of Public Health, 78,* 55-57.

Domino, G. (1981). Attitudes toward suicide among Mexican American and Anglo youth. *Hispanic Journal of Behavioral Sciences, 3,* 385-395.

Fromm, E., & Maccoby, M. (1970). *Social character in a Mexican village*. Englewood Cliffs, NJ: Prentice-Hall.

Garcia, H. D. C. (1981). *Bilingualism, confidence, and college achievement* (Report No. 318). Baltimore, MD: Center for Social Organization of Schools, John Hopkins University.

Gossett, J. T., Lewis, J. M., & Phillips, V. A. (1971). Extent and prevalence of illicit drug use as reported by 56,745 students. *Journal of American Medical Association, 21*(9), 1464-1470.

Guinn, R., & Hurley, R. (1976). A comparison of drug use among Houston and Lower Rio Grande Valley secondary students. *Adolescence, 11*(43), 455-459.

Hatcher, C., & Hatcher, D. (1975). Ethnic group suicide: An analysis of Mexican American and Anglo suicide rates for El Paso, Texas. *Crisis Intervention*.

Hispanic Policy Development Project. (1984). *Make something happen*. Washington, DC: Author.

Kimball, W. L. (1968). Parent and family influences on academic achievement among Mexican American students. *Dissertations Abstract International, 29,* 1965A. (University Microfilms No. 68-16, 550).

Levine, E. S., & Padilla, A. M. (1980). *Crossing cultures in therapy: Pluralistic counseling for the Hispanic*. Belmont, CA: Brooks/Cole.

Lindemann, C., & Scott, W. (1982). The fertility related behavior of Mexican-American adolescents. *Journal of Early Adolescence, 2*(1), 31-38.

Loya, F. (1976). *Suicide rates among Chicano youths in Denver, Colorado: A statistical and cultural comparison*. Unpublished paper, Center for the Study of Violence, Denver General Hospital.

Morales, A. (1984). Substance abuse and Mexican American youth: An overview. *Journal of Drug Issues, 14*(2), 297-311.

Myers, V. (1978). Drug-related sentiments among minority youth. *Journal of Drug Education, 8*(4), 327-335.

Nielsen, F., & Fernandez, R. M. (1981). *Hispanic students in American high schools: Background characteristics and achievement*. National Center for Education Statistics, Washington, DC: U.S. Government Printing Office.

Orozco, P. (1985). Teenage pregnancy: A trip to the dead zone. *Nuestro, 9*(1), 20-23.

Padilla, E., Padilla, A., Morales, A., Olmedo, E., & Ramirez, R. (1979). Inhalant, marijuana and alcohol abuse among barrio children and adolescents. *The International Journal of the Addictions, 14*(7), 945-964.

Rachal, J. V., Williams, J. R., Brehm, M. L., Cavanaugh, B., Moore, R. P., & Eckerman, W. C. (1975). *Final report: A national study of adolescent drinking behavior, attitudes and correlates*. Research Triangle Park, NC: Research Triangle Institute.

Ramirez, M. (1971). The relationship of acculturation to educational achievement and psychological adjustment in Chicano children and adolescents: A review of the literature. *El Grito: A Journal of Contemporary Mexican American Thought, 4,* 21-28.

Rogers, M. F., & Williams, W. W. (1987). AIDS in blacks and Hispanics: Implications for prevention. *Issues in Science and Technology,* 89-94.

Sanchez-Dirks, R. (1978). Drinking practices among Hispanic youth. *Alcohol and Health Resources World, 3,* 21-27.

U.S. Census Bureau (1980). *Provisional estimates of social, economic, and housing characteristics* (P.H.C. 80-F-1 Supplementary Report). Washington, DC: U.S. Department of Commerce.

U.S. Department of Health, Education, and Welfare (USDHEW). (1978). *Third special report to the U.S. Congress on alcohol and health* (Technical Support Document). Washington, DC: U.S. Government Printing Office.

U.S. Department of Health, Education and Welfare (USDHEW). (1981). Fourth special report to the U.S. Congress on alcohol and health (Technical Support Document). Washington, DC: U.S. Government Printing Office.

U.S. Department of Health and Human Services (USDHHS) (1981). *Fourth special report to the U.S. Congress on alcohol and health*. Washington, DC: U.S. Government Printing Office.

Vigil, J. D., & Long, J. M. (1981). Unidirectional or nativist acculturation-Chicano paths to school achievement. *Human Organization, 40,* 273-277.

The Mental Health of
Asian American Teenagers:
A Research Challenge

WILLIAM T. LIU
ELENA S. H. YU
CHING-FU CHANG
MARILYN FERNANDEZ

Introduction

More than 20 years have passed since William Peterson's land-mark article (1966) initiated the stereotype of success for Asian Americans. He characterized Japanese Americans as a group that had pulled itself up by its bootstraps to surpass even white Americans in educational and occupational attainment. In that same year, the December 26 issue of *U.S. News and World Report* also featured an article on the economic achievements of another Asian American subgroup—the Chinese, who also were characterized as hardworking, uncomplaining role models of diligence and achievement. All through the 1970s and 1980s, the popular press has continued to portray all Asian Americans as model minorities (e.g., Davidson, 1985; Green, 1984; Kasindorf, Chin, Weathers,

Foltz, Shapiro, & Junkin, 1982; McBee, 1984; McGrath, 1983; Spencer, 1986; Zabarsky, 1984; Zigli, 1984).

This "positive" stereotype has had some serious negative consequences for Asian Americans. First, it pits them against the more powerful minority groups, such as black and Hispanic Americans, and indirectly blames these other groups, rather than the social system, for their failure to "succeed." Second, it makes Asian Americans a convenient scapegoat for low-income and less educated white *and* minority Americans, who are led to believe that Asians took away their jobs or opportunities for college education. Third, it *trivializes* the social and mental health problems of Asian Americans either by implying that such problems are rare or nonexistent, or by suggesting that Asian Americans are able to take care of these problems "on their own." The result, of course, is that Asian Americans receive the lowest priorities in federal and state fundings for physical and mental health treatment and intervention programs, as well as for research and training programs. Fourth, it overlooks the immense diversity of the Asian American subgroups and the vast problems encountered by recent Southeast Asian refugees and new immigrants is accessing the educational and employment opportunities available in America.

The myth of Asian Americans as successful minorities is sustained only by ignoring the following facts: (a) the bifurcation in income, education, and occupations of Asian Americans in which a large percentage of them may be found in the lowest income, education, and occupation categories, followed by a smaller number in the highest brackets; (b) the unusually high percentage of households, persons, and unrelated individuals (who share a dwelling unit) living below the poverty level; (c) the low income return on education; (d) the prevalence of college overqualification among Asian Americans; and (e) the magnitude of mismatch between education and occupation (Azores, 1986-1987; Cabezas, Shinagawa, & Kawaguchi, 1986-1987; Kan & Liu, 1984; Li, 1980; Liu & Yu, 1985a; Liu & Yu, 1985b; Sowell, 1975; U.S. Commission on Civil Rights, 1978; Woodrum, 1981; Wu, 1980; Yu, Doi, & Chang, 1986).

The purpose of this chapter is to review available data relevant to the mental health in general, and suicide and depression in particular, of Asian American teenagers; pinpoint the limitations of existing data; and suggest new directions of research on this subject. To accomplish these objectives, U.S. Census data on the number of persons in mental hospitals and correctional institutions (so-called "treated prevalence") are presented, and *national* suicide data in the 15-24 year age group for two time periods are examined. Besides the apparent need for a descriptive database, such a comparison serves four other objectives: (a) to determine the magnitude and direction in treated prevalence and youth suicide between Asian and white Americans; (b) to examine the changes in suicide rate over time between the different groups; (c) to explore the plausible explanatory factors for the observed ethnic differences in youth suicide; and (d) to recommend ways of ascertaining and improving the accuracy of the information recorded on death certificates for Asian Americans.

Source of Data

Data for this chapter come from two principal sources: the Bureau of Census statistics and mortality files (based on death certificate records submitted by all 50 states) maintained by the National Center for Health Statistics (NCHS). The former data source frequently reports aggregate data for "Asian/Pacific Islanders" without the possibility of disaggregating into small subgroups, while the latter occasionally breaks down data only for the older subgroups of Asian Americans—namely, Chinese, Japanese, and Filipinos, but not for the newer groups of immigrants and refugees, such as Koreans, Vietnamese, Cambodians, and Laotians. Created in 1960, the National Center for Health Statistics is mandated to collect, analyze, and disseminate statistical and epidemiologic data on the health of the nation. However, because the size of the Asian American population remained numerically insignificant until recently, national mortality data for this special population prior to 1979 are difficult to analyze and interpret even though they have existed for some time at NCHS. Additionally, since analyses of such data require population denominators collected by the Bureau of the Census, the absence of intercensal estimates for Asian Americans in general, and Chinese and Japanese in particular, has severely limited the use of these records for research purposes. For these reasons, meaningful calculation of suicide rates can be made only for the years 1970 and 1980.

Furthermore, of the more than 40 Asian American subgroups enumerated in the last census, only the suicide statistics for Chinese and Japanese Americans will be presented in this paper for reasons of availability and usability of the data. This decision should not be interpreted to mean that the statistics obtained for these two older Asian American groups are error-free or in any way representative of the suicide patterns for all Asian Americans. In the strictest sense, the term Asian/Pacific Islanders is a meaningful concept only insofar as it identifies the geographic origins of a group of people who are visibly and culturally different from the majority white population. However, the population itself is made up of a number of diverse groups which, in many ways, are as different from one another as they are different from other races.

The Demographics of Asian American Teenage Population

Asian Americans are the fastest growing population in the United States today. From a total of only 1.5 million Asians and Pacific Islanders enumerated in the 1970 Census, the number has grown to 3.5 million in the 1980 Census, and was estimated at more than 5 million by 1985 (Gardner, Robey, & Smith, 1985). Factors accounting for most of this increase are immigration, births, and the inclusion of new groups in the census definition of "Asian/Pacific Islanders." According to the Immigration and Naturalization Statistics for Fiscal Year 1986, persons from Asian countries and the Pacific Islands accounted for close to 50% of all the immigrants entering the United States. This trend is expected to continue, other things being equal.

Unpublished data based on a 100% count of the U.S. Census show that there were only 89,342 Chinese Americans and 96,059 Japanese Americans between 15-24 years of age in 1970 (see Table 4.1). This age group represented 20.5% of the total Chinese American population and 16.2% of the total Japanese American population at the time. By 1980, the number of 15-24 year olds

TABLE 4.1: Total White, Chinese, and Japanese American Population and 15-24 Year Olds: 1970 and 1980 Census

Ethnicity and Age Group	1970	1980	% Change
White Americans, both Sexes			
All ages	177,748,975	188,371,622	+6.0
15-24 Year Olds	30,652,187	34,250,876	+11.7
Chinese Americans, both Sexes			
All Ages	435,062	806,040	+85.3
15-24 Year Olds	89,342	146,035	+63.5
Japanese Americans, both Sexes			
All Ages	591,290	700,974	+18.5
15-24 Year Olds	96,059	120,443	+25.4

[1]Data for 1970 are based on unpublished complete count (100%) of the 1970 U.S. Census data prepared by the Bureau of the Census for the National Center of Health Statistics. They are more reliable than the figures reported in some published 1970 Census reports that are based only on a 20% or 15% count.
[2]Data for 1980 are based on a 100% count of the 1980 U.S. Census data supplied by the Bureau of the Census to the Pacific/Asian American Mental Health Research Center.

increased by 63.5% (to 146,035) for Chinese Americans, and 25.4% (to 120,443) for Japanese Americans, compared to only an 11.7% increase for white Americans.

The 1980 Census data (as interpreted by Gardner, Robey, and Smith, 1985) reflects the diversity of the Asian American populations in nativity information. While the Japanese have an insignificant proportion of foreign-born persons in each age group, the Chinese and Filipinos have about an even split of native-versus foreign-born teenage populations and, for the newer immigrant and refugee groups (e.g., Korean, Asian Indian, and Vietnamese), foreign-born teenagers exceeded the 50% mark. Few of these foreign-born populations came before 1970. The growth of these teenage populations attributable to immigration contributes significantly to the formation of a unique cohort of Asian Americans—a socially created group of persons with age-differentiated sequences of shared experiences of a foreign origin. After all, these teenagers have lived part of their lives abroad and may continue to speak a language other than English. They can be expected to have experienced culture shock and some amount of identity problems after their arrival in the United States. As such, they represent a unique cohort of foreign-born persons in search of an American identity. Unfortunately, of the six major Asian subgroups, the NCHS suicide data only identifies Japanese, Chinese, and Filipinos separately, while data for Koreans, Vietnamese, and Asian Indians are simply categorized as "Other." Suicide data for the Filipinos are so incredibly low as to raise questions about the magnitude of errors in the dataset. Hence, only data for the Japanese and Chinese are presented in this chapter.

Census Estimates of Treated Prevalence

In the absence of any community survey of psychiatric disorders among Asian Americans anywhere in the United States, we resort to Census estimates of treated prevalence to obtain some information about the mental health of Asian American teenagers. These estimates show that insofar as inmates of mental hospitals and correctional institutions are concerned, Asian/Pacific Americans have an age-adjusted commitment rate (1.00 and 0.45 per thousand, respectively) that is lower than that reported for white Americans. The rate for Asian teenagers and young adults (15-24 years old) is about half of the rate shown for white Americans, about one-third of the rate reported for blacks, and about two-tenths lower than the low rates reported for the Spanish-speaking population.

In the absence of available statistics on the mental health of Asian American teenagers, we turn to data extracted from death certificates of all 50 states and submitted to the National Center for Health Statistics for analysis.

Age-Specific Suicide Rates

Table 4.2 shows the average annual age-specific and age-adjusted suicide death rates for white, Chinese, and Japanese Americans in 1980 and 1970, respectively. Following the convention of the National Center for Health Statistics where these data are managed, the U.S. population in 1940 was used as the standard for age adjustment.

TABLE 4.2: Average Annual Death Rates for Suicide, Per 100,000 Population, by Specified Race: United States, 1970 and 1980

| | 1970 | | | 1980 | | |
| | All Ages | | | All Ages | | |
	Crude	Age-adjusted	15-24 Year Olds	Crude	Age-adjusted	15-24 Year Olds
Whites						
Total	12.29	12.28	8.97	13.31	12.54	13.55
Male	17.75	17.90	13.79	20.57	19.41	21.91
Female	7.09	7.22	4.21	6.43	6.20	5.00
Chinese						
Total	10.89	11.60	2.98	8.27	7.97	6.39
Male	12.06	12.48	3.63	8.26	7.93	8.07
Female	9.60	10.45	2.92	8.28	8.02	4.65
Japanese						
Total	9.24	8.55	8.70	9.08	7.84	9.41
Male	10.68	10.01	11.97	12.57	11.08	14.09
Female	7.99	7.22	5.51	6.14	5.00	4.52

Source: Division of Vital Statistics, National Center for Health Statistics, unpublished data calculated by the authors.
[1]The numerator consists of 1980-1981 cumulative number of deaths, the denominator is based on the total enumerated of the 1980 United States Census.
[2]The numerator consists of 1960-1971 cumulative number of deaths, the denominator is based on the total enumerated of the 1980 United States Census.
[3]Excludes deaths of nonresidents of the United States.

Across time and for all ethnic groups in 1980, male suicide death rates in the 15-24 year age range have exceeded female rates. With a suicide death rate of 13.79 per 100,000 population in 1970 that increased to 21.91 per 100,000 in 1980, white American male youth have the highest suicide rates among the three ethnic groups compared. Over this time period, there was a 58.9% increase in suicide death rates among white male 15-24 year olds. The Chinese American male suicide rate increased more—by 122.3%—from 3.63 per 100,000 population in 1970 to 8.07 in 1980. Such a rapid increase may partly be a function of the low rate reported in the base year, 1970. By the same token, although Japanese American male suicide rates (11.97 per 100,000 in 1970 and 14.09 per 100,000 in 1980) have been higher than the Chinese rates, the rate of increase in suicide rates over time is not as dramatic as that found for Chinese Americans.

Given the population increase that each of the three ethnic groups has experienced between 1970 and 1980 (see Table 4.1), the question arises as to whether the increase in suicide rates may be a result of population growth. A closer examination of the data shows that the population increase is 13.7% for white males 15-24 years old, 63.1% for Chinese American youth of the same age group, and 30.6% for Japanese Americans. In short, the ratio of the rate of change in suicide death rates to the rate of population increase is highest for white American youth (4.3), lowest for Japanese Americans (0.58), and intermediate for Chinese Americans (1.9). Factors other than population growth explain the increase in suicide rates over time, although to a lesser extent among the Chinese youth than among white American youth.

By comparison, suicide death rates for white American females 15-24 years old have not changed significantly over the two census years (4.21 per 100,000 in 1970 compared to 5.00 in 1980) even though the population within this age range has increased by about 10 percent. Suicide death rates for Chinese American females increased by 59.2 percent, which is less than the 63.8 percent increase in the population of females in the same age group, while the suicide death rates for Japanese American females dropped slightly from 5.51 per 100,000 in 1970 to 4.52 per 100,000 in 1980, during which time the population had actually increased by 20.3 percent.

On the basis of either the 1970 or the 1980 age-specific suicide rates and the above ratios, some readers may conclude that suicide is not a major public health problem for Asian American youth compared with white Americans. However, an examination of the proportional mortality statistics over time gives a different picture of the findings.

Proportional Mortality for Selected Deaths

While the age-specific rate for any cause of death is calculated using the population size of a given group as the denominator and

TABLE 4.3: Proportional Mortality Rate for Suicide Among white, Chinese, and Japanese American 15-24 Year Olds, by Sex: 1970 and 1980

Race and Sex	1970	1980	% Change
White Americans			
Both Sexes	7.8	11.9	52.6
Male	8.1	12.9	59.3
Female	6.8	8.8	29.4
Chinese Americans			
Both Sexes	5.6	16.8	200.0
Male	4.9	15.1	208.2
Female	7.1	20.8	193.0
Japanese Americans			
Both Sexes	14.3	19.0	32.9
Male	14.2	21.3	50.0
Female	14.5	14.0	−3.4

Source: Unpublished data from the National Center for Health Statistics, Calculated by the authors.

the specific cause of death for that particular group as the numerator, proportional mortality for any cause of death is obtained by using the total number of deaths for any given population as the denominator and the specific cause of death as the numerator. Because of the differences in the denominator, it is possible for these two rates to give apparently contradictory information.

Table 4.3 presents the proportional mortality rates for suicide deaths by ethnicity in 1970 compared with 1980. One notes that *suicide accounts for a much larger proportion of deaths among Asian American youth in 1980 than among white Americans.* Among males, for instance, suicide represents 21.3% of all deaths for Japanese Americans, 15.1% for Chinese Americans, and only 12.9% for white Americans. Among females, it constitutes 20.8% of all deaths for Chinese Americans, 14% for Japanese Americans, and 8.8% for white Americans.

There is another way of examining the proportional mortality data in Table 4.3—that is, making within-group comparisons over time (see Table 4.4). In this case, the percentage change in average annual proportional mortality for Chinese Americans 15-24 year

TABLE 4.4: Average Annual Potential Years of Life Lost, in Percent and Rate Per 100,000 Population, by 10 Leading Causes of Death at Ages 15-24 Years: United States 1960-1971 and 1979-1981

Period and 10 Leading Causes	Whites			Chinese			Japanese		
	Number	Percent	Rate	Number	Percent	Rate	Number	Percent	Rate
1969-71									
10 Leading Causes, Total	1,858,698	100.09	—	2,145	100.0	—	2,948	100.0	—
Accidents	1,372,497	73.8	4,477.6	1,408	65.6	1,576.3	1,625	54.8	1,697.0
Suicide	178,642	9.6	582.8	173	8.1	194.0	542	18.3	565.7
Cancer	163,107	8.8	532.1	390	18.2	436.5	303	10.2	316.8
Heart Disease	48,252	2.6	157.4	65	3.0	72.8	130	4.4	135.8
Cerebrovascular Disease	29,055	1.6	94.8	65	3.0	72.8	173	5.8	181.0
Other	67,145	3.6	—	44	2.0	—	195	6.7	—
1979-81									
10 Leading Causes, Total	2,024,922	100.0	—	2,189	100.0	—	2,948	100.0	—
Accidents	1,479,963	73.1	4,321.0	975	44.5	667.6	1,712	58.1	1,421.1
Suicide	301,708	14.9	880.9	607	27.7	415.4	737	25.0	611.6
Cancer	139,555	6.9	407.4	390	17.8	267.1	282	9.6	233.9
Heart Disease	51,090	2.5	149.2	152	6.9	103.9	65	2.2	54.0
Cerebrovascular Disease	18,633	0.9	54.4	43	2.0	29.7	65	2.2	54.0
Other	34,060	1.7	—	22	1.0	14.8	87	2.9	—

Source: Unpublished data from the National Center for Health Statistics, calculated by the authors.

olds between 1969-1971 and 1979-1981 is striking (200% for both sexes) compared to white (53%) or Japanese Americans (33%).

However, it is important to stress that, to begin with, Japanese American proportional mortality rates had been very high in 1969-1971, and they remained high in 1979-1981, whereas the Chinese American rates were very low in 1969-1971 and they increased dramatically in 1979-1981. From a public health standpoint, this increase in proportional mortality rates over time for all three ethnic groups is cause for concern. It is therefore a misconception to rely solely upon the age-specific suicide rate of 15-24 year olds and conclude that Chinese American youth do not have a suicide problem. What is a "high" or "low" suicide rate depends on what group or what year is used as the reference point for comparison purposes.

The high proportional mortality rates found among Chinese Americans relative to their low age-specific death rates are most likely a consequence of other competing causes of death. As a rule, deaths due to accidents have always been a, if not *the*, major competing cause of death for persons in the age range of 15-24 years. So long as the proportional mortality rates for accidents remain very high, if not the highest of all causes of death, the proportion of deaths due to suicide can be expected to remain relatively low. This becomes apparent when one calculates the potential years of life lost for different causes of death, as shown in Table 4.4.

Potential Years of Life Lost

Using 5 of 10 leading causes of death for the United States, Table 4.4 presents the distribution of average annual potential years of life lost before age 85 for Chinese and Japanese who die at age 15 or older. Potential years of life lost before age 85 are calculated by totaling the remaining years until age 85 for each person who committed suicide in his/her youth (i.e., in the age range between 15-24 years). For example, a person dying at age 20 would contribute 65 years to the total, while one who dies at age 70 contributes only 15 years. With this indicator, it is possible to rank the different causes of death while including only deaths before age 85 and giving more weight to early deaths.

In terms of selecting health promotion and prevention priorities, the ranking of causes death according to potential years of life is more useful than ranking causes of death according to the total number of deaths. A death at the age of 20 or older has a different impact, at least to the family and to society at large, than a death at the age of 80 years.

Furthermore, because calculation of the potential years of life is affected by the population size as well as by the age-specific death rates, it is more interesting to compare the percentage of potential years of life lost between groups due to different causes than to look at the absolute figures themselves. Table 4.4 shows that all three ethnic groups have similar rankings of the potential years of life lost at age 15 or older for the 5 leading causes of death in the United States. Accidents head the list, followed by suicide. Thus suicide is a serious problem in the Asian American population just as it is in the white American population.

However, the groups differ greatly in the percentage of potential years of life lost due to a particular cause of death. Accidents, for example, accounted for 73% or nearly three quarters of the average annual potential years of life lost for white Americans who died at the age of 15 or older during 1979-1981, while they accounted for only 45% for Chinese Americans and 58% for Japanese Americans. On the other hand, suicide accounted for a higher percentage of potential years of life lost for Chinese (28%) and Japanese (25%) Americans, compared to only 15% among white Americans.

Those concerned with the identification of major public health problems among Asian Americans are well-advised to examine the distribution of potential years of life lost, as a first step to defining priorities. As a second step, rates of potential years of life lost should be considered for identifying trends over time.

Table 4.4 also shows the average annual potential years of life lost by 5 leading causes of death at ages 15-25 years in 1969-1971. The data indicate a higher percentage of potential years of life lost due to suicide for Japanese (18%) compared to Chinese (8.1%) and white Americans (10%). By 1979-1981, it is the Chinese youth who had the highest percentage of potential years of life lost to suicide (28%) compared to Japanese (25%) and white Americans (15%).

TABLE 4.5: **Average Annual Age-Specific and Age-Adjusted Deaths (1940 U.S. Standard Population) by suicide, in rate per 100,000, for specified Asian American groups, by nativity: United States, 1980**

	All Ages		
Ethnicity and Nativity	Crude	Age-Adjusted	15-24 Year Old
Chinese			
Native-born	2.9	3.5	5.2
Foreign-born	11.2	9.5	7.1
Japanese			
Native-born	5.5	5.2	8.1
Foreign-born	17.1	14.0	14.3

Source: Division of Vital Statistics, National Center for Health Statistics, unpublished data calculated by the authors.
[1]The numerator consists of 1979-1981 cumulative number of deaths, the denominator is based on the total enumerated of the 1980 United States Census.
*The rates are obtained with numerators that consist of less than 5 persons.

The Nativity Factor

Nativity, or the decedent's place of birth, is an important factor in Asian American mortality analysis. It is generally taken as a proxy measure for cultural upbringing and socioeconomic lifestyle, given the limited information available from the death certificate. In addition to age and sex, nativity is an important risk factor in the analyses of Asian American mortality data because among Chinese Americans 15-24 years of age, 60% are foreign-born, compared with 21.4% for Japanese Americans and 4.3% for white Americans. The variability in the proportion of foreign-born raises the question as to whether there are nativity differences in suicide mortality rates for Asian American youth compared with white Americans. Unfortunately, the nativity information is not available in the national mortality data tapes for 1969-1971. Analysis of the variable is thus confined only to the 1980 data set.

Table 4.5 shows that at each age group, the suicide death rate for foreign-born youth is consistently higher than that found for the native-born. In the 15-24 year age range, the rate for foreign-born Chinese is 7.1 per 100,000 population compared with 5.2 for native-born youth. For Japanese Americans, the nativity ratio is higher—the rate being 14.3 per 100,000 for the foreign-born youth compared with 8.1 for the native-born.

Clearly, suicide is a serious problem in the Asian American population, and more foreign-born youth are at risk than the native-born. Data on depression, if available, would be useful in pinpointing some of the underlying causes of suicide among Asian Americans. Unfortunately, to date we have found no study of depression among Asian American adolescents reported in the literature. Needless to say, any prevention efforts should pay close attention to the unique features of depression among foreign-born Asian American youth if we are to reduce effectively the overall suicide rates.

The Family Structure

In an attempt to find clues to increase our understanding of Asian American suicide rates, we examined the 1980 Census data on household type for Chinese and Japanese age 15 to 24. Table 4.6 shows that among U.S. born youth, the percentage of persons living in married couple households varies from 64.3% for Chinese Americans, 65.4% for Japanese Americans, to 67.5% for white Americans. However, the percentage of youth living alone, in group quarters, or in nonfamily households shows somewhat greater variability, with the Chinese having the largest percentage (25.6%) of the three groups living in the "other" type of households.

For foreign-born youth, the data in Table 4.6 is broken down by year of immigration. A larger percentage of Asian Americans who were between the ages of 15-24 in 1980 and who immigrated to the United States in the decade of the 1970s are either living in group quarters or in nonfamily households. Japanese American youth who immigrated during the 1970s have a disproportionately large percentage (around 13%) living alone, compared with the other two groups (no more than 5%).

Systematic studies on the family structure of recent immigrants are extremely few, if not non-existent. Problems exist in the study of Asian American families in the United States, foremost of which

TABLE 4.6: Household Type of 15-24 Year Olds for White, Chinese, and Japanese Americans, by Nativity and Year of Immigration: 1980 Census

Household Type	U.S. Born	N.A.[1]	Foreign-Born by Year of Immigration			
			1975-80	1970-74	1965-69	Prior to 1969
White (number)	(32929)	(357)	(394)	(218)	(210)	(296)
Percent	100.0	100.0	100.0	100.0	100.0	100.0
Married Couple	67.5	61.6	53.6	68.8	73.8	66.6
One spouse absent	13.5	18.2	25.6	24.8	15.7	11.5
Other						
Living alone	4.4	4.8	4.8	1.4	1.9	6.1
Group quarters	7.0	8.7	7.9	2.8	3.3	7.1
Nonfamily	7.7	6.7	8.1	2.3	5.2	8.8
Chinese (number)	(2907)	(72)	(2300)	(928)	(752)	(331)
Percent	100.0	100.0	100.0	100.0	100.0	100.0
Married Couple	64.3	62.5	55.5	69.8	70.9	65.3
One spouse absent	10.1	12.5	18.8	13.8	12.4	12.4
Other						
Living alone	5.5	2.8	3.7	3.0	3.5	4.5
Group quarters	10.7	12.5	11.2	6.4	8.4	9.7
Nonfamily	9.4	9.7	10.8	7.0	4.9	8.2

(Continued)

TABLE 4.6: (Continued)

Household Type	U.S. Born	N.A.[1]	Foreign-Born by Year of Immigration				
			1975-80	1970-74	1965-69	Prior to 1969	
Japanese (number)	(4861)	(294)	(585)	(108)	(81)	(255)	
Percent	100.0	100.0	100.0	100.0	100.0	100.0	
Married Couple	65.4	58.8	34.7	47.2	62.3	50.6	
One spouse absent	12.1	16.0	5.3	8.3	8.6	16.1	
Other							
Living alone	4.4	5.1	13.5	13.0	3.7	7.5	
Group quarters	9.0	9.8	26.3	17.6	11.1	10.2	
Nonfamily	9.1	12.2	20.2	13.9	13.6	15.7	

Source: Unpublished data from the 1980 Census tabulated by the authors. Data for Chinese and Japanese are based on the 5% Sample Microdata (A) tape, while data for white Americans are based on the .1% (B) sample tape.

[1]These are persons who cannot be said to have "immigrated" to the U.S. because they were born in U.S. Territories or possessions (and therefore *not* native-born). A small number of foreign-born persons for whom year of immigration information is missing may also be included in this category but the precise number cannot be ascertained.

*Percent do not add up to exactly 100 because of rounding errors.

is the transitional nature of any family in migration. Among other things, there is the difficulty of separating the prevailing patterns of family relations from the ongoing process of change in those relations. There is also the lack of descriptive information to cross-validate conclusions drawn from profiles derived from the U.S. Census. The 1980 Census showed that a typical Asian American immigrant family is a split household. Prolonged separation among members of the same family in two locales or countries is thus commonplace among Asian Americans. Are these family structures conducive to adolescent suicide? The paucity of systematic data on the family structure of Asian Americans and the risk factors for suicide in these special populations makes it possible for us to give any definitive answers at this juncture. But the available data we have gathered certainly pinpoints the directions for future research.

A Research Challenge

The study of suicide as a sociocultural phenomenon is a classic one, dating as far back as Durkheim's classic work (1951). His innovative approach to the study of suicide involves intersocietal comparisons of suicide statistics over time and among different segments of the population—an approach that emerged as a result of his concern over social integration and the nature of group cohesion.

Insofar as research on the mental health of Asian American teenagers is concerned, the work has not yet begun. Despite our efforts to review the literature, we failed to unearth a single piece of systematic study on depression among Asian American adolescents. This chapter is perhaps one of the first efforts at exploring the National Center for Health Statistic's archival death files to analyze interethnic differences in youth suicide rates among Chinese and Japanese, compared with white Americans. Previous efforts had been targeted to specific local areas, such as San Francisco (Bourne, 1973) or Hawaii, or other age groups instead of those between the ages of 15-24 years. It is obvious that we have barely scratched the tip of the iceberg on Asian American suicide at the national level.

What we have learned is that making interethnic comparisons at one point in time requires a certain among of caution in that when the suicide rates for the reference population (in this case, white American youth), have been high historically, Asian American rates always appear low by contrast. However, if one were to examine the Asian American suicide rates *per se* over time, one quickly discovers that these rates have increased dramatically. Asian Americans are not as free of health or social problems as one might be led to believe if one had relied solely on an Asian-white comparison of age-specific rates. The reasons for their increase have not been clearly understood, much less studied.

We must admit that, theoretically, we have no adequate explanation as yet for the lower age-specific suicide rates for Chinese and Japanese Americans as a group, compared to white Americans. One possibility is that overall rates for the 10 leading causes of death are lower for the two Asian American groups than for white Americans (Yu, Chang, Liu, & Kan, 1985). Similarly, their age-specific suicide statistics are also lower than that found for white Americans. Thus any Asian white comparison of rates would always lead to the conclusion that the former appear to have few health or social problems. Nonetheless, as we have demonstrated in this paper, whenever proportional mortality rates are used for purposes of comparison, a different picture emerges. Proportional suicide rates are higher for Asian Americans than for white Americans, and these rates have increased dramatically over a 10-year period.

An examination of the U.S. Census data indicates that Asian American youth are characterized by high enrollment in school, and data from the State of Illinois show that they have low dropout rates compared with white Americans (Yu, Doi, & Chang, 1986). The media have played an important role in highlighting the academic achievements of Asian American school-age youth, especially in math and science tests. What has been ignored is that "they have not done as well as whites . . . in a variety of tests of verbal abilities" (Hsia, 1988, p. 22). Also ignored is the psychological pressure and emotional scars that the young have suffered in order to sustain the expectations of parents and school teachers alike. Amidst the public stereotype of Asian American teenagers as the "model minority" lurked an uglier image of newly created street gangs in major cities on both the East and West coasts.

Sociologically, it is important to realize that over the last 20 years, the United States has experienced an unprecedented influx of Asian American immigrants whose educational levels and professional skills are at the highest levels ever compared to the earlier waves of Asians as well as European immigrants. In the United States today, the proportion of Asian Americans with four years or more of college is significantly higher than that for white Americans. Although the occupational return on education has not been as high for Asian Americans as one might expect had they been white Americans, large percentages of Chinese and Japanese Americans still hold high-prestige jobs compared with white Americans. This cohort of highly educated professionals is concentrated in the 40-55 year age range—the age of parenthood with children in school. At the same time, however, there is a large group of Asian Americans in the 40-55 year age range who have very little education and are confined to low-prestige service occupations in the ethnic ghettos. We know very little about their family and mental health problems, except perhaps for the work of Sung (1987). She identified the lengthy absence of both parents from home due to the long hours of work required to support the family as a major stressor in the life of Chinese American teenagers in New York's Chinatown. Sung believes, from her data, that one way the Chinese teenagers cope with the loss of familial and kinship support is to become gang members in an increasingly gang-organized Chinatown community. She cited the fact that all gang members she knew are foreign-born and are from one locale as evidence that peer group identity provides the teenagers with a sense of psychological security (Sung, 1987, p. 205).

In interview after interview with Asian American high achievers, we have learned from the media how the children explained their drive to excel in terms of the shame that can befall their parents should they fail, and the glory they bring to their families when they succeed. It comes as no surprise that we have a cohort of high-achieving Asian American parents who exert tremendous pressure on their children to become even more successful than they are. The intensified pressure, and the sudden awareness of Asian American teenagers about their self-identity problems, are likely causes of increased psychological turmoil, and possibly the higher suicide rates, which we are seeing. Native-born Chinese and Japanese in particular have a certain vulnerability in their self-concept in that most of them do not speak their parent's language and are still perceived by the society at large to be non-native Americans. However, foreign-born Asian American youths face perhaps even more inner turmoil because of the inevitable clash of values held by their immigrant parents and the larger society, especially their American peers. The most recent U.S. Census data we have examined indicate that a substantial percentage of Asian American youth are living without immediate familial support—a source of social support critical during the teenage years and early adulthood, especially for the uprooted (i.e., the foreign-born). What are the functional alternatives to the intact family for Asian American teenagers living in nonfamily situations? Much research remains to be conducted to examine the psychodynamics of the Asian American family, and the relationship between educational achievement, depression, and suicide among the young.

References

Azores, T. (1986-1987). Educational attainment and upward mobility: Prospects for Filipino Americans. *Amerasia, 13*(1), 39-52.

Bourne, P. G. (1973). Suicide among Chinese in San Francisco. *American Journal of Public Health, 63*(8), 744-750.

Cabezas, A., Shinagawa, L. H., & Kawaguchi, G. (1986-1987). New inquiries into the socioeconomic status of Filipino Americans in California. *Amerasia, 13*(1), 1-21.

Davidson, J. (1985, October 21). The mixed life of Asian pupils. *Chicago Tribune*, 1, 4.

Durkheim, E. (1951). *Suicide.* (J. A. Spaulding & G. Simpson, Trans.). New York: Free Press. (Original work published 1897)

Gardner, R. W., Robey, B., & Smith, G. (1985). Asian Americans: Growth, change, and diversity. *Population Bulletin 40*(4), 1-44.

Green, L. (1984, January 22). Super kids: Asian Americans *Sunday Chicago Sun-Times.*

Hsia, J. J. (1987). *Asian Americans in higher education and at work.* Hillsdale, NJ: Erlbaum.

Kan, S. H., & Liu, W. T. (1984). The educational status of Asian Americans: An update from the 1980 census. In N. Tsuchida (Ed.), *Issues in Asian and Pacific American Education.* (pp. 1-12) Minneapolis: Asian/Pacific American Learning Resource Center, published for the National Association for Asian and Pacific American Education.

Kasindorf, M., Chin, P., Weathers, D., Foltz, K., Shapiro, D, & Junkin, D. (1982, December 6). Asian Americans: A 'model minority.' *Newsweek*, 39-51.

Li, A. (1980). *Labor utilization and the assimilation of Asian Americans*. Unpublished doctoral dissertation, University of Chicago, Illinois).

Liu, W. T., & Yu, E. S. H. (1985a). Asian/Pacific American elderly: Mortality differentials, health status, and use of health services. *Journal of Applied Gerontology*, 4(1), 35-64.

Liu, W. T., & Yu, E. S. H. (1985b). Ethnicity, mental health, and the urban delivery system. In L. Maldonaldo & J. Moore (Eds.), *Urban ethnicity in the United States: New immigrants and old minorities* (Vol. 29) Urban Affairs Annual Review. Beverly Hills, CA: Sage.

McBee, S. (1984, April 2). Asian-Americans: Are they making the grade? *U.S. News and World Report*, 41-47.

McGrath, E. (1983, March 28). Education, Confucian work ethic. *Time Magazine*, 52.

Peterson, W. (1966, January 9). Success story, Japanese American style. New York Times Magazine.

Sowell, T. (1975). Affirmative action reconsidered: Was it necessary in academia? *Evaluative Studies* 27. Washington, DC: American Enterprise Institute for Public Policy Research.

Spencer, J. (1986, January 15). Why Fu Lien can read: For Asian Americans, learning is a family obligation. *Chicago Tribune*.

Sung, B. L. (1987). *The adjustment experience of Chinese immigrant children in New York City*. New York: Center for Migration Studies.

U.S. Commission on Civil Rights. (1978). *Social indicators of equality for minorities and women*. Washington, DC: U.S. Government Printing Office.

Woodrum, E. (1981). An assessment of Japanese American assimilation, pluralism, and subordination. *American Journal of Sociology, 87*, 158-169.

Wu, Y. L. (1980). *The economic condition of Chinese Americans*. Chicago: Pacific/Asian American Mental Health Research Center, Monograph 3.

Yu, E. S. H., Chang, C., Liu, W. T., & Kan, S. H., (1985). Asian-white mortality differences: Are there excess deaths? In M. M. Heckler (Ed.), *Report of the secretary's task force on black and minority health* (pp. 208-251) Washington, DC: U.S. Department of Health and Human Services.

Yu, E. S. H., Doi, M., & Fu Chang, C. (1986). *Asian American education in Illinois: A review of the data*. Chicago: Pacific/Asian American Mental Health Research Center.

Zabarsky, M. (1984, April). Asian Americans: The drive to excel. *Newsweek on Campus*, 4-7.

Zigli, B. (1984, April 25). Asian Americans beat others in academic drive. *USA Today*.

PART 2

Antisocial
Behavior/Violence/Delinquency

5

Violence and Minority Youth: An Ecological Perspective

NORA S. GUSTAVSSON

PALLASSANA R. BALGOPAL

Violence represents a threat to the mental health of minority youth. Depression, homicide, and suicide are three possible manifestations of violence. Using an ecological perspective, the authors will explore violence as it is experienced and manifested by minority youth. Based on this theoretical framework and supported by case examples, the impact of race and ethnicity in a capitalistic society on minority youth will be examined.

Violence can be an amorphous concept. It is most frequently associated with personal behaviors such as homicide, suicide, and child abuse. This conceptualization is narrow and supports the notion that violence is the fault of the individual, that there are few if any environmental conditions that support and promote violence, and that violent behavior is under the total control of the person. By placing violence in this context, both interventions and preventive strategies focus on changing the individual person.

A broader, more realistic definition that acknowledges the role played by forces beyond the direct control of the person might help to focus change efforts at larger targets. For the purposes of this discussion, the following definition of violence offers the most integrated view:

> Broadly, any act, whether overt or covert, that coerces or causes physical hurt, material loss or mental anguish, or that degrades human beings or that militates against human rights, dignity, and decency should be viewed as an act of violence. (Rajgopal, 1987, p. 5)

Social Manifestations of Violence

The social manifestations of violence are relatively easy to observe. Juveniles have a higher likelihood of being arrested for robbery and property crimes than any other age group and make up the largest proportion of offenders entering the criminal justice system (U.S. Department of Justice, 1988). In 1985, juveniles accounted for 27% of all arrests, 16.3% of all arrests for violent crimes such as murder, forcible rape, robbery, and assault and 30% of arrests of all serious property crimes such as burglary and motor vehicle theft (U.S. Department of Justice, 1986).

When juvenile arrests are disaggregated by race, disturbing trends can be identified. According to statistics from the Federal Bureau of Investigation, race is correlated with arrests. More than half of the teenagers arrested in 1983 for violent crimes were black, yet less than 15% of the population aged 14 to 17 was black (Flanagan & McGarrell, 1985).

The incarceration rates of juveniles also vary by race. Black males appear to suffer disproportionately high rates of incarceration, particularly in public correctional facilities. In 1985, 37% of the juveniles in public correctional facilities were black (U.S. Department of Justice, 1987). Using data from a number of sources, one research group reported a black male incarceration rate of 587.9 per 100,000 (Krisberg, et al., 1987). Hispanic males had a reported incarceration rate of 353.0 per 100,000. The white male incarceration rate was 154.8 per 100,000. The white male rate was approximately one quarter the rate for black males.

Females have a lower incidence of incarceration than males. However, when these rates are disaggregated by race, black females are at the greatest risk for incarceration in public correctional facilities. The black female rate of 76.9 per 100,000 is more than double the white female rate (33.2 per 100,000) and Hispanic female rate (31.3 per 100,000).

In 1982, the majority of residents in private correctional facilities were white (65%). Slightly more than half (54%) of all incarcerated white youth are in public correctional facilities while 71% of all incarcerated black youth and 73% of all incarcerated Hispanic youth are in public correctional facilities (Krisberg, et al., 1987).

Explicating Violent Youth

These aggregate numbers do not explain the over-representation of minority youth in the juvenile justice system, although there have been dozens of attempts to explain the criminal behavior of young people, particularly minority youth. These hypotheses can be broadly characterized into two main schools of thought. One school of thought focuses on the internal, psychological deficits in the personality composition of these adolescents and their families. The other school of thought focuses on the external, sociological environment of the adolescent. It should be noted that male adolescents have been the focus of much of the research in this area. This may be due to any number of factors ranging from the higher rates of arrest and incarceration of males to the pervasiveness of sexism in America.

Another approach, that could be considered part of the psychological school, suggests that delinquency is a typical aspect of adolescence, relating to the developmental tasks faced by the adolescent (see Rutter & Giller, 1984; Gold & Petronin, 1980; Mulvey & LaRosa, 1986). This research focuses on male adolescents. The contribution of the developmentalists to understanding the violent juvenile or the over-representation of minority youth in the juvenile justice system is limited.

The psychological school of thought suggests there is a relationship between child abuse and the violent behavior of the delinquent adolescent (Burgess & Conger, 1978; Gray, 1984; Hunner & Walker, 1981; Kratcoski, 1982). Retrospective studies of death row inmates, for example, have found that many of these individuals were victims of violent physical abuse (Lewis, et al., 1985; Pincus, Feldman, Jackson, & Bard, 1986).

Most of these studies suffer from serious methodological flaws such as the lack of a control group and failure to distinguish among a cluster of variables associated with child abuse, such as poverty and low socioeconomic status (SES). A study of 100 Dade County (Florida) juvenile offenders, for example, reported that delinquents were intellectually slower than their nondelinquent peers; scored lower on tests designed to measure moral development than their non-delinquent peers; suffered inadequate undersocialized personality disorders; and came from female headed, single-parent homes (U.S. Senate Subcommittee on Juvenile Justice, 1981).

The psychological school of thought does not adequately explain the over-representation of minority youth in the criminal justice system. There is little evidence to support the notion that there is a causal relationship between race and intelligence or race and the presence of sociopathy.

The sociological school of thought has studied a number of variables thought to be related to delinquency. Two of the more extensively researched variables are race and employment status. Blumstein (1982) suggests that minority youth engage in violent crime more frequently than their white peers. Huizinga and Elliot (1985) found no evidence to support the conclusions advanced by Blumstein. The conclusions of other studies (Dannefer & Schutt, 1982; Farnworth & Horan, 1980; Hindelang, 1978; Phillips & Votey, 1987) fail to establish evidence of a causal relationship between crime and race.

Employment status and criminal behavior has been a fertile field of research. Minority youth are over-represented among the unemployed. Recent research supports the notion that there is a relationship, although not a causal relationship, between crime and employment status (Becker, 1968; Christenson & Thornberry, 1984; Good, Pirog-Good, & Sickles, 1986). Duster (1987) warns that urban black youth are at great risk of joining a permanent underclass because of structural changes in the labor market, such as the flight of capital, technology change, and the level of skills required for entry-level positions. He predicts the public will shortly have to decide where to spend increasing amounts of its tax dollars

The choice is between building more prisons or developing career employment.

Neither the micro-level psychological deficits model nor the macro-level sociological model are able to establish a linear or causal relationship between adolescence and violent criminal activity and the over-representation of minority youth in the juvenile justice system. These same two schools of thought have attempted to explain another disturbing adolescent behavior, the self-destructive adolescent. The depressed adolescent is at risk for self-inflicted violence.

Adolescent Depression and Suicide

Homicide is the second leading cause of death for young people aged 15 to 24 (Children's Defense Fund, 1985). Suicide is the third major cause of death of young people (Wegman, 1985). American youth are being killed at an alarming rate. Minority youth seem to be at a greater risk for violence than their white counterparts. Black males have a 1 in 30 chance to be murdered while white males have a 1 in 178 chance (U.S. Department of Justice, Bureau of Justice Statistics, 1987).

Females are more likely to attempt suicide but less likely to succeed than are males (Kahn, 1987; Miller, Chiles, & Barnes, 1982). Anglo males are at the greatest risk for suicide. Data on the incidence of suicide among Hispanics is scarce. A 1985 (Smith, Mercy & Warren) study reported that suicides occur at a much younger age for Hispanics than for Anglos. Approximately one third of the Hispanics who committed suicide were under the age of 25 while less than 18% of the Anglos who committed suicide were under the age of 25. The psychological deficit school of thought attempts to explain adolescent suicide by examining variables such as depression, stress, communication, developmental tasks, and family dynamics. For adults, the latest trend in explanation comes from the field of neuroendocrinology. In the areas of affective, thought, and obsessive compulsive disorders, genetic or biological core deficits are assumed to be causal (National Institute of Mental Health, 1983). Since adolescence is marked by neurochemical changes, research among this population is problematic.

Suicide is a risk associated with depression. Depression may be endemic to a significant minority of adolescents. A 1975 (Albert & Beck) study of 7th-and 8th-graders reported a third of these young people were experiencing moderate to severe depression. Adolescence is a developmental stage characterized by dramatic changes. Feelings of depression are typical, and not necessarily indications of a pathological state. However, persistent and intense feelings of sadness may well mark the beginning of a pathological state.

Parents are assumed to play a significant causal role in the depression and/or suicide of their adolescent children. Adolescents who are the victims of maltreatment are reported to be at a greater risk for depression than their nonabused peers (Blumberg, 1981 Sturkie & Flanzer, 1987). The maltreatment of children is also assumed to play a causal role in the development of delinquency (Hunner & Walker, 1981). Just how maltreatment results in the development of depression and/or delinquency is not well understood.

Stress is also assumed to play a major role in adolescent suicide However, stress is an inherent aspect of "normal" adolescence. The conditions under which stress becomes pathological have yet to be explicated. The activities that frequently precipitate suicide attempts by adolescents involve disagreements, conflicts or problems with family members, school, or peers (Harkavy & Asnis 1985; Kahn, 1987; Tishler, McHenry, & Morgan, 1981).

Adolescent Developmental Tasks

The major developmental tasks of the adolescent may provide insights for understanding why this population faces such major threats to their mortality. The major developmental task for the adolescent according to Erikson (1968) involves issues of ego identity. Identity issues involving separation from parents, sexuality and vocational or academic competence come to the fore during the adolescent years. The relationships between the adolescent and his or her social system (i.e., family and peers) are characterized by major change.

The adolescent and the family struggle with the issues of control and autonomy. The adolescent strives to achieve independence from parental control and attempts to establish increasing levels of self-control (Youniss, 1980). As the adolescent moves away from the family, peers begin to assume greater importance. The normative model suggests that adolescents move from group activities with same-sex peers to more dyadic relationships with peers of the opposite sex (Conger & Peterson, 1984).

A third area of activity and possible conflict involves the development of vocational goals. The seminal research in this area has focused on male adolescents (Douvan & Adelson, 1966). Realistic academic or vocational planning requires the adolescent to have some knowledge about his or her interests and abilities as well as means for achieving the vocational goal.

The hostile environment faced by many minority youth may add barriers to the successful completion of the tasks of adolescence. Hispanic youth deal with additional pressures such as language barriers, value conflicts (that may be particularly troublesome for female Hispanics), and pressure to acculturate (Canino & Canino, 1980).

Violence and the Environment

Homicide and suicide are leading causes of death among adolescents. There is little doubt that these two behaviors represent striking manifestations of violence. But adolescents, especially minority adolescents, are subject to more pervasive forms of violence.

Adolescents are frequently the victims of violence. Public schools are especially dangerous places. About 7,000 schools face serious problems with crime, almost a quarter of a million young people are attacked at school in an average month, and more than 100,000 students are victims of robbery in an average month (U.S. Senate Subcommittee on Juvenile Justice, 1981).

The school system itself can be viewed as a perpetrator of violence, particularly for minority youth. In the public schools, minority youth are more likely to be victims of corporal punishment, more likely to be suspended or expelled, and more likely to be labeled as behavior disordered than Anglo youth (Children's Defense Fund, 1985). Each of these school-based actions victimizes or stigmatizes young people.

The home and school environment represent a potential threat to the physical and emotional safety of young people. But young people are subject to other sources of less obvious violence. Social injustice and exploitation are pervasive forms of violence perpetrated by economic, social, and political institutions. Infant mortality rates, for example, reflect a form of violence directed at the most vulnerable members of American society.

The United States ranks 17th in the world in its ability to keep its infants alive (Wegman, 1985). When race is disaggregated, the numbers change dramatically. The black infant mortality rate is almost twice the rate for white infants (U.S. Department of Health and Human Services, 1984).

Structural inequities that contribute to poverty, unemployment, and inadequated education can also be viewed as a form of violence. Children, especially black and Hispanic children, have become the poorest group of Americans. Those who seek work and are unsuccessful experience a form of violence that assails self-esteem and self-respect. Those unable to read above a 3rd-grade level after four years of high school are victims of a cruel form of violence and may go on to experience economic failure in the market place.

The Ecological Perspective

Minority youth face special hazards as they interact with the environment. Individuals influence and are influenced by social institutions. The interaction between the individual and the environment can be satisfying or marked by conflict. Minority youth who come to the attention of mental health agencies and juvenile courts are experiencing discord in their interactions with the environment.

Socialization through family, neighborhood, religious institutions, schools, advertising, and television encourages young people to believe they should work hard and excel in order to receive rewards. Realities such as inadequate housing, substandard schools, and racism make it difficult to succeed. Employment and vocational opportunities can be especially problematic. A high school diploma, due in part to the changing nature of work and the flight of capital, is no guarantee of employment. The U.S. Department of Labor (1984) reports the unemployment rate for black adolescents is in excess of 40%, more than twice as high as the rate for white adolescents. Wage levels for many of the jobs available to high school graduates are at a low level.

Despite these obstacles, many minority youth do excel and are actively recruited by institutions of higher education and by corporations as these institutions seek to abide by affirmative action regulations. These young people may leave their families, peers, and neighborhoods as a result of the recruitment efforts. This may have a negative impact on those left behind.

Minority youth who are not recruited for college or business may not be able to compete in the marketplace. They are ill equipped for the market place and may feel frustrated, depressed, and cheated. Some of their peers are in the same predicament and can offer acceptance, support, and recognition. Youths unable to find acceptance with peers or support within their families are at risk for serious depression.

The activities of the peer group are influenced by a number of variables. The recent media attention to youth gang involvement in the procurement and distribution of illegal drugs and the violence that frequently accompanies this activity has resulted in demands for stricter laws and a more visible police presence. These actions will prove ineffective as long as the huge profits from the sale of illegal drugs remain.

The following case examples help to illustrate the complex nature of violence as experienced and manifested by minority youth.

Maria R.

Maria, age 15, was a bilingual first-generation Mexican American. She was referred to a community mental health center by a hospital after making a suicide attempt. School records indicated that her academic performance was poor, she appeared depressed, and her attendance was sporadic. The school wanted to place Maria in an "alternate setting" where she would learn vocational skills.

Both of Maria's parents were employed outside of the home. Her father worked in construction and her mother worked in the garment industry. The family lived in a three-bedroom house, in a Southwestern city. Maria's two older brothers had moved out of the family home a year earlier. Maria had the primary child care responsibility for her two younger sisters and two younger brothers. She described her relationship with her siblings as strained. Maria had been dating a 19-year-old for the last six months. Since her parents did not approve of her dating, she kept this fact from them. She described her parents as "old fashioned" and nonresponsive to her needs and wishes. Her parents planned to send her to Mexico in a year and a half to marry a young man known by the family.

During the week of her suicide attempt Maria had argued with her parents about household responsibilities. Her relationship with her boyfriend was ending and she was told she would be suspended from school for nonattendance. Maria was found by her parents in an unconscious state after having cut both of her wrists.

Maria was seen at the mental health center for a month. During this time she began to verbalize feelings of anger concerning her inability to obtain the things she wanted, guilt over her wish to move away from her family, and resentment at the institutions that provided little support. Maria's development crisis, identity versus role confusion (Erikson, 1963), was further complicated by what she perceived to be her parents' ambivalence toward assimilation. Assimilation was viewed as both the means to achieving material success and cultural suicide if the assimilation process required a rejection of family and social values. Therapy was terminated when Maria's parents took her to Mexico to live with an aunt.

Research in adolescent suicide indicates that stressors play a significant role. Conflicts with parents, siblings, peers, and the school are common sources of stress. Minority youth face additional stressors, such as institutional racism, which serve to increase their risk for self-inflicted violence. These factors include a higher incidence of poverty, substandard schools and housing, and unemployment, which intensify the gap between the reality of life for these young people and the image portrayed on television. Conflicts resulting from acculturation, assimilation, and gender role identification add to the risks (Schinke, Schilling, Palleja, & Zayas, 1987). When these potential areas of conflict are either no resolved or are not achieved in an acceptable fashion, youngsters such as Maria find themselves in a no-win situation. There is no evidence to support the notion that assimilation, particularly in the economic and political arenas, is a reality for the majority of Mexican Americans (Feagin, 1989).

Ronald W.

Ronald, a black 17-year-old, was a twin. He and his twin sister, Olivia, lived with their mother in a two-bedroom apartment in a neighborhood marked by gang activity in a Northeastern city. Ronald's mother had been working as a nurse's aid for the last 12 years. She went to work outside of the home about a year after her husband was killed in an industrial accident. Ronald was in the 9th grade with little chance of promotion to the 10th grade. He rarely attended school. Olivia was in the 12th grade, an honor student, active in school clubs and in the local church. Olivia worked in a fast-food restaurant and did babysitting. Ronald was seeking work.

Mrs. W did not approve of Ronald's friends and feared they would get him "into trouble." She described them as "hoodlums" and drug users and instructed Ronald not to have contact with them. Ronald continued to have contact with his friends who were his primary source of support and safety. This lead to frequent verbal altercations between Ronald and his mother. Mrs. W was disappointed with Ronald's school performance. She had hoped Ronald would go to college and become a professional, something she and her husband had wanted to do but never had the opportunity to do. Mrs. W had asked her minister and the basketball coach at the youth center to speak with Ronald about his attitude and goals. Ronald refused to speak with them.

Ronald felt his mother compared him to Olivia and favored Olivia. Ronald listed his two major life goals as having "respect" and a well-paying job. When asked to name the people he respected, Ronald listed fictional characters from television and movies. Ronald did not have a specific plan for achieving a well-paying job.

Olivia earned a scholarship to a local college. Mrs. W was proud of Olivia's achievement and purchased a used car as a present for her. Ronald asked for the keys to the car so he could check the car's performance. Mrs. W told Ronald he was not allowed to use the car. She and Ronald had an unusually bitter argument and Ronald left the house in a rage. He met his friends, one of whom had just purchased a handgun. They decided to rob a local convenience store. During the course of the robbery, Ronald's 16-year-old friend shot and killed a store employee. Ronald was arrested and charged with robbery and murder.

Olivia was on her way toward achieving the American dream while Ronald awaited a court verdict. Mrs. W felt she failed in her task to give Ronald the strengths he would need to survive in a racist America, one of the major tasks of minority parents (Bowles 1988). Ronald was in trouble long before the incident at the convenience store. His family, friends, and teachers were not surprised at his arrest. Ronald had wanted a future marked by respect and a job. The prospects of achieving either of these goals are dim. Ronald's case scenario is not unique. It is pervasive in urban America. Given the situation, one could ask if it is justified to place total responsibility on Ronald's shoulders.

Implications

To effectively intervene with these young people and their families practitioners must be sensitive to, and understand, the constant struggle minority families encounter. Contemporary American life is characterized by social and economic inequities manifested by both personal and institutional racism.

Minority youth are often torn between the conflicting expectations of their families and their peer groups. Families and peer groups may offer support and a haven for the adolescent. In instances where the family and peer group hold divergent values there is a potential for internecine conflict between the two groups. The adolescent may then be placed in the position of having to choose between the two groups. This choice has major ramifications for the adolescent and is an area in which practitioners have to intervene to clarify choices or reduce the conflict. Such inter ventions have to be located both at the individual client's level as well as at the institutional and organizational levels.

The social institutions that affect the adolescent are in need of change. Public schools are a major purveyor of institutional racism. Years of research continue to demonstrate the role of schools in damaging minority youth (Carter, 1968; Kendall, 1983). In order to succeed in the job market, young people must be prepared to participate in the labor force. Since public schools generally provide part of this training ground, economic failure will continue to plague some minority young.

The segregated neighborhoods of America's minority poor can exacerbate the conflicts and challenges faced by minority youth and their families. The violent crime that frequently accompanies the drug business, for example, has made many urban areas dangerous for human beings. Some of the gangs of today are organized around the drug business and are using weapons with deadly results. The lure of huge profits from the sale of drugs adds another dimension to the conflict between the family and peer group.

Supports can be established to help adolescents (and their families) with their developmental tasks. The threats to the mental health of adolescents—especially minority adolescents—of suicide, substance abuse, racism, unemployment, homicide, early parenthood, depression, poverty, academic failures, and delinquency are amenable to intervention. The beginning of this intervention is relatively easy. The first step is to acknowledge the threat. The second step involves the development of a holistic approach, using an ecological perspective that offers the adolescent a realistic future (Johnson, 1985). Until these steps are taken, minority adolescents will continue to suffer disproportionate rates of morbidity and mortality from violence that is self-inflicted and society-inflicted.

References

Albert, N., & Beck, A. (1975). Incidences of depression in early adolescents: A preliminary study. *Journal of Youth and Adolescents, 4,* 301-307.

Becker, G. (1968). Crime and punishment: An economic approach. *Journal of Political Economy, 76,* 169-217.

Blumberg, M. (1981). Depression in abused and neglected children. *American Journal of Psychotherapy, 35,* 342-354.

Blumstein, A. (1982). On the racial disproportionality of United States prison populations. *Journal of Criminology and Criminal Law, 73,* 1259-1281.

Bowles, D. (1988). Development of an ethnic self-concept among blacks. In C. Jacobs & D. Bowles (Eds.), *Ethnicity and race: Critical concepts in social work* (pp. 103-113). Silver Spring, MD: National Association of Social Workers.

Burgess, R., & Conger, R. (1978). Family interaction patterns in abusive, neglectful, and normal families. *Child Development, 49,* 1163-1173.

Canino, I., & Canino, G. (1980). Impact of stress on the Puerto Rican family: Treatment considerations. *American Journal of Orthopsychiatry, 50,* 535-541.

Carter, T. (1968). The negative self-concept of Mexican-American students. *School and Society, 96,* 217-220.

Children's Defense Fund. (1985). *Black and white children in America.* Washington, DC: Author.

Christenson, R., & Thornberry, T. (1984). Unemployment and criminal involvement: An investigation of reciprocal causal structures. *American Sociological Review, 49,* 398-411.

Conger, R., & Peterson, A. (1984). *Adolescence and Youth* (3rd ed.). New York: Harper & Row.

Dannefer, D., & Schutt, R. (1982). Race and juvenile processing in court and police agencies. *American Journal of Sociology, 87,* 1113-1132.

Douvan, E., & Adelson, J. (1966). *The Adolescent Experience.* New York: John Wiley.

Duster, T. (1987). Crime, youth unemployment, and the black urban underclass. *Crime and Delinquency, 33,* 300-316.

Erikson, E. (1963). *Childhood and society* (2nd ed.). New York: Norton.

Erikson, E. (1968). *Identity: Youth and crisis.* New York: Norton.

Farnworth, M., & Horan, P. (1980). Separate justice: An analysis of race differences in court processes. *Social Science Research, 9,* 381-399.

Feagin, J. (1989). *Racial and ethnic relations* (3rd ed.). Englewood Cliffs, NJ: Prentice-Hall.

Flanagan, T., & McGarrell, E. (1985). *Sourcebook of criminal justice statistics.* Washington, DC: U.S. Government Printing Office.

Gold, M., & Petronin, R. (1980). Delinquent behavior in adolescence. In J. Adelson (Ed.), *Handbook of adolescent psychology* (pp. 495-535). New York: John Wiley.

Good, D., Pirog-Good, M., & Sickles, R. (1986). An analysis of youth crime and employment patterns, 1986. *Journal of Quantitative Criminology, 2,* 219-236.

Gray, E. (1984). *Child abuse: Prelude to delinquency?* Washington, DC: Office of Juvenile Justice and Delinquency Prevention.

Harkavy, J., & Asnis, G. (1985). Suicide attempts in adolescents: Prevalence and implications. *New England Journal of Medicine, 313,* 1290-1291.

Hindelang, M. (1978). Race and involvement in common law crimes. *American Sociological Review, 43,* 93-109.

Huizinga, D., & Elliott, D. (1985). *Juvenile offenders prevalence, offender incidence and arrest rates by race.* Boulder, CO: Institute of Behavioral Science.

Hunner, R., & Walker, Y. (Eds.). (1981). *Exploring the relationship between child abuse and delinquency.* Montclair, NJ: Allanheld & Osmum.

Johnson, R. (1985). Black adolescents: Issues critical to their survival. *Journal of the National Medical Association, 77*, 447-448.

Kendall, F. (1983). *Diversity in the classroom: A multicultural approach to the education of young children.* New York: Columbia.

Kahn, A. (1987). Heterogeneity of suicidal adolescents. *Journal of the American Academy of Child and Adolescent Psychiatry, 26*, 92-96.

Kratcoski, P. (1982). Child abuse and violence against the family. *Child Welfare, 61*, 435-444.

Krisberg, B., Schwartz, I., Fishman, G., Eisikovits, Z., Guttman, E., & Joe, K. (1987). The incarceration of minority youth. *Crime and Delinquency, 33*, 173-205.

Lewis, D., Moy, E., Jackson, L., Aronson, R., Restifo, N., Serra, S., & Simos, A. (1985). Biopsychosocial characteristics of children who later murder: A prospective study. *American Journal of Psychiatry, 142*, 1161-1167.

Miller, M., Chiles, J., & Barnes, V. (1982). Suicide attempters within a delinquent population. *Journal of Consulting and Clinical Psychology, 50*, 491-498.

Mulvey, E., & LaRosa, J. (1986). Delinquency cessation and adolescent development: Preliminary data. *American Journal of Orthopsychiatry, 56*, 212-224.

National Institute of Mental Health. (1983). *Special report on depression research.* Washington, DC: U.S. Department of Health and Human Services.

Phillips, L., & Votey, H. (1987). Rational choice models of crimes of youth. *Review of Black Political Economy, 16*, 129-186.

Pincus, J., Feldman, M., Jackson, L., & Bard, B. (1986). Psychiatric, neurological and psychoeducational characteristics of 15 death row inmates in the United States. *American Journal of Psychiatry, 143*, 838-845.

Rajgopal, P. R. (1987). *Social change and violence: The Indian experience.* New Delhi: Uppal.

Rutter, M., & Giller, H. (1984). *Juvenile delinquency: Trends and perspectives.* New York: Guilford.

Schinke, S., Schilling, R., Palleja, J., & Zayas, L. (1987. Prevention research among ethnic-minority group adolescents. *The Behavior Therapist, 10*, 151-155.

Smith, J., Mercy, J., & Warren, C. (1985). Comparison of suicides among Anglos and Hispanics in five Southwestern states. *Suicide and Life-Threatening Behavior, 15*, 14-26.

Sturkie, K., & Flanzer, J. (1987). Depression and self-esteem in the families of maltreated adolescents. *Social Work, 32*, 491-496.

Tishler, C., McHenry, P., & Morgan, K. (1981). Adolescent suicide attempts: Some significant factors. *Suicide and Life-Threatening Behavior, 11*, 86-92.

United States Department of Health and Human Services, National Center for Health Statistics. (1984). *Monthly vital statistics report* (Vol. 33, No. 3). Washington, DC: Author.

United States Department of Justice, Bureau of Justice Statistics. (1986). *Criminal victimization of the United States, 1986.* Washington, DC: Author.

United States Department of Justice, Bureau of Justice Statistics. (1987). *Bureau of justice statistics annual report.* Washington, DC: Author.

United States Department of Justice, Bureau of Justice Statistics. (1988). *Report to the nation on crime and justice.* Washington, DC: Author.

United States Department of Labor, Bureau of Labor Statistics. (1984). *Employment and earnings.* Washington, DC: Author.

United States Senate Subcommittee on Juvenile Justice. (1981). *The problem of juvenile crime* (Serial No. J-97-48). Washington, DC: Government Printing Office.
Wegman, M. (1985). Annual summary of vital statistics 1984. *Pediatrics, 76*, 861-871.
Youniss, J. (1980). *Parents and peers in social development: A Sullivan-Piaget perspective*. Chicago: University of Chicago Press.

6

In Pursuit of Affirmation:
The Antisocial Inner-City Adolescent

CHERYL L. THOMPSON

Inner-city life has long been associated with anti-social behavior (Whyte, 1965). Over the last 20 years the inner cities have become defined by the poverty and minority status of its residents. Life in the inner city has become increasingly more dangerous. Homicide is the leading cause of death for black adolescent males between 15 and 24 years of age. While black Americans constitute only 12% of the population they represent almost 50% of the prison population. Concurrently, the most frequent victim of criminal activity including robbery, rape, assault, burglary, and auto theft is also black. Fifty percent of all crime victims are black (Blackwell, 1985). Coupled with easy victimization is the experience of no protection from police authorities. Testimony from the Hearings Criminal Justice Subcommittee House Judiciary Committee reported that "blacks do not experience the police as present to protect them, but rather as 'an occupying force, an army'" (Roberts, 1987, p. 7). In fact, to call a policeman for protection can result in exacerbation of trauma. One need only to recall the recent series of events in New York City's 113th Police Precinct. Victims of crime seeking assistance have reported numerous episodes of verbal abuse as well as unnecessary use of force resulting in injuries sometimes serious enough to result in death.

Since 1968, the year of the riots, inner cities have experienced little growth that has impacted on its black residents. In fact, what has happened is that there has become a greater concentration of people who live at or slightly above the poverty level (World Almanac, 1989).

The flight of the middle class after the riots included the black middle class. The black middle-class flight meant that community role models had become less available to black youth. This made the ordinary awareness of avenues of success and achievement less apparent and therefore unobtainable. As a result, the heroes in the inner city became those men with cash, flashy cars, and no obvious employment.

Some of the factors long associated with juvenile crime such as low family income, large family size, parental criminality, low intelligence, and poor parenting behaviors (Masten & Garmezy, 1985), are the sociological explanations for much inner-city crime. For many social scientists, there is an assumption that sociological factors such as those stated above are a sufficient explanation to account for the antisocial behavior of inner-city youngsters (Bandura & Walters, 1959; Glueck & Glueck, 1962; Johnson & Szurek, 1952). However, the reliance on sociological factors to explain individual antisocial acts actually appears to perpetuate the activity because the adolescent remains unable to establish or experience a sense of personal identity (Erikson, 1968). This minimizes the possibility of becoming affirmed as worthwhile in more socially acceptable ways. Finally, the adolescent may become convinced that inner-city life has condemned him or her to a life of poverty, failure, and crime.

Inner-city antisocial behavior appears to represent the coalescence of discrimination, grinding poverty, and an intrapsychic constellation with wounded narcissism (Fromm, 1973) at its core. To avoid confusion about the definition of antisocial behavior, this chapter will limit its discussion to adolescents who have been detained at a youth detention facility or who have been incarcerated at a juvenile facility.

This chapter is divided into four parts: interpersonal and intrapsychic development that relate specifically to aspects of the black representational world, psychodynamic findings of psychological test results in forensic assessments, a case report of individual psychotherapy with an adolescent drug dealer and, finally, recommendations for intervention with inner-city antisocial adolescents.

The Development of the Black Representational World

The process of developing a cohesive and continuous sense of self (Kohut, 1977; Winnicott, 1986) is a complex process of repeated internalizations of external experiences coupled with an idiosyncratic or personal reworking so that the individual becomes his or her unique self. This process involves an interweaving of inner and outer reality with thoughts, feelings, actions, and interactions becoming increasingly complex and more clearly differentiated. This process in earliest infancy is concrete (Sharpe, 1937) and divided. Good experiences are stored separately from bad experiences. This process, called splitting, is a protective mechanism that guards the nascent ego from being overwhelmed (Kernberg, 1966) and protects the primary caretakers from excessive aggression (Klein, 1946). As this process unfolds, the infant shares and returns the reflections of his or her caretakers.

The black child must pass through this process, and incorporate into his definitions of self and other the cultural representations that further define the self. It has been demonstrated that by age three, black children clearly identify themselves as racial beings with some understanding of the social, psychological, and cultural implications (Clark 1963, 1965; McDonald, 1970) of their blackness.

With the imagery of blackness being primarily negative, there are many opportunities to develop impaired self-esteem and/or other forms of psychopathology. Parson (1985) hypothesizes that black Americans must develop a bicultural identity. He states this bicultural identity requires the synthesis of basically incompatible social values because of the differing cultural roots of African Americans and Euro-Americans as demonstrated in Table 6.1.

Parson further states:

The integrative task of bringing these basic inconsonant psychic elements and values into an harmonious, well-functioning, and sustaining identity system is extremely difficult, but with good early experiences in a protective family system (to include extended and adopted

TABLE 6.1: Black American Bicultural Value System

African Culture	Euro-American Culture
1. Time Perspectives	
Circular; emphasis on the past and present	Linear; emphasis on distant future planning
2. Concept of Self	
Psychological, physical, and spiritual well-being are dependent on the Community; affiliation; unity	Psychological, physical, social and spiritual well-being are dependent upon the individual; self-reliance; independence
3. Ownership	
Possession belongs to community; sociocentric; focus is on the non-material	Possession belongs to the individual; sociocentric focus is on the material
4. Authority	
Obedience to authority; respect for the aged indispensable to the young	Question and challenge authority; the aged are dispensable
5. Child Rearing	
Depend on extended family kinship	Socialization based primarily in the early years on the parents, especially the mother

Table adapted from Parson (1985). Reprinted with author's permission.

family members), integration of both African and American elements may result in a flexible self-identity, and may conceivably facilitate dialectical ego states. Thus such flexibility may make it possible for the black person to transcend social and economic oppression, while being enabled to move with relative freedom between inner and outer reality, between drive and object, between primary and secondary process thinking, and generally among id, ego, and superego derivatives . . . . These ego discordant elements may produce significant ego strength in black Americans, providing the family has succeeded in adequately protecting and sustaining the young evolving self from the ill effects of racism and its many derivatives (poverty, malnutrition, self-hate, etc). (Parson, 1985, p. 179)

The implications for the development of biculturality are adequate, sensitive, culturally aware parenting, coupled with concrete bicultural experiences. This would include as essential positive and instructive interactions with representatives of the culture one defines as American. For inner-city youth, the purveyors of the Euro-American culture are television, policemen, and teachers, because these children live in circumstances that are more racially and socially segregated than those that existed prior to Brown v. Board of Education, (1954). There is less opportunity for inner-city youth to integrate discordant cultural views, resulting in what Pinderhughes (1982) describes as a "victim system." That is, "the community becomes unable to sustain itself and in fact, serves an active disorganizing influence, as a breeder of crime and a source of even more powerlessness" (p. 109).

It is this author's contention that inner-city isolation and segregation from the larger community, including the black middle class; the perception of the police as maintainers of the victim system; and the failure of the education system to transmit cultural values come together with the media to deliver a message that acquisition without work can become a source of self-esteem enhancement. People can become defined by material possessions rather than by demonstration of character and principled life. This conviction, that material acquisition will lead to enhanced self-esteem regardless of the means of acquisition becomes a significant source of adolescent antisocial behavior where larceny and theft account for 45% of all juvenile crime (World Almanac, 1989). For many youngsters, however, crime represents a wish to participate in the culture as they understand it.

The cases that follow demonstrate the vulnerability and psychopathology that occurs when bicultural identification has no avenue of development.

Psychological Test Findings:

Case One:

Mary, age 16, was arrested for criminal conspiracy and kidnaping. At the time of arrest Mary was not enrolled in school; she had not attended school since 8th grade. She was living with a much older man whom she described as having "special talent from God." Mary stated that the two children who were kidnaped by

TABLE 6.2

Verbal Tests	Scaled Scores	Performance Tests	Scaled Scores
Information	2	Picture Completion	8
Similarities	5	Picture Arrangement	11
Arithmetic	8	Block Design	6
Vocabulary	6	Object Assembly	5
Comprehension	3	Coding	7
(Digit Span)	(10)		
	Verbal I.Q. Score	68	
	Performance I.Q. Score	82	
	Full Scale I.Q. Score	73	

her "common-law husband" were taken to provide company for her while he was working. This was a first arrest for Mary.

House - Tree - Person - opposite sex person are as follows:

The results of the Wechsler Intelligence Scale for Children-Revised (WISC-R) and the interviews suggest that Mary is an enormously vulnerable adolescent whose cognitive ability is unpredictable and unstable (see Table 6.2). Mary's figure drawings (see Figure 6.1) show some evidence of adolescent development such as the shapely adolescent female, however, all stages of psychosexual development are equally available to this young woman. This lack of phase-dominance in development left her vulnerable to joining with and believing in an "omnipotent other." It appears that her overwhelming loneliness and deprivation left her willing to engage in a kidnaping. She "wanted company."

Case Two:

Ruth, an 18-year-old black female was arrested for murder/manslaughter following a knifed fight in the street. Ruth, an orphaned and estranged adolescent had hoped this fight would result in her being accepted by her family. Ruth was genuinely shocked that the knife fight could result in death. Her adolescent conviction of immortality played a significant role in her willingness to fight with weapons. This was a first arrest for Ruth. Ruth's test results on the

Case One

Mary
16 yrs

Tree

Male
opposite sex person

House

Person
First drawing
Female

Figure 6.1. Case One Drawings

TABLE 6.3

Verbal Tests	Scaled Scores	Performance Tests	Scaled Scores
Information	7	Picture Completion	8
Digit Span	11	Picture Arrangement	10
Vocabulary	6	Block Design	8
Arithmetic	8	Object Assembly	8
Comprehension	6	Digit Symbol	10
Similarities	7		
	Verbal I.Q. Score	90	
	Performance I.Q. Score	92	
	Full Scale I.Q. Score	89	

Wechsler Adult Intelligence Scale-Revised (WAIS-R) are presented in Table 6.3.

Ruth attended high school until the 10th grade when she dropped out. Ruth's House—Tree—Person—Opposite sex person drawings (see Figure 6.2) demonstrate a lack of progressive psychosexual development, evidencing arrest before sexual differentiation could have occurred. This blurring reflects an inability to see herself as separate from a significant other.

These women demonstrated impairments in time perspective and self-concept that leave them easy victims as well prone to becoming victimizers.

These adolescents demonstrate the failures of each of the systems charged with their growth and development. The family, the school, and the community have not succeeded in providing an opportunity for growth and ego consolidation. Additionally, these children exhibit an object hunger, that appears to be the one thread of optimism. They are sufficiently needy for interpersonal contact, so that if they had contact with growth-promoting others, they could become rehabilitated. This finding, profound object hunger, is not present in every antisocial adolescent and therefore appears to be the differential determinant in whether an adolescent can be salvaged from a life of containment in penal institutions. The figure drawings as well as the explanations for their crimes demonstrate their compelling wish for affiliation as well as the

CASE TWO
Ruth
18 yrs

House

Opposite sex person

Tree

Person.

Figure 6.2. Case Two Drawings

impairments in ego function that would permit these specific anti-social actions.

Psychotherapeutic Intervention with a 19-Year-Old Male Drug Dealer

Kane (a pseudonym) was referred to me for psychological intervention one week after he had entered a special job training program in New York City. This program included high school courses with clerical job training. The young people admitted could not have reading or math test scores that exceeded Grade 5 on a standardized measure. Kane was quickly identified as much brighter than his classmates and as a behavior problem. He sat in class yawning loudly, sleeping, or just staring. It was the staring that was experienced as most distressing, as if he had "X-ray vision." His teachers complained that he seemed to look straight through them as if he were looking at their souls. At our first meeting, Kane presented as an immaculately groomed, thin, dark-skinned black male with an angry hostile expression. He had a muscular body reflecting a lot of time "working out."

Kane was extremely resistant to talking to me when he heard I was the psychologist. His first response was, "Now they think I'm crazy too."

Kane was told that his teachers and counselors wanted me to see him because they couldn't figure him out. They knew he was very smart, that he could ace this program with no sweat but that he seemed so angry that they were afraid he would fail.

Kane's response was to laugh. He said he had to pretend to read and write at a 5th-grade level in order to enter the program. He felt forced to enter the program because he was on probation for assault. In fact this was his last chance to avoid adult imprisonment. If he failed this program he could have his probation rescinded and be remanded to jail.

I asked him what "crazy" meant to him. Kane responded, "people who can't handle their own problems, people who don't have their stuff together." I responded by saying that I was concerned that his definition of crazy was so narrow that ordinary people who needed ordinary help couldn't ask for the help they needed.

This statement resulted in a lengthy tirade about people in that Kane expressed overwhelming distrust saying basically that anyone who trusts people should have their head examined because they are messed up. I responded to this tirade by saying that Kane seemed very disillusioned and hurt. That, somehow, trust had been stolen from him and that he would have to be helped to become able to trust a little again. Kane remained in that session with me for two and a half hours. He began to talk about his life. It became clear that Kane would never respond to the normal time constraints of the therapy hour. A decision was made to allow him to remain with me until he felt able to end. For the next 20 weeks we met at session times that varied from 30 minutes to three hours. Kane was informed that his sessions would end whenever he chose.

He shared a personal history of rejection and isolation. His mother, 15 years his senior, had not been able to parent him and her pregnancy was such a disappointment to her family that she and her son were not welcomed in the family. Kane states he started having trouble from the first day at school. He didn't listen, he fought with classmates and, by the age of 8, started playing hooky from school. He said the school called his mother almost every day. She became tired of the calls and tried to beat him, punish him, refuse to buy him things, not feed him, and so forth, but nothing really worked. Even at 19, he couldn't explain his behavior; it seemed beyond his control. By the age of 9, Kane was removed from his mother and placed in a residential setting. He did not see her or hear from her for two years. At age 11, he came home again, by now he knew how to pilfer purses and to steal items that could be quickly sold. By age 13 he was again removed and placed in a facility for delinquent boys. He remained until age 16. Upon release, he immediately found his mother. He told her he was wiser and now going straight. His mother is reported to have responded, "Kane I know you and you are just bad." Shortly after his return home he reconnected with antisocial characters and began to sell marijuana. Kane reasoned that since his mother didn't believe in him why shouldn't he do whatever he needed to survive? He went on to report that he earned a substantial sum of money. He had purchased a BMW that he drove without a driver's license. The family he lived with, a foster family who were blood relatives, were so pleased with the money he gave them, they asked no questions about its source.

However, a disagreement developed, resulting in gun play. The foster family became frightened and asked Kane to move. So at age 17, Kane was completely on his own. He found an apartment and continued to sell marijuana. He had a street name, a reputation for being armed but he still managed to steer clear of the police for the next year.

By 18, Kane began to sell crack (cocaine). He had two "spots" (locations from which he sold crack). He talked about crack as an "equal opportunity drug." He said this was the only drug that black people had an opportunity to make money selling. Kane boasted about the large quantity of cash he had amassed. This cash was stored in various containers in his apartment because he had no awareness of what to do with this money. He was questioned about the risks involved in his present lifestyle. He quickly talked about the risks. He felt unsafe in the streets unless he was armed. He stated he usually carried a .357 magnum or some other powerful automatic weapon. He also talked about his involvement with the police, stating at times they stopped him, had confiscated his car, and had taken some of his money. These accusations were not confirmable, but the mistrust he experienced became a focus for his therapy.

I explained to Kane that he could not come to school armed and that I was concerned about the tenuousness of his existence. It seemed to me that each day could be his last.

He acknowledged that his life had become unreal, he described it as, "Lights, Cameras, Action." He further said he never knew whether new people in his life were police plants, or competing drug dealers, or crack heads desperate for either drugs or money.

The dangerousness of his existence was acknowledged. His life indeed was the commodity he had sold for money. We talked about the choices between time and/or money. Kane had money he could not use and his life had the unreality of a movie, as he poignantly described, but he could never walk off the set. This avenue of exploration connected for him. He could see time and money existing in a dialectic and began to share that his real intention was to have power, prestige, and enough money to win his mother's attention and love.

When Kane became excited about his new insight, he wanted to share it with her. He was able to find her residing several states away. He went to visit, told her about his new path, and hoped for her approval. Her disappointment with him, in particular, and probably men in general, resulted in her once again rejecting his statements about change. Kane came back to the program with the icy hostile look he had in the beginning. He was confronted about his willingness to return to his self-destructive path because once again he was disappointed by his mother. Her disbelief was acknowledged and it was determined that he could demonstrate his changed behavior by not resuming his old lifestyle. Kane began to accept that trust for his mother would have to be at least as difficult for her as it was for him. He decided he would just have to prove himself.

Kane then planned his movement out of the drug trade. He felt that the first step needed to be a move to a neighborhood where he could be anonymous. The "spots" were closed without consequence. Kane explained that this is shaky business and customers just move on to the next "spot."

The morality of his activity was not focused upon because be seemed so hungry for approval, and disapproval seemed to exacerbate his antisocial tendency. Rather, each step to normalize his life was met with support and encouragement. His teachers and counselors were apprised of his wish to succeed and encouraged him to keep trying.

During this phase, Kane talked about feeling so small, so isolated, so out of place as a black male in a more normal (racially mixed) world. He talked about always being afraid that he would be assessed by the larger society as no good, as a criminal. We compared his mother's expectations and the community expectations to his sense of himself. Kane had an external self-definition that meant any person could affect his sense of himself.

Kane's clinical unfolding was dynamically similar to the other cases; the adolescent's self-esteem and self-definition reflect failures at ego integration.

Kane completed the training program and accepted an entry-level position. He was employed as a clerk in a household appliance store. At the end of six months, he was still employed. Kane was pleased to have a "normal 9 to 5" job. He was encouraged by his therapist and the staff to share an apartment with a classmate so that he could afford to start at the bottom and work his way up. At the end of the program, Kane had not completed the high school equivalency exam. By the 20th week in psychotherapy, Kane had become able to accept the treatment session as 45 to 50 minutes. Kane was helped by a multifaceted approach with staff providing encouragement for psychotherapy and support for every fledgling effort Kane initiated. Therapy was directive and supportive.

The inner-city adolescents described above have antisocial action as part of their development, but still have sufficient object hunger to be reached and possibly helped. Winnicott (1986) describes antisocial activity as a sign of hope. He stated, "Whenever conditions give a child a certain degree of new hope, then the antisocial tendency becomes a clinical feature and the child becomes difficult" (p. 92). For each of these youngsters, it seems hope of acknowledgment, reconciliation, or reunion was at the base of the specific antisocial act. For Winnicott,

> it is the mother's failure to teach the child to use the world creatively so that the child loses contact with objects but at the moment of hope, the child reaches out and steals an object. This is a compulsive act and the child does not know why he or she does it. (p. 93)

For all these children there was no planning, no understanding of consequences and clearly no sense of the permanence of the antisocial act. Each of these adolescents seemed motivated by an affiliative need gone awry. It is this need that is the beacon of hope in these adolescents.

Winnicott states, "The child absolutely requires an environment that is indestructible in essential respects . . . somehow the home sticks together and behind all this is the confidence that the child has in the relationship between the parents; the family is an ongoing concern" (p. 94). These families are not ongoing concerns. Thompson (1978) found that inner-city antisocial adolescents did not experience their families as secure or predictable. These families are the most vulnerable because nothing can be predicted. Poverty dictates mere survival, so that the most vulnerable receive the least support.

Black adolescents require greater effort from family, community, and institutions in order to develop adequate self-esteem because they must integrate two world views. The task becomes a greater burden when the youngsters also are entrenched in poverty.

Antisocial behavior is the responsibility of the entire society. All phases of a child's development need the support of the family, the community, and all institutions charged with their care. As the society changes, particularly since there are fewer two-parent families, we need more involvement from these institutions—not necessarily more money, but commitment, and willingness of the institutions to be the purveyor of Euro-American values within a context of respecting the black child's humanity as well as providing avenues to equal chances to succeed in socially acceptable endeavors. The individuals described in the case scenarios above still have hope and the capacity to have interpersonal connection. If this need is not nurtured, these adolescents will lose their ability to care and will become permanently lost. The drive to succeed, (White, 1960) to become affirmed, will continue to lead individuals down antisocial paths if no other path and no reliable guide can be found.

References

Bandura, A., & Walters, R. (1959). *Adolescent aggression.* New York: Ronald Press.

Blackwell, J. (1985). *The black community diversity and unity.* New York: Harper & Row.

Clark, K. (1963). *Prejudice and your child* (2nd ed.). Boston: Beacon.

Clark, K. (1965). *Dark ghetto.* New York: Harper & Row.

Erikson, E. (1968). *Identity: Youth and crisis.* New York: Norton.

Fromm, E. (1973). The anatomy of human destructiveness. New York: Holt, Rinehart & Winston.

Glueck, S., & Glueck, E. (1962). *Family environment and delinquency.* Boston: Houghton Mifflin.

Johnson, A., & Szurek, S. (1952). The genesis of antisocial acting out in children and adults. *Psychoanalytic Quarterly, 35,* 250-258.

Kernberg, O. (1966). Structural derivatives of object relationships. *International Journal of Psychoanalysis, 47,* 236-253.

Klein, M. (1946). Notes on some schizoid mechanisms. In J. Riviere (Ed.). *Developments in psychoanalysis.* London: Hogarth.

Kohut, H. (1977). *The restoration of the self*. New York: International Universities Press.

Masten, A., & Garmezy, N. (1985). Risk, vulnerability, and protective factors in developmental psychopathology. In B. B. Lakey & A. E. Kazden (Eds.), *Advances in clinical child psychology*. New York: Plenum.

McDonald, M. (1970). *Not by the color of their skins*. New York: International Universities Press.

Parson, E. (1985). The black Vietnam veteran: His representational world. In W. E. Kelly (Ed.), *Post-traumatic stress disorder and the war veteran patient. New York: Bruner/Mazel*.

Pinderhughes, E. (1982). The Afro-American family and the victim system. In M. McGoldrick, J. Pearce, & J. Giordorno, (Eds.), *Ethnicity and family therapy*. New York: Guilford.

Roberts, H. (1987). *The inner world of the black juvenile delinquent: Three case studies*. New Jersey: Lawrence Erlbaum.

Sharpe, E. (1937). *Dream analysis*. New York: Bruner/Mazel.

Thomas, A., & Sillen, S. (1974). *Racism & psychiatry*. New Jersey: Citadel.

Thompson, C. (1978). *Intrafamilial relationships in single parent low income families*. Unpublished manuscript.

White, R. (1960). *Competence and the psychosexual stages of development*. Nebraska Symposium on Motivation, 97-141.

Whyte, W. F. (1965). *Street corner society* (2nd ed). Chicago: University of Chicago Press.

Winnicott, D. (1964). *The maturational processes and the facilitating environment*. New York: International Universities Press.

Winnicott, D. (1986). *Home is where we start from*. New York: Norton.

World Almanac and Book of Facts. (1989). New York: Pharos Books.

7

Hispanic Adolescents and Antisocial Behavior: Sociocultural Factors and Treatment Implications

ORLANDO RODRIGUEZ
LUIS H. ZAYAS

Although Hispanic American adolescents appear to be at high risk for delinquency, substance abuse, conduct disorders, and other antisocial behavior given their demographic profile, little is known about the factors associated with antisocial behavior among these youth, or about culturally relevant treatment and prevention approaches. In this chapter, we review theories of antisocial behavior and consider sociocultural factors that must be integrated into these theories if they are to afford greater understanding of antisocial behavior among Hispanic youth. We also present a sociocultural model of Hispanic delinquency and discuss its program implications. Before proceeding, however, we note that much of the

Authors' Note: Research for this chapter was supported by Grant 1R01MH40387 of the Center for the Study of Violence and Anti-Social Behavior, National Institute of Mental Health, and Grant 2P01MH30569 A1, Minority Resources Branch, National Instituted of Mental Health. We are grateful to Maribel Vargas for her assistance in compiling data and information used in this chapter.

literature on Hispanics cited here is focused on Puerto Ricans and Mexican Americans. Despite the diversity among Hispanic immigrant groups, we believe that the realities facing the different Hispanic subgroups residing in inner cities are similar to those of mainland Puerto Ricans and Mexican Americans.

As considered in this chapter, the difference between an adolescent being adjudicated a delinquent or diagnosed as conduct disordered is a function of whether the juvenile justice system or the mental health system assesses his or her behavior. Not all youth with conduct problems are adjudicated as delinquents and many youth who commit offenses or are processed by the criminal justice system may not be conduct disordered; however, regardless of the label used, by descriptions of their behavior essentially the same or similar antisocial behaviors are involved.

Antisocial behavior as considered in this chapter and the extended sociocultural model of causation we propose encompass delinquent behavior, conduct disorders, and drug use. Our use of the term antisocial behavior conforms to the descriptions of conduct disorders and antisocial behavior found in the *Diagnostic and Statistical Manual of Mental Disorders* (DSM-III-R) (American Psychiatric Association, 1987): a persistent pattern of irresponsible behavior that often violates the rights of others and fails to conform to conventional social norms. Although substance use *per se* need not be antisocial, antisocial conduct has been linked to alcohol and drug abuse and other problem behavior (Block, Block, & Keyes, 1988; Jessor & Jessor, 1977; Kandel, 1978; Labouvie & McGee, 1986).

Space limitations preclude an extensive discussion of data on problem behavior rates among Hispanics. In general, little is known about the extent of antisocial behavior among Hispanics. The available evidence suggests that Hispanic youth are at greater risk of engaging in antisocial behavior than white youth, but that their prevalence rates are not as pronounced as those of blacks. Treatment and arrest data suggest that Hispanics' prevalence rates are closer to those of blacks (Banks, Rodriguez, & Burger, 1985; National Institute on Drug Abuse, 1987a; Rodriguez, 1988; Rodriguez, Burger, & Banks, 1984), while epidemiological survey data indicate prevalence rates only slightly higher than those for white (Elliott, Ageton, Huizinga, Knowles, & Canter, 1983; National Institute on Drug Abuse, 1987b; Rachal, Maisto, Guess, & Hubbard, 1982; Welte & Barnes, 1987). The contrasts shown by the two type of data may reflect differential treatment of Hispanics and whites by criminal justice and health services agencies (Chambliss & Nagasawa, 1969; Huizinga & Elliott, 1986; Krisberg, Schwartz, Fishman, Eisikovitz, & Guttman, 1986). Moreover, while antisocial behavior decreases as adolescents reach adulthood, Hispanic and other minority adolescents may be less likely than whites to reduce such involvements as they mature (Caetano, 1984; Rodriguez, Burger, & Banks, 1984).

We now turn to a discussion of how Hispanic antisocial behavior may be conceptualized. First, we briefly examine how current theories view youth antisocial behavior in general.

Antisocial Behavior Models

Existing theories of antisocial behavior constitute a useful point of departure for conceptualizing Hispanic antisocial behavior. However, the theories must be integrated with other conceptualizations relevant to the sociocultural situation of Hispanic youth. Although the theories differ on the factors they emphasize as central, most agree on the types that must be included. As indicated by Figure 7.1, most theories posit that disadvantaged status, low income, and discrimination, together with social environments that tolerate antisocial behavior, tend to weaken conventional bonding (the ability of families, schools, and other conventional institutions to control adolescents' antisocial behavior), and strengthen deviant peer bonding (the inclinations of peer groups to engage in such behavior). Weak conventional bonds and strong peer bonds directly influence antisocial behavior, but they may also foster a weak self-concept, a more proximate and psychological influence on antisocial behavior.

Disadvantaged Status

Most theories view delinquency as a reaction to disadvantaged class and ethnic position (Braithewaite, 1981; Datesman, Scarpitto, & Stephenson, 1975; Rutteer & Giller, 1983). In addition to class and ethnicity—structural factors that influence individuals' life chances—the neighborhood social environment provides

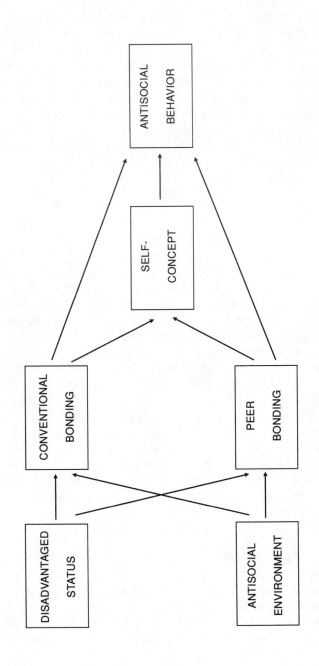

constraints or opportunities for delinquent involvement. More proximate factors, related to outcomes of interaction between the adolescent and his or her family, school, and peers, are found in other theories. Some formulations have elucidated the social-psychological processes by which disadvantaged status causes antisocial behavior. Among these are Cohen's (1955) theory of lower class reaction-formation to middle-class educational norms in the schools; Cloward and Ohlin's (1960) theory of reactions to lack of educational and occupational opportunity; and strain theory, which emphasizes discrepancies between achievement aspirations and expectations rather than expectations *per se* (Dembo, Blount, Schmeidler, & Burgos, 1986; Dembo, Farrow, Schmeidler, & Burgos, 1979; Elliott & Voss, 1974; Oetting & Beauvais, 1987; Simon & Gagnon, 1976).

Antisocial Environment

In some theories a social environment tolerant of crime and drug use is viewed as contributing to adolescents' involvement in delinquency (Conger, 1971; Smith, 1983). The crime-ridden neighborhood as a focus for providing examples and rationalizations for delinquency is found in Shaw and McKay's (1942) theory of social disorganization, and the theory of anomie and deviant behavior (Merton, 1957). In some conceptualizations, the social environment is viewed as providing opportunities for involvement in deviant behavior through the availability of behavior models to emulate. Thus drug use is more likely if drugs are available in the neighborhood (Dembo et al., 1979, 1986), and certain types of neighborhoods provide opportunities for youth to develop careers in organized crime (Cloward & Ohlin, 1960; Ianni, 1974).

In another conceptualization, some social environments engender subcultures with attitudes and perceptions conducive to delinquency and drug use among those so disposed. The concepts of delinquent subculture (Miller, 1958) and lower-class subculture (Banfield, 1970; Lewis, 1961; Rainwater, 1970; Suttles, 1955) reflect the views of a group-derived orientation emphasizing survival strategies based on bending the law (Hannerz, 1969; Liebow, 1967), focusing upon aspects of inner-city life that are unique to specific problem behaviors.

Conventional Bonding

Most theories view deviance as the result of failures by the family, school, and other conventional institutions to socialize youth to the conventional order (Jessor & Jessor, 1977; Kandel, 1980). When socialization is effective, youth develop conventional bonds: emotional attachment to the school and family, commitment to conventional activities, involvement in such activities, and belief in the moral order underlying conventional bonds (Elliott, Huizinga, & Ageton, 1985; Hirschi, 1969; Jessor & Jessor, 1977; Kandel, 1980; Kaplan, Martin, & Robbins, 1984).

Socialization in the family, that is, the patterns of supervision and discipline established by parents in early childhood, lies at the core of conventional bonding. Research has identified types of socialization problems that influence youth antisocial behavior. Parents sometimes may model aggression and substance use, sometimes criminality as well. In child rearing, parents may be inconsistent, harsh, or lenient, and often may rely on physical punishment, not engage in moral reasoning themselves, and fail to supervise (Glueck & Glueck, 1950; Martin, 1975; Patterson, 1981; Rutter & Giller, 1983; West & Farington, 1977). Patterson (1981) has also pointed out that parents may not follow through on sanctions for transgressions or rewards for good behavior, and may lack ways to deal effectively with problems and crises. Some families also may be unable to provide basic needs such as a sense of acceptance, security, affection, and emotional attachment (Anolik, 1981; Stott, 1982). In their work with delinquent black and Hispanic youth in New York City slums, Minuchin and his colleagues (Minuchin, Montalvo, Guerney, Rosman, & Schumer, 1967) identified parental failure to set family role boundaries as a major source of the antisocial behavior.

Peer Bonding

Research has identified peer bonding, the outcome of interaction between peers, as a critical element in explaining antisocial behavior. Deviance is influenced by one's peers through the same social-psychological mechanisms that operate in conventional bonding—namely, emotional attachment, and commitment to, and involvement in peer activities arising from socialization by peers into antisocial activities. The nature of delinquent socialization has been elaborated in social learning theory (Akers, 1977; Sutherland, 1947). Adolescents learn delinquency by modeling, exposure to friends delinquent behavior, peers' social approval for delinquent acts, and anticipated rewards for engaging in delinquency. Peer group influences on antisocial behavior are especially likely when there is weak bonding to the family and school (Elliott et al., 1985; Hirschi, 1969; Jessor & Jessor, 1977; Kandel, 1980; Kaplan et al., 1984). The assumption is that adolescent status is ambiguously defined by society, hence the strong reliance on the peer group to resolve identity problems (Coleman, 1976).

Self-Concept

More proximal to problem behavior and influenced by the more distal social factors discussed above is the adolescent's self-concept, that is, the overall sense of personal worth and efficacy (Bandura, 1982). Kandel (1974), Kaplan (1975), and Kaplan et al. (1984) include perceived self-worth as a factor in their conceptual approaches to adolescent drug use. Some clinicians suggest that, in assessing an adolescent with a conduct disorder, it is useful to consider the presence of an underlying major depressive disorder (Jensen, Burke, & Garfinkel, 1988; Mitchell, McCauley, Burke, & Moss, 1988). Boys with major depression often complain of problems of impulse control, anger and aggression, disturbed ideation, and parental conflict (Jensen et al., 1988). Children suffering from depression and presenting conduct disorders often come from families with paternal substance abuse and antisocial personality and maternal depression (Lahey, Piacentini, McBurnett, Stone, Hartdagen, & Hynd, 1988; Puig-Antich, 1982).

In conjunction with an examination of Figure 7.1, the discussion above suggests that models of antisocial behavior generally view adolescents as being influenced by factors at three experiential levels. At the individual level, negative self-concepts (e.g., low self-worth, external locus of control) directly influence antisocial involvements. At the social group level (i.e., the family, school, and peer group), negative outcomes of interaction with such groups influence antisocial involvement and also influence a negative self-concept. At the societal level, social class, ethnicity, and the neighborhood environments—vehicles for the distribution of life chances—indirectly influence antisocial behavior by affecting the ability of the family and other social groups to foster conventional bonds with the adolescent. How relevant is this conceptualization to the sociocultural situation of Hispanic adolescents?

Hispanic Antisocial Behavior: Elements of a Sociocultural Model

A major gap in theoretical models on delinquent behavior and drug use is a conceptualization of the specific social and cultural milieu in which social-psychological processes take place. Three broad areas of sociocultural differences are relevant to understanding the nature of Hispanic adolescent antisocial behavior and creating appropriate treatment and prevention strategies. One area concerns the unique cultural traditions possessed by Hispanics that differ from those of the American mainstream. Another area concerns the immigrant character of Hispanic inner-city populations, which often enmeshes them in the conflictive process of deciding whether to adhere to the norms and values of American society or to those of their parents' countries of origin. The third area concerns the nature of the sociocultural environment in inner-city neighborhoods, characterized by high levels of social disorganization and the preponderance of the lowest levels of the stratification ladder. Figure 7.2 suggests how sociocultural aspects of Hispanic social life may be integrated into existing conceptualizations to advance an extended sociocultural model of antisocial behavior among Hispanic youth. (The figure represents a heuristic rather than multivariate model. As the discussion below will show, the sociocultural concepts depicted are best understood as multidimensional contexts for understanding the effects of bonding and other factors on Hispanic youth).

Hispanic Cultural Traditions

Cultural traits inhibitory of antisocial behavior may be found in Hispanics' normative orientations toward the family. As a social organization, the traditional Hispanic family wields a pattern o

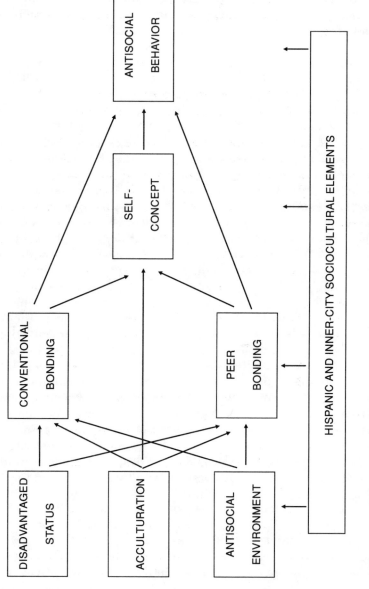

Figure 7.2. Extended Sociocultural Model of Hispanic Antisocial Behavior

influence and control over its members that may be effective in inhibiting antisocial behavior. Rogler and Cooney (1984) showed that there is more intensive interaction among intergenerationally linked Puerto Rican families than among a sample of American families. Another study found that Mexican American adolescents report more satisfaction with family relationships than is reported by Anglo adolescents (Schumm, McCollum, Bugaighis, Jurich, Bollman, & Reitz, 1988). Such solidarity implies that Hispanic families may create patterns of conventional behavior even when other factors may dispose adolescents toward deviance.

The intensive interactions that signal solidarity among Hispanic families have been related to familism, that is, adherence to the value of the family as a system in support of the institution itself (Rogler & Cooney, 1984; Sabogal, Marin, Otero-Sabogal, VanOss Marin, & Perez-Stable, 1987; Zayas & Palleja, 1988). The existence of familism in Puerto Rican tradition has been amply documented by a large number of island-based studies (Landy, 1959; Roberts & Stefani, 1949; Rogler & Hollingshead, 1975; Tumin & Feldman, 1961; Wolf, 1952) and in other Hispanic groups (Andrade, 1980; Fernandez-Marina, Maldonado-Sierra, & Trent, 1958; Garrison & Weiss, 1979; Gurak, 1981; Gurak & Kritz, 1984; Penalosa & Mc-Donagh, 1966).

It is hypothesized that when people strongly adhere to familism they are more likely to accept family control and thus the children are less likely to involve themselves in antisocial acts, or if an antisocial act is committed, they are more likely to be brought into line by invoking the threat of dishonor and humiliation to the family. Child rearing beliefs and practices that encourage strict respect and obedience for parents and deference to authority are common in many Hispanic cultures and may act to buffer youth from delinquent behavior (Busch-Rossnagel & Zayas, in press). In support of this, Buriel, Calzada, and Vasquez (1982) found that adherence to traditional cultural values among Mexican American male adolescents was an effective insulation from delinquency. Even among adolescents whose low socioeconomic status, absent fathers, troubled family relationships, discrepancies in the level of acculturation between themselves and their parents, and delinquent peer influences place them in situations of antisocial behavior risk, the value of families may be invoked by parents or other family members to restrain any propensity to engage in such behavior.

Another aspect of Hispanic culture, traditional beliefs about gender roles, may also help explain antisocial behavior. The traditional male role emphasizes masculine traits such as independence, personal honor, physical prowess, loyalty to family, respect for the aged, and protection of females and children; traditional behaviors for the female role include less freedom than is allowed the male and more dependency (Trankina, 1983). The complementary nature of these gender roles may lead to a greater propensity for adolescent males than females to engage in anti-social behavior. In his review of literature on delinquent and antisocial behavior among Hispanic adolescents and of demographic data on homicide and violent crimes, Rodriguez (1988) suggests that the comparatively low rates of delinquency and violent crimes among Hispanic females, in comparison to females of other ethnic groups, may point to the influence of Hispanic cultural norms regarding masculine and feminine behavior. The imbalance between male and female violence (Horowitz, 1982; Rodriguez, 1988) and substance abuse (Caetano, 1984) suggests that the norms governing the relations between the sexes may shelter females from situations in which they might engage in antisocial behavior, but encourage such behavior among males.

Acculturation

Early delinquency theory was concerned with the role of assimilation difficulties among European immigrants (Sellin, 1938; Thomas, 1969; Znaniecki & Thomas, 1927). More recent research on Hispanic immigrants emphasizes the role of acculturation as a major factor in all aspects of Hispanic life in the U.S. Acculturation refers to the process whereby the behaviors and attitudes of an immigrant group undergo change as a result of contact and exposure to the new dominant culture (Berry, 1980; Padilla, 1980). This process may be relevant to explaining Hispanic delinquency and other deviant behaviors (Anderson & Rodriguez, 1984). Recently, models of social-psychological stress and Hispanic health (Vega, Hough, & Miranda, 1985; Vega, Warheit, & Meinhardt, 1985) have offered greater understanding of the influence of the acculturation process on problem behaviors. Earlier, Born (1970) had termed the conflict arising from immigrants' efforts to adapt to and resolve or minimize their differences with the host culture as acculturative stress. In the model proposed by Vega and his colleagues, immigration, social isolation, acculturation to a new social and structural milieu, and resulting cultural conflict are pivotal factors in creating stress and dysfunction. One result may be that the discrepant levels of acculturation between parents and children yield a sense of marginality, depression, and despair in youth. Another result, arising from Minuchin et al.'s (1967) model of multiproblem families, may be the loss or blurring of boundaries and roles in the structure of Hispanic families in which traditional cultural values are not upheld, parental child-rearing practices are weakened, and maladaptive patterns of behavior are tolerated or encouraged.

In their study of drug use among adolescent Cuban-Americans, Szapocznik, Kurtines, and Fernandez (1980) suggest that the problems resulting from the process of acculturation are an important influence on whether a person gets involved in drug use. They suggest that the discrepancy between the parents' and the adolescent's level of acculturation will cause conflict for the adolescent and, therefore, a greater dependency on the peer group. Adolescents in this situation may turn to drug use as a way of resolving acculturation conflicts with parents. Fitzpatrick (1971) hypothesized this with respect to Puerto Rican youth, and Beauvais, Oetting, and Edwards (1985) observed the same relationship in their study of drug use among Native Americans.

The influence of acculturation on antisocial behavior may not adequately be described by a simple statement of bivariate relationship. Some of its dimensions may indirectly increase while others may inhibit antisocial behavior. For example, acculturated adolescents may be more knowledgeable of the workings of American society, perceive more economic and educational opportunities, and thus be less inclined to antisocial behavior. On the other hand, disparities in the level of acculturation between parents and children may be associated with delinquent behavior. Disparities are likely to occur between first-generation parents and second-generation children because the latter are more exposed to influences of the host culture and society in school and the mass media (Szapocznik & Kurtines, 1980; Szapocznik, Kurtines, & Fernandez,

1980). Unacculturated families may lack knowledge of accepted behavior norms in the United States and may be less likely to socialize their children adequately. This may influence antisocial behavior by weakening family and school bonds.

Inner-city Environment and Subculture

For Hispanics as well as blacks, ethnicity often coincides with lower class status and inner-city residence. As noted earlier, there exist several conceptualizations of antisocial behavior based on the notion of the antisocial environment—the neighborhood that offers opportunities for delinquency and/or presents youth with the choice of mainstream versus "street" orientation (Hannerz, 1969). These conceptualizations abstract, from observations of inner-city environments, normative patterns that are viewed as universal to all lower class environments. There has been great controversy in the social science literature about the extent to which subcultural approaches to delinquency reflect middle-class bias (see Curtis, 1975 for discussion of the issue).

Insofar as the antisocial environment view is valid, it should be applicable to poor or inner-city residents in general, not just Hispanics. However, some observers have argued that concepts such as social disorganization or lower class subculture are posed at too high a level of abstraction. It is argued that for subcultural approaches to be useful, conceptualizations cannot ignore the rich variation in the norms and perceptions of lower class individuals and must link such subcultural views to specific antisocial behaviors. For example, central to Moore's (1978) analysis of *barrio* delinquency in East Los Angeles is the notion of the territorially defined, intergenerationally linked gang. This is not applicable to Hispanic delinquency in other cities. Similarly, Edelman's (1984) observations in the South Bronx, pointing to the existence of violence and fear of violence as central factors in inducing delinquency among some Puerto Rican adolescents and in avoiding it among others, may not be generalizable to groups in other inner cities. Intricate norms and perceptions emerging from the unique experiences of Hispanics and other ethnic groups in specific cities cannot be adequately captured by the abstract concepts, such as social disorganization or lower class subculture, that have usually been applied to inner-city settings.

Program Implications

With an enhanced understanding of the unique sociocultural factors impinging on Hispanic youth, two additional questions emerge. First, how relevant are current interventions to the unique situation of Hispanic adolescents? Second, how can these approaches be modified to reflect the needs and specific conditions of Hispanic youth? In this section, we review the approaches typically utilized to treat and prevent antisocial behavior and discuss modifications required to make these techniques more relevant for Hispanic youth. The principles we use to recommend modifications are based on those advanced by Rogler, Malgady, Costantino, and Blumenthal (1987) in their discussion of what is meant by culturally sensitive mental health services for Hispanics. They suggest that services to Hispanics must be reviewed with three considerations in mind: the accessibility of traditional treatments to Hispanic clients; the selection and altering of a traditional treatment according to perceived features of Hispanic culture; and the extraction of elements from Hispanic culture for use as an innovative treatment tool.

Interventions to prevent or treat antisocial behavior may be classified into three broad groupings: family, community-group, and individual approaches. Below we review the first two types: family and community-based approaches, as we consider them more relevant than individual treatment to the sociocultural situation of Hispanic youth. Because of the preeminence of the Hispanic family in the life of the individual, interventions that exclude the family and the community context in which the adolescents exist may be the least effective. The Hispanic mental health literature has touched upon this quite often (Canino, 1982; Canino & Canino, 1980; Hardy-Fanta & McMahon-Herrera, 1981; Juarez, 1985; Zayas & Bryant, 1984). We exclude from our classification nontreatment approaches such as deterrence and incapacitation. Although whether to treat or punish is a thorny issue, ethnicity enters the discussion only insofar as minorities are more likely to be punished than treated.

Family-Focused Interventions

Much of the literature on the causation, prevention, and treatment of antisocial behavior, delinquency, and conduct disorder has identified family structure and processes as perhaps the single most important factor (Rankin & Ellis, 1987). Interventions focused on the family of antisocial adolescents that are described in the literature are numerous, for example: Alexander & Parsons, 1982; Barton & Alexander, 1981; Hanson, Henggeler, Haefele, & Rodick, 1984; Henggeler, 1982; Henggeler, Rodick, Bourduin, Hanson, Watson, & Urey, 1986; Minuchin, 1974; Patterson, Chamberlain, & Reid, 1982; Szapocznik, 1983; Szapoczik, Kurtines, Foote, & Perez-Vidal, 1986). Empirical evaluations of these approaches indicate considerable success in treating adolescents with problem behaviors.

In order to make these approaches relevant to Hispanic adolescents and their families, features of the Hispanic culture governing familial relations, principally familism and family solidarity, should be addressed in the treatment of antisocial youth. Beginning with the use of bilingual therapists, any intervention designed to address the Hispanic family must also include recognition of child rearing practices that emphasize deference to and respect for the parents, of sibling relationships that often are hierarchically structured according to birth order and gender roles, and of family obligations that encourage family solidarity at the expense of individual achievement. Many clinical writers (e.g., Canino & Canino, 1980; Zayas & Bryant, 1984) observe that the therapeutic approach with Hispanic families must acknowledge and support the intense family bonds that are culturally prescribed for Hispanic families.

Alertness to possible discrepancies between adolescents and parents in acculturation is of paramount importance in any program proposing to treat Hispanic youth. The difference in acculturation between first-generation Hispanic parents and their more acculturated offspring sets up the possibility for conflict in their value orientations. Generational differences may result in or exacerbate family functioning problems, and the conflict generated by such differences may be solved by antisocial behavior on the part of the youth and sometimes the parents as well.

Szapocznik and colleagues have advanced two family-focused treatment models specifically for Hispanics. Operating from the conviction that acculturation presents the immigrant Hispanic family with disruptions in its closely-knit structure, bicultural effectiveness training (Szapocznik, Santiesteban, Kurtines, Perez-Vidal, & Hervis, 1984; Szapocznik, Santiesteban, Rios, Perez-Vidal, Kurtines, & Hervis, 1986) is targeted at intergenerational and intercultural family-adolescent conflicts. Essentially a psychoeducational approach based on structural family therapy (Minuchin, 1974), bicultural effectiveness training encourages the development of more harmonious family relations by appreciation of both original Hispanic cultural values and behaviors and those of the adopted mainstream American culture. The other approach, Family Effectiveness Training, has been employed with families of preadolescents at risk for future conduct disorders (Szapocznick, Santiesteban, Rios, Perez-Vidal, & Kurtines, 1986). It is intended to reestablish family structural properties that have become dysfunctional.

Both of these models conform to the concepts advanced by Rogler et al. (1987) in that they have been made accessible by the developers to the needs of Hispanic immigrant families, using as a selection criterion the importance of the family in Hispanic culture. Further, the two models also share in common the belief that family treatment for antisocial youth need not isomorphically reflect patterns of the culture that are not functional in either the native or adopted culture.

Community-Based Interventions

Another approach to the treatment of antisocial youth is found in community-based programs that utilize a combination of group and family interventions. This approach operates from the principle that the intervention should be conducted within the social and geographic environment most familiar to the adolescent. The intent is to insure that the pro-social behavior that is encouraged is carried over from home to school to community, thereby avoiding situations in which the improved behavior is isolated to one of another situation in which the adolescent functions. Community-based approaches also permit interventions to be provided to a large grouping of adolescents and their families. Often, however, community-based models do not adhere to any specific set of treatment techniques and find entry into the adolescent's life through the family, school, community, or peer group (Kazdin, 1987a, 1987b). Feldman, Caplinger, and Wodarski (1983) describe a large-scale community intervention program that found that experienced therapists leading groups deliberately composed of both antisocial and conventionally-oriented adolescents and using behavioral techniques were most successful in promoting pro-social behavior. In another example, Haapala and Kinney (1988) have described an intensive home-based family preservation service that seeks to avoid out-of-home placement for status-offending adolescents. The availability of family counselors located within the community and who carry small caseloads of families allows for the integration of family treatment approaches combined with access to community services.

Intervention programs based in schools also have shown considerable promise (see Clements, 1988 for a review). In such programs, youth in junior high schools presenting conduct disorders who have not "graduated" to more serious antisocial behaviors requiring intervention by juvenile justice authorities are treated to prevent further problems. Most treatments try to improve school attendance and performance using behavioral methods in the school and peer group as well as family treatment (Lane & Murakami, 1987).

Clements has observed that treatment strategies must build the necessary community structures and involve as many informal supports as possible (1988, pp. 300-301). In line with this assertion, community-based programs directed to Hispanic youth and communities require attention to the importance of the family in the youths' lives but also those features of their culture of origin that can enhance ethnic and community pride. The use of paraprofessionals, which has been shown effective given the scarcity of trained professionals in these communities (Gordon & Arbuthnot, 1988), can have positive effects not just because they are a real, immediate source of manpower in poor communities but also because they can offer role models for the youth by the paraprofessionals' involvement in the betterment of their communities.

To be relevant to the sociocultural situation of Hispanic youth, community-based programs should involve Hispanic families' roles in the treatment of antisocial youth. By asking Hispanic parents to articulate aspects of the Hispanic culture that govern personal and family behavior that highly acculturated youth seldom understand, such group and community programs serve an important educative function in helping youth understand their own families (Zayas & Palleja, 1988). Similarly, because Hispanic youth are raised to respect and revere their parents and adult relatives, the inclusion of parents and other extended family members reinforces family solidarity. Hispanic professionals and paraprofessionals themselves who have successfully negotiated a bicultural identity also may assist the youth and families in retaining valued aspects of the Hispanic culture while adopting new behavioral strategies of the host culture.

Ethnic pride programs including appreciation of ethnic heroes, awareness of the popular and fine arts of the Hispanic culture, and learning of cultural traditions will enhance development of identity among these youth. The work of Costantino, Malgady, and Rogler (1985) represents an attempt to incorporate this idea into a systematic clinical framework. First applying the notion of Puerto Rican folktales to children with behavioral problems, the concept was then applied to interventions with adolescents, utilizing the notion of Puerto Rican folk heroes and heroines as role models.

Summary

We have reviewed explanatory theories of antisocial behavior and shown that these models are useful points of departure for understanding how antisocial behavior comes about among minority group youth in American cities. Toward the objective of making these models more relevant to the realities facing Hispanic adolescents we have modified them by including three broad areas of the Hispanic youth experience: Hispanic cultural values and traditions, the concept of acculturation, and the social class and inner-city character of a large segment of the Hispanic population in the United States. We have also reviewed two types of antisocial behavior prevention and treatment approaches—family- and community-based interventions—that seem to us to adhere to the criteria of cultural sensitivity advanced by Rogler et al. (1987). We hope that our discussion will encourage practitioners and social scientists interested in Hispanic and minority youth to base their approaches on the latter's sociocultural reality.

References

Akers, R. L. (1977). *Deviant behavior: A social learning perspective*. Belmont, CA: Wadsworth.

Alexander, J. F., & Parsons, B. V. (1982). *Functional family therapy*. Monterey, CA: Brooks/Cole.

American Psychiatric Association. (1987). *Diagnostic and statistical manual of mental disorders* (3rd ed., revised). Washington, DC: Author.

Anderson, N., & Rodriguez, O. (1984). Conceptual issues in the study of Hispanic delinquency. Hispanic Research Center, Fordham University: *Research Bulletin* 7(1-2).

Andrade, S. (1980). Family planning of Mexican Americans. In M. Melville (Ed.). *Twice a minority: Mexican American women* (pp. 17-32). St. Louis: C. V. Mosby.

Anolik, S. A. (1981). Imaginary audience behavior and perceptions of parents among delinquent and nondelinquent adolescents. *Journal of Youth and Adolescence, 10,* 443-454.

Bandura, A. (1982). Self-efficacy mechanism in human agency. *American Psychologist, 37,* 122-147.

Banfield, E. (1970). *The unheavenly city*. Boston: Little, Brown.

Banks, L., Rodriguez, O., & Burger, W. (1985). Crime rates among Hispanics, blacks and whites in four U.S. cities. Paper presented at the meeting of the Eastern Sociological Society, Philadelphia.

Barton, C., & Alexander, J. F. (1981). Functional family therapy. In A. S. Gurman & D. P. Kniskern (Eds.), *Handbook of family therapy* (pp. 403-443). New York: Brunner/Mazel.

Beauvais, F., Oetting, E. R., & Edwards, R. W. (1985). Trends in drug use of Indian adolescents living on reservation: 1975-1983. *American Journal of Drug and Alcohol Abuse, 11*(3 & 4), 209-229.

Berry, J. (1980). Acculturation as varieties of adaptation. In A. Padilla (Ed.), *Acculturation, theory, models, and some new findings*. Boulder, CO: Westview.

Block, J., Block, J. H., & Keyes, S. (1988). Longitudinally foretelling drug usage in adolescence: Early childhood personality and environmental precursors. *Child Development, 59,* 336-355.

Born, D. (1970). Psychological adaptation and development under acculturative stress: Toward a general model. *Social Science and Medicine, 3,* 529-547.

Braithewaite, J. (1981). The myth of social class and criminality reconsidered. *American Sociological Review, 43,* 36-57.

Buriel, R., Calzada, S., & Vasquez, R. (1982). The relationship of traditional Mexican-American culture to adjustment and delinquency among three generations of Mexican-American male adolescents. *Hispanic Journal of Behavioral Sciences, 4,* 41-55.

Busch-Rossnagel, N. A., & Zayas, L. H. (in press). Hispanic Adolescents. In R. Lerner, A. Peterson, & J. Brooks-Gunn (Eds.), *Encyclopedia of Adolescence.* New York: Garland.

Caetano, R. (1984). Ethnicity and drinking in Northern California: A comparison among whites, blacks, and Hispanics. *Alcohol and Alcoholism, 18,* 1-14.

Canino, I. (1982). The Hispanic child: Treatment considerations. In R. M. Becerra, M. Karno, & J. I. Escobar (Eds.), *Mental health and Hispanic Americans: Clinical perspectives* (pp. 157-168). New York: Grune and Stratton.

Canino, I., & Canino, G. (1980). Impact of stress on the Puerto Rican family: Treatment consideration. *American Journal of Orthopsychiatry, 50,* 535-541.

Chambliss, W., & Nagasawa, R. (1969). On the validity of official statistics: A comparative study of white, black, and Japanese high school boys. *Journal of Research on Crime and Delinquency, 6,* 71-77.

Clements, C. B. (1988). Delinquency prevention and treatment: A community centered perspective. *Criminal Justice and Behavior, 15,* 286-305.

Cloward, R., & Ohlin, L. E. (1960). *Delinquency and Opportunity: A Theory of Delinquent Gangs.* Glencoe, IL: Free Press.

Cohen, A. K. (1955). *Delinquent boys.* New York: Free Press.

Coleman, J. S. (1976). The school to work transition. In *The teenage unemployment problem: What are the options?* Washington, DC: U.S. Government Printing Office.

Conger, J. J. (1971). A world they never knew: The family and social change. *Daedulus, 100,* 1105-1138.

Costantino, G., Malgady, R. G., & Rogler, L. H. (1985). *Cuento therapy, folktales as a culturally sensitive psychotherapy for Puerto Rican children.* Maplewood, NJ: Waterfront.

Curtis, L. (1975). *Violence, race and culture.* Lexington, MA: D.C. Heath.

Datesman, S. K., Scarpitto, F. R., & Stephenson, R. M. (1975). Female delinquency An application of self and opportunity theories. *Journal of Research in Crime and Delinquency, 12,* 107-123.

Dembo, R., Blount, W. R., Schmeidler, J. & Burgos, W. (1986). Perceived environmental drug use risk and the correlates of drug use and non-use among inner city youths: The motivated actor. *International Journal of the Addictions, 21* 977-1000.

Dembo, R., Farrow, D., Schmeidler, J. & Burgos, W. (1979). Testing a causation model of environmental influences on the early drug involvement of inner city junior high school youths. *American Journal of Alcohol Abuse, 6,* 313-336.

Edelman, M. (1984). Exploratory study on delinquency avoidance in the South Bronx. Hispanic Research Center, Fordham University: *Research Bulletin, 7*(1-2).

Elliott, D. S., Ageton, S., Huizinga, D., Knowles, B. A., & Canter, R. J. (1983). *The prevalence and incidence of delinquent behavior.* Boulder, CO: Behavioral Research Institute.

Elliott, D. S., Huizinga, D., & Ageton, S. (1985). *Explaining Delinquency and Drug Use.* Beverly Hills, CA: Sage.

Elliott, D. S., & Voss, H. L. (1974). Delinquency and dropout. Toronto: D. C. Heath.

Feldman, R. A., Caplinger, T. E., & Wodarski, J. S. (1983). *The St. Louis conundrum: The effective treatment of antisocial youth.* Englewood Cliffs, NJ: Prentice-Hall.

Fernandez-Marina, R., Maldonado-Sierra, E. D., & Trent, R. D. (1958). Three basic themes in Mexican and Puerto Rican family values. *The Journal of Social Psychology, 48,* 167-181.

Fitzpatrick, J. (1971). *Puerto Rican Americans: The meaning of migration to the mainland.* Englewood Cliffs, NJ: Prentice-Hall.

Garrison, V., & Weiss, C. I. (1979). Dominican family networks and United States immigration policy: A case study. *International Migration Review, 13,* 264-282.

Glueck, S., & Glueck, E. T. (1950). *Understanding juvenile delinquency.* New York: Commonwealth Fund.

Gordon, D. A., & Arbuthnot, J. (1988). The use of paraprofessionals to deliver home-based family therapy to juvenile delinquents. *Criminal Justice and Behavior, 15,* 364-378.

Gurak, D. T. (1981). Family structural diversity of Hispanic ethnic groups. Hispanic Research Center, Fordham University: *Research Bulletin, 4*(2-3).

Gurak, D. T., & Kritz, M. M. (1984). Kinship networks and the settlement process: Dominican and Colombian immigrants in New York City. Hispanic Research Center, Fordham University: *Research Bulletin, 7*(3-4).

Haapala, D. A., & Kinney, J. M. (1988). Avoiding out-of-home placement of high-risk status offenders through the use of intensive home-based family preservation services. *Criminal Justice and Behavior, 15,* 334-348.

Hannerz, V. (1969). *Soulside.* New York: Columbia University.

Hanson, C. L., Henggeler, S. W., Haefele, W. F., & Rodick, J. D. (1984). Demographic, individual, and family relationship correlates of serious and repeated crime among adolescents and their siblings. *Journal of Consulting and Clinical Psychology, 52,* 528-538.

Hardy-Fanta, C., & McMahon-Herrera, E. (1981). Adapting family therapy to the Hispanic family. *Social Casework, 62,* 138-148.

Henggeler, S. W. (Ed.). (1982). *Delinquency and adolescent psychopathology: A family-ecological systems approach.* Littleton, MA: Wright/PSG.

Henggeler, S. W., Rodick, J. D., Bourduin, C. M., Hanson, C. L., Watson, S. M., & Urey, J. R. (1986). Multisystem treatment of juvenile offenders: Effects on adolescent behavior and family interaction. *Developmental Psychology, 22,* 132-141.

Hirschi, T. (1969). *Causes of delinquency.* Berkeley: University of California Press.

Horowitz, R. (1982). *Honor and the American dream: Culture and social identity in a Chicano community.* New Brunswick, NJ: Rutgers University Press.

Huizinga, D., & Elliott, D. S. (1986). Juvenile offenders, prevalence, offender incidence, and arrest rates by race. Paper prepared for the Meeting on Race and the Incarceration of Juveniles, Wingspread Foundation, Racine, Wisconsin.

Ianni, F. (1974). *Black mafia.* New York: Simon & Schuster.

Jensen, J. B., Burke, N., & Garfinkel, B. D. (1988). Depression and symptoms of attention deficit disorder with hyperactivity. *Journal of the American Academy of Child and Adolescent Psychiatry, 27,* 742-747.

Jessor, R., & Jessor, S. L. (1977). *Problem behavior and psycho-social development: A longitudinal study of youth.* New York: Academic Press.

Juarez, R. (1985). Core issues in psychotherapy with the Hispanic child. *Psychotherapy, 22,* 441-448.

Kandel, D. B. (1974). Drug and drinking behavior among youth. *Annual Review of Sociology*. New York: Annual Reviews, Inc.

Kandel, D. B. (1978). Convergence in prospective longitudinal surveys of drug use in normal populations. In D. B. Kandel (Ed.), *Longitudinal Research on Drug Use* (pp. 3-38). New York: John Wiley.

Kandel, D. B. (1980). Drug and drinking behavior among youth. *Annual Review of Sociology*. New York: Annual Reviews, Inc.

Kaplan, H. B. (1975). *Self-attitude and deviant behavior*. Pacific Palisades, CA: Goodyear.

Kaplan, H. B., Martin, S. S., & Robbins, C. (1984). Pathways to adolescent drug use: Self-derogation, peer influence, weakening of social controls, and early substance abuse. *Journal of Health and Social Behavior, 25*(3), 270-289.

Kazdin, A. E. (1987a). *Conduct disorders in childhood and adolescence*. Newbury Park, CA: Sage.

Kazdin, A. E. (1987b). Treatment of antisocial behavior in children: Current status and future directions. *Psychological Bulletin, 102*, 187-203.

Krisberg, B., Schwartz, I., Fishman, G., Eisikovitz, Z. & Guttman, E. (1986). *The incarceration of minority youth*. Manuscript, Hubert H. Humphrey Institute of Public Affairs, University of Minnesota.

Labouvie, E. W., & McGee, C. R. (1986). Relation of personality to alcohol and drug use in adolescence. *Journal of Consulting and Clinical Psychology, 54*, 289-293.

Lahey, B. B., Piacentini, J. C., McBurnett, K., Stone, P., Hartdagen, S. & Hynd, G. (1988). Psychopathology in parents of children with conduct disorder and hyperactivity. *Journal of the American Academy of Child and Adolescent Psychiatry, 27*, 163-170.

Landy, D. (1959). *Tropical Childhood: Cultural Transmission and Learning in a Rural Puerto Rican Village*. Chapel Hill: University of North Carolina Press.

Lane, T. W., & Murakami, J. (1987). School programs for delinquency prevention and intervention. In E. K. Morris & C. J. Braukmann (Eds.), *Behavioral approaches to crime and delinquency: A handbook of application, research, and concepts*. New York: Plenum.

Lewis, O. (1961). *The children of Sanchez*. New York: Random House.

Liebow, E. (1967). *Tally's corner: A study of negro street corner men*. Boston: Little, Brown.

Martin, B. (1975). Parent-child relations. In F. D. Horowitz (Ed.), *Review of child development research* (Vol. 4). Chicago: University of Chicago Press.

Merton, R. K. (1957). *Social theory and social structure*. Glencoe, IL: Free Press.

Miller, W. (1958). Lower class culture as a generating milieu of gang delinquency. *Journal of Social Issues, 14*(3), 5-19.

Minuchin, S. (1974). *Families and family therapy*. Cambridge, MA: Harvard University Press.

Minuchin, S., Montalvo, B., Guerney, G., Rosman, B., & Schumer, F. (1967). *Families of the slums*. New York: Basic Books.

Mitchell, J., McCauley, E., Burke, P. M., & Moss, S. J. (1988). Phenomenology of depression in children and adolescents. *Journal of the American Academy of Child and Adolescent Psychiatry, 27*, 12-20.

Moore, J. (1978). *Homeboys*. Philadelphia: Temple University Press.

National Institute on Drug Abuse. (1987a). *Demographic characteristics and patterns of drug use admissions to drug abuse treatment programs in selected states.* Rockville, MD: Division of Epidemiology and Statistical Analysis.

National Institute on Drug Abuse (1987b). *Use of selected drugs among Hispanics: Mexican Americans, Puerto Ricans, Cubans.* Rockville, MD: Division of Epidemiology and Statistical Analysis.

Oetting, E. R., & Beauvais, F. (1987). Common elements in drug abuse: peer clusters and other psychological factors. *Journal of Drug Issues, 17*(1 & 2), 133-151.

Padilla, A. (1980). The role of cultural awareness and ethnic loyalty in acculturation. In A. Padilla (Ed.), *Acculturation, theory, models, and some new findings.* Boulder, CO: Westview.

Patterson, G. R. (1981). *Coercive family processes.* Eugene, OR: Castala.

Patterson, G. R., Chamberlain, P., & Reid, J. B. (1982). A comparative evaluation of a parent-training program. *Behavior Therapy, 13,* 638-650.

Penalosa F., & McDonagh, E. C. (1966). Social mobility in a Mexican-American community. *Social Forces, 44,* 498-505.

Puig-Antich, J. (1982). Major depression and conduct disorders in prepuberty. *Journal of the American Academy of Child and Adolescent Psychiatry, 21,* 118-128.

Rachal, J. V., Maisto, S. A., Guess, L. L., & Hubbard, R. L. (1982). Alcohol use among youth. In *Alcohol consumption and related problems* [Alcohol and Health Monograph No. 1]. Rockville, MD: National Institute on Alcohol Abuse and Alcoholism.

Rainwater, L. (1970). *Behind ghetto walls.* Chicago: Aldine.

Rankin, J. H., & Ellis, L. E. (1987). The preventive effects of the family on delinquency. In E. H. Johnson (Ed.), *Handbook on crime and delinquency prevention* (pp. 257-277). Westport, CT: Greenwood.

Roberts, L., & Stefani, L. R. (1949). *Patterns of living in Puerto Rican families.* Rio Piedras, P. R. Editorial Universitaria.

Rodriguez, O. (1988). Hispanics and homicide in New York City. In J. F. Kraus, S. B. Sorenson, & P. D. Juarez (Eds), *Proceedings, Research Conference on Violence and Homicide in Hispanic Communities* (pp. 67-84). Los Angeles: UCLA Publication Services.

Rodriguez, O., Burger, W., & Banks, L. (1984). Crime rates among Hispanics, blacks, and whites in New York City. Hispanic Research Center, Fordham University: *Research Bulletin, 7*(1-2).

Rogler, L. H., & Cooney, R. S. (1984). *Puerto Rican Families in New York City: Integenerational Processes.* Maplewood, NJ: Waterfront.

Rogler, L. H., & Hollingshead, A. B. (1975). *Trapped: Families and Schizophrenia* (2nd ed.). Huntington, NJ: Krieger.

Rogler, L. H., Malgady, R. G., Costantino, G., & Blumenthal, R. (1987) What do culturally sensitive mental health services mean? The case of Hispanics. *American Psychologist, 42,* 565-570.

Rutter, M., & Giller, H. (1983). *Juvenile delinquency: Trends and prospects.* Baltimore, MD: Penguin.

Sabogal, F., Marin, G., Otero-Sabogal, R., VanOss Marin, B., & Perez-Stable, E. J. (1987). Hispanic familism and acculturation: what changes and what doesn't? *Hispanic Journal of Behavioral Sciences, 9,* 397-412.

Schumm, W. R., McCollum, E. E., Bugaighis, M. A., Jurich, A. P., Bollman, F. R., & Reitz, J. (1988). Differences between Anglo and Mexican American family members on satisfaction with family life. *Hispanic Journal of Behavioral Sciences, 10,* 39-53.

Sellin, T. (1938). *Culture conflict and crime: A report of the subcommittee on delinquency of the committee on personality and culture.* New York: Social Science Research Council.

Shaw, C. R., & McKay, H. D. (1942). *Juvenile delinquency and urban areas.* Chicago: University of Chicago Press.

Simon, W., & Gagnon, J. H. (1976). The anomie of affluence: A post Mertonian conception. *American Journal of Sociology, 82*(2), 356-378.

Smith, W. C. (1983). Contemporary child saving: A study of juvenile justice decision-making. *Juvenile and Family Court Journal, 34,* 63-74.

Stott, D. (1982). *Delinquency: The problem and its prevention.* New York: SP Medical and Scientific Books.

Sutherland, E. H. (1947). *Principles of criminology.* Philadelphia: J. B. Lippincott.

Suttles, G. (1955). *The social order of the slum.* Chicago: University of Chicago Press.

Szapocznik, J. (1983). Conjoint versus one-person family therapy: Some evidence for the effectiveness of conducting family therapy through one person. *Journal of Consulting and Clinical Psychology, 51,* 889-899.

Szapocznik, J., & Kurtines, W. M. (1980). Acculturation, biculturalism, and adjustment among Cuban Americans. In A. Padilla (Ed.), *Acculturation, Theory, Models and some New Findings*(pp. 139-159). Boulder, CO: Westview.

Szapocznik, J., Kurtines, W. M., & Fernandez, T. (1980). Bicultural involvement and adjustment in Hispanic-American youth. *International Journal of Intercultural Relations, 4,* 353-365.

Szapocznik, J., Kurtines, W. M., Foote, F., & Perez-Vidal, A. (1986). Conjoint versus one person family therapy: Further evidence for the effectiveness of conducting family therapy through one person. *Journal of Consulting and Clinical Psychology, 54,* 395-397.

Szapocznik, J., Santiesteban, D., Kurtines, W., Perez-Vidal, A., & Hervis, O. (1984). Bicultural effectiveness training: A treatment intervention for enhancing intercultural adjustment in Cuban-American families. *Hispanic Journal of Behavioral Sciences, 6,* 317-344.

Szapocznik, J., Santiesteban, D., Rios, A., Perez-Vidal, A., & Kurtines, W. (1986). Family effectiveness training for Hispanic families: Strategic structural systems intervention for the prevention of drug abuse. In H. P. Lefley & P. B. Pederse (Eds.), *Cross cultural training for mental health professionals.* Springfield, IL: Charles C Thomas.

Szapocznik, J., Santiesteban D., Rios, A., Perez-Vidal, A., Kurtines, W., & Hervis, O. (1986). Bicultural effectiveness training (BET): An intervention modality for families experiencing intergenerational/intercultural conflict. *Hispanic Journal of Behavioral Sciences, 8,* 303-330.

Thomas, W. I. (1969). *Unadjusted girls with cases and standpoint for behavior analysis.* Montclair, NJ: Patterson-Smith.

Trankina, F. J. (1983). Clinical issues and techniques in working with Hispanic children and their families. In G. J. Powell, J. Yamamoto, A. Romero, & A. Moral

(Eds.), *The psychosocial development of minority group children* (pp. 307-329). New York: Brunner/Mazel.

Tumin, M. M., & Feldman, A. S. (1961). *Social class and social change in Puerto Rico.* Princeton, NJ: Princeton University Press.

Vega, W. A., Hough, R. L., & Miranda, M. R. (1985). Modeling cross-cultural research in Hispanic mental health. In W. A. Vega & M. R. Miranda (Eds.), *Stress and Hispanic mental health* (pp. 1-29) (DHHS Publication No. ADM 85-1410). Washington, DC: U.S. Government Printing Office.

Vega, W. A., Warheit, G. J., & Meinhardt, K. (1985). Mental health issues in the Hispanic community: The prevalence of psychological distress. In W. A. Vega & M. R. Miranda (Eds.), *Stress and Hispanic mental health* (pp. 30-47) (DHHS Publication No. ADM 85-1410). Washington, DC: U.S. Government Printing Office.

Welte, J. W., & Barnes, G. M. (1987). Alcohol use among adolescent minority groups. *Journal of Studies on Alcohol, 48*(4), 329-336.

West, D. J., & Farrington, D. P. (1977). *The delinquent way of life.* London: Heinemann.

Wolf, K. L. (1952). Growing up and its price in three Puerto Rican subcultures. *Psychiatry, 15,* 401-433.

Zayas, L. H., & Bryant, C. (1984). Culturally sensitive treatment of adolescent Puerto Rican girls and their families. *Child and Adolescent Social Work Journal, 1,* 235-253.

Zayas, L. H., & Palleja, J. (1988). Puerto Rican familism: Implications for family therapy. *Family Relations, 37,* 260-264.

Znaniecki, F., & Thomas, W. I. (1927). *The Polish peasant in Europe and America.* New York: Knopf.

PART 3

Sexuality

8

High Risk Sexual Behavior Among Black Adolescents

ALGEA HARRISON

Premarital sexual experience among adolescents has increased (Allan Guttmacher Institute, 1981). This increase in sexual activity was accompanied by a trend in increased permissiveness in premarital sexual standards (Singh, 1980). Reviews of relevant literature on sexual permissiveness concluded that peers were more permissive than parents, adolescents were influenced more by peers than parents, and sexual behavior of adolescents was consistent with that of peers (Shah & Zelnik, 1981). Generally, young black males have a more permissive attitude than black females towards premarital sex (Delcampo, Sporakowski, & Delcampo, 1976). Today's adolescents, for a variety of reasons, engage not only in increased sexual activity, but also in high risk sexual behaviors. High risk sexual behavior refers to sexual intercourse without birth control. This chapter discusses three related issues: (a) demographic information indicative of the involvement of black adolescents in high risk sexual behavior; (b) conceptual explanations as to why black adolescents engage in high risk sexual behavior; and (c) society's response to the social problems that emerge as a consequence of their behavior.

Demographic Information

During the 1980s, an estimated 12 million of the 21 million teens in the United States were sexually active (Moore & Erickson, 1985). Fifty-four percent of those under 18 years of age and 23% of those under 16 years of age have had premarital sexual experience (McAdoo, 1986). For black adolescents age 19 and under, the most dramatic change occurred during the 1970s. As of 1971, 78% of black females under the age of 19 had had sexual intercourse; no equivalent data for black males are available. As of 1979, 89% of black males and females in the United States under age 19 had had sexual intercourse (Moore, 1986).

The failure of black adolescents to practice safe sex (sexual intercourse with birth control) is of major concern to families, the community, and the larger society. The incidence of births to teenage mothers indicates the failure to prevent conception. In 1980, among mothers 15 to 19 years of age, 87% of the black and 33% of the white births were outside of marriage (Moore, 1986). In 1986, the birth rates (per 1,000 population for specified group) for unmarried black women between the ages of 15 and 19 years was 89.9 (U.S. Bureau of the Census, 1987). Sixty percent of the births to blacks were to unmarried women and 31.6% of the births to all black women were to those aged 15 to 19 years. Of black males age 15 to 19, 42.8% were fathers. Indeed, it has been suggested that these behavior patterns for black women are forerunners of patterns for white women and that soon, for all races, parenting will be separated from marriage just as sex was separated from marriage in previous decades (Rossi, 1985).

Having a child at such an early age has been found to interfere with opportunities for a more productive, satisfying life for black mothers (Furstenberg, Brooks-Gunn, & Morgan, 1987). A pattern of early pregnancies for young women, most of whom are unwed, increases the likelihood of their dropping out of school, thus interfering with educational opportunities and preparation for careers (Alan Guttmacher Institute, 1981). Further, the increase in teenage pregnancy has been a major determinant in the growth of black female households and the feminization of poverty in the black community (Pearce & McAdoo, 1981). In 1985, 47% of all black households were maintained by women, compared with 26% of all white households (U.S. Bureau of the Census, 1986). Contrary to the thinking of some, the maintenance of a household by a single female is not in and of itself pathological. The difficulty is the economic status of the household because of the limited labor market opportunity and other factors that handicap the only wage earner. In 1986, 50% of black female households were below poverty level (U.S. Bureau of the Census, 1988). Moreover, of blacks in poverty, 60.9% were in female-maintained families compared with 27.8% of whites (U.S. Bureau of the Census, 1988).

Conceptual Explanations

Numerous explanations have been offered for the increase in high risk sexual behaviors among black adolescents. Often these explanations have limited empirical underpinnings; Diepold and Young (1979), in their critical review of three decades of empirical studies on adolescent sexual behavior, concluded that findings often are based on less than adequate research techniques and experimental designs. Nevertheless, like most complex issues, the relevant and valid explanations are complicated and multifaceted. Two of the most prevalent explanations will be discussed with the recognition that they are intertwined; separately they are partial causes, and additively they are not the absolute in determinants. The explanations are grouped under the headings of (a) social systems and (b) sexual ideology of the community.

Social Systems

Today's black adolescent is bombarded with media messages that encourage sexual adventure with little note of negative consequences (Moore & Erickson, 1985). Indeed, social structures such as the media are conceived as being the major determinants of the increase in high risk sexual behavior among black adolescents. In other words, social scientists and nonprofessionals recognize that societies are structured with social institutions, systems, and organizations that influence the behavior of individuals and groups. The health care, economic, and educational systems, and mate availability/sex ratio are presented for the relevance and validity of their roles as determinants of high risk sexual behavior among black adolescents.

Health Care System

The health care system has been seen incorrectly by high risk sexual behaviors in three ways: (a) increased availability of health care so that young persons are physically maturing earlier; (b)increased availability of safe abortions; and (c) increased availability of birth control information. Forty-one percent of black girls aged 15 and younger are sexually active and are at high risk for pregnancy (Moore, Simms, & Betsey, 1987). By their 18th birthdays, 20% of black females have become mothers (Pitt, 1985). Before the pervasive influence of the formal operations period, which is not universally attained, adolescents have difficulty thinking systematically and abstractly about the future, according to the Piagetian model of cognitive development. The formal operations period is characterized by the ability of the individual to think in the abstract and test hypotheses, by the ability to think ahead and approach the solving of problems in a systematic manner, and by the ability to think about the process of thinking and how to make one's thinking more efficient (Zigler & Finn-Stevenson, 1987). For adolescents not in this period, cognitive limitations undermine their ability to plan for and use contraception. At the same time, improvement in health care and nutrition has seen a lowering of the age of menarche, the first menstrual period. The secular trend, a term that describes the changes in physical growth over time as found in large samples of populations, indicates the age of maturation of girls has decreased six months each decade (Zigler & Finn-Stevenson, 1987). This change in the hormonal system stimulates, along with other environmental elements, interest in sexual activity. Currently one third of American girls experience menarche before or during their twelfth year and every year about 1.2 million girls between the ages of 10 and 14 become pregnant. Thus contemporary adolescents are at risk for unwanted pregnancies because of mixed levels of maturity in two domains, cognitive and physical.

Antiabortion voices claim that the availability of abortions exacerbates the situation. In their view, fear of pregnancy does not deter adolescents from engaging in premarital sexual relations. Adolescents of today do not care if they get pregnant because they can always have an abortion. Cross-cultural investigations do not support this position. In England, Canada, France, Sweden, and the Netherlands, abortion services for adolescents are free or subsidized (Jones, 1986). These countries have lower adolescent abortion and birth rates than the United States and make confidential, low-cost, effective birth control available to adolescents (Jones, 1986).

Educational information regarding birth control is increasingly available and different methods are advertised openly in drug stores and supermarkets. A segment of the American public, however, still believes that knowledge and availability of contraceptives encourage sexual experimentation among adolescents (Delcampo, Sporakowski, & Delcampo, 1976; Udry, 1971). Kanter and Zelnik (1972) found that 77% of sexually active black and white adolescents in a national U.S. sample had never used or seldom used birth control. Diepold and Young (1979), in their review, indicated that black, as compared to white, adolescents had an earlier age of onset of sexual intercourse, a higher rate of premarital intercourse, a poorer understanding of the biological aspects of pregnancy, and a later age for beginning the use of contraceptives. Thus the availability of birth control does not necessarily contribute to the increase in teenage pregnancy, rather, it is the lack of use of birth control.

Educational System

Similarly, the educational system has been indicted as a contributor to higher risk sexual behavior among black adolescents because the number of sex education classes available in public schools has increased. (Moore, Simms, & Betsey, 1987). From the perspective of a vocal minority, sex education classes increase the likelihood of adolescents engaging in premarital sex. However, data from two national surveys indicate that young people who have had sex education are not more likely to have sexual intercourse than those who have never taken a course. In fact, sexually active young women who have had sex education classes are less likely to become pregnant than their counterparts who have had no such instruction (Zelnik & Young, 1982). Sex education classes should begin before the young person becomes sexually active, since 45% of the first premarital pregnancies occur in the first six months of sexual activity (Allan Guttmacher Institute, 1981). Studies of sex education programs have found that students' reproductive knowledge increases, yet students' personal morality is not affected (Moore, Simms, & Betsy, 1987). Further, school-based health clinics have been effective in reducing teenage pregnancy (Zabin, 1986). Results of an evaluation of a three-year school-based clinic involving 1,700 students in grades 7 through 12 indicated that girls involved in the program were more likely to postpone first intercourse, to seek birth control before first sexual intercourse, and to attend birth control clinics, than were girls who were nonparticipants.

Economic System

The economic activity of the labor market has been seen as one of the causes of the increase in the incidence of unmarried mothers among black adolescents. In previous years couples usually married when an unplanned child was on the way. Currently, black teen mothers between 15 and 17 are more likely to remain unmarried (93%) as compared to whites (45%) in the same circumstances (Height, 1985). Further, black males have increasing difficulty in obtaining employment and therefore are viewed as less desirable marriage partners by black females and are themselves reluctant to marry (Moore, Simms, & Betsy, 1987).

The economic system has not only fostered an increase in unemployment among black males, but also an increase in employment among black females. The steady increase in the past three decades of the cost of living has placed a tremendous economic burden on families and an increasing number of mothers have entered the labor market. As a result, a large percentage of young persons are without adult supervision for a greater portion of the day. Young persons have increased opportunities to engage in sexual experimentation. Adult supervision sometimes is a deterrent to premature physical intimacy (Hanson, O'Connor, Jones, & Blocker, 1981).

The availability of Aid to Dependent Children has been seen as a contributor to the increase in female heads of households (Moore, Simms, & Betsy, 1987). The governmental policy of payment of funds to females when they become mothers is seen by some critics as encouraging teenagers to become mothers so they can be independent of their parents. Although a proportion of young single mothers leave their parents' homes and establish a household, no qualifiable evidence supports the idea that government assistance is a major motivating factor of these women. Five developed nations (England, Canada, France, Sweden, and the Netherlands) have higher welfare benefits than the United States, but lower teen birth rates. The rate of teen sexual activity in these countries is similar to that of the United States, but rates of pregnancy and childbirth are far lower (Jones, 1986).

Sex Ratio Imbalance

The male/female sex role imbalance has been interpreted as a causative factor in the increase in high risk sexual behavior among black adolescents and black persons of all ages (Guttentag & Secord, 1983; Jackson, 1971; Staples, 1988; Tucker, 1987; Tucker & Mitchell-Kernan, in press). Scholars have proposed that the increase in births to unwed mothers in the black community is the result of a shortage of male partners to marry. This shortage is due to a number of factors, including a large percentage of incarcerated black males, drug traffic, and the increase in infant mortality rates. The imbalance between the number of males and females results in males having more opportunities for sexual intercourse without having to make commitments. The gender in great demand in the dyad has more power in the relationship (Tucker & Mitchell-Kernan, in press) and the gender in oversupply will engage in high risk sexual behavior to initiate and maintain the relationship.

Sexual Ideology of the Community

Writings on the black community suggest a more permissive attitude among blacks than whites on premarital sexual relations (Ladner, 1972; Staples, 1981). Evidence is accumulating that a community's commitment to a cultural norm and the strength of its social controls will influence individual or family commitment to the norm (Rubin, 1981). A community's norm has the potential power to exercise influence over individual members of the community. Ladner's (1972) study of northern, urban, lower socioeconomic status female adolescents found that these young persons believed that the rite of passage into womanhood was having a baby. In other words, these young persons perceived the community norm for becoming a woman as having a baby. Subsequently, other writers inferred or noted the comment among their subjects (e.g., Falk, Gispert, & Baucom, 1981; McAdoo, 1986). Thus the explanation of the sexual ideology of the community as a major determinant of high risk sexual behavior among adolescents has accelerated. This position is not clearly supported by empirical evidence. Often this ideology is inferred from findings on related questions on attitudes of the community. For example, some of the related findings are (a) that black children are not rejected because of the marital status of their parent, (Staples, 1971); (b) females who were affiliated with a same-sex peer group, as compared to those who were not, did not feel as rejected by the people around them if they became premaritally pregnant (Rubin, 1981); and (c) that there is a greater tolerance of nonmarital childbearing (Moore, Simms, & Betsy, 1987). These findings have been interpreted as the black community having a permissive attitude towards unplanned preg-nancies among unmarried adolescents.

Juxtaposed to this permissive ideology is the prevailing sex-role attitude among 13-to 19-year-olds. Using a national probability sample, Canter and Ageton (1984) found that black male and female adolescents had a more traditional sex-role attitude than whites. The more traditional attitudes of black female adolescents were noticeable on ideological items (e.g., men do not cry at mov-ies). The traditional attitudes toward sex roles assume that major decisions in a dyad are made by the male partner; therefore if a male insists on sexual activity in the relationship, the female should acquiesce. This attitude among some black adolescents combined with the consistent findings from national surveys that black males have more permissive attitudes toward sexual rela-tions (Singh, 1980) and less knowledge of birth control methods than black females (Delcampo, Sporakowski, & Delcampo, 1976; Moore & Erickson, 1985), makes for predictable consequences.

Nevertheless, the female is not always the innocent, exploited victim. Other studies report that some young mothers began to have sexual relations willingly because of emotional involvement, curiosity, or simply because they did not see any reason for waiting until marriage (Falk, Gispert, & Baucom, 1981; Furstenberg, 1976; Furstenberg, Brooks-Gunn & Morgan, 1987). As reported, a major-ity of adolescent black women are more conservative than black males regarding premarital sexual intercourse. Given the reported incidence of sexual activity, it is obvious that black female adoles-cents had acquired one set of ideology and lived by another. This ambivalence about their sexual code makes it difficult for these young women to deal realistically with the consequences of their sexual behavior.

One of the factors that contributes to this ambivalence is the black female's perspective of parental attitudes. Analysis of data from a national probability sample of 15-to 19-year-old women suggests some insights into the influence of parents (Shah & Zelnik, 1981). Sexually active black women whose views had been influenced by their parents' disapproval of premarital sex were least likely (52%) to use contraception; and most likely (50%) to become premaritally pregnant. In contrast, women with views resembling those of their friends are more likely to use contraceptives. Fear of their parents' discovery is a major reason most adolescents delay their visit to a family planning clinic until a year or more after starting intercourse (Zabin & Clark, 1981). Furstenberg and colleagues (1987), in a study of urban black adolescents, found that the young people's mothers were not hesitant to discuss birth control. Ninety-three percent of mothers reported having given birth control information to their daughters; however, directions regarding birth control were sometimes vague. Among black female adolescents, a factor that appears to predict consistent birth control usage is the young women's self-assessment of compliant behavior with other medications and a life-style of organizing and planning daily activities (Litt, 1985). Thus the willingness to lead and past reinforcement for an organized life increases the likelihood that the black female adolescent will commit to the use of birth control.

Finkel and Finkel (1978), in a study of contraceptive utilization among a sample of sexually active black males in urban high schools, found that a majority of the young men were classified as ineffective contraceptors. Data showed that 31.1% of young black males rarely used condoms and 23.6% never used them. The major explanations for not using them were: "using condoms was not important" (27%); "didn't have one," (22%); "partner was protected" (20%); and "didn't think partner could become pregnant" (13%).

Similarly, Rivara, Sweeney, and Henderson (1985) studied black teenage fathers of lower socioeconomic status and their non-father peers. No significant differences were found between the two groups for age of first intercourse (mean = 12.5 years), frequency of intercourse in the last year, knowledge about the risk of pregnancy, the effectiveness of contraceptives, and negative attitudes about contraceptives. The non-father adolescents, however, perceived pregnancy as disruptive of their plans for school, job, and marriage. On the other hand, adolescents who were fathers generally came from a home environment in which teenage pregnancy was common, accepted, and perceived to be minimally disruptive in the lives of persons involved. Hendrick and Fullilove's (1983) sample of black adolescent fathers, as compared to controls who had never been fathers, were more likely to have an external locus of control and to be non-churchgoers, and less likely to use birth control. Thus black male adolescents are more likely to practice birth control if they are in a stable romantic relationship (Furstenberg, 1976), have an internal source of control, and have plans for and commitments to the future.

Societal Responses

The societal problems created by high risk sexual behaviors among black teenagers have been discussed above (e.g., increase in unwanted pregnancy, feminization of poverty) along with some of the responses to the problems (e.g., increases in birth control information and sex education classes, availability of school-based clinics). Pertinent to the black adolescent are the responses of the black community. This issue is discussed along with the probable effects of the current efforts to limit the availability of abortions.

Black Community

The prevailing view of not rejecting a person because of his or her parents' marital status has enhanced the humanness of the black community and enabled often confused adolescents to find solace and compassion. Concordant with this view was the attitude that the birth of children was best confined to a marital situation. These attitudes were dominant guidelines to adolescent behaviors in the decades of the 1940s, 1950s, and early 1960s when the values and attitudes of the rural, Southern, agricultural society dominated families, the community, churches, schools, and so forth. Although teenage pregnancy and female heads-of-house

holds existed, they were not the dominant mode of family groupings. The black population has become more urbanized and economically vulnerable, has witnessed a decline in the influence of
the black church, and has grown increasingly susceptible to contemporary trends that are pervasive in the larger society. With the
rise of high risk sexual behaviors among adolescents, major civic,
social, and political organizations have become increasingly vocal
in their views of expected and appropriate behaviors for young
persons. In recent years, the Urban League and the National Association for Advancement of Colored People, the two largest civic
organizations in the black community, have convened meetings
and workshops at local and national levels to address the issue.
Importantly, the National Urban League's program addresses the
black male adolescent (Pitt, 1985). Young black males are encouraged to act responsibly in relationships to avoid fathering children.
Such programs have been initiated by parent groups, national
black fraternities and sororities, and professional organizations.
The underlying assumption is that the community immediate to
the adolescent will have an impact on her or his attitude and
behavior. Regrettably, there are no systematic program evaluations
of these efforts.

Abortion

A major thrust currently is underway by a large segment of the
American population to limit the availability of abortions. A growing number of black female adolescents have abortions to avoid
unwanted births. From 1972 to 1978, the abortion rate for black
females age 12 to 19 was 17.4 (per 1,000) and 51.2 (Ezzard, Cates,
Kramer, & Tietze, 1982). For young persons 15 years of age and
under, in 1978 the abortion rate was 24.4. Importantly, the number
of deaths from illegal abortions among black teenagers decreased
after the legalization of abortion (Russo, 1986). Reports from a
study of teenage fertility rates between 1970 and 1974 showed that
the combination of family planning programs and abortion helped
adolescents to avoid unwanted births. Generally, adolescents did
not substitute abortion for methods of contraception, but each has
contributed to lower birthrates (Ezzard, Cates, & Schulz, 1985).

If current antiabortion campaigns are successful, then an increase in birthrates among black adolescents is predictable. Indeed,

it can be speculated, but not currently documented, that the increase in tempo of the abortion opponents may be a contributing factor to the increase in birthrates among black adolescents. This scenario certainly will exacerbate social problems in the black community.

Summary and Conclusions

The involvement of black adolescents in high risk sexual behavior has increased. Subsequently, births to teenagers have risen. Social systems, irresponsible personal behaviors, and sexual ideology for the black community have been discussed as possible reasons for these increases. The problems accompanying high risk sexual behavior among adolescents have prompted formation of school-based health clinics, and increased the availability of birth control information and sex education classes. Importantly, the black community has organized programs and activities to address the issue; however, there is a lack of empirical documentation of these efforts. The antiabortion campaign probably has caused undocumented and predictably negative consequences as shown in related demographic figures for this group. Efforts should begin to plan for contingency actions to avoid unwanted pregnancies if safe low-cost abortions become inaccessible to those young persons.

Among black adolescents, the need for information and programs addressing the importance of individual control over one's life is evident. Often black adolescents need positive role models and sympathetic caring persons in their lives to give them direction towards a more productive life-style. More research on the psychological mechanisms involved in the decision to engage in high risk sexual behavior clearly is needed.

References

Allan Guttmacher Institute (1981). *Teenage pregnancy: The problem that hasn't gone away.* New York: Author.

Canter, R. J., & Ageton, S. S. (1984). The epidemiology of adolescent sex-role attitudes. *Sex Roles, 11,* (718), 657-677.

Delcampo, R. L., Sporakowski, M. J., & Delcampo, D. S. (1976). Premarital sexual permissiveness and contraceptive knowledge: A racial comparison of college students. *The Journal of Sex Research, 12*(3), 180-192.

Diepold, J., & Young, R. D. (1979). Empirical studies of adolescent sexual behavior: A critical review. *Adolescence, 14*(53), 45-64.

Ezzard, N. V, Cates, W., Jr., Kramer, D. G., & Tietze, C. (1982). Race-specific patterns of abortion use by American teenagers. *American Journal of Public Health, 72,* 809.

Ezzard, N. V., Cates, W., Jr., & Schulz, K. K. (1985). The epidemiology of adolescent abortion in the United States. In P. Sachdev (Ed.), *Perspectives on abortions* (pp. 73-88). Metuchen, NJ: Scarecrow Press.

Falk, R., Gispert, M., & Baucom, D. H. (1981). Personality factors related to black teenage pregnancy and abortion. *Psychology of Woman Quarterly, 5*(5) 737-746.

Finkel, M. L. & Finkel, D. J. (1978). Male adolescent contraceptive utilization. *Adolescence, 13*(51), 443-451.

Furstenberg, F. F. (1976). *Unplanned parenthood.* New York: Free Press.

Furstenberg, F. F., Brooks-Gunn, J., & Morgan, S. P. (1987). *Adolescent mothers in later life.* Cambridge: Cambridge University Press.

Guttentag, M., & Secord, P. F. (1983). *Too many women: The sex ratio question.* Beverly Hills, CA: Sage.

Hanson, R. O., O'Conner, M. E., Jones, W. H., & Blocker, T. J. (1981). Material employment and adolescent sexual behavior. *Journal of Youth and Adolescence, 10*(1), 55-60.

Height, D. (1985, March). What must be done about children having children. *Ebony,* p. 76.

Hendrick, L. E. & Fullilove, R. E. (1983). Locus of control and the use of contraception among unmarried black adolescent fathers and their controls: A preliminary report. *Journal of Youth and Adolescence, 12*(3), 225-233.

Jackson, J. (1971). But where are all the men? *Black Scholar, 3*(4), 34-41.

Jones, E. F. (1986). *Teenage pregnancy in industrialized countries.* New Haven, CT: Yale University Press.

Kanter, J. F. & Zelnik, M. (1972). Sexual experience of young unmarried women in the United States. *Family Planning Perspectives, 4,* 9-18.

Ladner, J. (1972). *Tomorrow's tomorrow: The black woman.* Garden City: Doubleday.

Litt, I. F. (1985). Know thyself—Adolescents' self-assessment of compliance behavior. *Pediatrics, 75*(4), 693-696.

McAdoo, H. P. (1986, November). *Adolescent attitudes about premarital sexuality and pregnancy.* Paper presented at the National Council of Family Relations Annual Meeting, Detroit, MI.

Moore, K. (1986, October). Facts on births to U.S. teens. *Facts at a glance.* Washington, DC: Child Trends, Inc.

Moore, D. S., & Erickson, P. I. (1985). Age, gender, and ethnic differences in sexual and contraceptive knowledge, attitudes, and behaviors. *Family and Community Health, 8*(3), 38-51.

Moore, K. A., Simms, M. C., & Betsey, C. L. (1987). *Choice and circumstance.* New Brunswick, NJ: Transaction Books.

Pearce, D., & McAdoo, H. (1981). *Women and children: Alone and in poverty.* Washington, DC: National Advisory Council on Economic Opportunity.

Pitt, E. (1985). National Urban League initiates male responsibility campaign. *Children and Teens Today, 5*(10), pp. 3-4.

Rivara, F. P., Sweeney, P. J., & Henderson, B. F. (1985). A study of low socioeconomic status, black teenage fathers and their non-father peers. *Pediatrics, 75*(4), 648-656.

Rossi, A. (1985). Gender and parenthood. In A. Rossi (Ed.), *Gender and the life course* (pp. 161-192). New York: Aldine.

Rubin, R. H. (1981). Attitudes about male-female relations among black adolescents. *Adolescence, 16*(61), 159-174.

Russo, N. F. (1986). Adolescent abortion: The epidemiological context. In G. B. Melton (Ed.), *Adolescent abortion* (pp. 40-73). Lincoln, NB: University of Nebraska Press.

Shah, F., & Zelnik, M. (1981). Parent and peer influence on sexual behavior, contraceptive use, and pregnancy experience of young women. *Journal of Marriage and the Family,* (May), 339-348.

Singh, B. K. (1980). Trends in attitudes toward premarital sexual relations. *Journal of Marriage and the Family,* (May), 387-393.

Staples, R. (1971). *The black family: Essays and studies.* Belmont, CA: Wadsworth.

Staples, R. (1981). *The world of black singles.* Westport, CT: Greenwood.

Staples, R. (1988). Race and marital status: An overview. In H. P. McAdoo (Ed.), *Black families* (pp. 173-175). Beverly Hills, CA: Sage.

Tucker, B. (1987). The black male shortage in Los Angeles. *Sociology and Social Research, 71*(3), 221-227.

Tucker, B., & Mitchell-Kernan, C. (in press). Sex ratio imbalance among Afro-Americans: Conceptual and methodological issues. In R. Jones (Ed.), *Black adulthood and aging.* Berkeley, CA: Cobbs & Henry.

Udry, R. J. (1971). *The social context of marriage.* Philadelphia: J. B. Lippincott.

U.S. Bureau of the Census. (1986). Statistical Abstracts of the United States: 1987 (107th edition): Table 56. Washington, DC: U.S. Government Printing Office.

U.S. Bureau of the Census. (1987). Statistical Abstracts of the United States: 1988 (108th edition): Table 1-32, No. 87. Washington, DC: U.S. Government Printing Office.

U.S. Bureau of the Census. (1988). Poverty in the United States: 1986. *Current Population Reports,* Table 1 and 3, series P-60, No. 160, Washington, DC: U.S. Government Printing Office.

Zabin, L. S. (1986). The Alan Guttmacher Institute. *Children and Teens Today Newsletter, 6*(12), 2-4.

Zabin, L. S., & Clark, S. D. (1981). Why they delay: A study of teenage family planning clinic patients. *Family Planning Perspectives, 13*(5), 205-217.

Zelnik, M., & Young, J. K. (1982). Sex education and its association with teenage sexual activity, pregnancy and contraceptive use. *Family Planning Perspectives, 14*(3), 117-126.

Zigler, E. F., & Finn-Stevenson, M. (1987). *Children: Development and social issues.* Lexington, MA: D. C. Heath.

9

Social Support and Teen Pregnancy in the Inner City

BRENDA G. MCGOWAN

AMY KOHN

Introduction

The total number of births to teenagers in the United States has declined almost 20% in the past generation from 594,000 in 1960 to 478,000 in 1985. During the same period the birth rate for young women aged 15-19 declined substantially from 89.1 per 1,000 in 1960 to 51.3 per 1,000 in 1985, while the birth rate for those aged 10-14 increased very slightly from 0.8 per 1,000 in 1960 to 1.2 per 1,000 in 1985 (U.S. Bureau of the Census, 1987). Although the birth rate among black teens aged 15-19 in 1985 (97 per 1,000) was more than double that of whites of the same age (42.8 per 1,000), the decline in the birth rate among young black women from 1960 to 1985 (37.6%) closely paralleled the decline among young white women (39.8%) (Children's Defense Fund, 1988; Moore, Simms, & Betsey, 1986). Despite these trends suggesting a significant decline in teenage births,[1] the amount of public attention directed to teen

Authors' Note: The research on which this article is based was supported by grants from the Kenworthy-Swift Foundation and New York Community Trust.

TABLE 9.1: Teenage Births in the United States by Marital Status, 1960–1985

	1960	1970	1975	1980	1985
All					
Total Live Births (000)	4,258	3731	3144	3612	3761
Percent of Births to Women Under 20	13.9	17.6	18.9	15.5	12.7
Birth Rate[a] Women Age 15-19	89.1	68.3	55.6	53.0	51.3
Unmarried					
Total Live Births (000)	224.3	398.7	447.9	665.7	828.2
Percent of Births to Women Under 20	40.9	50.1	52.1	40.8	33.8
Birth Rate[a] Unmarried Women, Age 15-19	15.3	22.4	23.9	27.6	31.6
Percent of Teen Mothers Unmarried	15.4	30.5	39.2	48.4	58.6

[a]Per 1,000 women

Source: United States Bureau of the Census, 1987 (pp. 60, 62). (Data from the National Center for Health Statistics.)

pregnancy, particularly in minority communities, has increased dramatically in recent years.

Several factors contribute to this widespread perception of teen pregnancy as a social problem. First, although teenage birth rates have declined, the proportion of out of wedlock births among adolescents has continued to expand, as illustrated in Table 9.1. Moreover, there has been a substantial increase in the number of unmarried teens who engage in premarital sexual activity and in the number who become pregnant. Approximately 4 out of 10 white and Hispanic females and 6 out of 10 black females are sexually active by age 18, and approximately 4 out of 10 whites and 6 out of 10 blacks become pregnant at least once by age 20. The

TABLE 9.2: Teenage Birth Rates by Marital Status of Mother and Race/ Ethnicity of Child, 1970–1985 (Births per 1,000 young women, age 15-19)

	Whites		Blacks		Hispanics		All Races	
	Total	Un-married	Total	Un-married	Total	Un-married	Total	Un-married
1970	57.4	10.9	147.7	96.9	NA	NA	68.3	22.4
1980	44.7	16.2	100.0	89.2	82.2	39.7	53.0	27.6
1985	42.8	20.5	97.4	88.8	NA	NA	51.3	31.6

Source: Children's Defense Fund, 1988. (Based on data from the National Center for Health Statistics).

proportion of teen pregnancies ending in abortion increased from 20.0% in 1972 ($N = 191,000$) to 40.0% in 1984 ($N = 401,128$) (Hayes, 1987). These trends challenge traditional beliefs about appropriate sexual behavior among unmarried adolescents.

Second, despite recent trends (See Table 9.2) indicating that out of wedlock births may be increasing faster among white teens than among minority youth, the proportion of black adolescents who became pregnant and bore children out of wedlock (88.8 per 1,000) was still over four times that of white adolescents (20.5 per 1,000) in 1985. The rate of out of wedlock childbirth among Hispanic teens (39.7 per 1,000) was more than double that of whites (16.2 per 1,000) in 1980 (Children's Defense Fund, 1988).

Third, several important research reviews have been released documenting the negative social and economic correlates and consequences of teenage childbearing. (See, for example, Alan Guttmacher Institute, 1981; Moore & Burt, 1982; Hayes, 1987). Although some teenage parents and their children fare very well, it has been repeatedly demonstrated that adolescent mothers are less likely to complete their education, more likely to be poor, unemployed and dependent on welfare, and more likely to have unstable marriages and increased numbers of unplanned children. The children of teen mothers face increased developmental and health risks and are more likely to become adolescent parents themselves. Although it is difficult to separate the effects of low socioeconomic status commonly associated with teenage parenting from the independent

impact of young childbearing, the collective impact of recent research has been to increase public awareness of the high social
costs of this phenomenon both for the individuals involved and for
society at large. The fiscal costs are equally troubling. Expenditures
for Aid to Families with Dependent Children (AFDC) and other
welfare-related benefits for those who had been teen mothers was
estimated at over $16 billion in 1985 (Kamerman & Kahn, 1988).

Although it has been argued that teen childbearing is not necessarily deleterious (Chilman, 1988; Furstenberg, 1976; Furstenberg
and Crawford, 1978), and may in fact represent a normative, alternative life course that is viable because of strong kin networks
within the black community (Hamburg, 1986; Ladner, 1971; Stack,
1974; Staples, 1981), questions are now being raised about whether
traditional extended family supports are sufficient to overcome the
tremendous structural disadvantages posed by early childbearing
among black youth in low-income urban areas (Edelman, 1987;
Wilson, 1987). Similar concern has been raised about the capacity
of Hispanic families who have moved from their home communities to urban centers to perpetuate extended family values and ties
and provide the help required at times of need (de Anda & Becerra,
1984; Fitzpatrick, 1981).

Commenting on the high rates of teenage childbearing in the
black community, Eleanor Holmes Norton has noted:

> These figures would be easier to bear if our strong extended family
> tradition had survived more often. Extended families are not uncom-
> mon in the black community today, but their incidence is much lower
> than it was, for example, in the rural South of our historic roots. . . .
> The marvelously protective extended family units that were as strong
> among blacks as among any other group in this country are not
> widespread enough today to give the children of young and poor
> single mothers the chance they must have for a decent life. (Quoted in
> Moore, Simms, & Betsey, 1986, pp. 2-3).

In this chapter we shall briefly review available research regarding the ways that social support may mediate the consequences o
teenage pregnancy and then present the results of a study designec
to examine social supports and depression in a sample of low
income, black and Hispanic pregnant teens in New York City.

Role of Social Support

Despite varying definitions, it is generally agreed that social support is a multidimensional concept referring to some combination of the emotional, informational, material, and/or instrumental help potentially available or actually provided to individuals to assist with life tasks and buffer environmental and personal stress. As research about the direct and indirect associations between social support, physical and mental health, and social functioning began to accumulate in the 1970s, investigators concerned about the negative consequences of single parenthood and early childbearing quite naturally started to study the impact of various dimensions of social support on these phenomena. As a consequence there is now a rather substantial body of research pointing to the beneficial effects of social supports on pregnant and parenting teens.

To illustrate, in a study of 86 pregnant adolescents, Barrera (1981) found that satisfaction with the current support system was the strongest single predictor of adjustment. Reporting on a study of parental acceptance/rejection by 50 teenage mothers, Colleta (1981) noted that the most consistent predictor of maternal behavior was the total amount of support mothers received. Based on a comparative study of 62 pregnant, 63 parenting, and 60 nonpregnant or parenting teens, Barth, Schinke and Maxwell (1983) concluded that "teenage pregnancy and motherhood (at least in the first year) are not in and of themselves as psychologically incapacitating as often thought" (p. 481). Instead, they reported, socioeconomic status and social supports were the more powerful predictors of adolescent well-being.

Similar findings about the importance of social support in mediating the potential negative consequences of early childbearing have been reported by a number of authors. (See, for example, Colletta, 1981; Presser, 1980; Zitner & Miller, 1980). In what is probably the most comprehensive review to date of research on the association between social support and parenting, Crockenberg (1988) concluded that all but one of the many studies that have examined this relationship in adolescent populations suggest a positive link between social support and maternal behavior. Based on a review of studies pointing to social isolation among neglectful and abusive parents (See, for example, Polansky, Ammons, & Gaudin, 1985), she also concluded that social support may reduce the possibility of such behavior in parents who are at risk because of their own developmental history.

Findings such as these have led many authors and clinicians to recognize the potential value of mobilizing natural supports to mediate the stress associated with adolescent parenting and to propose various professional interventions designed to strengthen teens' social support systems (Barth & Schinke, 1984; de Anda & Becerra, 1984; Fine & Pape, 1982; Weatherley & Cartoof, 1988). The study reported below was initiated in the first phase of what had been designed as a three-year project to develop and test a clinical assessment tool that could be used to evaluate level of risk for inadequate parenting reflected in the social supports available to pregnant teens.[2]

Study Subjects

The sample consisted of 50 adolescents who were in their sixth or later month of pregnancy and planning for their first full-term birth. Thirty (60%) were patients at Harlem Hospital prenatal clinic and 20 (40%) were patients at a Maternity-Infant Care Clinic in the Bushwick section of Brooklyn. These sites were selected to insure that subjects would be drawn from neighborhoods with a high incidence of the social problems such as poverty, single parenthood, limited educational attainment, welfare dependency, and unemployment that Ricketts and Sawhill (1988) have since described as characterizing underclass areas. One-third of the residents of Central Harlem received some form of public assistance in 1988 as did 41% of those in Bushwick (Gager, 1988). Table 9. presents selected characteristics of live births in the Central Harlem and Bushwick health districts compared to New York City as whole in 1985. It will be noted that even in a city with a high proportion of low-income minority residents, these health districts have a disproportionate number of births to mothers who are black or Hispanic, unmarried, adolescent, and dependent on Medicaid.

TABLE 9.3: Selected Characteristics of Live Births by Health Center District, New York City, 1985

					Percent of Total Births				
	Total Live Births	His- panic Descent	Non- white Child	Under 2500 grams	Late or No Pre- natal Care	Out of Wed- lock	On Medi caid	Teen Mother	Mother Not H.S. Grad
New York City	188,542	28.5	42.1	8.5	17.2	38.9	35.8	11.2	26.5
Central Harlem	2,014	7.9	91.6	17.3	38.2	82.2	72.5	20.5	39.1
Bushwick	4,094	55.4	43.9	9.7	21.9	59.6	66.6	20.1	49.6

Source: Adapted from tables in C. T. Gager, (1988). *Twelve Health Center Districts in Need: A Birth Atlas.* New York: Population Studies Unit, Community Service Society.

Although the study focused deliberately on low-income, minority teens, those with serious psychiatric, medical, or substance abuse problems were excluded from the sample because the intent was to study the social supports of relatively "normal" pregnant women under the age of 20. Study subjects who met sample criteria were selected on a random basis from the lists of those scheduled for clinic appointments on specific days during the data collection period (July to December, 1986). Only one identified as appropriate for inclusion in the sample refused to be interviewed.

Demographic Characteristics

The subjects ranged in age from 11 to 19 years. The median age was 17.8 and the mean was 17.1. Thirty-four (68%) defined themselves as black; 14 (28%) as Hispanic;[3] and two (4%) as white or other. Twelve (24%) were Catholic; 22 (44%) were Protestant; and 16 (32%) said they had no religion. Forty-four (88%) of the subjects were single; five (10%) were married; and one was divorced. Twenty-three (46%) were attending school and four (8%)

were employed outside the home. Ten (20%) of the total had graduated from high school.

Half of the respondents had lived at their current address less
than two years and 18 (36%) less than one year. During the month
preceding the interview, the subjects had lived with from one to
eight people ($\bar{x}$ = 3.5). Over half (58%) lived with their mothers,
and two-thirds (66%) were in households that included one or
more siblings. Less than one-quarter lived in households that included their own fathers (24%) or the babies' fathers (20%). Other
relatives were present in 10 (20%) of the subjects' households, but
only 3 (6%) lived in households that included a grandmother.

In addition to the persons residing in their immediate households, two-thirds of the respondents (N = 28) said they had one or
more relatives living nearby whom they saw regularly. Almost
one-third (N = 16) saw these relatives daily.

Exposure to Early Childbearing

The teenagers in the sample generally reported extensive exposure to childcare and young pregnancy. On a scale of one (high) to
four (low) regarding the number of other girls they knew who
were approximately their own age and who were pregnant or had
children, the median response was 1.0 and the mean, 1.8. Of the 43
subjects who knew the age at which their own mothers first had a
child, 31 (72.1%) said their mothers had been in their teens (median
age = 18.0). Twenty-one (42%) of the respondents said that one or
more of their siblings already had a child. The median age for their
sisters' first births was 18.0. Thus the early age of first childbirth
for the young women in the sample appears quite consistent with
the patterns established for females in their families of origin.

Identified Fathers

The identified fathers (N = 49) ranged in age from 16 to 31 ($\bar{x}$ =
20.8). Thirty-two (65.3%) were described as black; 12 (24.5%) as
Hispanic; 1 (2%) as white; and 4 (8.2%) as other. Twenty-eight
(58.3%) were employed, and 13 (26.5%) were currently attending
school. Only 16 (39%) of those for whom education was known
(N = 41) were high school graduates. Nine (18.4%) had children by
other women; eight had one other child, and one had three.

At the time of conception, the duration of the respondents' rela-
onship with the alleged fathers ranged from one month to seven
ears ($\bar{x}$ = 25 months). Ten (20%) of the subjects were living with
e fathers of their babies. Fewer than one-third (N = 16), including
ose already married, expected to be married in the future. How-
er, almost three-quarters described their relationship with the
bies' fathers as very (N = 29) or somewhat (N = 6) close, and all
: the identified fathers had been informed about the pregnancy.

ttitudes Toward Pregnancy

When asked to recall how they felt when they discovered they
ere pregnant, only 16 (32%) reported being at all upset. On a scale
: one (positive) to four (negative) regarding their own feelings
out the pregnancy, the respondents' median score was 2.0.
espite these relatively positive responses, half of the subjects
ought about not going through with the pregnancy, suggesting at
ast some initial ambivalence.

The reactions of other significant persons in their social net-
orks to their pregnancies were generally perceived to be positive.
venty-six percent of the respondents' mothers and 81% of the
bies' fathers were reported to be "very" or "somewhat" pleased
out the pregnancy. Approximately 9 out of 10 of the respon-
nts' sisters and friends were also described as responding posi-
ely. Although there were notable differences in the perceived
actions to pregnancy by age of respondent, it seems clear that
erall these teenagers felt they received very positive reinforce-
ent for their pregnancies.

Social Supports

A modification and elaboration of the Arizona Social Support
terview Schedule (ASSIS) developed by Barrera (1981) was used
measure various components of social support. this instrument,
hich has been used in at least one prior study of pregnant teens,
easures total and unconflicted network size; support system
embers; specific functions served; need for support; and re-
rted satisfaction. Test-retest correlation of the total network size

measure in a prior study of college students was reported to be $r(43) = .88$, $p < .00$ (Barrera, 1981).

Number and Utilization Rate

There was a correlation of .86 between the number of the sub jects' potential and actual social supports. The number of potentia help givers listed ranged from 0 (2%) to 7 (10%). The median anc mean numbers of potential helpers cited were both 4.0 (S.D. = 1.7) The numbers of persons actually asked for help during the pas month also ranged from 0 (2%) to 7 (4%). The median number o persons cited was 3.0 ($\bar{x} = 3.2$, S.D. = 1.7). For this population th ratio of actual to potential helpers was thus relatively high ($\bar{x} = .79$ S.D. = .22). This indicates that the subjects make high usage of th number of potential supports available to them. Only 10 (20.4% requested assistance from half or fewer of their potential support during the past month whereas 23 (46%) had utilized everyone i the potential support network during the past month. There wa no relationship between age or ethnicity and number and utiliza tion of social supports or other support variables.

Number and Relationship of Helpers by Function

The respondents were asked to list those to whom they would g for various types of companionship or help and how frequentl they actually went to these people during the past month. Th specific support functions probed were as follows: (a) Material Ai ("If you needed to borrow things like $10 or food or clothing, t whom would you go?"); (b) Personal Talk ("If you wanted to tal to someone about personal or private things, to whom would yo go?"); (c) Recreation ("When you like to do fun things or relax . . with whom do you do this?"); (d) Physical Assistance ("If yo needed help with shopping, a ride somewhere, moving or carryin heavy objects . . . to whom would you go?"); (e) Advice ("If yo needed advice on an important matter, to whom could you go?")

These pregnant teenagers identified only a small number of p tential helpers available to serve each support function. The mea numbers reported were as follows: Material Aid, 1.42; Person Talk, 1.56; Recreation, 1.52; Physical Assistance, 1.42; and Advic 0.84. However, there were significant differences in the types

TABLE 9.4: Multidimensionality of Helping Relationships (N = 50)

Relationship	Mean Number of Functions Potentially Served
Mother (*n* = 35)	2.6
Father (*n* = 27)	1.4
Brother (*n* = 12)	1.3
Sister (*n* = 19)	1.9
Baby's Father (*n* = 32)	2.6
Grandmother (*n* = 9)	1.1
Other Relative (*n* = 26)	1.3
Baby's Father's Family (*n* = 7)	2.1
Friend (*n* = 27)	1.9

functions different members of the respondents' social networks were expected to fill. These expectations generally conformed with very traditional age and sex role expectations.

As demonstrated in Table 9.4, sample members also were selective about the range of functions they expected different network members to serve. It will be noted that the mean number of potential functions ranged from 1.1 for grandmothers (*n* = 9) to 2.6 for mothers (*n* = 35) and babies' fathers (*n* = 32). The mean number for all of the persons in the respondents' social networks was 1.9. No correlations were noted between the amount of help actually provided by network members and the number of functions served.

Quality of Helping Relationships

The overwhelming majority described themselves as "very" or "somewhat" close to the persons described as available to serve various support functions. The mean number of persons identified as very close was 2.18 (*S.D.* = 1.35), and the mean number identified as somewhat close was .80 (*S.D.* = .86).

It should also be noted that a small but significant minority said they felt they had to "pay a price" (i.e., were made to feel uneasy or unhappy) when they asked various members of their social network for help. Not surprisingly, respondents were most likely to feel they had to pay a price in those relationships they depended on most (mothers, 20%; and baby's fathers, 16%) for help. This suggests that the support networks of these pregnant teenagers are not unconflicted.

The degree of reciprocity in potential helping relationships cited by the respondents varied widely. When asked how frequently each of the potential helpers went to the respondent for help or advice on personal matters, the subjects distinguished carefully among the various members of their support networks. There was wide variation in the degree of mutual helping described, but these differences again generally reflected traditional age and relationship norms. The subjects' responses indicate that their relationships with the babies' fathers are the most reciprocal and their relationships with their own fathers, the least. Over three-quarters of the sisters and friends whom they can approach for help are said to seek help from them at least occasionally, as do approximately 60% of the subjects' mothers who are available to help.

Need for Help and Level of Satisfaction

In order to measure need for different types of help, subjects were asked to indicate how much they needed or wanted assistance in each functional area during the past month. Similarly, to measure satisfaction with the support they received, they were asked whether they would have liked more, the same amount, or less assistance in each area during the past month. Table 9.5 summarizes the responses to each question. It will be noted that these young women, all of whom live in poverty conditions and have few available supports, expressed surprisingly little need for various types of assistance and were generally quite satisfied with the support they received.

The only type of support that over one-third thought they needed "quite a bit" was the chance to talk to people about personal things. There was a moderate correlation of .40 between need to talk and need for advice. There were also moderate correlations between the levels of satisfaction expressed with the amount of support available for physical assistance and for personal talk (.48), advice (.45), and recreation (.43), and between the amount of support available for personal talk and for recreation (.38). These correlations suggest that subjects may not differentiate "satisfaction" by function as clearly as they do other aspects of helping.

TABLE 9.5: Level of Expressed Need and Satisfaction by Function (*N* = 50)

	Personal Talk	Physical Assistance	Advice	Material Assistance	Recreation
Need					
Quite A Lot	38%	22%	24%	12%	20%
A Little	40%	42%	56%	40%	28%
Not At All	22%	36%	20%	48%	52%
Satisfaction (Amount of support preferred)					
More	14%	28%	24%	30%	20%
Same Amount	64%	46%	42%	52%	46%
Less	18%	26%	34%	18%	34%

Although the subjects indicated a higher level of need for personal talk and advice than for other types of help, only 14% expressed a desire for more opportunity for personal conversation than they received; and although 24% would have liked more advice, one-third would have liked less than they received. In contrast, although almost half said they did not need any material assistance and only 12% thought they needed quite a lot, 30% would have liked more than they received.

These responses again demonstrate the respondents' capacity to differentiate among the types of support that are needed and are available to them. At the same time the fact that 30% or fewer expressed a desire for more help of any kind suggests that these subjects have very low expectations of the help that can and should be available to them.

Incidence of Depression

The Generalized Contentment Scale (GCS) developed by Hudson (1982) and used repeatedly in clinical and research trials was selected to measure the degree of depression in the respondents. This is a 25-item summated rating scale designed to yield a score ranging from 0-100 with higher scores indicating an increased degree or severity of depression. The cutting point designed to indicate the presence or absence of a clinically significant depression is a score of 30. Since the standard error of measurement for this scale is 4.26, those scoring below 25 can generally be defined as not manifesting a significant level of depression and those scoring 35 or above should generally be defined as clinically depressed. Clinical experience has indicated that those scoring above 70 may be suicidal and those scoring above 50 may have suicidal ideation (Hudson, 1982).

Given these cutting points, the respondents' scores on the GCS indicated that 8 (16%) were at risk (25-34) and in need of further evaluation and 29 (58%) were clinically depressed (35+). Moreover, 11 of the latter group scored above 50 and 4 above 70, suggesting that almost one-third (30%) of the total sample could have suicidal ideation or be actively suicidal. The median score for all respondents was 39.5.

The very troubling conclusion that approximately three-quarters of these young women must be defined as depressed or at risk of depression is consistent with the clinical observations of the research interviewer. It is also consistent with the denial and poor self-esteem reflected in the respondents' low aspirations for themselves and limited expectations of others in their social networks. Yet it is even more sobering when one recalls that potential respondents with known histories of serious medical, psychiatric, or substance abuse problems were deliberately excluded from the sample.

There was no association between age or ethnicity and score on the GCS within the study population. There were negative correlations between need for talk and level of depression (-.33) and between satisfaction with the opportunities for recreation presented and level of depression (-.37). These findings are clinically persuasive because depressed teenagers may not recognize their need to talk with others about personal matters and may view recreational opportunities as a demand rather than a pleasure.

Of most interest from the perspective of this study was the strong negative correlation between the number of respondents' potential social supports and their level of depression as measured by the GCS (-.54). No causal relationship can be assumed because these variables are clearly interactive. However, this finding highlights the importance of assessing the risks of depression in pregnant adolescents who claim few social supports.

Conclusion

Perhaps the most striking finding is the utter poverty of the lives of most of those whom we studied. Selection of sample sites was designed to insure that respondents would have limited financial resources. What was not expected was that so many of the respondents' lives would be equally devoid of other instrumental, social, and emotional resources. The fact that these young women generally depend on a very small circle of intimates to meet all of their support needs and are quite satisfied with the limited help they receive, suggests that they lead rather narrow, constricted lives and have few aspirations for anything better. Similarly, the fact that none mentioned a representative of a formal institution (e.g., teacher, religious leader, or health worker) as a potential source of support indicates that they have only marginal ties to the larger social community. These findings underscore Wilson's (1987) observations about the troubling levels of social dislocation and isolation in depressed inner-city neighborhoods today that deprive young people of any opportunity for sustained interaction with those who demonstrate mainstream patterns of behavior and provide the contacts and socialization required for social mobility.

Thus it is not surprising to learn that the respondents themselves and others in their social networks view their pregnancies positively. Teen pregnancy is clearly defined as a normative event in the population sampled and there are few, if any, competing claims on these youngsters' energies and hopes. These findings lead us to side strongly with those who argue that the "teen pregnancy problem" cannot be addressed until society is prepared to offer all young people the educational, economic, and social opportunities that make delay of pregnancy a desirable personal goal. (See, for example, Edelman, 1987; Hayes, 1987; Wilson, 1987; Chilman, 1988). Those who see no future role for themselves except as mother and lover have little reason to postpone childbirth, an event commonly defined as symbolizing entry into adulthood. It is unlikely that we can stem the growth of teen pregnancies until we understand the function it serves for those at risk and provide realistic alternatives.

The finding that study respondents are deeply embedded in their own very small social networks also leads us to conclude that to be successful with this population, pregnancy prevention efforts must be directed towards teenagers' entire social networks, not just to the adolescents themselves. As long as teenagers believe that pregnancy will be perceived as a positive life event by those most important to them, it is unrealistic to expect sex education or family planning programs sponsored by secondary institutions to have any real impact on their aspirations or behavior.

The study finding of most immediate concern is the high prevalence of depression among the population surveyed. Maternal depression is likely to create serious problems in parenting. Therefore, we must assume that the children of those teen mothers who are seriously depressed are very much at risk. What cannot be determined from the current study is the degree to which the depression noted predates the pregnancy in this population and/or persists after childbirth. This question must be answered to determine how best to address this problem.

Study findings regarding the limited number of potential and actual supports available to these pregnant teens raise questions about the wisdom of the recent policy shift toward emphasizing reliance on family members for the care of youth and others in need. Additional research is needed to determine that tasks are best handled by informal, and that by formal supports, as well as the optimal size network required to meet the needs of teen mothers adequately. What seems clear, however, is that there is a limit to the amount of support that low-income, minority mothers living on a marginal level themselves can be expected to provide to teenage daughters and their babies. Similarly, it is questionable how much support the identified fathers will be able or willing to provide after the babies are born. Since these are the primary persons on which the pregnant teens in this sample depend, concern must be raised about the adequacy of their potential supports after childbirth. As Schilling (1987) has wisely noted, informal social supports, like other resources, may be inequitably distributed—to the disadvantage of those most in need.

Finally, given the focus of the current volume and recent attention to the salience of ethnicity in the design and delivery of services to populations at risk (Jenkins, 1981; McGoldrick, Pearce, & Giordano, 1982; Green, 1982; Jacobs & Bowles, 1988), it is important to emphasize that there were no significant differences between blacks and Hispanics in relation to any of the major study variables. This finding suggests that the commonalities among poor inner-city adolescents may be far more significant determinants of behavior than ethnic differences. It is also very consonant with Wilson's (1987) observation that Hispanics in urban areas are now beginning to experience many of the same social problems that plagued inner-city black communities. The implications of this conclusion seem clear. To reduce the negative consequences of adolescent pregnancy and address the other social dislocations of the inner city, we must provide the economic resources and structural supports that promote social mobility and integration for all youth in communities at risk.

Notes

1. In August 1990 the National Center for Health Statistics reported that the teenage birth rate had increased from 1985 to 1988, making the total higher than it had been at any time since 1975. It is too early to determine whether this reversal in birth rate trends will be substained.

2. The originator of this project was our colleague and friend, Francine Sobey, Professor, Columbia University School of Social Work, who died prior to the start of data collection. The authors, unfortunately, were able to assume responsibility only for completing the first phase of this work that had been so important to her.

3. Because of concern about the potential number of undocumented aliens, site administrators requested that the interviewers not inquire about country of origin.

References

Barrera, M., Jr. (1981). Social support in the adjustment of pregnant adolescents. In B. H. Gottlieb (Ed.) *Social networks and social support* (pp. 69-95). Beverly Hills, CA: Sage.

Barth, R. P., & Schinke, S. P. (1984). Enhancing the social supports of teenage mothers, *Social Casework, 65,* 523-531.

Barth, R. P., Schinke, S. P., & Maxwell, J. S. (1983). Psychological correlates of teenage motherhood, *Journal of Youth and Adolescence, 12*(6), 471-487.

Chilman, C. S. (1988). Never-married, single adolescent parents. In C. S. Chilman, E. W. Nunnally, & F. M. Cox (Eds.), *Variant family forms* (pp. 17-38). Newbury Park, CA: Sage.

Children's Defense Fund. (1988). *A children's defense budget, 1989.* Washington, DC: Author.

Colletta, N. D. (1981). Social support and the risk of maternal rejection by adolescent mothers, *Journal of Psychology, 109,* 191-197.

Crockenberg, S. (1988). Social support and parenting. In H. Fitzgerald, B. Lester, & M. Yogman (Eds.), *Theory and research in behavioral pediatrics*, (pp. 141-174) (Vol. 4.) NY: Plenum.

de Anda, D., & Becerra, R. M. (1984). Support networks for adolescent mothers, *Social Casework, 65*(3), 172-181.

Edelman, M. W. (1987). *Families in peril*. Cambridge, MA: Harvard University Press.

Fine, P., & Pape, M. (1982). Pregnant teenagers in need of social networks: Diagnostic parameters. In I. R. Stuart & C. F. Wells (Eds.), *Pregnancy in adolescence* (pp. 80-104). New York: Van Nostrand Reinhold.

Fitzpatrick, J. P. (1981). The Puerto Rican family. In C. H. Mendel & R. W. Haberstein, (Eds.), *Ethnic Families in America: Patterns and Variations* (2nd ed.), (pp. 189-214). New York: Elsevier.

Furstenberg, F. (1976). *Unplanned parenthood: The social consequences of teenage childbearing*. New York: Free Press.

Furstenberg, F., & Crawford, A. (1978). Family support: Helping teenage mothers to cope, *Family Planning Perspectives, 10*, 322-333.

Gager, C. T., with the assistance of C. Brellochs, T. J. Rosenberg, & J. Wessler. (1988). *Twelve health center districts in need: A birth atlas*. New York: Population Studies Unit, Community Service Society.

Green, J. W. (1982). *Cultural Awareness in the Human Services*. Englewood Cliffs, NJ: Prentice-Hall.

Alan Guttmacher Institute (1981). *Teenage pregnancy: The problem that hasn't gone away*. New York: Author.

Hamburg, B. A. (1986). Subsets of adolescent mothers: Developmental, biomedical, and psychosocial issues. In J. B. Lancaster & B. A. Hamburg (Eds.), *School-age pregnancy and parenthood*, (pp. 115-146). New York: Aldine.

Hayes, C. D. (Ed.). (1987). *Risking the future: Adolescent sexuality, pregnancy and childbearing* (Vol. 1). National Research Council. Washington, DC: National Academy Press.

Hudson, W. W. (1982). *The clinical measurement package*. Homewood, IL: Dorsey.

Jacobs, D., & Bowles, D. D. (Eds.). (1988). *Ethnicity and race: Critical concepts in social work*. Silver Springs, MD: National Association of Social Workers.

Jenkins, S. (1981). *The ethnic dilemma in social services*. New York: Free Press.

Kamerman, S. B., & Kahn, A. J. (1988). *Mothers alone*. Dover: Auburn House.

Ladner, J. (1971). *Tomorrow's tomorrow*. New York: Doubleday.

McGoldrick, M., Pearce, J. K., & Giordano, J. (1982). *Ethnicity and family therapy*. New York: Guilford.

Moore, K. A. & Burt, M. R. (1982). *Private crisis, public cost: Policy perspectives on teenage childbearing*. Washington, DC: Urban Institute.

Moore, K. A., Simms, M. C., & Betsey, C. L. (1986). *Choice and circumstance: Racial differences in adolescent sexuality and fertility*. New Brunswick: Transaction Books.

Polansky, N. A., Ammons, P. W., & Gaudin, J. M. (1985). Loneliness and isolation in child neglect, *Social Casework, 66*, 38-47.

Presser, H. B. (1980). Sally's corner: Coping with unmarried motherhood, *Journal of Social Issues, 36*, 107-129.

Ricketts, E. B., & Sawhill, I. V. (1988). Defining and measuring the underclass *Journal of Policy Analysis and Management, 7*(2), 316-325.

Schilling, R. F., II. (1987). Limitations of social support, *Social Service Review, 61*(1), 19-31.

Stack, C. (1974). *All our kin: Strategies for survival in a black community*. New York: Harper & Row.

Staples, R. (1981). The black American family. In C. H. Mendel & R. W. Haberstein (Eds.), *Ethnic families in America: Patterns and variations (2nd ed.), (pp. 217-244). New York: Elsevier.*

U.S. Bureau of the Census. (1987). *Statistical Abstract of the United States: 1988* (108th ed.). Washington, DC: U.S. Department of Commerce.

Weatherley, R. A., & Cartoof, V. G. (1988). Helping single adolescent parents. In C. S. Chelman, E. W. Nunnally, & F. M. Cox (Eds.), *Variant family forms* (pp. 39-55). Newbury Park, CA: Sage.

Wilson, W. J. (1987). *The truly disadvantaged*. Chicago: University of Chicago Press.

Zitner, R., & Miller, S. H. (1980). *Our youngest parents: A study of the use of support services by adolescent mothers*. New York: Child Welfare League of America.

Black Teens Parenting in the Inner City: Problems and Recommendations

SANDRA Y. LEWIS

In recent years, the dramatic increase in the number of teenage parents has become a topic of research and discussion within the fields of health, education, psychology, and social welfare. Professionals in these varied fields have noted the disturbing physical, emotional, developmental, and financial consequences arising when the tasks of caring for and cultivating the development of a child are added to the young person's work of mastering the developmental phase of adolescence. The result is a potentially damaging situation for both the adolescent parent and their child. Add to this potentially damaging situation the elements of black inner-city life and the chances that there will be harmful effects for the parent and child are significantly increased. The challenges faced by black teen parents in the inner city are phenomenal, particularly for the teen mother who usually bears the primary responsibility for the child. In this chapter, problems faced by black teen mothers in the inner city and recommendations for their resolution are outlined. In order to set the scene for this discussion, adolescent development, the general challenges faced by any teen parent, and the conditions of black inner-city life are reviewed.

Adolescence: A Phase of Development

Adolescence, marked by the onset of puberty or entering the teen years, is a dynamic phase. Puberty is the beginning of marked physical changes, a most significant one being the capacity to reproduce. The overall developmental tasks of this phase are identity formation (Erikson, 1968) and preparation for adult independence. Other more specific tasks include developing one's personal moral philosophy through evaluation of values learned during childhood; defining vocational interests and beginning to set a career path; preparing for intimate interpersonal relationships; forming a personal and social role (Bryt, 1979); and solidifying a sexual identity (Kestenbaum, 1979). This general course of development is significantly altered for the adolescent girl who becomes a parent.

The Consequences of Adolescent Parenthood

The physical fact that the adolescent has reproduced in no way indicates readiness to rear children (i.e., to care for and facilitate a child's growth and development). Most teenage parents have yet to develop a sense of their identity and life goals. Early introduction to parenthood interrupts their development.

Adolescent parents experience delays in completing their education (Barret & Robinson, 1985; Card & Wise, 1978; Furstenberg, 1976; McGee, 1982). Though many attempt to complete their education, they may eventually drop out due to the demands of parenting. This decreases the probability that the adolescent will acquire the skills necessary for employment and economic self-sufficiency. Their development is compromised, as they may be unable to meet the demands of a society that requires advanced education and skills (Gibbs, 1984). They end up in menial, low-paying jobs (Barret & Robinson, 1985; Card & Wise, 1978).

Adolescent mothers are at high risk for medical complications of pregnancy. Factors such as low socioeconomic status, physical immaturity, poor nutrition, and inadequate prenatal care (often occurring with adolescent pregnancy) increase their medical risk

(Menken, 1980). Problems such as toxemia, prolonged labor, and anemia are common among teenage mothers (Menken, 1980; Robertson, 1981). Their babies often have low birth weight (Menken, 1980) and, as such, are more susceptible to various handicaps or even death. Baldwin and Cain (1980) indicate that children of teen parents suffer more cognitive deficits, are more likely to become teen parents themselves, and are more adversely affected when the teen father is not involved. When the father is involved, babies evidence less behavior problems (Barret & Robinson, 1985).

Pregnancy and parenthood can be linked to complications in the adolescent's emotional development. Adolescent mothers may feel intense joy at the thought of caring for and loving an infant (Hatcher, 1973) whose return of love is perceived as unconditional. The baby becomes the adolescent mother's expression of her need to remain dependent or to satisfy her unmet dependency needs (Fisher & Scharf, 1980). She may see nourishing the baby as nourishing herself or being nurtured by her mother. Boundaries between mother and baby may become blurred. Or, the baby may be the girl's proof of autonomy or womanhood (Hatcher, 1973; Ladner, 1971).

In all likelihood the relationship between the teen parents is transformed. Marriage is not likely to be a successful alternative. Teen marriages are associated with greater likelihood of dropping out of school, welfare dependency, and marital instability (Card & Wise, 1978; Furstenberg, 1976; McGee 1982).

Teenage parenthood has also been associated with difficulties in regulating family size (Furstenberg, 1976). Those who bear children in their teens tend to have more children, to have them closer together, and have more unwanted children (Trussel & Menken, 1978) than those who wait until their 20s. They are also more likely to exceed their family size preference (Card & Wise, 1978).

In summary, teenage parenthood yields negative consequences for the teen mother (Card & Wise, 1978) and child. It interrupts her development and taxes her internal resources. The stresses of adolescence and mothering are compounded, spawning the need for a number of support services. McGee (1982) notes the most needy young mother is likely to be poor or on welfare, lacking family support, and lacking adequate housing. This profile is further complicated by minority status and other conditions of inner-city life described below.

The Realities of Black Inner-City Life

It has been well-documented in the literature (Billingsley, 1968; Edelman, 1989; Franklin, 1982; Hill, 1989; Hines, 1988; Hines & Boyd-Franklin, 1982; Nobles & Goddard, 1989) that black inner-city life is plagued by poverty, racism, unemployment, inadequate housing, homelessness, poor education, poor health care, and the drug culture. The circumstances of inner-city life lead black families to seek government support to obtain food, shelter, medical attention, and education and job training. Governmental assistance such as welfare or temporary shelter is not likely to be sufficient to meet a family's basic needs and is less likely to help them better their circumstances. The family's life cycle is punctuated by numerous crises and their adaptive abilities are stretched beyond what is thought to be humanly possible (Hines, 1988). They become vulnerable to emotional, physical, and environmental crises. Pinderhughes (1982) describes the resulting phenomenon as the "victim system" (p. 109). Barriers to educational and other opportunities limit chances for skill development and employment. When this occurs one is unable to adequately provide for oneself and/or one's family. Family relationships become stressed, which retards individual growth and hence the capacity of individuals to organize communities that offer adequate resources. The resultant disorganized community, with inadequate employment, educational, financial, and housing resources, breeds crime and other forms of pathology (Pinderhughes, 1982).

Though there has not been a systematic analysis of the impact of inner-city life upon the development of black adolescents (Franklin, 1982), some writers have indicated that such conditions impede individual as well as family and community development (Hines, 1988; Pinderhughes, 1982). Inner-city life forces one to develop coping strategies that may be maladaptive in mainstream society (Pinderhughes, 1982) and may serve to perpetuate one's condition (Hines, 1988). The adolescent's attempt at independence and control over his or her life may be marked by oppositional behavior, materialism, or even withdrawal. The stresses of inner-city life truncate the adolescent's successful completion of crucial developmental tasks, namely differentiation of self, establishment of oneself in work, and development of intimate peer relationships (Hines, 1988).

These observations lead one to concur with Gibbs (1984) in her description of black youth as an "endangered species" (p. 6). When one considers these startling factors and the challenges faced by any adolescent mother, the life of a black teen mother in the inner-city presents many issues.

Black Teen Mothers in the Inner City: A Special Issue

A Black teen mother in the inner city is surrounded by the conditions noted above. Though she may hope for the ideal American dream of happy married life, stable home, and healthy family, her hopes are dimmed by the harsh realities of her environment (Franklin, 1982). She may become dependent on the welfare system for financial and medical supplements that do not meet her needs or those of her child. The inadequacy of housing and financial resources often leads to frequent moves by a teen and her infant (Furstenberg, Brooks-Gunn, & Morgan, 1987). Homelessness is familiar to black inner-city life (Hill, 1989) and black teen mothers are unfortunately susceptible to this condition.

Edelman (1989) gives a detailed description of poor black families' limited access to adequate health care. Poverty, along with cutbacks in Medicaid, have played a major role in the declining health status of black infants and children. Thus the black teen mother living in the impoverished inner-city is likely to be faced with difficulties in securing proper health care for herself and her child. Her child faces far greater health risks than white children (Edelman, 1989).

As noted earlier, poor black families interface with a number of governmental and social agencies to meet their basic needs. Many report intrusive prying by these agencies. Child welfare authorities can be particularly threatening due to their power to remove children and place them in foster care (Boyd-Franklin, 1989). In my clinical experience, I have found this to be a fear of many black teen mothers. This fear may reinforce an already low sense of confidence in her ability to provide for her child. She often fears that the all-consuming demands of meeting basic survival needs and parenting may lead her to lose control and neglect or abuse her child. Thus she would become the reason authorities would re-move her child.

My clinical experience also reveals that, when asked about their wishes for their children's futures, black teen mothers express the desire to have their children grow up healthily, complete school, establish themselves in careers and have an ideal family complete with a happy marriage and healthy children. However, they fear the lack of resources (e.g., economic, social support) will prohibit their children from achieving these goals. They fear their children will be swayed by the quick highs and fast money of the drug culture and end up dead or in jail. They also often express the fear their children will repeat their mistake and become parents much too soon.

This latter fear is often the story of the teen's life. They, like their mothers and sometimes their grandmothers, became parents much too soon. Boyd-Franklin (1989) notes that often, in black families, when a teenager gives birth, her offspring may be reared as her sibling. The grandmother may be referred to by the child as "Mommy" or "Mama" while the actual mother is referred to by her first name. Though this arrangement may prove advantageous while the teenager is young, as she becomes an adult and wants to take over as mother of her child, neither her mother nor child may be agreeable to this change in roles (Boyd-Franklin, 1989). This pattern, too, may have multigenerational roots (Bowen, 1976). The teen mother may have been reared by her grandmother, having more of a sibling relationship with her own mother. Her mother's assumption of the role as mother to the teen's child may be the mother's opportunity to function as "mother." Such blurring of roles is frequently the making of family conflicts. The result may be decreased family support for a child and young mother continu-ally struggling with developmental and parenting issues in an environment that breeds crisis. The loss of family increases their vulnerability to physical and/or emotional disorder unless there are other resources (e.g., other family, social services) to help the teen mother and her child buffer themselves against crises.

Following is a case example that illustrates a number of issues noted above, as they occurred in the life of one black teen mother parenting in the inner city. This case illustrates the cycle of crises faced by this mother as well as the resources that proved useful in helping her master these crises.

Case Example

Dawn, age 14, resided with her mother and three younger brothers. She has a history of foster placements with various relatives and was allegedly sexually abused by her mother's live-in paramour. At age 14, Dawn became pregnant, as her mother had at age 14. Dawn's pregnancy progressed with some complications. The small size of the fetus per sonogram evaluation led physicians to question her due date and Dawn was required to have a number of sonograms. During the 7-10 days before she delivered, her cervix began to dilate and she was hospitalized. Concerns about the baby continued. The first time Dawn went into labor, her labor was halted due to concerns over prematurity. After an amniocentesis revealed the fetus had reached term, Dawn's labor was induced and she delivered a 5 lb. 11 oz. boy. Due to the inadequacy of her mother's home, child welfare authorities placed Dawn and her son with a maternal aunt.

Dawn and her aunt had a conflictual relationship as well as financial problems. Dawn was unable to get back into school. She eventually left her aunt's home and proceeded on a course of moving from one place to another. She was able to receive public assistance and help from the baby's father's family. However, the father also had responsibility for a second baby born approximately three weeks after Dawn's son.

Within one year after her son's birth, Dawn had a second trimester abortion. This proved to be quite a difficult experience for her. She had denied pregnancy for months, though her therapist questioned her about the possibility due to her irregular periods. Within months after the abortion, Dawn was diagnosed with a "cervical dysplasia" and had to undergo a copolscopy.

Dawn had utilized both individual and parent-child group psychotherapy but discontinued. She occasionally calls and visits her former psychotherapist. During one visit, she revealed that her great-grandmother had died, her mother had disappeared, and her grandmother was psychiatrically hospitalized.

Dawn and her son now live with a cousin, his wife and six children. She works occasionally but depends primarily on welfare support. She is now involved in a federally-funded program through the Welfare Department, which aims to help teen parents become self-sufficient.

Contacts with Dawn's son reveal him to be a bright, verbal, pleasant, and aware little boy whose play is quite imaginative. Though she is at times challenged by him, she has found appropriate means of disciplining him and encouraging his growth. At times when she has needed a break, she has put him in the care of trustworthy relatives. Though she continues to face many challenges, Dawn manages to secure the resources she needs.

Dawn's case may seem extreme, yet it is very much the norm of black teen mothers parenting in the inner city. These young parents have a number of service needs.

Services for Black Teen Parents

The needs of black teens who are parenting in the inner city are rooted in the social issues of poverty and racism that have spawned problems such as unemployment, poor education, poor housing, poor health and nutrition, and the drug culture. For the black teen parent, inner-city life, the tasks of adolescence, and the responsibility of child rearing represent a fierce, stress-inducing combination, often resulting in a vicious cycle of crises. Black teen parents need community leaders and organizations to make their neighborhoods safe. Their high probability of poor health due to poverty leaves them in greater need of health-related services during and after pregnancy. They are likely to need assistance securing adequate housing. Gibbs (1984) notes that, in order for the teen to complete her education, child care services are essential. Thus these services play a role in breaking the cycle of black teen parents dropping out of school, failing to develop essential skills for employment, becoming unemployed and depending on welfare for a long term. Career education and training also are imperative to eventual economic self-sufficiency for the black adolescent parent.

Since it is highly probable that the black adolescent parent initially will be forced to seek welfare assistance, welfare policies must be such that teens do not get caught in the cycle of dependence. McGee (1982) notes concern that welfare policies often allow a teen mother to establish her own household when she is too young to manage the responsibility. This leaves her at higher risk for experiencing a greater number of problems.

Black teen parents in the inner-city need various counseling and support services such as family planning, parenting skills, support groups, and individual counseling. Since the problem of teen parenting is often a multigenerational issue, interventions that involve grandparents are indicated. Of course, though black teen fathers in the inner city have not been discussed here, their needs for adequate education, employment, and other services to facilitate adequate parenting must be addressed. They must be involved in programs with their female counterparts.

Lastly, prevention programs are especially essential to black teens in the inner city. The realities of their environment severely complicate their development. Coordinated community efforts are imperative to address environmental issues. Primary and secondary prevention programs aimed at preventing teenage pregnancy as well as unemployment, poor health, involvement in the drug culture, and poor education must be addressed.

Recommendations and Summary

The needs of black teens parenting in the inner city dictate development of comprehensive service programs (Gibbs, 1984; McGee, 1982; Salguero, Yearwood, Phillips, & Schlesinger, 1980), or at least strong linkages between existing service agencies to coordinate utilization of their resources. These teens require availability of and easy accessibility to health, educational, social, and psychological services (McGee, 1982), as well as family support. Services should include: (1) pregnancy testing; (2) maternal counseling regarding options; (3) prenatal and postnatal care; (4) referral to needed health services or provision of health services; (5) family planning counseling and services; (6) educational and vocational referrals and/or services; (7) mental health services; (8) assistance with housing; (9) child care or referral to child care; (10) transportation and outreach; (11) education about parenting and life skills; (12) parent-child interaction groups; (13) outreach to and counseling with families of teen parents; (14) liaison with or involvement of the welfare department; and (15) pregnancy prevention. Services must be extended to teen mothers, teen fathers, and their families. McGee (1982) cites a comprehensive program located in prior elementary school in Michigan. The program includes child care, a preschool, and family resource center. Various forms of education and counseling are provided to teen mothers, teen fathers, and their parents. These include academics, parenting education, and job preparation.

Currently in Chicago, Illinois; Camden, New Jersey; and Newark, New Jersey, there are federally funded programs (Ott, 1988) that aim to break the welfare dependency cycle among teen mothers and help them become economically self-sufficient. The programs assist teen mothers in linking to needed medical or psychological services, completing their education, getting job training and job placement, and securing child care. Transportation, parenting education, life skills education and planned parenthood classes are provided.

This chapter has detailed the plight of black teens parenting in the inner city. Their needs as well as recommendations for meeting them have been outlined. Though the major recommendation has been for comprehensive service programs, I agree with Gibbs (1984) that the ultimate resolution rests with implementation of social policies that demonstrate concern for families and the annihilation of racism and poverty in our society. Until this can be achieved, it is incumbent upon professionals to dedicate their skills and effort to break the cycle of problems faced by black teens parenting in the inner city.

References

Baldwin, W., & Cain, V. S. (1980). The children of teenage parents. *Family Planning Perspectives, 1,* 34-43.

Barret, R. L., & Robinson, B. E. (1985). The adolescent father. In S. Hanson & F. Bezette (Eds.), *Dimensions of fatherhood* (pp. 353-368). Newbury Park, CA: Sage.

Billingsley, A. (1968). *Black families in white America.* Englewood Cliffs, NJ: Prentice-Hall.

Bowen, M. (1976). Theory in the practice of psychotherapy. In P. J. Guerin (Ed.), *Family therapy: Theory and practice* (pp. 42-90). New York: Gardener.

Boyd-Franklin, N. (1989). *Black families in therapy: A multisystems approach.* New York: Guilford.

Aryt, A. (1979). Developmental tasks in adolescence. In S. C. Feinstein & P. L. Giovacchini (Eds.), *Adolescent Psychiatry: Developmental and Clinical Studies* (Vol. 7) (pp. 136-146). Chicago: University of Chicago Press.

Card, J. J., & Wise, L. L. (1978). Teenage mothers and teenager fathers: The impact c early childbearing on the parents' personal and professional lives. *Family Plar ning Perspectives, 10,* 199-207.

Edelman, M. W. (1989). Black children in America. In J. Dewart (Ed.), *The state black America* (pp. 63-76). New York: National Urban League.

Erikson, E. H. (1968). *Identity, youth and crisis.* New York: Norton.

Fisher, S. M., & Scharf, K. D. (1980). Teenage pregnancy: An anthropological, soci logical, and psychological overview. In S. C. Feinstein, P. L. Giovacchini, J. (Looney, A. Z. Schwartzberg, & A. D. Sorosky (Eds.), *Adolescent psychiatry: Deve opmental and clinical studies* (Vol. 8, pp. 393-403). Chicago: University of Chicag Press.

Franklin, A. J. (1982). Therapeutic interventions with urban black adolescents. I E. E. Jones & S. J. Korchin (Eds.), *Minority mental health* (pp. 267-295). New Yor Praeger.

Furstenberg, F. F. (1976). The social consequences of teenage parenthood. *Fami Planning Perspectives, 8,* 148-164.

Furstenberg, Jr., F. F., Brooks-Gunn, J., & Morgan, S. P. (1987). *Adolescent mothers later life.* Cambridge: Cambridge University Press.

Gibbs, J. T. (1984). Black adolescents and youth: An endangered species. *America Journal of Orthopsychiatry, 54,* 6-21.

Hatcher, S. L. (1973). The adolescent experience of pregnancy and abortion: developmental analysis. *Journal of Youth and Adolescence, 2,* 53-102.

Hill, R. B. (1989). Critical issues for black families by the year 2000. In J. Dewa (Ed.), *The state of black America* (pp. 41-61). New York: National Urban League.

Hines, P. M. (1988). The family life cycle of poor black families. In B. Carter M. McGoldrick (Eds.), *The changing family life cycle: A framework for family therap* (2nd ed.), (pp. 513-544). New York: Gardener.

Hines, P. M., & Boyd-Franklin, N. (1982). Black families. In M. McGoldrick, J. I Pearce, & J. Giordano (Eds.), *Ethnicity and family therapy* (pp. 84-107). New Yor Guilford.

Kestenbaum, C. J. (1979). Current sexual attitudes, societal pressure, and t middle-class adolescent girl. In S. C. Feinstein & P. L. Giovacchini (Eds.), *Adol cent psychiatry: Developmental and clinical studies* (Vol. 7, pp. 147-156). Chicag University of Chicago Press.

Ladner, J. (1971). *Tomorrow's tomorrow: The black woman.* Garden City, NY: Doub day.

McGee, E. A. (1982). *Too little, too late: Services for teenage parents.* New York: Fo Foundation.

Menken, J. (1980). The health and demographic consequences of adolescent pre nancy and childbearing. In C. S. Chilman, *Adolescent pregnancy and childbearir Findings from research* (pp. 177-205). Washington, DC: U.S. Department of Heal and Human Services.

Nobles, W. W., & Goddard, L. L. (1989). Drugs in the African-American communi A clear and present danger. In J. Dewart (Ed.), *The state of black America* (p 161-181). New York: National Urban League.

Ott, D. (1988, January 26). Camden program seeks to break the welfare cycle. *T Philadelphia Inquirer,* pp. 1-2B.

Pinderhughes, E. (1982). Afro-American families and the victim system. In M. Mc-Goldrick, J. K. Pearce, & J. Giordano (Eds.), *Ethnicity and family therapy* (pp. 108-122). New York: Guilford.

Robertson, E. G. (1981). Adolescence, physiological maturity, and obstetric outcome. In K. G. Scott, T. Field, & E. G. Robertson (Eds.), *Teenage parents and their offspring* (pp. 91-101). New York: Grune & Stratton.

Salguero, C., Yearwood, E., Phillips, E., & Schlesinger, N. (1980). Studies of infants at risk and their adolescent mothers. In S. C. Feinstein, P. L. Giovacchini, J. G. Looney, A. Z. Schwartzberg, & A. D. Sorosky (Eds.), *Adolescent psychiatry: Developmental and clinical studies* (Vol. 8, pp. 404-421). Chicago: University of Chicago Press.

Trussel, J., & Menken, J. (1978). Early childbearing and subsequent fertility. *Family Planning Perspectives, 10,* 209-218.

11

Pregnant and Parenting Black Adolescents: Theoretical and Policy Perspectives

WILLIAM MARSIGLIO

JOHN H. SCANZONI

Introduction

During the past few decades, high pregnancy and fertility rate among black adolescents, and the related upswing in the propor tion of black households headed by young single women, hav become increasingly central issues in the social and political de bates over the quality of life and life chances for young blacl Americans (Smith, 1988; Wilson, 1987). Interest in these issues ha been heightened also by the growing concern among the public a large, the social service community, and researchers over the prev alence of adolescent pregnancy and childbearing[1] in general. Th recent two-volume report *Risking the Future,* commissioned by th National Academy of Sciences in 1987, is the most compreher sive project to date addressing these issues. While it does not e> plore fertility-related events in the context of the black communit directly, the report examines black-white differences in sexualit abortion, pregnancy, childbearing, and family formation pattern Without dismissing the seriousness of the problem within th black community, the findings of this report also help refute the popular myth that teenage pregnancy and childbearing are primarily or exclusively "black" problems (Furstenberg, 1987).

The aim of this chapter is to review and assess recent research, social interventions, theory, and policy that deal with postconception fertility events among black adolescents.[2] First, we describe recent demographic trends and explanations for marital and nonmarital pregnancy, abortion, childbearing, and family formation patterns among adolescent blacks in the United States. Second, we discuss how the social and subcultural context influences the quality of life and life chances of pregnant and parenting black adolescents. Finally, we illustrate how competing theoretical views on life-course patterns shape the issues pertaining to the well-being of young blacks who are responsible for teenage pregnancies and births and the well-being of their children. In this context, we discuss some of the implications these theoretical interpretations have for contemporary policy and programmatic initiatives.

Fertility-Related Events among Black Adolescents: A Social Demographic Perspective

Social demographers have used numerous national data sources during the past two decades to document rates of black adolescent pregnancy, abortion, childbearing, and family formation (Furstenberg, 1987; Moore, Sims, & Betsey, 1986; see also Hofferth & Hayes, 1987 for a review of the relevant data sets). In addition to documenting these patterns for blacks, a concerted effort has been made to identify and explain racial differences in fertility-related outcomes and behaviors. Because others have written about these issues extensively (Hayes, 1987; Hofferth & Hayes, 1987; Moore, Simms, & Betsey, 1986), we provide only a brief summary.

Previous research has shown that black adolescent pregnancy and childbearing rates have been extremely high during the past two decades. For example, one conservative estimate based on several national data sources for 1981 suggested that among black females, 40.7% experienced a pregnancy (marital and nonmarital) before the age of 18 and 63.1% became pregnant before their 20th birthday (cited in Hofferth and Hayes, 1987, p. 420). The

comparable figures for whites were 20.5% and 39.7%, respectively
Among black teens who become pregnant, about 41% choose to
have an abortion while 47% of whites who became pregnant have
an abortion.

Among black women in 1986, 7% of 15-17 year olds and 14.1% o
18-19 year old women gave birth to a child irrespective of their
marital status at conception or birth (Moore, 1988). These figures
are slightly lower than comparable 1970 figures that represent the
period immediately preceding the legalization of abortion, 10.1%
and 20.5% respectively. While adolescent birthrates may have actu
ally declined slightly in recent years, the percentage of births born
to women outside of wedlock has increased significantly for both
blacks and whites. The percentage of live first births conceived and
born out of wedlock to 15-19 year old black women in the early
1980s has increased sharply during the past 30 years (O'Connell &
Rogers, 1984). Whereas 46.6% of live births to 15-19 year old black
women were conceived and born out of wedlock during 1950-1954
a conservative estimate for 1980-1981 was 87.9%. Moore (1988
reports the figure as 90% for 1988. This trend represents almost
90% increase in the proportion of first-born black babies conceive
and born out of wedlock and is partly accounted for by the fac
that in 1980-1981 only 8.5% of young black women married pric
to the birth of their nonmaritally conceived first child in contrast t
18.3% in 1950 and 19.8% in 1965-1969. Thus the vast majority c
young black pregnant women have been reluctant to marry durin
the past several decades. Adolescent blacks today are only half a
likely to "legitimate" a pregnancy in this way than they were 20 c
30 years ago. Moreover, in 1984, black females 15-19 had almos
four times as many births out of wedlock as did whites (Nationa
Center for Health Statistics NCHS, 1986), although these rates an
converging due largely to the elevated rate of out of wedlock birth
to whites. Almost all of these 15-19 year old black mothers kep
their child; less than 1% of them opted for adoption in 1982 accorc
ing to national estimates, whereas 7.4% of young white and othe
women allowed adoption (Bachrach, 1986).

While most research on teenage childbearing has focused on fir
births, the pace of repeat childbearing among young mothers ar
the implications of additional births is an important issue as we
Using a national sample of women aged 18-26 in 1983, Mott (198
found that 30% of black women who had their first child at age

or younger had an additional birth within 24 months and 45% had another birth within 36 months. An inverse relationship existed between the age of black mothers at first birth and the probability of an additional birth within the 2- and 3-year intervals. For example, 21% of black mothers who had their first child when they were either 17 or 18 had an additional child within 24 months, and 34% had another child within 36 months. An important finding of this study was that age at first childbearing was not related to the probability of having a second birth within 24 or 36 months for whites when a series of background factors were controlled; however, age at first childbearing was a significant predictor of repeat childbearing among blacks. Because the relationship between age at first childbearing and subsequent fertility among blacks persisted in a multivariate context, Mott concluded that these racial differentials must be due to "relatively subtle cultural, social or economic variations" and not simply factors such as marriage rates, desire for children, and other standard sociodemographic and socioeconomic factors associated with race.

Since young mothers' household living arrangements will influence their available resources, it is instructive to describe those arrangements. Using 1980 Census data, Trent & Harlan (1987) reported the following patterns among black teenage mothers: mother-husband (9.3%); mother-only (10%), mother-parents (26.7%); mother-mother (36.2%); mother-other relatives (13.5%); and other (4.3%). Almost 86% of the households in which a teenage mother was living on her own, and 61% of households where the teen mother was living with her mother, were categorized below the federal poverty line. On the other hand, teen mothers who fared the best economically were those who lived with both parents since only 26.7% of these types of households were living in poverty.

Not surprisingly, similar fertility and family formation patterns to those noted earlier were found when adolescent fathers were examined. One national study reported that 14.8% of young black males 20-27 years of age in 1984 had fathered a child when they were a teenager with 14.2% having been responsible for a nonmaritally conceived first child (Marsiglio, 1987). Twenty-three percent of this sample of adolescent fathers were 11-16 years of age when their nonmaritally conceived child was born. Furthermore, only 15% of the black fathers responsible for a nonmaritally conceived child lived with their child shortly after the child's birth.

Prevailing Explanations

Attempts to explain these fertility-related patterns for blacks have frequently used white patterns as a benchmark (Hofferth, 1985). A structural explanation of these patterns stresses the implications of poor economic conditions of many black youth and families (Betsey, Holister, & Papageorgiou, 1985; Freeman & Holzer, 1985; Johnson & Sum, 1987; Moore, Simms, & Betsey, 1986; Sandefur & Tienda, 1988; Wilson & Neckerman, 1986). According to this model, dismal economic conditions shape individuals' attitudes and expectations as well as curtail their human capital potential. The opportunity costs associated with a school-age pregnancy or birth are therefore not as high for those raised in a disadvantaged economic background as they would be for individuals from a more affluent environment. Moreover, the obstacles preventing young parents from establishing a formal and stable coresidential arrangement, with or without getting married, appear to be formidable due to the perceived or actual poor economic prospects of many young black fathers. Young black male high school dropouts and graduates age 20-24 experienced a 61% and 52% reduction, respectively, in their real annual earnings between 1973 and 1984 (Johnson & Sum, 1987). In 1984, only 12% of these black male dropouts and 30% of the high school graduates had earnings above the three-person poverty line.

While the structural model focuses on the impact of structured inequalities that affect blacks disproportionately, such as those due to the restructuring of the economy, the major thesis of a second—subcultural—model is that blacks as a group, to a large extent irrespective of class, tend to espouse different sexuality and family-related values, norms, and attitudes. These views in turn produce unique pregnancy, childbearing, and family formation patterns. From this perspective, the black community is thought to hold less traditional views about adolescent sexual activity, marriage, and early childbearing than do whites. These views may be the strongest in urban ghetto areas since young black males (and females) residing here encounter considerable peer pressure to engage in early sexual activity (Ladner, 1971; Staples, 1978; see also Fursten-berg, Brooks-Gunn, & Morgan, 1987). Black youth also report a desired age for childbearing that is younger than their desired age for marriage and a greater willingness to consider nonmarital childbearing (Abrahamse, Morrison, & Waite, 1988; Cherlin, 1981; Clark, Zabin, & Hardy, 1984; Heiss, 1981; see also Moore, Simms, & Betsey, 1986). Given this constellation of values and norms, engag-ing in early sexual activity, having a nonmarital pregnancy and birth, and opting for a pregnancy resolution/family formation de-cision that does not involve marriage or a coresidential arrange-ment, have all been more viable options among blacks than whites because blacks have been stigmatized less severely by their same-race reference groups (Moore, Simms, & Betsey, 1986; Zelnik, Kan-ter, & Ford, 1981).

A third explanation, and one that is illustrated in Figure 11.1, suggests that both social structural and subcultural factors are im-portant and interrelated. This model posits that housing segrega-tion and the decline of the urban industrial base, especially within impoverished neighborhoods inhabited by blacks, facilitates the emergence and perpetuation of a subcultural climate wherein less conventional values and norms about the appropriate context and timing of sexuality/fertility flourish and less traditional values and norms regarding the institutions of education, work, and fam-ily prevail. While impressionistic evidence suggests that this model as applied to the inner city has a rather strong following in popular culture, it is sometimes questioned in the research commu-nity. For instance, at least one ethnographer has shown that it is common for inner-city black communities to facilitate the informal establishment of paternity and the informal involvement of the young father in child support arrangements (Sullivan, 1985; see also Adams & Pittman, 1988; Stack, 1974). Such a pattern suggests that the black community may have informal mechanisms that produce results similar to the more institutionalized strategies found more typically among whites. The extent to which this inte-grated model has similar implications for blacks living in predom-inately middle-class neighborhoods outside the central city is a challenging empirical question that deserves research attention. It is interesting to note in this context that some evidence suggests that family income is not related to adolescent childbearing among black females (Hogan & Kitagawa, 1985) or males (Hanson, Morrison, & Ginsburg, 1989).

Quality of Life and Life Options

Much has been written about the negative social, psychological, health, and economic consequences associated with pregnant and childbearing adolescents, both in the academic literature (Hayes, 1987; Hofferth & Hayes, 1987) and the popular media (Diamant, 1986; Klein, 1984). Although Frazier had described it in 1939, the public began to view early childbearing among blacks as an issue during the mid 1960s when a relationship was alleged between black family structure and poverty (Glazer, 1965; Moynihan, 1965). During the 1980s, public recognition of and reaction to adolescent pregnancy/fertility patterns (and related behavior patterns) for both blacks and whites has elevated these issues collectively to the status of a social problem, although the prevailing public view may still be that this problem is one restricted primarily to inner-city areas with large black populations. The perceived seriousness of this social problem, from the perspective of specific class and racial groups, will depend in part upon the assessment of two factors. To what extent do early fertility-related events violate norms regarding the sequencing of institutionalized life-course transitions, and to what extend do these events negatively affect the short- and long-term life options and quality of life for a large number of adolescents (and their children)?

A conceptual model for our review is presented in Figure 11.1. It illustrates how a variety of factors may affect the well-being and life options of pregnant and parenting teens. This model also indicates the significance of limited resources. The first and most important pertain to structural features of our society and local communities (e.g., labor market opportunities, gender ratios, and poverty and school completion rates). On an aggregate level, a recent study indicated that high poverty rates, low social completion rates, low public welfare expenditures, and high unemployment rates were significant predictors of state adolescent fertility rates in the United States (S. L. Zimmerman, 1988). Social policies and programs designed to assist youth in life-course transition

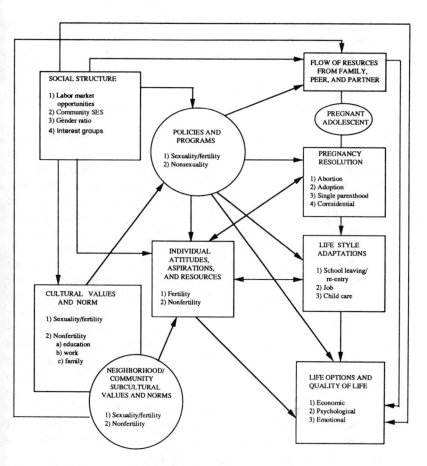

Figure 11.1. Conceptual Model for Pregnant and Parenting Adolescents'
Life Options and Quality of Life

areas, both fertility-related (e.g., child care, abortion, supplemental
child support provided by the government as an incentive for
young fathers to complete high school) and nonfertility-related
(e.g., GED programs, work-skills training programs, remedial education), are an important component of the social structure, as are
more general public policies dealing with welfare expenditures.

The second variable involves the subcultural values and norms
characteristic of blacks in general and local communities inhabited

by blacks in particular. The values/norms of interest here relate to the acceptability and appropriate timing of sexual activity and fertility relative to other life-course transitions and developmental stages (e.g., completing high school, marriage, stage of moral development). In addition, nonfertility-related values/norms dealing with the education, work, and family institutions will influence how early pregnancies and childbearing are handled. While a critical, thorough analysis of values and norms within the black community is beyond the scope of our purposes here, it is important to recognize that considerable debate exists as to the extent to which social class distinguishes the belief and normative systems among blacks as it does among whites (Furstenberg, 1987; Marsiglio, 1989, Moore, Simms, & Betsey, 1986). Given this debate, we draw a distinction between the types of values and norms most representative of blacks as a racial minority group from those specific to a given community/neighborhood. We feel the latter will be more important in shaping individuals' attitudes, life aspirations, and fertility-related behaviors, especially when the proportion of blacks living in the area is high (see Hogan & Kitagawa, 1985; Wilson, 1987).

Black community values and norms, particularly those found within the immediate neighborhood, also should influence the flow of nonmaterial support/advice and tangible resources from family and peers to pregnant teens and adolescent parents. This support will be utilized when teens make pregnancy resolution decisions (e.g., abortion, adoption, single parenthood, coresidential or marriage commitments) and life-style adaptations to accommodate their new circumstances (e.g., dropping out or reentering school, finding a job, altering leisure activities with friends, performing childcare tasks).

Although pregnancy resolution and family formation decisions are likely to have short- and long-term implications for the lives of young parents and their children, and perhaps other relatives as well (Hofferth & Hayes, 1987; see also Brazzell & Acock, 1988, for a series of references on specific consequences), little research has considered the decision-making process in these areas (see Hofferth, 1987b, for a social demographic perspective). Previous research with young unmarried pregnant women indicated that significant others were involved at various stages of the pregnancy resolution process (Cortroneo & Krasner, 1977; Evans, Selstad, &

Welcher, 1976; Freeman, 1978; Hudis & Brazzell, 1981; Rosen, 1980; M. K. Zimmerman, 1977). Rosen (1980) found in her study of 432 unmarried pregnant women (black and white) under 18 years of age, that the mothers of these teenagers assumed a prominent role in the pregnancy resolution process in more than 50% of the cases. Parents also appeared to be more important than peers in influencing prospective mothers' behaviors (Hudis & Brazzell, 1981; Rosen, 1980).

The notion that black families are generous in their level of assistance to teenage and young adult single mothers, more so than are whites, is an idea entrenched in the literature and public discourse although it is based more on impressionistic rather than empirical evidence. One national study in 1984 of black and white young mothers age 19-26 (only some of whom had given birth to a child while they were a teenager), did find that participation in a kin support network (either living in an extended family situation, or receiving half or more of one's total income from kin, or receiving unpaid childcare from kin) was much more common for black than white young mothers (Hogan, Hao, & Parish, 1988). While blacks were more likely to coreside with adult kinfolk than whites—the primary means by which they were involved in a kin support network—they were less likely to receive substantial income support after controlling for marital status, fertility history, and kin proximity. The researchers concluded that the prevailing notion about black family support patterns should be qualified. Extended family support systems are an important source of assistance for black families, but black families are not particularly well-suited to cope with the difficulties associated with single parenthood. Black families are probably more likely than whites to be involved in extended support arrangements because they find themselves disproportionately involved in situations that require additional assistance.

In addition to the flow of advice and resources from family and peers, pregnancy resolution decisions are likely to be influenced directly and indirectly by three additional factors: social structure (especially labor market opportunities for black youth), fertility-related policies/programs, and individuals' own personal attitudes, aspirations, and resources. The particular choice an individual/couple makes about resolving a pregnancy and, if need be, choices made about formal or informal family formation arrangements, will in turn influence the kinds of life-style changes that will be adapted as a response to new life circumstances and contingencies. The life-style adaptations that are required, and the extent and manner in which they are supported formally and informally, will affect individuals' life options and quality of life economically, psychologically, and emotionally, both in the short- and long-term. Finally, individuals' own attitudes, aspirations, and resources also will shape individuals' life experiences in the areas of work, education, and family.

Most of the research that examines the relationship between early childbearing and young parents' life options and quality of life has concentrated on the social and economic consequences of fertility-related events from a social demographic or life-course perspective for young mothers (Hofferth, 1987c) and to a much lesser extent, young fathers (Marsiglio, 1987; Parke & Neville 1987). Some research has assessed how young single black women's parenting styles, coping strategies, and available resources influence children's developmental outcomes (Franklin 1988; see also Hofferth, 1987d). Unfortunately, little attention has been given to the possible psychological and emotional ramifications of early childbearing and social support for young parents (Colletta & Lee, 1983; Thompson, 1986).

At present, we know a great deal about the consequences associated with early childbearing for the population as a whole but our understanding of how racial factors influence adolescent child bearing is not as well developed. Our knowledge of the latter is sketchy at best because researchers have not been able to specify empirically how social structural and social psychological factors are interrelated in this area. More specifically, data collection efforts and research designs have not adequately measured or controlled for socioeconomic status, ecological factors, and subcultural value and normative systems. The question of whether racial differences exist in the type and magnitude of consequences associated with teenage childbearing also remains unanswered (Furstenberg, 1987).

The available evidence indicates that compared to black women who do not have a child during their teen years, black teenage mothers are less likely to complete high school and become self sufficient economically (Furstenberg, Brooks-Gunn, & Morgan 1987; Mott & Marsiglio, 1985). Based on a national sample of women 20-26 years of age in 1983 who had been teenage mothers, Mott and Marsiglio found that among black women, 93% of those who had not become mothers had completed high school (either diploma or GED), whereas only 55% of mothers whose baby was conceived before and born after leaving school for the last time (last drop-out date or graduation) had completed their high school education. The economic hardships associated with adolescent childbearing may also be exacerbated for teenage mothers because they are less likely to limit their family size and more likely to be single mothers (Furstenberg, 1987; Hofferth, 1987c; Mott, 1986). The relationship between marriage as a response to a nonmarital conception and future economic status is complex; it appears though that marriage may enhance a teenage mother's long-term financial situation if the marriage lasts, but marriage may actually produce negative long-term results if divorce occurs, because women who marry and/or move away from their parental home may tend to curtail their educational careers and/or have larger families (Furstenberg & Crawford, 1978; Hofferth, 1987c; McLaughlin, Grady, Billy, Landale, & Winges, 1986).

Research suggests that becoming a mother at a young age has a negative impact on women's later economic well-being net of pre-existing social background factors, a relationship that is mediated primarily by lower educational attainment and larger family size (Hofferth, 1987c). However, in their 17-year follow-up study of 300 teenage black mothers in Baltimore, Furstenberg, Brooks-Gunn, & Morgan (1987) note that the long-term consequences of early motherhood for these women, now in their 30s, were not as dismal as stereotypical images might suggest. Nonetheless, Furstenberg (1987) provides a sobering observation on the life options of many young black women and men. He suggests that black community leaders may be correct in their assessment that the source for early childbearing among many black youth is their despair over future opportunities because the opportunity costs associated with early childbearing are rather low.

After reviewing the few longitudinal studies that have examined the psychological consequences of teenage childbearing, Thompson (1986) concluded that adolescent mothers experience a reduction in their psychological well-being after the birth of their child. This relationship persisted over time irrespective of the number or spacing of children and after controlling for initial differences in mother's education, parental socioeconomic status, and psychological well-being. In her own research with a sample of primarily disadvantaged young mothers who had their child when they were 20 or younger in the late 1970s (the children were infants at the time of the interview), Thompson found that black mothers were less likely to report maternal stress than whites and that this difference was not due to differences in social support. This study also found that more social support is not necessarily better. Perceived support from friends, female siblings, and relatives was related to higher levels of psychological distress, while support from a male partner had the opposite effect. Meanwhile, Colletta and Lee (1983) concluded, based on their study of 64 black adolescent mothers, that social support was positively associated with a decrease in stress and an increase in self-esteem.

In addition to the potential consequences of early childbearing for young black parents, some research has focused on the negative consequences for the children of black teenage mothers. According to Hofferth's (1987d) extensive review, most research has found a direct relationship between mother's age at childbirth and child outcomes, such as intelligence scores on standardized instruments, retention in grade, and socioemotional development (to a lesser extent and with mixed findings for boys and girls), but the magnitude of these relationships has been quite small. A number of studies also have found that the influence of mothers' age on child outcomes has been mediated by family structure, maternal education, and family size. However, little is known about the processes by which these intervening variables influence child outcomes (Franklin, 1988; Hofferth, 1987d). Given the variety of research design limitations that characterize this literature (Hofferth, 1987d), we are unable at this time to draw firm conclusions about the parenting behaviors of young black mothers and the manner in which the complex set of interrelated factors associated with early childbearing influence the child's quality of life and life options. Nonetheless, it seems reasonable to assume that a child's quality of life and life chances will be affected adversely by economic difficulties the young parents encounter, irrespective of the origin of the parents' curtailed economic opportunities or the nature of the transmission process.

Theory and Policy:
Long- and Short-Term Perspectives

From a sociological perspective the theoretical interpretation of these issues, and the accompanying policy initiatives that address them, will depend upon whether static or dynamic aspects of society, the individual life course, and families are emphasized. Ahistorical, homeostatic models consistent with the functionalist tradition (Scanzoni, Polonko, Teachman, & Thompson, 1989) tend to perceive pregnant adolescents, as well as those who become single parents, as deviant because they violate institutionalized norms regarding the sequencing of events involving fertility, education, and marriage. Thus from a static, dominant culture life-course perspective, pregnant and childbearing adolescents experience personal hardships and confront society with a social problem because their fertility-related behavior occurs outside the social controls imposed by institutions of education, work, and family. These "off-time" events tend to be disruptive for both individuals and society because the social system is not designed to accommodate the special needs of pregnant and parenting teens. This theoretical orientation stimulates conservative policy, the intent of which is to ensure the maintenance of the social system by promoting conformity to the prevailing norms regarding pregnancy resolution and family formation. However, this position muddles the relevant issues if an adolescent becomes pregnant since "deviancy" is subject to multiple interpretations. For example, individuals who elect to have an abortion may be viewed as deviant in one respect, but at the same time they are ridding themselves of their deviant pregnant adolescent status. Likewise, cultural scenarios are subject to subcultural influences whereby marrying to "legitimize" a nonmarital conception may actually be perceived as deviant behavior within some sectors of society.

On the other hand, a more dynamic interpretation of life-course patterns, and one sensitive to subcultural influences, would focus on inherent, ongoing dialectical processes that tend to involve competing interest groups (Elder, 1985). Following Simmel and Weber, a fundamental assumption of this dynamic interpretation of the life-course model is that individuals and groups behave in a goal-oriented fashion (i.e., to achieve their own interests as they perceive them within their social environment). Hence to characterize their behavior as "deviant" is to misconstrue totally its theoretical and practical significance. A dialectic orientation does *not* assume merely one appropriate cultural scenario or normative structure for a given area of social life. Thus this model provides the basis for a *progressive* policy approach that is responsive to the fluid character of life-course patterns and varying forms of families (Cherlin, 1983; Scanzoni, 1983; 1989).

Peters and McAdoo (1983) observe that for decades blacks have been moving away from dominant family values, largely because their economic deprivation has made those values/norms unworkable. More recently, growing numbers of whites also have been shifting away from conventional normative patterns because they too find them unworkable. However, for both whites and more advantaged blacks, the "unworkability" is owing not so much to deprivation as it is to what several observers label as *individualism* (Bellah, Madsen, Sullivan, Swidler, & Tipton, 1985; Buunk, 1985; Francouer, 1983; Morgan & Scanzoni, 1987), (i.e., rather than conform to dominant values regarding sexuality and parenting confined to permanent monogamous marriages, persons increasingly pursue sexual/parental interests that they define as vital to them). However, a critical issue arises because most adolescents and some adults (black and white) possess neither the economic nor subjective resources to cope effectively with issues central to pregnancy and parenting.

Reactions of conservative interest groups to this state of affairs are significant in shaping both U.S. policy (broad goals and objectives regarding desirable states) as well as programs (specific mechanisms aimed at attaining those states) in the realm of adolescent pregnancy and childbearing. In the conservative view, if adolescents were to say *no* to sex (i.e., conform to dominant culture traditional norms), then current problems would eventually disappear. As Bauer (1986) make clear, the long-term policy goal of conservatives is a *return* to widespread endorsement and enforcement of adolescent chastity. However, conservatives are aware that it is difficult for them to enforce their view of sexuality at this time.[3] Nevertheless, alongside their long-term policy objective, their short-term policy is to oppose specific programs that would in any way seek to legitimize what they consider deviant cultural norms, namely, that responsible sexuality is good in and of itself, quite apart from any specific arrangements such as marriage (Francouer, 1983). Thus, for example, their opposition to abortion coupled with their refusal to negotiate wide-ranging adolescent contraception programs (Bauer, 1986), leads to the hypothesis that their alleged concern for fetal rights may be a smokescreen to enforce conformity to chastity norms.

From the progressive standpoint, abortion access is an important *short-term* programmatic option to pregnant adolescents' dilemmas. For example, the proportion of teen pregnancies ending in abortion since 1973, the year of the Roe versus Wade decision, has increased by almost 66%. The availability of abortion also has lowered the probability that a teenage female facing a nonmarital conception will have an out of wedlock child or marry in response to her pregnancy (Hofferth, 1987b). At the same time, conservatives and progressives have fashioned an uneasy web of cooperation on some short-term programs to aid pregnant and parenting adolescents, though for very different long-term reasons. Although neither set of interest groups wishes to legitimize the institutionalization of pregnant and parenting adolescents' fertility patterns, both acknowledge (sometimes reluctantly) the need for certain short-term programs. These include, for instance, support of programs such as Title IX of the Education Amendments (1972). This legislation prohibits schools receiving federal funds from discriminating against students on the basis of pregnancy, childbearing, or marital status. Although it is difficult to determine the exact impact of this change, Mott & Maxwell (1981) reported that a higher proportion of adolescent mothers in the late 1970s remained in school compared to their counterparts a decade earlier. In addition to Title IX, an extensive array of programs have been implemented in communities across the country during the past ten years that address pregnant and parenting teens. Some of the more notable ones include programs to improve life planning, life-skills training, alternative schools, employment programs, family care programs, role models and mentoring programs, comprehensive care programs, and adoption services (Hofferth, 1987e). The breadth of these programs reflects the varied perspectives that guide the respective intervention efforts. Professionals working within the context of these programs have focused on issues such as the health consequences of mothers and children, drop-out rates among pregnant and parenting teens, problems of young-parent families, rapid repeat pregnancy rates, increased reliance on abortion, and the increasing use of public assistance by teen mothers.

The life-options approach is an important feature of many of these programs; the basic thrust of this strategy is to help adolescents and young adults develop a stronger commitment to, and a more optimistic view of, their future educational and work plans. Programs that are successful in furthering the educational career of young black mothers are likely to improve the well-being of teen mothers' children as well, although more research is needed to understand how additional schooling for young mothers actually brings about improved child outcomes (Franklin, 1988; Hofferth, 1987d).

Conservatives and many progressives favor making adolescent fathers more accountable for their fertility by incorporating them into programs for pregnant and parenting youth. For example, a Reagan administration program sought to establish paternity and enforce child support payments among as many young fathers as possible (Savage, 1987). However, given the economic difficulties many young black fathers experience in meeting their child support obligations, it would seem that a more constructive approach to promoting male responsibility would be to maximize young black fathers' potential for long-term financial contributions, rather than focusing on meager short-term contributions. This could be accomplished by crediting young males for their efforts to finish high school and/or receive job training (Adams & Pittman, 1988). Such a strategy would provide disadvantaged young fathers with the incentive and an opportunity to fulfill their obligations to their child while at the same time advancing their own life options (see Cherlin, 1988).

While conservatives would welcome greater male involvement in the lives of their child and partner, particularly if it involved marriage, they may be reluctant to modify Aid to Families with Dependent Children (AFDC) regulations to accomplish this goal. In this context, research indicates that public expenditures do *not* increase the pregnancy rate although abortion and family formation decisions may be affected (Hofferth, 1987e). Current AFDC policies in some states act as a disincentive for parents to live together since the young mother's eligibility for AFDC assistance and food stamps is jeopardized if her partner lives with her

(Adams & Pittman, 1988). Since a larger proportion of black women than white women are poor, this policy is likely to have a greater impact on families of blacks than whites. Although only a small proportion of black teenage fathers live with their nonmaritally conceived child after their child is born, some evidence suggests that more would do so if they were given the opportunity (Marsiglio, 1988, 1989; Marsiglio & Menaghan, 1990).

If a policy objective is to have young fathers play a more active role in the support and care of their children, the recently completed Teen Father Collaboration project (Klinman, Sander, Rosen, & Longo, 1986) provides a model for organizing services to assist young fathers. The National Urban League's (1987) campaign for Male Responsibility represents another promising strategy that alerts young black males to the responsibilities of fatherhood. Eight communities across the United States participated in the Teen Father project. Local agencies offered young fathers a variety of services that included vocational training, job placement, assistance in completing their education, individual counseling, parenting skills classes, prenatal classes, group and couples' counseling, and a grandparents' support group. Overall, the programs were influential in encouraging high school dropouts to return to school and/or obtain a GED. The project also was successful in enabling young fathers to secure part-time or full-time jobs. These kinds of programs may be particularly useful for disadvantaged young black fathers who are high school dropouts and lack employment skills (see Johnson & Sum (1987) for specific education and work-related recommendations). While many progressives see these kinds of programs as ameliorative in the short run, they argue that Americans must begin thinking about programs that are integrated into a broader, long-term, coherent public policy aimed at improving the well-being of both black and white families. Policy is politics (Boulding, 1985; Steiner, 1981) and it is becoming apparent that government policies regarding families must address the needs of blacks and whites simultaneously. Progressives argue that long-term sexuality and parenting policies need not be either conformist or hedonistic. In Sweden, for example, a policy goal is aimed at enhancing *responsible* sexuality and parenting regardless of legal status (Popenoe, 1987; see also Jones et al., 1986). In the United States there is must evidence documenting irresponsibility among married persons in terms of sexual and physical abuse of children (see Finkelhor, Gelles, Hotaling, & Straus, 1983; Haugaard & Reppucci, 1988; Russell, 1984). Hence legality is *not* a proper license for parenthood, as conservatives assert. Consequently, progressives' long-term goals for a modern society are to promote the idea that a *responsible* person, regardless of race or marital status, does not parent unless he or she first is socioeconomically *autonomous,* and second possesses sufficient socioemotional well-being to nurture properly his or her child.

Consistent with these long-term objectives, and contrary to conservative dominant culture norms regarding men's and women's work and family roles, programs would be aimed at promoting gender equity for adolescents as well as adults (Dornbusch & Strober, 1988). Progressives argue that adolescents will not be motivated to eschew having babies (or having unprotected sexual intercourse for that matter) unless alternative status awards are accessible. These kinds of programs would involve both macro- and micro-oriented strategies. At the macro-oriented structural level, the entire educational system of the United States, beginning with preschool experiences, is in need of evaluation and reformation. In spite of the Jeffersonian tradition that education is supposed to provide entry into the occupational system, conservatives and progressives concur that currently it ill serves most girls and boys of all races. However, progressives differ from conservatives in that they wish to restructure the educational experiences of girls and boys—beginning in the preschool years—so that gender equity is a central theme of those experiences. These structural changes would be reinforced by fresh cultural values. Central to these values is the idea that every woman (as well as every man) must be economically autonomous. The cultural value of women' economic autonomy must of course be accompanied by program aimed at making connections between restructured educational experiences and the labor market. That goal would be accompanied by a corresponding emphasis on male responsibility for and effectiveness in both parenting and routine household tasks. The ultimate policy goals would be to work towards gradual reductions in current gender differences in participation throughout economic, parenting, and household matters. While these gender equity policies should be promoted for all racial groups, such policies must also be sensitive to the dyer educational and unemploy ment circumstances which affect young black males disproportionately.

As suggested above, an emphasis on gender equity would be a core element of renewed educational structures, and it is within these structures that micro-oriented experiences would occur reinforcing these emerging values. Among these experiences would be programs aimed at training women and men to negotiate with each other over sexual and relationship issues from a position of relative strength based on women's economic autonomy. These programs would be aimed at making persons effective problem solvers in general, not just in the primary relationship sphere. In keeping with the reality that all social policy is based ultimately on faith, progressives believe that these kinds of micro-oriented training experiences, combined with restructured macro-oriented patterns, would reverse current trends toward pregnancy and parenting among persons ill suited for either.

Notes

1. The terms adolescent or teenage pregnancy and childbearing have become entrenched in the popular press/media and the scholarly literature. However, the indiscriminate use of these terms has often produced an oversimplified and distorted view of the relevant issues for the lay population as well as the academic community. From a life-course perspective it is important to consider the timing of fertility-related events relative to other life-course transitions such as marriage and completion of high school. It is misleading, for example, to lump 19-year-old parents responsible for a maritally conceived child, who are high school graduates with no previous desires to continue their schooling, with 16-year-old, unmarried high school students who have aspirations to at least obtain a college degree. Inevitably some of the statistics we report will not differentiate these types of individuals. Given the broad scope of our review we do not restrict ourselves to a particular segment of youth who are responsible for pregnancies and births as teenagers; however, we are concerned primarily with pregnancies and births that affect youth who have not made a "formal" commitment to one another prior to conception (marriage or a coresidential arrangement) and/or have not completed high school before conception occurs.

2. Because we focus on events subsequent to the acknowledgment of a pregnancy, we do not incorporate into our discussion the expansive body of literature on sexual activity or pregnancy prevention strategies (for reviews see Furstenberg, Morgan, Moore, & Peterson, 1987; Hofferth, 1987a; 1987e).

3. One image of conservative control of sexually related matters can be found in Atwood (1985).

References

Abrahamse, A. F., Morrison, P. A., & Waite, L. J. (1988). Teenagers willing to consider single parenthood: Who is at greatest risk? *Family Planning Perspectives, 20*(1), 13-24.

Adams, G., & Pittman, K. (1988). *Adolescent and young adult fathers: Problems and solutions.* Washington, DC: Adolescent Pregnancy Prevention Clearinghouse Report, Children's Defense Fund.

Atwood, M. (1985). *The handmaid's tale.* New York: Houghton Mifflin.

Bachrach, C. A. (1986). Adoption plans, adopted children, and adopted mothers. *Journal of Marriage and the Family, 48,* 243-253.

Bauer, G. L. (1986). *The family: Preserving America's future.* Washington, DC: White House Group on the Family.

Bellah, R. N., Madsen, R., Sullivan, W. M., Swidler, A., & Tipton, S. M. (1985). *Habits of the heart: Individualism and commitment in American life.* Berkeley: University of California Press.

Betsey, C. L., Holister, R. G., Jr., & Papageorgiou, M. R. (1985). *Youth employment training programs: The YEDPA years.* Washington, DC: National Academy Press.

Boulding, K. E. (1985). *Human betterment.* Beverly Hills, CA: Sage.

Brazzell, J. F., & Acock, A. C. (1988). Influence of attitudes, significant others, and aspirations on how adolescents intend to resolve a premarital pregnancy. *Journal of Marriage and the Family, 50,* 413-425.

Buunk, B. (1985). Alternative life-styles from an international perspective: A transatlantic comparison. In E. D. Macklin & R. H. Rubin (Eds.), *Contemporary families and alternative lifestyles.* (pp. 303-330) Beverly Hill, CA: Sage.

Cherlin, A. (1981). *Marriage, divorce, remarriage: Social trends in the United States.* Cambridge: Harvard University Press.

Cherlin, A. (1983). Family policy: The conservative challenge and the progressive response. *Journal of Family Issues, 4,* 427-438.

Cherlin, A. (1988). The weakening link between marriage and the care of children. *Family Planning Perspectives, 20,* 302-306.

Clarke, S. D., Jr., Zabin, L. S., & Hardy, J. G. (1984). Sex, contraception and parenthood: Experience and attitudes among urban black young men. *Family Planning Perspectives, 16,* 77-82.

Colletta, N. D., & Lee, D. (1983). The impact of support for black adolescent mothers. *Journal of Family Issues, 4,* 127-143.

Cortroneo, M., & Krasner, B. R. (1977). A study of abortion and problems in decision-making. *Journal of Marriage and the Family, 3,* 69-76.

Diamant, A. (1986, May 18). Teen-age pregnancy and the black family. *The Boston Globe Magazine,* 19-47.

Dornbusch, S. M., & Strober, M. H. (1988). *Feminism, children and the new families.* New York: Guilford.

Elder, G. H. (1985). Perspectives on the life course. In G. H. Elder (Ed.), *Life course dynamics: Trajectories and transitions, 1968-1980* (pp. 23-49) Ithaca, NY: Cornell University Press.

Evans, J. R., Selstad, G., & Welcher, W. H. (1976). Teenagers: Fertility control behavior and attitudes before and after abortion, childbearing or negative pregnancy test. *Family Planning Perspectives, 8*, 192-200.

Finkelhor, D., Gelles, R., Hotaling, G. T., & Straus, M. A. (1983). *The darker side of families: Current family violence research*. Beverly Hills: Sage.

Francouer, R. T. (1983). Religious reactions to alternative life styles. In E. D. Macklin & R. H. Rubin (Eds.), *Contemporary families and alternative lifestyles* (pp. 379-399) Beverly Hills, CA: Sage.

Franklin, D. L. (1988). The impact of early childbearing on developmental outcomes: The case of black adolescent parenting. *Family Relations, 37*, 268-274.

Frazier, E. F. (1939). *The negro family in the U.S.* Chicago: University of Chicago Press.

Freeman, E. W. (1978). Abortion: Subjective attitudes and feelings. *Family Planning Perspectives, 8*, 148-164.

Freeman, R. B. & Holzer, H. J. (1985). Young blacks and jobs—what we now know. *The public interest, 78*, 18-31.

Furstenberg, F. F., Jr. (1987). Race differentials in teenage sexuality, pregnancy, and adolescent childbearing. *The Milbank Quarterly, 65*(2), 381-403.

Furstenberg, F. F., Jr., Brooks-Gunn, J., & Morgan, S. P. (1987). *Adolescent mothers in later life*. New York: Cambridge University Press.

Furstenberg, F. F., Jr., & Crawford, A. G. (1978). Family support: Helping teenage mothers to cope. *Family Planning Perspectives, 10*, 322-333.

Furstenberg, F. F., Morgan, S. P., Moore, K. A., & Peterson, J. L. (1987). Race differences in the timing of adolescent intercourse. *American Sociological Review, 52*, 511-518.

Glazer, N. (1965). A sociologist's view of poverty. In M. S. Gordon (Ed.), *Poverty in America* (pp. 12-26) San Francisco: Chandler.

Hanson, S. L., Morrison, D. R., & Ginsburg, A. (1989). The antecedents of teenage fatherhood. *Demography, 26*(4), 579-596.

Haugaard, J. J., & Reppucci, N. (1988). *The sexual abuse of children*. San Francisco: Jossey-Bass.

Hayes, C. (1987). *Risking the future: Adolescent sexuality, pregnancy, and childbearing* (Vol. 1.). Washington, DC: National Academy Press.

Heiss, J. (1981). Women's values regarding marriage and the family. In H. McAdoo (Ed.), *Black families* (pp. 186-197) Beverly Hills, CA: Sage.

Hofferth, S. L. (1985). Children's life course: Family structure and living arrangements in cohort perspective. In G. H. Elder (Ed.), *Life course dynamics: Trajectories and transitions, 1968-1980* (pp. 75-112) Ithaca, NY: Cornell University Press.

Hofferth, S. L. (1987a). Factors affecting initiation of sexual intercourse. In S. L. Hofferth, & C. Hayes (Eds.), *Risking the future: Adolescent sexuality, pregnancy, and childbearing* (Vol. 2), pp. 7-35. Washington, DC: National Academy Press.

Hofferth, S. L. (1987b). Teenage pregnancy and its resolution. In S. L. Hofferth, & C. Hayes (Eds.), *Risking the future: Adolescent sexuality, pregnancy, and childbearing* (Vol. 2), pp. 78-92. Washington, DC: National Academy Press.

Hofferth, S. L. (1987c). Social and economic consequences of teenage child-bearing. In S. L. Hofferth, & C. Hayes (Eds.), *Risking the future: Adolescent sexuality, pregnancy, and childbearing* (Vol. 2, pp. 123-144). Washington, DC: National Academy Press.

Hofferth, S. L. (1987d). The children of teen childbearers. In S. L. Hofferth, & C. Hayes (Eds.), *Risking the future: Adolescent sexuality, pregnancy, and childbearing* (Vol. 2, pp. 174-206). Washington, DC: National Academy Press.

Hofferth, S. L. (1987e). The effects of programs and policies on adolescent pregnancy and childbearing. In S. L. Hofferth, & C. Hayes (Eds.), *Risking the future: Adolescent sexuality, pregnancy and childbearing* (Vol. 2, pp. 207-263). Washington, DC: National Academy Press.

Hofferth, S. L., & Hayes, C. (1987) *Risking the future: Adolescent sexuality, pregnancy, and childbearing* (Vol. 2). Washington, DC: National Academy Press.

Hogan, D., Hao, L., & Parish, W. L. (1988). *Race, kin networks, and assistance to mother-headed families* (Working Paper No 1988-30). University Park: Pennsylvania State University: Institute for Policy Research and Evaluation, Population Issues Research Center.

Hogan, D., & Kitagawa, E. (1985). The impact of social status, family structure, and neighborhood on the fertility of black adolescents. *American Journal of Sociology, 90*, 825-855.

Hudis, P. M., & Brazzell, J. F. (1981). Significant others, adult-role expectations, and the resolution of teenage pregnancies. In P. Ahmed (Ed.), *Pregnancy, childbirth, and parenthood* (pp. 167-187) New York: Elsevier.

Jones, E. F., Forrest, J. D., Goldman, N., Henshaw, S., Lincoln, R., Rosoff, J. I., Westoff, C. F., & Wulf, D. (1986). *Teenage pregnancy in industrialized countries.* New Haven, CT: Yale University Press.

Johnson, C., & Sum, A. (1987). *Declining earnings of young men: Their relation to poverty, teen pregnancy, and family formation.* Adolescent Prevention Clearinghouse Report. Washington, DC: Childrens' Defense Fund.

Klein, J. (1984, February 6). Babies having babies. *New York*, 45-53.

Klinman, D. G., Sander, J. H., Rosen, J. L., & Longo, K. R. (1986). The teen father collaboration: A demonstration and research model. In A. B. Elster & M. A. Lamb (Eds.), *Adolescent fatherhood* (pp. 155-170). Hillsdale, NJ: Lawrence Erlbaum.

Ladner, J. (1971). *Tomorrow's tomorrow: The black woman.* Garden City, NJ: Doubleday.

Marsiglio, W. (1987). Adolescent fathers in the United States: Their initial living arrangements, marital experience and educational outcomes. *Family Planning Perspectives, 19*(6), 240-251.

Marsiglio, W. (1988) Commitment to social fatherhood: Predicting adolescent males' intentions to live with their child and partner. *Journal of Marriage and the Family, 50*, 427-441.

Marsiglio, W. (1989). Adolescent males' pregnancy resolution preferences and family formation intentions: Does family background make a difference for black and whites. *Journal of Adolescent Research, 4*, 214-237.

Marsiglio, W. & Menaghan, E. (1990). Pregnancy resolution and family formation: Understanding gender differences in adolescents' preferences and beliefs. *Journal of Family Issues, 11*, 313-333.

McLaughlin, S. D., Grady, W. R., Billy, J. O. G., Landale, N. S., & Winges, L. D. (1986). The effects of the sequencing of marriage and first birth during adolescence. *Family Planning Perspectives, 18*(1), 12-18.

Moore, K. A. (1988). *Facts at a glance: November.* Washington, DC: Child Trends, Inc.

Moore, K. A., Simms, M. C., & Betsey, C. L. (1986). *Choice and circumstance: Racial differences in adolescent sexuality and fertility.* New Brunswick, NJ: Transaction Books.

Morgan, M., & Scanzoni, J. H. (1987). Religious orientations and women's expected continuity in the labor force. *Journal of Marriage and the Family, 49,* 367-379.

Mott, F. L. (1986). The pace of repeated childbearing among young American mothers. *Family Planning Perspectives, 18*(1), 5-12.

Mott, F. L., & Marsiglio, W. (1985). Early childbearing and completion of high school. *Family Planning Perspectives, 17,* 234-237.

Mott, F. L., & Maxwell, N. L. (1981). School-age mothers: 1968 and 1979. *Family Planning Perspectives, 13,* 287-292.

Moynihan, D. P. (1965). *The negro family: The case for national action.* Washington, DC: Office of Policy Planning and Research, U.S. Department of Labor.

National Center for Health Statistics (1986). Vital Statistics of the United States. Advanced report of final natality statistics. *Monthly Vital Statistics Report, 34*(6), September 1985 and *34*(4), July, 1986.

National Urban League (1987). *Adolescent male responsibility: Pregnancy prevention & parenting program: A program development guide.* New York: National Urban League.

O'Connell, M., & Rogers, C. C. (1984). Out-of-wedlock births, premarital pregnancies and their effect on family formation and dissolution. *Family Planning Perspectives, 16*(4), 157-162.

Parke, R. D., & Neville, B. (1987). Teenage fatherhood. In S. L. Hofferth, & C. Hayes (Eds.), *Risking the future: Adolescent sexuality, pregnancy, and fertility* (Vol. 2, pp. 145-173). Washington, DC: National Academy Press.

Peters, M. F., & McAdoo, H. F. (1983). The present and future of alternative lifestyles in ethnic American cultures. In E. D. Macklin & R. H. Rubin (Eds.), *Contemporary families and alternative lifestyles* (pp. 288-307) Beverly Hills, CA: Sage.

Popenoe, D. (1987). Beyond the nuclear family: A statistical portrait of the changing family in Sweden. *Journal of Marriage and the Family, 49,* 173-184.

Rosen, R. H. (1980). Adolescent pregnancy decision-making: Are parents important? *Adolescence, 15,* 43-54.

Russell, D. E. H. (1984). *Sexual exploitation: Rape, child sexual abuse, and workplace harassment.* Beverly Hills, CA: Sage.

Sandefur, G. D., & Tienda, M. (1988). *Divided opportunities: Minorities, poverty, and social policy.* New York: Plenum.

Savage, B. D. (1987). *Child support and teen parents.* Washington, DC: Adolescent Pregnancy Prevention Clearinghouse, Children's Defense Fund.

Scanzoni, J. H. (1983). *Shaping tomorrow's family: Theory and policy for the 21st century.* Beverly Hills, CA: Sage.

Scanzoni, J. H. (1989). Alternative images for public policy: Family structure versus family struggling. *Policy studies review, 8,* 599-609.

Scanzoni, J. H., Polonko, K., Teachman, J., & Thompson, L. (1989). *The sexual bond: Rethinking families and close relationships.* Newbury Park, CA: Sage.

Smith, J. P. (1988). Poverty and the family. In G. D. Sandefur, & M. Tienda (Eds.), *Divided opportunities: Minorities, poverty, and social policy.* (pp. 141-172) New York: Plenum.

Stack, C. (1974). *All our kin: Strategies for survival in a black community.* New York: Harper & Row.

Staples, R. (1978). *The black family: Essays and studies* (2nd ed.). Belmont, CA: Wadsworth.

Steiner, G. (1981). *The futility of family policy.* Washington, DC: Brookings Institute.

Sullivan, M. (1985). *Teen fathers in the inner city: An exploratory ethno-graphic study.* New York: Vera Institute of Justice.

Thompson, M. S. (1986). The influence of supportive relations on the psychological well-being of teenage mothers. *Social Forces, 64,* 1006-1024.

Trent, K., & Harlan, K. (1987). *Household structure among teenage mothers in the United States.* Paper presented at the American Sociological Association Meetings, Chicago, IL.

Wilson, W. J. (1987). *The truly disadvantaged: The inner city, the underclass, and public policy.* Chicago: University of Chicago Press.

Wilson, W. J., & Neckerman, K. M. (1986). Poverty and family structure: The widening gap between evidence and public policy issues. In S. H. Danziger, & D. H. Weinberg (Eds.), *Fighting poverty: What works and what doesn't.* (pp. 232-259) Cambridge, MA: Harvard University Press.

Zelnik, M., Kantner, J. F., & Ford, K. (1981). *Sex and pregnancy in Adolescence.* Beverly Hills, CA: Sage.

Zimmerman, M. K. (1977). *Passage through abortion: The personal and social reality of women's abortion experiences.* New York: Praeger.

Zimmerman, S. L. (1988). State level public policy choices as predictors of state teen birthrates. *Family Relations, 37,* 315-321.

PART 4

Substances:
Use and Abuse

12

Social Competence as a Framework for Addressing Ethnicity and Teenage Alcohol Problems

EDITH M. FREEMAN

Social competence involves a lifelong striving toward coping effectively with new developmental challenges. Moreover, it implies that socially mature individuals seek out, rather than simply react to, new opportunities for growth and self-improvement (Barth, 1986; Gilchrist, 1981). The concept connotes, therefore, a positive, self-actualizing view of human potential similar to that of existential philosophy (Meador & Rogers, 1984). Any problem, such as adolescent substance abuse for example, can be viewed as an individual's ineffective efforts to achieve a satisfactory level of social competence. This perspective directs attention to multiple factors that can prevent or impair competence in adolescents as well as affect intervention once the lack of competence and substance abuse have become a problem.

Substance abuse among teenagers is a major problem today; estimates of the numbers who use alcohol on a monthly basis range from 25% to 60% (Rachal, Maisto, Guess, & Hubbard, 1982). In fact, larger numbers of adolescents also are using other drugs of choice such as cocaine and marijuana, or combining those drugs with alcohol (Freeman, Logan, & McRoy, 1987). While substance abuse is endemic among the general population of youth, it has some unique characteristics among minorities. For instance, some researchers have found the overall use of alcohol and other drugs to be lower among black teenagers than among white youth, and the age of onset to be later (e.g., Harford, 1985). The long-term consequences of chemical dependency, however, are considerably more serious for black youth and other minorities.

"Cirrhosis mortality rates among black men and women, even within the age range from 25 to 34 years, are several times higher than for white men and women of the same age" (Harford, 1985). Among Indian people, alcohol has been found to be a contributor to 90% of all homicides and 80% of suicides (Gunther, Jolly, & Wedel, 1985). Finally, higher alcohol and other drug use by Mexican American youth is associated with lower grades, increased school drop-out rates, and high unemployment in adulthood (McRoy, Shorkey, & Garcia, 1985).

Given these consequences related to mortality and impairment of social competence among minority teenagers, there is a need for more effective mental health services. Information about the influence of race or ethnicity on substance abuse treatment is also inadequate (Wright, Kail, & Creecy, 1989); it has failed to clarify ways to enhance the competence of minority youth related to their developmental needs and multiple environmental stressors.

This chapter explores the theoretical linkage between racial factors and social competence in black teenagers, and the role of substances in coping with environmental stress. The discussion includes the author's research on the cultural relevance of one facility's mental health groups for black and white youth based on theories of social competence. In addition, implications of the findings for social work practice are addressed.

Theoretical Underpinnings of Social Competence

This section is focused on theories related to the development of social competence in general, the relationship between competence and substance abuse, and the influence of these issues on the life experiences of black youth. Each area has been addressed in more detail within specialized literature (Botvin, Baker, Renick, Filazzola, & Botvin, 1984; Gilchrist, 1981; Harford, Lowman, & Kaelber, 1982; Heller & Swindle, 1983; Kinder, Pape, & Walfish, 1980; Robin & Foster, 1984; Robins, Murphy, & Breckenridge, 1968). For this reason, the following discussion summarizes the findings and conclusions from this literature.

The Development of Social Competence

Whittaker and colleagues noted two essential aspects of social competence: the possession of life skills and access to responsive social supports. Life skills "refer to competencies beyond intellectual knowledge that are needed to act effectively in social environments and social roles" (Whittaker, Schinke, & Gilchrist, 1986). Having social skills during adolescence as well as the ability to do career planning and gain access to resources for mental health and developmental needs are examples of age-specific life skills. Life skills are learned through meaningful contacts with adults and peers who comprise the adolescent's social support system (Barth, 1983). Gottlieb (1983) defined social supports as "verbal and/or nonverbal information or advice, tangible aid, or action that is proffered by social intimates or inferred by their presence and has beneficial emotional or behavioral effects on the recipient." Support also consists of feedback, problem solving efforts, modeling, meaningful social interaction, and acceptance (Gilchrist, 1981; Heller & Swindle, 1983; Matus & Neuhring, 1979).

The theoretical underpinnings of these concepts are part of the ecological paradigm and general systems theory. The relationship between the environment and the individual is viewed as dynamic and reciprocal; each influences the other as "the active growing individual" and the ever-changing context (Bronfenbrenner, 1970). Whittaker, Schinke, & Gilchrist (1986) note that a central implication of this paradigm for human services practice is the need to enhance social supports and teach life skills when these properties are absent from or impaired by the environment.

Similarly, Barth (1986) linked social competence in children and adolescents to cognitive behavioral and problem-solving theories.

Cognitive behavioral theory emphasizes social interactions with parents, peers, and professional caregivers as a process for helping youth to develop competence and the "teaching of social skills to help them obtain the rewards they need from their social environment or ecology" (Barth, 1986). The theory highlights both the cognitive and behavioral changes necessary for competent performance. Cognitive changes refer to knowledge, emotions, motivation, and problem-solving skills. Behavioral changes include shifts in verbal and motor activities related to individual *and* interpersonal dimensions. The two types of changes are directly linked; for instance, cognitively based problem-solving skills are implemented behaviorally through a series of prescribed activities.

Problem-solving may take the form of a preventive, crisis, or interventive response to the need for social competence at the individual and social network level. The theory discourages victim blaming; the focus is on transitions as opportunities for improving problem-solving skills (Barth, 1986; Bright & Robin, 1981; Camp & Bash, 1981). In summary, social competence is the individual's increasing ability to initiate and respond to new life experiences and role expectations with a repertoire of problem-solving and coping skills, and is not viewed in terms of the absolute presence or absence of those abilities.

Social Competence and Substance Abuse

The above focus on transitions implies a direct linkage between competence and developmental theory. This theory is useful for conceptualizing the process through which alcohol and other drugs may be used by adolescents to cope with new role expectations. Jessor and Jessor (1975) concluded that growing up can involve drinking as "part of a whole other complex dynamic of taking on adult roles such as getting a job and learning to drive." Research has shown that only having adult models present who are either abstinent or fit within the broad category of problem drinkers means the adolescent has few opportunities to observe models who are able to use alcohol responsibly (Harford, 1985). Observing models is a primary method for learning about and taking on more adult-like roles during this period.

The linkage between the gradual development of competence and substance abuse is particularly complex for two additional reasons. Adolescence involves a transition period of heightened anxiety and stress due to new role expectations and major physical changes. Self-esteem and self-image not only change, but previously familiar ways of coping may no longer be useful. New means of coping are sought out, including the use of alcohol and other drugs. These substances can be rewarding developmentally: they make youth feel they are like their peers and provide a false sense of maturity while also masking the underlying stress and anxiety.

Second, in these situations developmental tasks are more likely to be unaddressed or addressed inadequately because chemical abuse temporarily diverts attention from them and thus arrests development. Recovery and treatment at a later age require the individual to go back to that point in his or her development and to work through the unaddressed issues while *not* using substances. Only then can he or she recover fully from the addiction, develop the competencies that were missed during adolescence, and move toward young adulthood. These competencies include separation from the family of origin, friendship and loyalty issues, identity, courtship and adult love relationships, and career planning (Freeman & McRoy, 1986).

Social Competence and Coping Among Black Youth

An effective treatment program for teenage substance abusers in general requires attention to any gaps in their development and social competence that result from chemical dependency. With black youth, development and coping may be complicated by additional factors related to race and ethnicity. Such factors are part of the sociocultural context; they include social or environmental stress, social health, and social adaptation. Most theories are not useful in helping workers to understand these phenomena in their work with black youth. General systems, developmental, and symbolic interaction theories can be expanded beyond their conventional use, however, to consider this context.

Social Stress

Hardy-Fanta (1986) concurred with the above observation about the limitations of most theories because "only secondary attention is given to environmental stress." Sources of environmental or social stress for blacks include the following substantive problems: poverty, powerlessness, inadequate housing, unemployment or underemployment, poor health and lack of access to resources, and racism. During childhood, the stress from these problems often is experienced indirectly. Adult caretakers more directly confront, cope with, and attempt to modify the adverse conditions that many black and other minority group families face (Crawley, 1988). By adolescence, however, individuals gain more direct exposure to and develop their own interpretations of those situations. In addition, they are expected to develop adult-like coping patterns.

Models for adult coping responses can be found within the cultural community as well as the media. The current media emphasis is on many pseudo-adult means of coping, such as the use of substances, without the accompanying information necessary for problem solving: for anticipating the consequences related to competence and positive functioning. Systems theory is useful for clarifying the impact of social stress and the availability of environmental resources on black youths' development and use of substances. The theory must be expanded to examine all social stressors as primary factors that can contribute to a state of homeostasis or resistance to change by the interacting systems. This steady state reinforces *barriers* to competence or *positive* coping without the use of substances and to recovery once a problem has developed.

Social Health

A related concept, social health, has been used to clarify aspects of competence related to Hispanics and is generalizable to black youth (Hardy-Fanta, 1986). The concept should be distinguished from that of mental health. The latter focuses on an individual's psychiatric and interpersonal problems often while ignoring environmental and institutional obstacles to social competence. The Diagnostic and Statistical Manual-III (DSM-III) is an example of a psychiatric classification system that employs this more narrow perspective of a person's mental health status (Williams, 1981). Some mental health programs, consequently, do not consider cultural factors in assessing problems or in designing and implementing their treatment strategies. This practice "perpetuates the deficit model of ethnicity that social work is trying to dispel" (Hardy-Fanta, 1986).

Social health does focus on a racial or ethnic group's collective coping responses to adverse social stress, and emphasizes a strengths perspective that is more consistent with social work values. For instance, a practitioner who understands the concept of social health would explore with a black adolescent how others of the same background have developed competence or coped with social stress without chemical dependency. Sources of positive coping might include a sense of group identity, tangible supports such as housing or access to a job, or opportunities to experience an emotionally supportive mentor relationship. A group's ability to provide this type of coping model, sources of competence, and positive group-concept either in symbolic or literal terms is a measure of its social health. Thus symbolic interactionism is a useful theory for clarifying the concept of social health (Manns, 1981).

Social Adaptation

Similarly, social adaptation is a more positive way of conceptualizing an *individual's* responses to social stress. Attempts to cope with stress and develop an adequate level of competence can be functional or dysfunctional depending on the point of reference. For example, the ability to externalize some of the causes of environmental stress is functional and appears to be critical for the psychological health of black youth. This type of cultural reality testing is often supported by the individual's ethnic group. However, the same process may be viewed as dysfunctional and radical from the perspective of the dominant group or the white practitioner.

Adaptations that do not allow an individual to achieve life goals can be considered dysfunctional; for instance, substance abuse, teenage pregnancy, and dropping out of school may result from dysfunctional efforts to cope with social stresses such as power-lessness, poverty, loss of hope, and racism (Chestang, 1980). The avoidance of help for addressing these problems also may be considered dysfunctional and an indication of deficits in social competence. Examples of positive social adaptations include seeking out and utilizing positive role models who demonstrate how to use substances responsibly, and the use of social supports to enhance life skills and social competence.

Help-seeking skills may be useful for encouraging black youth to obtain formal services as well as help from culturally-relevant natural supports in order to prevent and treat substance abuse. Such skills are age-specific; thus developmental theory directs attention to black youth's social adaptations to limited employment opportunities and to the impact on their competence in the world of work along with other developmental tasks. This theory and others that have been discussed encourage attention to an important question: To what extent do mental health services for black teenage substance abusers focus on these aspects of the social context and on their developmental needs? Although some information has been gleaned from practitioners' anecdotal experiences with clients, qualitative research is useful for exploring this area more systematically.

An Exploratory Study

The author conducted a qualitative study that utilized a modified version of Tripodi and Epstein's (1980) variables for evaluation by content analysis. Those researchers identified nine criteria of content analysis, "that when applied to process records, could conceivably make analysis more systematic and enhance the validity and reliability of the inferences drawn from those records of practice." Their methods were modified in the present study in the following ways: (1) audio tapes were used as the source of data analysis in order to make the process more empirical; (2) the focus of the analysis was on the types of concerns and needs that the members brought to their treatment group rather than on the therapeutic activities of the group facilitators, although inferences were drawn about the cultural relevance of their interventions; and (3) only seven of Tripodi and Epstein's (1980) variables were used because of the nature of the small exploratory study. Steps related to reliability measures and defining the study materials were omitted. The sample and setting will be discussed before the study methodology involving Tripodi and Epstein's (1980) variables is described.

Sample and Setting

The sample consisted of three open-ended groups of teenage substance abusers in a mental health facility in the Midwest where the author served as a consultant. One group consisted of inpatient clients and the other two served clients on an outpatient basis. Group members ranged in age from 14 to 18, with the average age being 16 years. A total of 83 youths were seen in the groups over the four-month study period. Approximately 75% were male and the remaining were female; while the racial composition was 66% white, 23% black, and 11% Hispanic.

The facility drew adult and teenage clients from many diverse areas of the metropolitan region based on formal and informal contracts with juvenile court, several Employee Assistance Programs, and a Health Maintenance Organization. In addition, informal ties with several local school districts within the area resulted in an ongoing referral source for teenage clients. The facility's substance abuse services included alcohol education, detoxification, antiabuse treatment, individual and group services for teenagers and adults, "I Can Cope" groups for families, and 12 step programs. Periodic audio taping of group sessions was done routinely for staff training and supervision purposes; a random sample of these tapes was used for the study. The two cofacilitators were a 29-year-old white female with an MSW degree and a 35-year-old black male alcohol counselor with a BA degree in psychology. Clients were in the inpatient group for periods from 30 to 60 days, and then often became members of outpatient groups for aftercare. The outpatient groups typically ran approximately 8 to 10 weeks. Group size ranged from 12 to 15 members.

Specifying Monitoring Standards

Monitoring standards are dimensions that reflect the expected activities, behaviors, and content to be exhibited by workers and clients (Tripodi & Epstein, 1980). As such, standards imply the ideals against which performance is measured. In the mental health facility in which the treatment groups were conducted, the monitoring standards included the clients' abilities to acknowledge that they have a problem in controlling their use of substances, to refrain from using substances, to stay involved in all aspects of their recovery program in the treatment contract, and to follow school, work, or legal requirements 100%. Workers were expected to confront clients when they were not in compliance or "working their programs," and to provide support and education to enhance their efforts to maintain sobriety.

Specifying Sources of Data and Their Availability

Tripodi and Epstein (1980) emphasize that records of interviews should be consistently available over time, across cases, and across workers through a systematic process of recording. For this reason, it was decided that a random sample of audio tapes of the three treatment groups would be used for doing the content analysis in this study. Forty-eight tapes were available for a four-month period during which each group was taped once per week; however, only 41 of those tapes were clear enough to be usable. One-half or 20 of the tapes were selected randomly for inclusion in the study. This included tapes of eight inpatient and 12 outpatient sessions.

Estimating the Authenticity of Documents

Documents are authentic to the extent that they are representative of what actually transpires in treatment sessions, according to Tripodi and Epstein (1980). The audio tapes used in this study were transcribed into written records for the content analysis. Each written transcript was reviewed by at least two persons and the necessary changes were made to insure that the transcriptions were valid representations of the audio tapes.

Defining the Units of Analysis

The unit of analysis refers to the informational units that are categorized or coded including sentences, thought units, and thematic content areas (Tripodi & Epstein, 1980). In this study, each audiotaped group session constituted a unit of analysis. Members were identified by name in the written transcripts, and then case records were used to identify each member's racial background. Thus it was possible to analyze differences and similarities in their concerns across racial groups. Black youth were not present in six of the sessions.

Operationally Defining Analytic Categories

Categories for analysis are the types of variables represented in records of treatment sessions; they should be mutually exclusive and exhaustive. In qualitative research, the categories and their behavioral referents come from studying the documents to be analyzed and are not predetermined (Tripodi & Epstein, 1980). Once identified, specific instructions should be written about what information should be considered or ignored. From reviewing written transcripts of the sessions, seven types of client concerns or analytic categories were identified. They included meeting the expectations of others, defining who the individual is, coping with stress and anxiety, handling interpersonal conflicts, testing to see if the individual can resist using substances, deciding how to handle peer pressures to use substances, and questioning who could be trusted to understand their worries and to be loyal when they made mistakes.

Each of these analytic categories was operationally or behaviorally defined. For instance, concerns about meeting others' expectations was defined as "identifying a discrepancy or conflict between how a member viewed his or her roles and responsibilities and the stated ideas of important peers, family members, or other adults." Testing to see if the individual can resist using substances was defined as "intentionally placing oneself in a social situation (such as a previous high-stress event or party) in which others may be using substances or the member might be tempted to do so during early periods of recovery (1-6 months)." Once those categories were operationally defined, the written transcripts were reviewed more systematically. Descriptive notations were made about any group interactions to which one of the analytic categories seemed to apply.

Findings and Discussion

Tripodi and Epstein's (1980) eighth and ninth variables are collecting, tabulating, and presenting the data, and comparing the findings against the monitoring standards. The findings from this exploratory study indicate that a model of social competence is needed that is more relevant to the life experiences of black adolescents with substance abuse problems. Although the small nonrepresentative sample used in the study prohibits generalization of the findings to other clients, the black clients in these treatment groups expressed concerns that were both similar to and different from those of members from other racial groups. Ninety-six percent of the members (across racial groups) indicated they had concerns about meeting others' expectations, trust-loyalty issues, and interpersonal conflicts with significant others. Their concerns are age-appropriate developmental tasks that are a reality for all teenagers.

Those concerns are consistent with Whittaker, Schinke, & Gilchrist's (1986) description of life skills that were previously discussed as an important aspect of competence. The expectations of others related to life skills that were most often discussed by group members included maintaining a job or school attendance and making responsible decisions (problem-solving). The sources of those expectations most frequently were parents, school authorities, probation officers, and extended family members in that order. Similarly, the group members' concerns about trust-loyalty issues and interpersonal conflicts seemed to have implications for their awareness and use of these social supports. Ninety-one percent of the members (across racial groups) were able to provide numerous examples of their help-avoidance behaviors or lack of competence in using natural supports. Members questioned the loyalty of parents, peers, and role models who confronted them about their substance abuse, but also doubted whether those supports were doing enough to help in the members' efforts to achieve sobriety.

In one example, a member who had been invited to a "keg" party felt his family and the group members lacked faith in him when they questioned whether he might be tempted to drink beer if he went to the party. Another individual who had dropped out of school expressed anger when members pointed out that she was using the same excuses about problems on the job that she had used about her earlier problems in school. Moreover, she was unable to use their experiences to anticipate how this pattern might threaten her sobriety until a later session when she had been fired from her job.

In addition to these common experiences with competence and problems in recovery, some differences were noted among group members. Many of the white adolescents (85%) indicated that conflicts over meeting the expectations of peers, parents, or role models was a major factor in their abuse of substances. Most of the black and Hispanic youth in the groups (98%), however, discussed concerns about their identity or self-concept as a major factor in their use of substances and the rewards of alcohol in minimizing environmental stresses. Sources of their stress included a sense of hopelessness about the racism that they had encountered, particularly in their school and work experiences.

Some of these youth (51%) indicated they had not been given the option of attending an alternative school when they were expelled for using substances or other behavioral problems, while they believed most of their white peers were encouraged to enroll in such programs. Eight of the black youth (44%) referred to older relatives who had not worked for long periods or who could only find part-time work and cited this as the reason they had given up on finding jobs themselves. The hopelessness expressed by relatives made it difficult to believe their lives could be different and encouraged them to use alcohol for coping and self-medication. These racial differences in members' reasons for drinking and the potential threats to recovery are consistent with other research findings (Harford, 1985; Harper, 1983; Klatsky, Seizelaub, Landy, & Friedman, 1983).

When these findings are compared with the monitoring standards for clients in this facility (see p. 256), it is clear that the standards are inadequate for capturing the real-life experiences of the clients. They do not consider the contextual factors that seem to be affecting members' abilities to acknowledge they lack control in using substances and to refrain from using. In summary, coping with conflicting expectations and acquiring life skills by teenagers in general, and handling social stress related to racism by black youth were not being addressed adequately in these groups.

Implications for Practice

Similarly, the monitoring standards for the workers seem to be inadequate in terms of the process of treatment in the groups. The leaders' responses to members' concerns about developmental and cultural issues appropriately conveyed support and empathy. Those responses were consistent with the monitoring standards for workers that were previously described. They were acknowledged as useful by group members from time to time, but they did not encourage problem-solving activities as a next step.

In one of the situations noted previously, a member insisted that going to a "keg" party would prove he could resist using alcohol. The leaders might have raised questions about how he would be able to tell if his resistance was decreasing and what alternative steps could be taken if that happened. They also could have pointed out that he had placed himself in a no-win situation, and then invited other members to identify what his dilemma was and to share similar experiences. Using group process in this manner can be more effective than having the facilitators confront a member.

When black youth in the groups indicated they used alcohol to self-medicate against their experiences with racism, the leaders might have encouraged them to talk about those experiences more fully in order to get in touch with their pain and how it had affected them. Exploring whether they had choices in how they reacted to those experiences, and steps for identifying cultural models for coping with environmental stress without alcohol might have encouraged mutual aid and natural helping within the group and in the community.

These practice examples illustrate the usefulness of a more systematic approach to improving both substance abuse services and the training of social workers. Table 12.1 includes a revised set of monitoring standards for clients that may be useful for training helping professionals as well as for designing and evaluating treatment programs. A comprehensive training program focused on those areas could include knowledge and value dimensions, and should allow opportunities for experiential learning such as role playing and values clarification exercises. Evaluation of the cultural-relevance of group services after staff training and program implementation can be done informally based on feedback from clients and colleagues about how well the areas included in Table 12.1 are addressed over time. Formal evaluation could be accomplished by the periodic use of research procedures such as the one described in this chapter (Tripodi & Epstein, 1980).

Based on Whittaker, Schinke, & Gilchrist's (1986) major categories of social competence, Table 12.1 identifies subcategories to be included under life skills and natural supports, and it indicates how the categories are culturally relevant and linked to substance abuse issues for black youth. The standards may be useful in work with adolescents from other racial groups as well. Subcategories under each life skill can be evaluated "yes" or "no" based on whether they are being accomplished, while subcategories under natural supports can be evaluated on a continuum from "can identify" to "can use." These more comprehensive standards reflect the theoretical underpinnings of social competence that were discussed earlier along with the concerns expressed by members of the treatment groups in this study. A final practice implication is that when resources for enhancing clients' competence and the recovery process are not present in the environment, practitioners should advocate and help to create the necessary social changes. Useful strategies may range from helping to change discriminatory school policies, to mediating family conflicts about role expectations, to increasing employment and job opportunities.

TABLE 12.1: Monitoring Standards Related to the Social Competence of Black Youth with Substance Abuse Problems

Life Skills*	Natural Supports*					

Ability to meet changing role responsibilities and developmental tasks related to the social context of the individual without the use of alcohol.

(1) Awareness and an ability to discuss developmental roles and tasks including adult-like behaviors such as use of substances, learning to drive, etc.:

- family relationships including separation from the family of origin,
- peer relationships or friendship/loyalty issues, same-sex or opposite-sex love relationships, identity or sense of self and self-esteem, and
- education/career/employment responsibilities now and in terms of future planning.

(2) Awareness of and ability to cope with *social stress*, its impact on the handling of developmental tasks/roles, and cultural patterns in those influences (with alternatives to substance abuse).

(3) Use of problem-solving skills

- talking about or clarifying issues related to (1) and (2), above (positive risk-taking)
- presenting or responding positively to alternative solutions
- anticipating and planning related to potential consequences

Ability to identify and utilize relationships with social intimates (including the family) to develop life skills and meet new role expectations through growth and risk-taking experiences, without the use of alcohol.

The person is able:

To identify			To use		
0	1	2	3	4	5

(1) Culturally relevant role models that demonstrate the racial/ethnic group's *social health* and responsible use of alcohol or abstinence from other drugs.

(2) Resources for coaching and monitoring the development of culturally relevant life skills

- for seeking treatment for substance abuse, for staying involved in and completing treatment
- for reinforcing a plan of lifelong recovery
- for addressing new role expectations and developmental tasks (see number (1) under "Life Skills").

(3) Resources for tangible needs

- food, clothing, work, transportation, money, housing, and child care for infants of teenage parents.

(Continued)

262

- accepting and giving advice
- trying out new ways of responding or handling issues and role responsibilities (without the use of substance)
- accepting and providing feedback about the issues and how they are being reacted to
- self-correcting or catching oneself in ineffective problem-solving or coping—including threats to recovery
- generalizing problem-solving to other issues and future concerns (making connections, doing prevention), developing a lifelong plan for continued sobriety.

(4) Improving coping patterns (social adaptation)
  - acknowledging social stress and its sources
  - acknowledging how the use of substances can help one deny, ignore, mask, or cope dysfunctionally with stress
  - clarifying new role expectations and developmental tasks along with environmental and cultural resources (school, work, legal, health, relationships, spiritual) for coping without substances
  - identifying the circumstances when coping patterns are likely to fail and relapse or other dysfunctional coping will occur
  - identifying a range of positive coping patterns that can be used for individual stress management (relaxation, physical activity, meditation, time out, etc.).

(4) Advice, problem-solving consultation, and feedback on threats to sobriety, managing environmental or social stress, or coping patterns.

(5) Emotional support, acceptance, nurturance in meaningful relationships for a positive self-concept and improved social adaptation in terms of racial issues.

---

*This bimodal conceptualization of social competence comes from Whittaker, Schinke, & Gilchrist (1986). The subcategories under each represent the author's efforts to clarify and build on those two concepts.

Conclusion

Assumptions underlying the concept of social competence provide an alternative perspective about substance abuse and developmental problems of black adolescents. Those assumptions can be useful to social workers and other helping professionals because they are consistent with an ecological perspective and a nondeficit model of ethnic practice. They help to identify monitoring standards for evaluating worker and client activities and direct attention to the cultural context in which resources for and barriers to effective recovery can be found.

References

Barth, R. P. (1983). Social support for adolescents and families. In J. K. Whittaker & J. Garbarino (Eds.), *Social support networks: Informal helping in human services.* Hawthorne, NY: Aldine.

Barth, R. P. (1986). *Social and cognitive treatment of children and adolescents.* San Francisco: Jossey-Bass.

Botvin, G., Baker, E., Renick, N., Filazzola, A., & Botvin, E. (1984). A cognitive-behavioral approach to substance abuse prevention. *Addictive Behaviors, 9,* 137-147.

Bright, P. B., & Robin, A. L. (1981). Ameliorating parent-adolescent conflict with problem-solving communication training. *Journal of Behavior Therapy and Experimental Psychology, 12,* 275-280.

Bronfenbrenner, U. (1970). *Two worlds of childhood.* New York: Russell Sage.

Camp, B. W., & Bash, M. A. S. (1981). *Think aloud: Increasing social and cognitive skills—A problem-solving program for children (primary level).* Champaign, IL: Research Press.

Chestang, L. W. (1980). Character development in a hostile environment. In M. Bloom (Ed.), *Life span development* (pp. 40-50). New York: Macmillan.

Crawley, B. (1988). Black families in a neo-conservative era. *Family Relations, 37,* 415-419.

Freeman, E. M., Logan, S. L., & McRoy, R. (1987). Treatment for teenage alcohol problems: Survey of mental health agencies. *Arete, 12,* 21-32.

Freeman, E. M., & McRoy, R. (1986). Treatment strategies for adolescent drinking problems. *Proceedings of the 31st International Institute on Prevention and Treatment of Alcoholism* (pp.160-168). Rome, Italy: International Council on Alcohol and Addictions.

Gilchrist, L. D. (1981). Social competence in adolescence. In S. P. Schinke (Ed.), *Behavioral methods in social welfare* (pp. 61-80). New York: Aldine.

Gottlieb, B. H. (1983). *Social support strategies: Guidelines for mental health practice.* Beverly Hills, CA: Sage.

Gunther, J. F., Jolly, E. J., Wedel, K. (1985). Alcoholism and the Indian people: Problem and promise. In E. M. Freeman (Ed.), *Social work practice with clients who have alcohol problems* (pp. 214-228). Springfield, IL: Charles C Thomas.

Hardy-Fanta, C. (1986). Social action in Hispanic groups. *Social Work, 31,* 119-123.

Harford, T. C. (1985). Drinking patterns among black and non-black adolescents: Results of a national survey. In E. M. Freeman (Ed.), *Social work practice with clients who have alcohol problems* (pp. 276-291). Springfield, IL: Charles C Thomas.

Harford, T. C., Lowman, C., & Kaelber, C. T. (1982, April) *Current prevalence of alcohol use among white and black adolescents.* Paper presented at the National Council on Alcoholism Conference, Washington, DC.

Harper, F. D. (1983). Alcoholism treatment and black Americans: A review and analysis. In T. D. Watts & R. Wright (Eds.), *Black alcoholism: Toward a comprehensive understanding* (pp. 71-84). Springfield, IL: Charles C Thomas.

Heller, K., & Swindle, R. W. (1983). Social networks, perceived social support, and coping with stress. In R. Felner, J. Moritsugu, & S. Farber (Eds.), *Preventive psychology: Theory, research and practice* (pp. 87-103). Elmsford, NY: Pergamon.

Jessor, R., & Jessor, S. L. (1975). Adolescent development and the onset of drinking. *Journal of Studies on Alcohol, 36,* 27-32.

Kinder, B., Pape, N., & Walfish, S. (1980). Drug and alcohol education programs: A review of outcome studies. *International Journal of the Addictions, 15,* 1035-1054.

Klatsky, A. L., Seizelaub, A., Landy, C., & Friedman, G. (1983). Racial patterns of alcohol beverage use. *Alcoholism: Clinical and Experimental Research, 7,* 372-377.

Manns, W. (1981). Support systems of significant others in black families. In H. P. McAdoo (Ed.), *Black families* (pp. 238-251). Beverly Hills, CA: Sage.

Matus, R., & Neuhring, E. M. (1979). Social workers in primary prevention: Action and ideology in mental health. *Community Mental Health Journal, 15,* 33-40.

McRoy, R. G., Shorkey, C. T., & Garcia, E. (1985). Alcohol use and abuse among Mexican-Americans. In E. M. Freeman (Ed.), *Social work practice with clients who have alcohol problems* (pp. 229-241). Springfield, IL: Charles C Thomas.

Meador, B. D., & Rogers, C. R. (1984). Person-centered therapy. In R. J. Corsini (Ed.), *Current psychotherapies* (pp. 142-195). Itasca, IL: Peacock.

Rachal, J. V., Maisto, S. A., Guess, L. L., & Hubbard, R. L. (1982). Alcohol use among youth. In *Alcohol and health monograph no. 1.* (DHHS Publ. No. (ADM) 82-1190, 55-95). Washington, DC: U.S. Government Printing Office..

Robin, A. L., & Foster, S. L. (1984). Problem-solving communication training: A behavioral family system approach to parent-adolescent conflict. In P. Karoly & J. Steffen (Eds.), *Adolescent behavior disorders: Foundations and contemporary concerns* (pp. 195-240). Lexington, MA: D. C. Heath.

Robins, L., Murphy, G. E., & Breckenridge, M. B. (1968). Drinking behavior of young urban Negro males. *Quarterly Journal of Studies on Alcoholism, 29,* 657-684.

Tripodi, T., & Epstein, I. (1980). The use of content analysis to monitor social worker performance. *Research techniques for clinical social workers* (pp. 103-120). New York: Columbia University Press.

Whittaker, J. K., Schinke, S. P., & Gilchrist, L. D. (1986). The ecological paradigm in child, youth, and family services: Implications for policy and practice. *Social Service Review, 61,* 355-376.

Williams, J. B. W. (1981). DSM-III: A comprehensive approach to diagnosis. *Social Work, 26,* 101-106.

Wright, R., Kail, B. L., & Creecy, R. F. (1989). Culturally-sensitive social work practice with black alcoholics and their families. In S. Logan, E. M. Freeman, & R. G. McRoy (Eds.), *Social work practice with black families: A culturally specific perspective* (pp. 203-221). New York: Longman.

13

The Role of Family Factors in the Primary Prevention of Substance Abuse Among High Risk Black Youth

URA JEAN OYEMADE
VALORA WASHINGTON

Drug abuse, particularly in the black community, is one of the most serious and perplexing problems facing America today. Not only does addiction result in higher rates of high school dropouts, unemployment, crime, and incarceration for the current generation, but the children of substance abusers are more likely to become abusers and eventually end up as members of a growing underclass (Hawkins, Lishner, & Catalano, 1985; National Institute on Alcohol Abuse and Alcoholism, 1987).

In this paper we present the scope of the problem, identify factors that affect drug abuse rates, and present an ecological model for primary prevention. Our focus is on how these psychodynamic and environmental factors affect substance abuse. We will review the research within a theoretical model, and suggest the most effective components for a primary drug abuse prevention program for families.

Scope of the Problem

Nationally, the 1980s were marked by a decline in the rate of overall illicit drug use within the school-aged population. For example, cocaine use was down from 16.9% to 15.2% between 1986 and 1987 (Johnston, O'Malley, & Bachman, 1988). However, the United States still has the highest rates of illicit drug use among the world's industrialized nations. More than one-half (57%) of the 1987 high school seniors had tried an illegal drug, and more than one-third had tried a drug other than marijuana. Furthermore, the least change in drug use took place among students whose parents had never been to high school, a drop of only 2.7% versus a 13% drop for those whose parents had some graduate education.

The figures are even more foreboding for low-income minorities. For example, the number of youth in the District of Columbia who use alcohol has increased by more than 20% during the past six years, up from 46% to 76% (COBA Associates, 1987). Also, while cocaine was previously used more by college graduates (11% versus 4% for those who had not completed high school), by 1985 the situation was reversed (Johnston, O'Malley, & Bachman, 1988). Only 3% of college graduates said they used cocaine in the last month, while 10% of people who never finished high school said they used the drug. Also, metropolitan substance abuse services report that most crack users appearing at hospitals and treatment centers are low-income minorities. Crack seems to have become entrenched in inner-city areas.

Perhaps the most dire vision of the future concerns the intravenous users of heroin, a drug that has remained predominantly the preserve of those with low incomes who live in the inner city. These people are now at high risk for exposure to the acquired immunodeficiency syndrome (AIDS) virus because they share needles.

In reviewing the epidemiology of substance abuse, two major factors indicate usage levels: supply and demand. Clearly, the availability of drugs in any community has significant impact on their use. As the supply of cocaine has increased, so has its consumption. Heroin distribution apparently has been targeted to low-income minority communities (Jurith, 1989). The increase in availability and the drop in the price of cocaine has been directly related to the increase in use during the last 7 years.

The supply of illicit substances is affected by production, both locally and in foreign countries, as well as by laws and activities to control the supply. The Anti-Drug Act of 1986 (P.L. 99-570), is aimed at curbing the supply by monitoring international borders more closely, working with other national governments, increasing enforcement, and punishing drug distributors more stringently. Additionally, the law provides for the support of research, treatment, and prevention programs. However, although central efforts such as these have increased, the epidemic of cocaine and other substance usage is still present, thus demonstrating that supply control efforts alone are not enough to stem a drug epidemic. Demand must be reduced or the lure of great profits will simply continue to attract new suppliers.

Factors that Affect Drug Abuse Rates

In general factors that affect drug abuse can be categorized as physiological, psychodynamic, and/or environmental. The physiological causes of drug abuse are negligible, however. The other two categories—psychodynamic and environmental factors—clearly account for the greatest proportion of abusers. These influences are thought to be the major reason for the disproportionate involvement of black youth in substance abuse today. Psychodynamic factors include those mental disorders that lead to instability and, subsequently, drug addiction. Environmental factors, which have been the subject of much research in recent years, include influences such as one's family, socioeconomic level (SES), peer group, stress, racism, inadequate schools, and unemployment.

The demand for illegal drugs is exacerbated by a host of psychodynamic and environmental factors operating within the black community. Primm (1987) has identified these as:

- The history of racism in the United States that began with the forced exile of slaves from Africa;
- High unemployment rates and lack of job and career opportunities that lead to poverty;
- Disproportionate arrest rates of blacks on drug charges;

- Drug abuse policies and get-tough laws;
- The economics of drug distribution versus alternative careers;
- The hopelessness of ghetto life;
- Lifestyles that reject menial or subsistence jobs in favor of hustling in the dramatic world of drug dealing;
- Peer pressure;
- Cultural and class conflicts;
- Inadequate educational preparation and high drop-out rates;
- Rising material, social, and success expectations and aspirations;
- The breakdown of family life;
- Welfare policies that encourage single-parent households;
- Frustration from continuing discrimination and rejection;
- Responsiveness to the dominant culture's media imperative for instant gratification; and
- Stress.

Psychodynamic Factors

A wide array of personality traits have been linked with early or frequent substance abuse:

- rebelliousness (Bachman, Johnson, & O'Malley, 1981; Kandel, 1982),
- nonconformity to traditional values (Bachman, Johnson, & O'Malley, 1981; Jessor & Jessor, 1977),
- high tolerance of deviance,
- resistance to traditional authority,
- a strong need for independence, and
- normlessness (Jessor, 1976; Jessor & Jessor, 1975; Paton & Kandel, 1978).

Smith and Fogg (1978) reported that on measures of personal competence and social responsibility (such as obedience, diligence, and achievement orientation), nonusers scored highest and early users scored lowest. Also, frequent drug users scored lower on measures of well-being, responsibility, socialization, self-control, tolerance, achievement, and intellectual efficacy (Smith & Fogg, 1978; Wexler, 1975). Similarly, Labouvie (1986) found that the experience of strained social relationships and a heightened sense of powerlessness or helplessness may induce adolescents to rely more heavily on substance abuse as a means to achieve emotional self-regulation without much effort, ability, or sense of control on their part.

In a study of 234 black families in Oakland, California, parents and children who were involved in substance abuse expressed feelings of loneliness, isolation, anomie, and frustration (Nobles, Goddard, Cavil, & George, 1987). These researchers also suggest that poor self-esteem seems to be a key variable in the onset of substance abuse. On the other hand, certain factors and behaviors tend to inhibit substance abuse. Among these are commitment to school and education, and belief in society's general expectations, norms, and values (Krohn, Massey, Laner, & Skinner, 1983).

While these research results suggest a positive relationship between drug abuse and a variety of psychodynamic factors, in general, personality characteristics have been found to be less predictable of substance abuse than behavioral or interpersonal factors (Kandel, 1978).

Family and Environmental Factors

The family undoubtedly is the single most important arena for the socialization of its members throughout childhood. Hence, the family is probably the most significant factor in the motivation of adolescents' substance abuse behavior. Hirschi's social control theory suggests that parents have a direct, independent effect on the adolescent's daily behavior, regardless of whether or not the youth interacts with delinquent friends (Glynn, 1981; Hirschi, 1969). Other investigators also have shown that the family is more influential than the peer group throughout adolescence (Blum, Henry, & Sanford, 1971; Clausen, 1966; Coleman, 1961; Larsen, 1972, 1974; Solomon, 1961).

In a developmental model, Kandel, Kessler, and Margulies (1978a) postulate three stages of drug use (initiation into hard liquor, then use of marijuana, followed by use of other illicit drugs) from the perspective of four conceptual clusters (parental influences, peer influences, adolescent's beliefs and values, and involvement in certain activities). Thus Kandel and her colleagues include major sources of interpersonal influence as well as the relevant intrapersonal characteristics of the adolescent (see Figure 13.1).

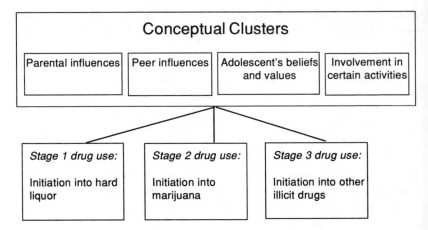

Figure 13.1. Model of Family and Peer Influence on Adolescent Drug Use
SOURCE: Kandel, Kessler, & Margulies. (1978a).

These researchers (Kandel, Kessler, & Margulies, 1978b) discuss three ways interpersonal influences may operate:

1. Directly—One person influences the behavior of another by providing a model, appropriate reinforcement, or an intimate relationship.
2. Indirectly—One person influences the development of another's values, attitudes, or behaviors over a period of time although not in a strictly linear way.
3. Conditionally—One source of influence affects a focal person's opportunity or susceptibility to be influenced by another.

Moreover, Kandel and her colleagues (1978a) suggest that these influences are transmitted primarily through imitation (the adolescent imitates another person's behavior) and reinforcement (the teenager feels accepted or otherwise rewarded for performing the desired behavior). These researchers contend that this interpersonal process provides the foundation, explicitly or implicitly, for many of the studies conducted on family/peer influences on adolescent drug abuse.

Thus the literature will be reviewed in this paper from the focus on the three stages of drug use outlined by Kandel and her associates. Most of the studies included black and white samples in urban and suburban settings. Some relied only on adolescent reports, while others also involved family retrospective reports.

Stage 1: Initiation into Hard Liquor

The literature confirms that parents play a substantial and even quite specific role in influencing adolescent initiation into the use of hard liquor. The child's knowledge of parents' drinking patterns typically seems to be the most important predictor of adolescent drinking patterns (Maddox, 1970). In addition, Lawrence and Vellerman (1974) found that the most significant factor influencing adolescent alcohol use was not whether or how often one or both parents drank, but how much they drank each time (i.e., whether they drank to intoxication or had a single drink).

A reasoned, democratic parenting style may have a positive effect on adolescent drug abuse, including the use of alcohol (Braucht, Brakarsh, Follingstad, & Berry, 1973). These researchers noted that adolescent alcohol users usually had parents whose interactions with their teenage children were extreme: they were over- or under-dominating or rejecting, laissez faire or liberal, or exhibited prolonged periods of strict control. In contrast, there is also some evidence to support the notion that good parent-child relationships have a positive influence on adolescent nondrinking. McBride (1978) suggests that positive family relations, and positive involvement with the family, discourage initiation into adolescent drug use; and, in contrast, that family friction and fights may encourage use.

Stage 2: Initiation into Marijuana

Kandel and her colleagues (1978b) found that parents have an extremely small influence on adolescent marijuana use. Unlike the evidence with the use of hard liquor, adolescent initiation into marijuana was "virtually unrelated" to any type of drug use on the part of parents. What little parental influence was found appeared to be based on parental attitudes and the closeness of their relationship with their children. Parents whose relationships with their children were strong enough to enable them to forbid or strongly discourage marijuana use and still hold the relationship together were more successful in minimizing initiation than parents whose attitudes and behavior suggested a more permissive stance.

Indeed, positive parent-child relationships may tend to decrease marijuana use (Brook, Whiteman, & Gordon, 1983). Specific variables associated with less teenage marijuana use included the child's perception of strong parental support and greater involvement with parents; the strength and importance of the family and degree of satisfaction the adolescent derives from the family; the strength of family efforts to meet the emotional needs of the adolescent; and a parental relationship that is affectionate and child-centered.

Stage 3: Initiation into Other Illicit Drugs

Adolescent initiation into the use of drugs other than marijuana appears to be strongly related to parental influences and, in particular, the quality of the parent-child relationship (Kandel, Kessler, & Margulies, 1978a, 1978b). When the adolescents reported feeling close to their families, there was a low likelihood of initiation into other drugs. Conversely, strict controls and parental disagreement about discipline predicted higher likelihood of initiation. Parental drug use (including alcohol) again, was an important predictor of adolescent abuse of drugs.

One study specifically supports the Kandel, Kessler, and Margulies data that suggest a strong relationship between parental use of legal and illegal psychoactive, mood-changing drugs and adolescent use of similar illegal psychoactive substances (Smart & Fejer, 1972). This juvenile manifestation of adult behavior is deemed to be a reflection of "generational continuity."

Additional findings indicate that in drug abusing families, the members appeared more rigidly fixed or stereotyped in their respective roles, that is, the father was more powerful and unfriendly while the mother was more actively helping (Kandel, Kessler, & Margulies, 1978a, 1978b). In general, the nonabusing families were perceived as warm rather than simply rigidly controlling and indifferent. Other factors these researchers found to be associated with absence of drug abuse were greater assignments of household tasks to the children, less generous monetary allowance, more of parents' time spent in activities with children, greater likelihood of church attendance, and use of noncontact punishment (or only an occasional spanking).

New Research Substantiates
the Role of the Family

The literature indicates that parents have the most influence on their adolescent children's drug use in Stages 1 and 3 (alcohol abuse and illicit drug abuse). Another study, conducted by Oye-made (1985), lends further support to the role of environmental factors. In that study, 134 income-stratified, randomly selected black adolescents and their families in Washington, DC were interviewed. These families were divided into four categories describing the behavior of one adolescent family member: academic achiever, nonacademic achiever, juvenile delinquent (often a substance abuser), or teenage parent. Interview questions focused on family values and childrearing practices.

Family Values

In brief, this study revealed that successfully coping families (parents of adolescent academic or nonacademic achievers) had higher aspirations for their children and also expected them to achieve more than did the less successful families. Aspirations and expectations for achievement were fairly well matched for adolescents in the successful families.

With respect to family values in less successful families, parents of juvenile delinquents placed a moderate emphasis on material goods and were more nontraditional in moral values. They were moderate in cultural identity and had the poorest attendance at religious services. Families of teen parents, on the other hand, placed high importance on material goods and were more traditional in moral values. This group also did not have a high attendance rate at religious services.

Child Rearing Practices

When child rearing practices are examined closely, the results reveal that families of juvenile delinquents and teen parents used more negative reinforcement, had fewer rules for peer interaction and general discipline, and were more authoritarian (i.e., discipline and rules were set and enforced without explanation).

This authoritarian style of discipline, which relies heavily on external controls, may appear to work with younger children (i.e., young children follow the rules). However, the real consequences of authoritarian child rearing styles are only fully realized in adolescence. By puberty, most children raised in authoritarian households still have not internalized the families' values. These adolescents begin to assert their independence from parental control—but often in directions that make success difficult if not impossible to achieve.

Findings from Oyemade (1985), and other similar studies, consistently show that families who offer positive discipline, a nurturing home environment, parental supervision, and strong religious values are more likely to have children who are achievers. In contrast, families who use negative, authoritarian disciplinary measures and who have lower religious service attendance rates tend to have children who exhibit less successful coping behaviors such as juvenile delinquency, teenage pregnancy, or substance abuse.

One caution is in order at this point. Some of the child rearing practices and associated delinquent behaviors now being observed in so many black communities should not be interpreted as representative of the traditional black culture. Nobles and his colleagues (1987) assert that the black family cultural orientation has shifted, in the course of one generation, to a drug culture that is antithetical to the traditional African-American culture.

One result of this shift: An erosion of the historically viable black cultural system in some families. Traditionally, the black family valued mutual aid, adaptability, natural goodness, respect, responsibility, unconditional love, cooperation, work orientation, religion, and kinship networks. With the shift to the drug culture, selfishness, materialism, paranoia, individualism, manipulativeness, distrust, and other destructive values have taken the place of more positive, traditional values. This erosion of values may be one explanation for the increase in substance abuse in the black community.

Other Environmental Factors

Two other environmental factors made significant distinctions between the groups in the Oyemade studies—availability of essential services and socioeconomic status. Families of teen parents and juvenile delinquents (including substance abusers) had significantly fewer essential services (transportation, municipal, protective, health care, and religious) available to then than did parents of children who were achievers. Moreover, the socioeconomic status (as measured by home ownership, parental education, current and past year income, earnings from jobs as opposed to public assistance, and occupational status of spouse) was significantly lower for families with teen parents or juvenile delinquents than for parents of achievers.

A three-generation perspective adds yet another dimension to the topic. The occupational status of grandparents was highest for nonacademic achievers and lowest for teen parents and juvenile delinquents. This finding suggests much less intergenerational mobility for the latter two groups. Consistent with previous studies, families with teen parents and juvenile delinquents were often found in the lower SES groups. Indeed, social and demographic factors may account for a majority of the variance associated with these adolescent behaviors.

Another finding with regard to socioeconomic status also sheds light on the issue of substance abuse. Significantly more parents of adolescent achievers reported that their earnings were from a job (as opposed to public assistance ($p < .001$).

Family composition and the home's interpersonal environment clearly are major contributors to child outcomes, although these factors have not been studied in as much detail as status characteristics such as education, occupation, and home ownership, which also are critical variables (Coleman, 1967; Jencks, 1972).

Unquestionably, lower socioeconomic status serves to *exclude* black children from many of the activities in the American culture that are important for success and to *deprive* them of the resources necessary to function in the institutions of the mainstream of American life. Therefore, many black children reared in lower SES families fail to achieve because of limited access and other barriers that usually are manifested in the form of racial and class discrimination, particularly in the educational system and in the job market. The Oyemade study (1985) results support this position. Adolescents who failed to demonstrate positive achievements also had fewer essential services such as transportation, health care, and protective services, all of which could have enabled them to participate more actively in mainstream culture activities.

Another independent variable that differentiated between groups in the Oyemade study was geographic mobility. Interestingly, the families of academic achievers and teen parents were less geographically mobile than were those of nonacademic achievers and juvenile delinquents. It appears that residential stability has a positive effect upon school performance. In contrast, as Edwards (1976) points out, the mobile student is forced to "prove himself" to peers in each new context. This frequently involves excessively hostile or antisocial behaviors that could lead to encounters with law enforcement authorities.

Single-parent households often have been associated with poor academic achievement, delinquent behavior, and teenage pregnancy (Scott-Jones, 1984). However, while a greater number of juvenile delinquents and teen parents were from single-parent families, the differences were not significant in Oyemade's results (1985).

In examining the factors that might mitigate the negative effects of the environment, the question was raised as to whether kin networks play a role in adolescent success. The effects of the extended family (whether relatives or fictive kin) have not clearly been identified. Scanzoni (1977) attempted to assess the effect of relatives on black social mobility. He found that adolescents were neither particularly helped nor hindered by relatives in the teens' attempts to "get ahead in life." The Oyemade findings (1985) are somewhat conflicting as well. On the other hand, the extended families of juvenile delinquents were involved with teenage family members significantly less than were the other groups. However, juvenile delinquents received more support from their immediate families.

Perhaps juvenile delinquents needed more help from their immediate families to get out of trouble. If so, the theory that family isolation leads to less positive outcomes for children is supported. For example, if help is needed for child care of financial resources, for example, and those resources are not available in the immediate family, these needs may go unmet. Therefore, delinquent behaviors (such as selling drugs to obtain desired material goods) may be the result, because children home alone without supervision are more likely to get into trouble.

The likelihood that this scenario happened in the families in Oyemade's work (1985) is further enhanced by the finding that families of juvenile delinquents and teenage parents also had access to fewer essential outside services. Most of these families were from the lowest income level, raising the probability that their needs may have gone wanting. In contrast, families of academic achievers were involved in a regular exchange of help within the extended and immediate families.

The psychodynamic and environmental data reveal several factors that place the young black population at risk for life problems including substance abuse and teenage pregnancy:

- Family history of antisocial behavior or criminality
- Family history of alcohol abuse
- Family management problems
- Children's early antisocial behavior and hyperactivity
- Parents' drug use and positive attitudes toward use
- Children's academic failure
- Little family commitment to education
- Adolescent alienation, rebelliousness, and lack of bonding to society
- Friends who do drugs
- Favorable community attitudes toward drug use
- Easy first use of and access to alcohol and other drugs
- Low religious participation.

An Ecological Model for Primary Prevention

Given the large number of risk factors, the goal of primary prevention is a challenging one necessitating an ecological approach that takes into account all aspects of the child's environment including the school, peers, family, and the wider society. While many prevention programs have targeted peers and school-based interactions, few have focused on the family and often those are aimed at, or at least more accessible to, the middle-class community (e.g., Parent Effectiveness Training).

Any serious effort toward prevention must take into account the family and societal predictors of later drug use. First, programs must be targeted at *young* children and their families, because the research clearly indicates the roots of drug abuse are found in child rearing practices and other factors affecting value formation and internalization of positive values and self-discipline during the early years.

Prevention programs also must address the needs and life-styles of a variety of families. Different strategies should be devised in order to reach these diverse groups. These strategies need to take into account factors such as differences in child rearing practices (e.g., black parents tend to be strict and direct with discipline); religious orientation (blacks tend to use religion as a means to improve their ability to cope with the stresses of life); the variations in orientation toward attending meetings with different social classes; and the problem of the disproportionate numbers of black males who become involved in substance abuse (for example, there is a need to socialize black males to resist the discrimination of racism they will encounter in society; that is, black males are automatically suspected as delinquents).

All parents want the best for their children. Substantive efforts must be made to enable them to achieve their goal. Programs within the community, such as Head Start, churches, child care, job training, and Work Incentive, can all be invaluable in the process. Preschool programs such as Head Start are an ideal target for primary drug-abuse prevention efforts. Family management, child rearing, communication skills, consistent interaction and involvement with the child, and interpersonal skills could be the focus of these efforts. Head Start's Parent Involvement Program already includes several activities that help alleviate many sources of stress such as poverty, unemployment, and lack of job and career development (Washington & Oyemade, 1987). Although a host of factors are important, programs aimed at meeting some basic needs of families and at modifying parenting styles hold the most promise for success. A four-pronged approach for primary prevention has been developed and the model is already being implemented in Howard University's School of Human Ecology. These approaches include stress management, resource identification, family social support, and family education.

Family Stress Management

All families need to develop strategies to resist stress and manage their reaction to it. In a comprehensive primary prevention program, families would build their emotional strengths so they could avoid or at least ward off the negative effects of a stressful situation (e.g., knowledge of drug use). Families then would learn how to react to stress in ways that are growth-enhancing rather than in ways that make the situation even worse (i.e., encourage appropriate rather than destructive family responses to a child's encounter with law enforcement officials).

Family Resource Identification

This program component consists mainly of a referral source that is readily accessible to all target families. Information on neighborhood, city, state, and federal programs and agencies is compiled, taking into account transportation and other factors. In addition, suggestions to work with the schools are offered. Sources for assistance include the Urban League, YMCA, police, human services department, home economics extension service, child care centers, Head Start programs, and local churches.

Family Social Support

Target families are invited to neighborhood meetings held bi-monthly. They are encouraged to invite friends, relatives, and neighbors. These meetings involve discussions, films, and resource people to help deal with specific problems and other family-related issues. Such meetings help strengthen and even expand social networks in the community. Schools, churches, community centers, or other convenient public buildings house the groups, who are encouraged to continue to meet even after the conclusion of the program.

Family Education

This aspect of the program draws on findings from the research on the effects of different child rearing practices and coping skills. Parents are encouraged to become more aware of their own coping patterns and interpersonal behaviors. More effective, positive coping and parenting strategies are introduced and practiced so participants can feel comfortable with making changes in their family relationships. The intensity of such a program usually necessitates meetings twice a week.

*   *   *

We know a great deal about which family variables are most critical for raising children who are achievers (and that variables lead to less successful lives). While parenting and family-life skills programs still are few in number, these programs nevertheless can help reduce the incidence of youthful drug abuse. Programs of the type described here offer several advantages:

- They emphasize healthy life-styles and prevention of problems rather than reacting to drug abuse or other difficulties after the fact.
- They assume that families are in control of their own destinies.
- They are accessible, affordable, and transportable.
- They have the potential to make a profound impact on the well-being of families.

References

Bachman, J. G., Johnson, J. D., & O'Malley, P. M. (1981). *Monitoring the future: Questionnaire responses from the nation's high school seniors.* Ann Arbor, MI: Survey Research Center.

Blum, R. H., Henry, W. E, & Sanford, N. (Eds.). (1971). *The dream sellers.* San Francisco: Jossey-Bass.

Braucht, G. N., Brakarsh, D., Follingstad, D., & Berry, K. L. (1973). Deviant drug use in adolescents: A review of psychosocial correlates. *Psychological Bulletin, 79,* 92-106.

Brook, J. S., Whiteman, M., & Gordon, A. S. (1983). Stages of drug use in adolescence: Personality, peer, and family correlates. *Developmental Psychology, 19,* 269-277.

Clausen, J. A. (1966). Family structure, socialization and personality. In M. L. Hoffman & L. W. Hoffman (Eds.), *Review of child development research II.* New York: Russell Sage.

COBA Associates. (1987). *Research and evaluation services for the D.C. school-based substance abuse prevention and intervention initiative* (Contract #JA86470). Washington, DC: Department of Human Services, District of Columbia Government.

Coleman, J. S. (1961). *The adolescent society.* Glencoe, IL: Free Press.

Coleman, J. S. (1967). *Equality of educational opportunity.* Washington, DC: U.S. Office of Education.

Edwards, O. L. (1976). Components of academic success: A profile of achieving black adolescents. *Journal of Negro Education, 45,* 408-422.

Glynn, T. F. (1981). From family to peer: A review of transitions of influence among drug-using youth. *Journal of Youth and Adolescence, 10,* 363-383.

Hawkins, J. D., Lishner, D., & Catalano, F. (1985). Childhood predictors and the prevention of adolescent substance abuse. In T. Glynn, et al. (Eds.), *Etiology of drug abuse: Implications for prevention.* (NIDA research monograph 56, pp. 75-126). Washington, DC: U.S. Department of Health and Human Services.

Hirschi, T. (1969). *Causes of delinquency.* Berkeley: University of California Press.

Jencks, C. (1972). Inequality: A reassessment of family and schooling in America. New York: Basic Books.

Jessor, R. (1976). Predicting time of onset of marijuana use: A developmental study of high school youth. *Journal of Consulting Clinical Psychology, 44,* 125-134.

Jessor, R., & Jessor, S. L. (1975). Adolescent development and the onset of drinking: A longitudinal study. *Journal of the Study of Alcohol, 36,* 27-51.

Jessor, R., & Jessor, S. L. (1977). *Problem behavior and psychosocial development: A longitudinal study of growth.* New York: Academic Press.

Johnston, L. D., O'Malley, P. M., & Bachman, J. G. (1988). *Drug abuse among American high school students, college students, and other young adults: National trends through 1987.* Washington, DC: National Institute on Drug Abuse.

Jurith, E. (1989). Controlling access to narcotic substances. In Oyemade, et al. (Eds.), *Proceedings of the Human Ecology Forum. The ecology of substance abuse: Toward primary prevention among high risk youth.* Washington, DC: HDAMHA.

Kandel, D. (1978). Convergences in prospective longitudinal surveys of drug use in normal populations. In D. Kandel (Ed.), *Longitudinal research on drug use: Empirical findings and methodological issues.* Washington, DC: Hemisphere-John Wiley.

Kandel, D. B. (1982). Epidemiological and psychosocial perspectives on adolescent drug use. *Journal of American Academic Clinical Psychiatry, 21,* 238-347.

Kandel, D., Kessler, R., & Margulies, R. (1978a). Adolescent interaction into stages of drug use: A developmental analysis. In D. Kandel (Ed.), *Longitudinal research on drug use: Empirical findings and methodological issues.* Washington, DC: Hemisphere-John Wiley.

Kandel, D., Kessler, R. C., & Margulies, R. S. (1978b). Antecedents of imitation into stages of drug use: A developmental analysis. *Journal of Youth and Adolescence, 7,* 13-40.

Krohn, M., Massey, J., Laner, R., & Skinner, W. (1983). Social bonding theory and adolescent cigarette smoking: A longitudinal analysis. *Journal of Health and Social Behavior, 24,* 337-349.

Labouvie, E. W. (1986). Alcohol and marijuana use in relation to adolescent stress. *International Journal of Addictions, 21,* 333-345.

Larsen, L. E. (1972). The influence of parents and peers during adolescence: The situation hypothesis revisited. *Journal of Marriage and Family, 34,* 67-74.

Larsen, L. E. (1974). An examination of the salience hierarchy during adolescence: The influence of the family. *Adolescence, 9,* 317-332.

Lawrence, T. S., & Vellerman, J. D. (1974). Correlates of student drug use in suburban high schools. *Psychiatry, 35,* 129-136.

Maddox, G. L. (Ed.). (1970). *The domesticated drug: Drinking among collegians.* New Haven, CT: College and University Press.

McBride, D. (1978). *Parental and peer influences on adolescent drug use.* Rockville, MD: National Institute on Drug Abuse.

National Institute on Alcohol Abuse and Alcoholism. (1987). *Alcohol health and research world, 2.* Washington, DC: National Institute on Alcohol Abuse and Alcoholism.

Nobles, W., Goddard, L. L., Cavil, W. E., & George, P. Y. (1987). In *The culture of drugs in the black community* (pp. 10-36). Oakland, CA: Black Family Institute.

Oyemade, U. J. (1985). Achievement of black adolescents in academic and non-academic areas. In *Proceedings of symposium: The ecology of black adolescents.* Symposium Conducted at the Meeting of the Society for Research in Child Development, Toronto, Canada. Chicago: University of Chicago Press.

Paton, S., & Kandel, D. B. (1978). Psychological factors and adolescent illicit drug abuse: Ethnicity and sex differences. *Adolescence, 13,* 187-200.

Primm, B. J. (1987). AIDS: A special report. In J. Dewart (Ed.), *The state of black America 1987* (pp. 139-166). New York: National Urban League.

Scanzoni, J. H. (1977). *The black family in modern society: Patterns of stability and security.* Chicago: University of Chicago Press.

Scott-Jones, D. (1984). Family influences on cognitive development and school achievement. In E. W. Gordon (Ed.), *Review of research in education* (pp. 54-81). Washington, DC: American Educational Research Association.

Smart, R. G., & Fejer, D. (1972). Drug use among adolescents and their parents: Using the generation gap in mood modification. *Journal of Abnormal Psychology, 70,* 153-166.

Smith, G. M., & Fogg, C. P. (1978). Psychological predictors of early use, late use, and non-use of marijuana among teenage students. In D. B. Kandel (Ed.), *Longitudinal research on drug use: Empirical findings and methodological issues.* Washington, DC: Hemisphere-John Wiley.

Solomon, D. (1961). Adolescents' decisions: A comparison of influence from parents with that from other sources. *Journal of Marriage and Family Living, 23,* 393-396.

Washington, V., & Oyemade, U. J. (1987). *Project Head Start: Past, present and future trends in the context of family needs.* New York: Garland.

Wexler, M. (1975). Personality characteristics of marijuana users and non-users in a suburban high school. *Cornell Journal of Social Relations, 10,* 267-282.

14

American Indian Adolescents: Combating Problems of Substance Use and Abuse Through a Community Model

E. DANIEL EDWARDS
MARGIE EGBERT-EDWARDS

Introduction

Alarming statistics have recently surfaced from current research studies regarding substance abuse problems among American Indian youth. Recent evidence has shown that problem drinking is quite prevalent among adolescents and even younger Indian children (Beauvais & LaBoueff, 1985, p. 149). Their research with over 1400 American Indian youth has shown that 82% of Indian adolescents report having used alcohol at least once as compared to 66% of non-Indian youth sampled at the same time. In addition, 50% of the Indian adolescents reported that they had used alcohol in the recent past as compared with 27% of the non-Indian population. Much of the use of alcohol among Indian adolescents appeared to be heavy, with incidents of blackouts and extremely drunk behavior being reported. These authors also reported on a 1982 study with young American Indian children between the ages of 9 and

12. Over 33% of these Indian children, representing seven different reservations, indicated they had used alcohol (Beauvais & La-Boueff, 1985; pp. 147-148). While reports of usage were light, this early experimentation with alcohol is a definite concern to American Indian people today.

Because of this concern, a number of Indian tribes are becoming more involved in documenting, understanding, and addressing factors that impact the use and misuse of alcohol among their people. While reliable data regarding incidence of substance abuse among American Indian people are surfacing (Beauvais & La-Boueff, 1985; Oetting, Beauvais, & Edwards, 1988), recommendations are also surfacing for education, prevention, and treatment approaches to address the needs of American Indian youth. Oetting, Beauvais, & Edwards, (1988) have definite ideas about what types of programs will succeed in changing or modifying alcohol use among Indian youth. They indicate, according to their research, that the following "good ideas" will fail: (1) a simple program aimed at improving self-esteem will fail; (2) a program based on the idea that alcohol is used as a substitute for social acceptance will fail; (3) a program based on the idea that alcohol is taken by depressed, anxious, or otherwise emotionally disturbed youth will fail; (4) a program that uses "socially acceptable" people to reach deviant youth will fail; (5) a program that provides cultural ceremonies and doesn't follow through to ultimately change peer clusters will fail; (6) recreational or social activities that do not actively and completely exclude alcohol use will fail.

"What, then will work? Strong and effective programs that (1) increase family strength, (2) lead to improved school adjustment, (3) create hope for the future, and (4) change peer clusters to discourage alcohol abuse" (Oetting, Beauvais, & Edwards, 1988, p. 99).

The authors of this paper believe that the comprehensive programs advocated by Oetting and colleagues would be enhanced if they included a strong, positive cultural enrichment and identification component.

This paper advocates a comprehensive community approach to the substance use problems of American Indians. The approach recommends a coordinated prevention, education, and treatment model for American Indian youth, their families, and their communities. Such an approach relies heavily on implementation of the

American Indian value that respects knowledge and wisdom. American Indian people traditionally strive to attain knowledge that will help them live in harmony with nature and in accordance with their religious beliefs. There is a cultural expectation that all knowledge will be used wisely in promoting positive living experiences for the benefit of individual Indian youth, their families, clans, and tribes.

This paper also advocates the use of group decision making, another traditional value of American Indian people.

In order to achieve the goals of such an approach, emphasis in Indian communities must be upon understanding the issues and problems confronting Indian adolescents that may contribute to their substance use and may impact effective treatment plans. Treatment approaches should be comprehensive in nature and include community prevention approaches; coordinated school prevention approaches; family prevention/treatment approaches; and individual and group prevention/treatment approaches.

Indian Adolescents:
Problems That May Contribute to Substance Use

Many Indian adolescents have lived with drinking/drug behaviors to the extent that they see them as "Indian" behaviors. Some adolescent Indian males view heavy drinking as a "rite of passage to masculinity" and the means of proving that they are "real" Indians. Early experimentation with sniffing, smoking, and drinking are common among many Indian youth. Indian children have not incorporated high school graduation into their life-styles as a realistic, attainable goal. To the contrary, early experimentation with substances often interferes with attainment of educational degrees.

Indian communities in the past have had difficulty acknowledging the extent of their substance use and abuse problems. Indian youth do not necessarily view substance use and abuse as negative, pathological, or interfering with their lives. In some situations, substance use and abuse are seen as components of Indian life-styles. A myth is perpetuated that "everyone" participates in substance use. In reality, many Indian people do not use alcohol and drugs.

Indian youth often see drinking activities as "where the action is." This is where they associate with other youth. Many Indian youth live in situations where they have too much leisure time, few employment opportunities, and limited commitment to education. They often turn to experimentation with substances to relieve boredom.

There are many differences of opinion on Indian reservations and in Indian communities regarding appropriate responses to substance use and abuse. Some Indian people advocate abstinence and encourage all Indian people to "live life drug-free." Others advocate for responsible drinking behaviors; and others prefer to leave such decisions to individuals. Indian youth do not have clear-cut values to guide them in making decisions regarding substance use.

In addition to meeting the normal expectations for adolescent development, Indian youth must deal with issues related to poverty, racism, and identification with their "Indianness." Many Indian youth have experienced discrimination, particularly in towns bordering their Indian lands; others display uncertainty regarding questions such as "What is an Indian?" and "How does an Indian behave?" Indian youth often respond to these developmental issues by participating in substance use.

Many Indian youth have witnessed traumatic experiences that have emotionally impacted their development. One Indian leader has indicated that most Indian children have lost two significant people by the time they reach six years of age. Many of these losses have been alcohol-related. Indian youth have limited opportunities to discuss these losses with people who could be helpful to them. Residues of sadness, powerlessness, and helplessness are associated with these traumatic events. Indian youth may resort to substance use to relieve themselves of this pain.

Traditional Indian child rearing customs have been eroded in terms of their effectiveness. The traditional support of entire communities in child rearing responsibilities is difficult to effect. Indian youth have few controls or models to guide them in their development. Substance use behaviors are often ignored rather than attended to by parents and other responsible adults.

Indian Adolescents:
Issues That May Impact Effective Treatment Plans

Many Indian adolescents have not been taught how to express feelings or utilize words that express feelings. Adolescents experience feelings of powerlessness. They lack confidence in their ability to exert power and control over their lives. They lack opportunities to associate with successful American Indian people who can be appropriate role models.

When parents are involved in substance use behaviors, it is difficult to involve them in the treatment plans of their children. Many Indian parents are reluctant to talk with social workers about the problems their children are experiencing. Indian parents often believe that the social worker is using the child as an instrument to get to the parent—to talk with the parents about parental drinking behaviors.

Many Indian people have well-developed expectations about interacting with one another. It is not appropriate to embarrass or shame an Indian family or tribal member by bringing problems of their children to their attention.

Many Indian social workers are employed with programs that serve their own tribal groups. It is difficult for these social workers to confront relatives or peers about the problems of their adolescent children. If Indian social workers are recovering alcoholics, they often feel uncomfortable talking with relatives and friends about drinking behaviors of their adolescent children; "everyone" on the reservation knows that the social worker was once a problem drinker.

Indian and non-Indian social workers who develop treatment programs for Indian youth often are criticized for taking on or assuming too much responsibility. Helping people often become discouraged because of this criticism, and potentially helpful programs are disbanded.

Resources often are limited to address adolescent drinking problems. Detoxification centers have not proven effective in some Indian communities. These centers are being replaced by "healing centers" where the focus is on healing everyone within the community and the community itself, and making it legitimate and acceptable to not drink.

Community crises may motivate a community to seriously address problems associated with substance abuse. Multiple deaths (particularly of youth) in one or more serious traumatic accidents may affect substantial members of the community to where Indian people and organizations will say "enough"—and mobilization of all community resources may be geared toward addressing substance abuse problems at all levels.

Substance abuse programs seem to be most effective in those reservations and Indian communities where leaders, including tribal council members, are supportive. Also essential is the support of the Indian elders and spiritual community leaders.

In many Indian communities there is a cadre of Indian and non-Indian professional and lay people who are willing to mobilize support from enough community people and resources to surmount the criticism and continue program developments to meet substance use and abuse problems "head on." Many exciting programs are developing to address problems of substance use and abuse among Indian youth. Some of these will be discussed in this paper.

Community Prevention Approaches

American Indian communities are recognizing the importance of involving the entire community in social problems impacting their reservations and communities. As indicated above, this approach relates well to Indian traditional and cultural problem-solving methods.

In order to develop community-oriented prevention/treatment approaches, the following factors should be considered:

1. Support must be generated from all aspects of the community including tribal leadership and elders.
2. A needs assessment or community assessment of substance use and abuse among all components of the community is essential.
3. A thorough tabulation and interpretation of the assessment data are imperative. These findings must be reported to the entire community

4. All members of the Indian community should be invited to participate in the formation of task groups to address each of the important
   issues identified in the assessment.

5. Membership of task groups should include American Indian youth,
   their parents, community leaders, professional people, members of
   social service agencies including substance abuse treatment centers,
   and traditional Indian people from all age groups, with particular
   emphasis upon inclusion of the "elders" of the community.

6. Every agency and unit within the community that has or can develop
   a role in addressing substance abuse problems and accessing funding
   sources should be included. Input must be solicited from every component of the community in order for this approach to be effective.
   Some examples of effective and innovative programs from a variety
   of Indian communities include the following:

Minneapolis, Minnesota: Soaring Eagles

This group was organized in 1983 to promote the development
of leadership abilities of Indian youth in the Minneapolis area. It
now provides social, cultural, and educational activities for youth
between the ages of three and 20. Alternative activities to substance use are promoted. Supportive relationships are developed
with other Indian youth and adults who do not use or abuse substances. Educational achievement and attainment are encouraged
and positively reinforced. Positive enhancement of self-image and
identification with "Indianness" are encouraged. Individual goals
are set by each group member to accomplish during this year.
Service to younger youth and community is encouraged. Family
activities are held on a regular basis. An annual summer family
retreat to a nearby Indian reservation is an important component
of this program. Transportation to and from the Social Center is
provided for all youth requiring this service.

Ignacio, Colorado: Indian Youth "Drug Busters"

This program was developed with the cooperation of two VISTA
volunteers, the Southern Ute Tribe, and the community of Ignacio,
Colorado. The program is supervised by adults but run primarily
by youth group members who call themselves "Drug Busters."

Among their group-supported activities are the following: a 320-mile annual run from southern Colorado to Denver where the youth deliver a message to the Governor and Legislature related to their concerns about substance abuse and the importance of curbing the problems and providing alternative activities; monthly meetings to which all youth are invited; movie trips to a nearby city; drug-free parties and dances including an all-night New Years' Eve party; renovation of an old building to serve as a teen center; and fund-raising activities. A 25-minute video has been prepared describing this project and can be obtained from the Southern Ute Tribe, Box 294, Ignacio, Colorado, for the cost of the postage (Indian Kids Lead Third Annual 325-Mile Run Against Drugs, 1986).

Alaska: Chevak Village Youth Association

This organization came into being to provide primary prevention services to reduce several social problems of the Village including alcohol and drug abuse. The Association serves not only youth and young adults but the entire community. The youth are responsible for generating the large proportion of their budget. They sponsor many activities to offer constructive alternatives to boredom and substance use for all age groups in the Village. They also sponsor community "festival" activities in the spring and the fall. Community service is an important component of their organization. Many young people are involved in the leadership and voluntary service roles required to accomplish the goals of the Association (McDiarmid, 1983).

Helping Programs Achieve Their Goals

While there is little argument about the importance of dealing effectively with the problems of American Indian youth substance use, there often are serious differences of opinion as to who should be responsible for directing such programs and how they should be conducted. It is vital to build cooperative relationships with all agencies and groups working on behalf of American Indian people and particularly American Indian youth. Conflict should be professionally addressed and resolved through utilization of community boards, councils, and other resources. Addressing conflicts immeliately and in an up-front professional manner will help control development of vested interests, schisms, or divisiveness that so often influence the development of new programs. Participation and input from Indian youth and their parents are important. Representatives from these groups should be active members of task groups or councils that are designated with the role of addressing adolescent drinking problems. Helping adults appreciate the contributions youth can make to such programs is pertinent to the success of these proposals. Involvement of all formal organizations dealing with adolescents also is crucial in implementing sound prevention and treatment programs. These organizations include but should not be limited to, tribal councils and other Indian organizations, schools, social service programs, Indian Health Service programs, tribal and municipal police departments and courts, religious organizations, self-help groups such as those sponsored through Alcoholics Anonymous (A.A.), and all other resources that affect or could affect American Indian youth.

Another important consideration is the element of patience. Many successful community programs take years to develop. Viable projects always are in a state of flux. Input and recommended changes must always be welcome. Mistakes should be corrected but not overly criticized. Cooperation and growth are highly valued on individual, group, and community levels. With such an approach, there should be community pride in the success of each component of the program.

Coordinated School Prevention Approaches

Fortunately, public concern about alcohol and drug use and abuse in our country has continued to increase over the past three decades (Kumpfer, 1988). Nationally, there has been an increase in the number of medical facilities that are treating youth and adult substance users. Treatment costs are skyrocketing. High use and rising treatment costs may be contributing to community interest in recommending more prevention strategies to reduce substance abuse—particularly among youth.

The schools are in a particularly viable position to approach substance prevention at all levels. Many prevention programs have originated in the schools—several of which have been in response to national efforts. One of the problems with national efforts is that they often do not allow for the unique needs, characteristics, and problems of individual communities and schools. Some approaches that have been developed are:

1. Drug education programs. These early programs were developed around "scare tactics," many of which were not credible to youth. More recent efforts have found successful interventions when factual knowledge is presented by a credible communicator, who focuses on short-term consequences and risk factors (Kumpfer, 1988).

2. Affective and interpersonal education programs. These programs emphasize increased positive self-concept and development of coping skills. While these programs have usually not demonstrated effectiveness in reducing substance abuse, they are rarely detrimental and may be heading in the right direction towards a more concentrated emphasis (Kumpfer, 1988).

3. Alternative programs. These programs seek to involve youth in "alternative highs." They teach new skills, reduce boredom, and enhance bonding to communities. One of the important components of these programs is that they seek to encourage bonding with nonusers who participate in the activities (Kumpfer, 1988).

4. Behavioral prevention programs. These programs teach behavioral techniques that are designed to help youth resist peer influences to use drugs and alcohol. Research reports show disappointing results particularly among high risk students (Kumpfer, 1988).

5. Coordinated, comprehensive school approaches. Until recently, most prevention approaches have relied on a primary single strategy approach. The coordinated community approach emphasizes many different programs or components in an integrated, supportive format. One such program, PATHE (Gottfredson 1984, Gottfredson & Gottfredson, 1987), is demonstrating positive results. This program utilizes the services of a "school prevention coordinator" and a core school team approach. Its major goals are to provide a positive school climate, improve school involvement and bonding, and increase academic performance, while reducing substance abuse behaviors. Another project following this model is currently funded in the Davis School District through the Social Research Institute at the University of Utah's Graduate School of Social Work. This research is in its initial stages and no research reports have been issued to date.

In order to make a coordinated school prevention program effective, several challenges must be met. Among these challenges are the following:

1. Programs must be organized with a well-defined theory base.
2. The programs must be integrated into the school program and receive support from all existing school personnel.
3. The programs must be expertly designed. Goals must be concretely identified. Objectives must be conceptualized in ways that promote evaluation.
4. Evaluation measures must be prioritized.
5. Inservice training must be ongoing.
6. Rewards and recognition for goal achievement must be available and forthcoming on a regular basis for all participants.
7. Programs must be conceived and receive endorsements for long-term intervention.
8. Programs must be administered by mature, well-respected school personnel who have the support of administration, their education peers, students, and the community.
9. School administrators and staff must be willing to look at institutional factors (barriers) that may affect the successful accomplishment of a goal; interpersonal frustrations between administrators, teachers, students, and parents that raise concern; and personal frustrations that may result when cooperation or results are not forthcoming as quickly as may be desired (Kumpfer, 1988).

What May Work
With American Indian Youth

There are over 500 American Indian tribes in the United States. There are 287 American Indian reservations and approximately 200 Alaskan native villages (Stewart, 1987). Indian people also live in a variety of Indian land situations, in rural and urban areas, and many Indian people are mobile—changing their residences often.

Each Indian tribe is in a unique situation and impacted by a variety of circumstances over which they have varying degrees of control. For these reasons, a coordinated community/school approach is believed to be capable of addressing the unique needs of these Indian communities and each community's right to self-determination.

Such a community/school approach could be successful in impacting Indian youth decisions regarding use of drugs or alcohol. It would be designed to address community issues impacting tribal and school administrators. Some of the goals of the approach would be to promote a positive school climate and encourage youth to remain in school—finding it an enjoyable place to be. It could also promote bonding among tribal members and all participants in the school setting—including parents. Another of the goals would be to provide opportunities for individual tribes and communities to identify their own goals, obstacles to goal achievement, and methods for goal attainment. The program would be designed to increase student participation in all aspects of the school system, through which an increase in positive self-concepts, positive peer group relationships, and school achievement could result. Ultimately, such a program could achieve long-term goals of increased knowledge regarding substance use and abuse, decisions to not participate in drugs or alcohol, increased peer support, and greater realization of individual, community, and tribal potential. Another long-range goal would be to evaluate the effectiveness of these coordinated community/school programs in achieving these goals.

Procedures for implementing a coordinated community/school approach would include the following:

1. Hire knowledgeable and competent project staff and consultants.
2. Identify evaluation measures that are appropriate for use with an American Indian population. One such instrument could be the Oetting, Edwards, & Beauvais, (1985) "Children's Drug Use Survey" that assesses alcohol, marijuana, inhalants, and pill usage among minority and nonminority children. This survey was planned to be self-administered and, according to the authors, is "short, easy to read and structured so that it does not encourage drug use." Other measurements may include data regarding arrests, convictions, and disciplinary actions for alcohol and drug use. School problem behavior indicators also could be identified, including truancy, poor grades, drop-out rates, and graduation rates. Academic achievement indica-

tors, including grade point averages, and any standardized test data may be helpful.

3. Organize and train school prevention/coordinating teams. Membership should include all interested students, student body officers, parents, school staff, community agencies, and community "elders."

4. Organize support teams for each goal or project identified by the school prevention/coordinating team. Among the teams that could be considered are the following:

   a. Student/School Concerns Support Team. This team could address problem behaviors and academic problems of the general student body and possibly high risk students. The team could also look at school organization issues such as the extent to which school rules are clear, fair, and appropriately administered; the manner in which punishments are given; the availability of teaching resources; administration/teacher cooperation; and administrator/teacher attitudes towards students.

   b. Student Leadership Team. This task force should include student leaders and nonleaders from all representative groups in the student body. One of the purposes of this team would be to plan a variety of activities that would be of interest to all groups of students represented in the student body. These activities should include social opportunities, community service projects, and educational activities. Programs to improve educational performance should also be addressed.

   c. Parent Leadership Team. These teams should consist of parents who are representatives of the wide variety of different backgrounds of the student body and the community. Both professional and lay people should be included. Promoting parent involvement in the program is the major goal of this team.

   d. Curriculum Support Team. This team would be responsible for reviewing the curriculum and making recommendations that would lead to improved school relationships and academic functioning of all students. This team would also be responsible for reviewing drug and alcohol prevention programs currently utilized and making suggestions for modification. The team would also be responsible for services that would help improve academic performance of students.

   e. Tribal/Community Team. Tribal Council and other community leaders would be asked to identify activities that would be supported by the tribe and community to support the goals of the community/school approach.

f. "Elders" Team. This team would be helpful in identifying ways in which American Indian elders could be involved in this program. Elders may be beneficial in enriching the curriculum and in sharing their knowledge and wisdom. They may also serve as tutors, volunteers within the classrooms, and foster grandparents.

g. Other Teams. Home Room Teams could support a goal of making every student feel wanted and important in the school system. A Music Team, Drama Team, or Art Team could promote encouragement of student involvement in the development of their artistic talents. A Rodeo Team or Cross Country Team could relate to the recreation and physical activity needs of Indian youth.

Evaluation

An extremely important component of a community/school approach would be evaluation of the accomplishments of the program goals. Everyone should be made aware of the importance of the research being conducted. Reports of evaluations should be shared openly and honestly with all members of the community.

Family Prevention/Treatment
Approaches

American Indians have traditionally been very supportive of immediate, extended, and clan family members. In order to capitalize on this important value, the following suggestions are offered:

1. Involve as many family members as possible in any planning or treatment intervention. With American Indian families, participants could also include clan and other tribal members.

2. Identify and work through nondrinking family members. Take time to find the most appropriate and helpful family or clan members who can provide substance-free activities and support for Indian youth.

3. Help family members become aware of all resources in the community that could be beneficial to them in preventing and treating any substance abuse problems. Help them access these resources in ways that are beneficial to them.

4. Hold out "hope" to the family.

5. Deal more with behavior than with feelings. This is particularly important with those American Indian people who have had limited experience expressing feelings. Dealing with the behavior and helping them identify behavioral changes they would like to achieve may be more beneficial than focusing intently on expression of feelings.

6. Parent education is strongly emphasized throughout our country at the present time. The Northwest Indian Child Welfare Institute has developed a program titled "Positive Indian Parenting: Honoring our Children by Honoring our Traditions." This program has developed parenting principles in ways that apply specifically to American Indian people.

In order to help parents understand how to discuss issues related to substance abuse with their children, the following suggestions are offered:

1. Parents should encourage their children to participate in healthy activities that can serve as alternatives to experimenting with or using substances.

2. Adults should model appropriate drinking behaviors. Parents should be instructed as to possible behaviors on their part that may contribute to their children's drinking. Parents should be encouraged to not drink and drive; not drink when pregnant; not drink under unsafe conditions; and not make light of getting drunk. Parents should also be encouraged to not ask their children to bring them or fix them a drink.

Parents should have opportunities to practice and gain confidence in talking with their children about substance experimentation and use. A particularly important discussion could address the topic of "the advantages of drinking something nonalcoholic." Some of the advantages that children and parents may identify in such a discussion could include the following:

1. You may be less apt to make a fool of yourself on a date.

2. Your parents may be more willing to let you use the car or truck.

3. You may make a good impression on people who matter to you.

4. You would be more likely to stay out of trouble with the law, teachers, parents, and others.

5. You will have more money to spend on other items such as a stereo, records, clothes, recreational equipment, a car or truck, or a college education.
6. You may lose weight or maintain an adequate weight.
7. You are more apt to be in control of yourself.

Group and Individual Prevention/Treatment Approaches

Many American Indian youth would benefit from a positive individual relationship with a professional person. Others would enjoy the opportunity to participate in a group experience with their peers.

Factors to consider in providing appropriate individual and group services to American Indian youth include the following:

1. Focus on establishing relationships with Indian youth that convey honest and genuine concern. Listen to them. Deal appropriately with their resistance. Encourage their participation.
2. Document and reflect their behavior appropriately. Concretely identify their successes and positive changes in attitudes, values, and behavior.
3. Don't accept excuses. Don't put Indian youth down. And never give up.
4. Confront the problem drinking behavior. Assist American Indian youth to confront their own problem drinking behaviors.
5. Teach American Indian youth problem-solving skills. Help them identify problems they are creating for themselves, possible solutions, consequences of such actions, and realistic goals.
6. Seek the assistance of professional or lay counselors and peers who could be beneficial to American Indian youth. Such people as A. A. members, clergymen, treatment program counselors, and physicians may be in a position to be of help to Indian youth. Relationships with other non-substance-using American Indian youth are critical to the success of these programs.
7. Utilize the services of American Indian medicine people as appropriate.
8. Help Indian youth find their own alternative activities to drinking. These may be highly individualistic and could include participation

in school and recreational activities, volunteer work, employment, and community activities.

9. Assist American Indian youth to acquire academic skills necessary for their success. Remedial programs, tutoring programs, peer counseling, and other services may be individually appropriate for Indian youth.

10. If necessary, a young person may benefit from the opportunity to participate in a day-care treatment program or an inpatient treatment program. A foster home placement or group home placement may also be beneficial. Halfway house programs may be appropriate for some youth.

Recreational and physical education groups are important to American Indian youth. Any individual or group recreational/sports activity could be appropriate. Youth leadership training groups also could be beneficial. Youth may participate on community committees, organize volunteer programs, help tutor young children, provide services to elders, and assist in any unique project for their particular community.

"Theme Centered" groups can be interesting, educational, and growth-motivating for youth. Some of the themes to which these groups could relate are future goals, men's issues, women's issues, educational goals, vocational goals, self-esteem enhancement, stress identification and management, and other topics that are of interest or problematic to the youth involved.

Summary

Traditional values of American Indians promote physical and mental well-being among all Indian people. Indian tribes and organizations today are advocating coordinated community approaches to address the problems of substance use and abuse among their youth. The focus of such programs must provide for community support and involvement, coordinated school approaches, programs for parents and families, and group and individual services for youth.

In order to establish effective community programs, formal and informal organizations serving Indian communities must be involved in all stages of their planning and programming. The projects must involve all interested community individuals—including youth, parents, and "elders." Such an approach will coordinate both prevention and treatment approaches and provide strong evaluation programs to identify and reinforce those programs that are most effective in goal achievement. These evaluations will be required to identify what works. Effective programs should be shared with all Indian communities throughout the United States.

These coordinated community efforts can involve Indian people in positively identifying and supporting programs that enhance their value systems, culture, and traditions in ways that will benefit all Indian people, including youth and their families.

References

Beauvais, F., & LaBoueff, S. (1985). Drug and alcohol abuse intervention in American Indian communities. *International Journal of the Addictions, 20*(1), 139-171.

Gottfredson, G. D. (1984). Standards for program development evaluation plans. *Psychological Documents, 14*(32).

Gottfredson, G. D., & Gottfredson, D. C. (1987). *Using organization development to improve school climate* (Report No. 17). Center for Research on Elementary and Middle Schools, Baltimore, MD: The Johns Hopkins University.

Indian kids lead third annual 325-mile run against drugs. (1986). *Linkages for Indian Child Welfare Programs, 4*(5), 1-4.

Kumpfer, Karol L. (1988). *Challenges to prevention programs in schools: The thousand flowers must bloom.* Unpublished manuscript, University of Utah, Graduate School of Social Work.

McDiarmid, G. W. (1983). Community and competence: A study of an indigenous primary prevention organization in an Alaskan Village. *White Cloud Journal, 3*(1), 53-74.

Oetting, E. R., Beauvais, F., & Edwards, R. (1988). Alcohol and Indian youth: Social and psychological correlates and prevention. *Journal of Drug Issues, 18*(1), 87-102.

Oetting, E. R., Edwards, R., & Beauvais, F. (1985). Reliability and discriminant validity of the children's drug-use survey. *Psychological Reports, 56*, 751-756.

Positive Indian parenting: Honoring our children by honoring our traditions. Portland, OR: Northwest Indian Child Welfare Institute.

Stewart, P. (1987). *Nations within a nation: Historical Statistics of American Indians.* Westport, CT: Greenwood.

15

Hispanic Adolescents and Substance Abuse: Implications for Research, Treatment, and Prevention

MELVIN DELGADO

Introduction

There is little doubt that substance abuse has tremendous impact on the Hispanic community in the United States. Its impact is far wider than the adolescent abusing drugs—his or her family, neighbors, and community also are impacted. However, the topic, although receiving greater attention in the professional and mass media, has not benefited from a systematic study. The primary goal of this chapter is to provide a clearer understanding of alcohol and other drug abuse among Hispanic youth. This will be accomplished through the following: (1) demographic profile of Hispanics—this will provide the reader with a foundation concerning

Authors' Note: This chapter is based, in part, upon a report coauthored with Sylvia Rodriguez-Andrew (1989), titled *Hispanic Adolescents and Substance Abuse,* under contract with the Office of Substance Abuse Prevention, ADAMHA. Address of the author: Boston University School of Social Work, 264 Bay State Road, Boston, MA 02215 who we are talking about when we say "Hispanic community"; (2) review of the literature on Hispanic adolescent substance abuse—this section will address nine key aspects; (3) emerging characteristics of high risk Hispanic youth—with a special focus on family and socioenvironment; and (4) recommendations for research, treatment, and prevention.

Demographic Profile of Hispanics

The Hispanic population in the United States can be best categorized as follows: (1) experiencing rapid increase in size; (2) highly concentrated in certain states, regions, and urban areas; (3) young; (4) primarily consisting of three Hispanic ethnic groups; and (5) low educational achievement. These factors have profound implications for substance abuse prevention, intervention, and research.

1. Rapid increase in the number of Hispanics: According to the 1980 U.S. Census Bureau, there are approximately 14.6 million Hispanics living in the United States. Mexican Americans (60%) represent the largest group, followed by Puerto Ricans (14%) and Cubans (6%) (Weyr, 1988). Other Hispanic groups combined account for approximately 20% of the total Hispanic population (Ford Foundation, 1984).

Between 1970 and 1980, the Hispanic population in the United States increased by 61% compared to 11% for the general population; this increase, which by most estimates has continued into the 1980s, is attributed to high fertility and immigration (Ford Foundation, 1984). The 1980 fertility rate of Hispanic women, for example, age 15-44 was 95.4 per 1,000—approximately 32 points higher than that of white, non-Hispanic women (62.4) and 5 points higher than black women (90.7). (Ford Foundation, 1984).

The impact of immigration and the number of undocumented Hispanics in the United States has received increased public attention within the past two years. The difficulty in reaching and counting this population, particularly in large urban areas presents a serious challenge in the field of human services and substance abuse in particular.

2. Geographic distribution of Hispanics: The states of California (31.1%), Texas (20.4%), New York (11.4%), Florida (5.9%), and Illinois (4.4%), account for 73.2% of all Hispanics in the United States. California, Texas, and New York account for almost two-thirds of the total Hispanic population (Ford Foundation, 1984).

Hispanics are the most urbanized ethnic group in the United States with 83% living in urban areas compared to 77% for blacks and 66% for whites; approximately half of all Hispanics live in 10 metropolitan areas with Los Angeles (2 million) and New York (1.5 million) having the highest number in the United States (Ford Foundation, 1984).

3. Youthfulness of Hispanic population: One-third of the Hispanic population in the United States is under the age of 15, compared to approximately 20% of the general population. Puerto Ricans and Mexican Americans, with a median age of 22, represent the youngest Hispanic groups, and Cubans, with a median age of 38, the oldest; as a group, Hispanics have a median age of 23, compared to 25 for blacks and 31 for the general population (Ford Foundation, 1984).

4. Low educational achievement of Hispanics. It is in education that the gap in achievement between Hispanics and other groups is the widest and most serious. As it will be noted in other sections of this chapter, schools very often are the primary focus of Hispanic substance abuse prevention efforts. However, as noted by the National Commission on Secondary Schooling for Hispanics (1984), it will require a prodigious national effort to make this system more responsive to Hispanic students, particularly in the following areas:

   a. The schools Hispanics attend very often are crowded, poorly equipped, and have lower per pupil budgets than other schools in their areas.

   b. Hispanics are often over-age for their grade levels because of language problems in earlier years. Thus almost 1 in 4 of all Hispanics who enter high school are over-age.

   c. Two-thirds of Hispanics attend schools where over half of the students are of color.

   d. Over the next 20 years, Hispanics will become the majority of the school population and the majority of the work force in many areas of the country.

e. Between 1976 and 1983, combined SAT scores for Mexican Americans increased by 22 points (686-708) and Puerto Ricans increased their scores by 4 points (761 to 765).

The primary consequences of the above conditions is that the Hispanic drop-out rate is extremely high. For example, New York City, widely regarded as having the best educational attainment level for Puerto Ricans in the United States, has an estimated drop-out rate that ranges from a low of 41.7% to a high of 80% (Fitzpatrick, 1987).

Review of the Literature on Hispanic Adolescent Substance Abuse

Before proceeding to analyze the literature on Hispanic adolescent substance abuse, there are five key factors that seriously impede a comprehensive understanding of the impact of alcohol and other drugs on Hispanic adolescents and their community (Gilbert & Alcocer, 1988; Humm-Delgado & Delgado, 1983). These factors can be classified as follows: (1) lack of specificity on what is meant by "Hispanic"; (2) a tendency to combine "Hispanics" with other people of color into a category of "minority"; (3) confusion related to age and gender regarding the findings and implications for services; (4) shortcomings in research methodology and sample selection; and (5) limitations related to use of statistics based upon population in treatment.

An analysis of the existing literature on Hispanic adolescents' alcohol and other drug use has been the recent topic of several authors. Three reviews focus exclusively on the extent of alcohol use among Hispanic youth (Gilbert & Alcocer, 1988; Singer, 1987), and more specifically among Mexican Americans (Gilbert & Cervantes, 1986a, 1986b). The extent of substance abuse among the various Hispanic adolescent groups has been examined by Humm-Delgado and Delgado (1983). Hispanic adolescent treatment issues were described by Delgado (1988), while Gilbert (1987) and Galan (1988) examined prevention themes. Theoretical considerations focusing on Mexican American youth have been addressed by Morales (1984). Despite general consensus that little is known about Hispanic adolescents and substance abuse, the absence of data clearly challenges researchers and practitioners to narrow this gap.

For the purposes of reviewing the literature, the following categories will be presented: (1) age groups represented in the literature; (2) ethnic subgroups represented in the literature; (3) gender represented in the literature; (4) substances studied; (5) survey settings; (6) geographic locations; (7) treatment approaches; (8) acculturation and substance use; and (9) evaluation instruments and research designs.

1. Age groups represented in the literature: It is interesting to note that the subject of age has not been clearly defined in the literature. Invariably, the category of age is usually assigned a "general" label such as "youth," "adolescent," "high schooler," "early adolescent," "secondary schooler," "12th grader," or "junior high schooler." Needless to say, this seriously limits the generalizability of the findings.

When age groups are reported in the literature, the following age ranges highlight the difficulty of determining who is in the sample selection: 9-17 (Bloom & Padilla, 1979; Padilla, Padilla, Morales, Olmedo, & Ramirez, 1977; Rodriguez-Andrew, 1985); 9-19 (Cruz, 1987); 6-12, (Szapocnik, Kurtines, Foote, Perez-Vidal, & Hervis, 1983); 8-21 (Jackson, Carlisi, Greenway, & Zalesnick, 1981); 12-20 (Szapocnik, Kurtines, Foote, Perez-Vidal, & Hervis, 1983); 10-19 (Del Valle, 1987); 14-22 (Amsel et al., 1971); 13-17 (Stybel, Allen, & Lewis, 1976; Santos De Barona & Simpson, 1984; Singer, 1987); under 18 (Curtis & Simpson, 1976); 18-31 (Jimenez, 1980); 18 and older (Joseph, 1973); under 21 (Page, 1980); 20-50 (Neff, Hoppe & Perea, 1987); mean of 15.5 (Perez, Padilla, Ramirez, Ramirez, & Rodriguez, 1979).

2. Groups represented in the literature: Hispanic groups in the literature vary, with most authors categorizing their study simply as "Hispanic." As already noted, the practice of aggregating diverse Hispanic groups is a major obstacle in understanding the extent of

current information and refining future research. When specified, Mexican Americans represent the largest Hispanic ethnic group in the professional literature. Puerto Ricans represent the second most researched group, while Cubans, in turn, represent the third most researched group.

3. Gender represented in the literature: Gender, like age and Hispanic background, has not received sufficient attention in the literature. A large percentage of published articles invariably do not make reference to gender. Nevertheless, a number of studies have attempted to examine the impact of gender as part of the sample selection. Only one article has focused on females (De Chello, 1987); most rely exclusively on males.

Trotter's (1982) comparison of Anglo and Mexican American college students from a similar geographical location found lower levels of usage among both Mexican American males and females than their Anglo counterparts. Mata's (1986) survey of Texas rural youth also found a higher frequency of alcohol use among Anglos (63%) than Mexican Americans (56%). While Anglo males reported a higher frequency of alcohol use (63%), than Mexican American males (61%), the difference in use was slight. Among females, the differences were greater, 65% of Anglo females reported alcohol use compared to 51% of Mexican American females.

Studies based in Miami have highlighted the point that Cuban males (like Mexican American males) have a higher likelihood of abusing drugs than their female counterparts (Page, 1980; Santisteban & Szapocnik, 1982; Szapocnik, et al., 1983). Similar observations have been made pertaining to Puerto Rican male adolescents (Colon, 1987; DiBartolomeo, 1980; Robles, Martinez & Moscoso, 1979; Velez-Santori, 1981).

4. Substances studied: Without question, the research literature has focused on the study of alcohol use and abuse among Hispanic adolescents. This may be the result of an interplay of several key factors: (1) availability of alcohol and its relative low cost makes its study of prodigious importance; (2) special scholarly efforts at studying this problem through special publications on the topic (nine of the 26 articles cited are the result of two special journal issues); (3) availability of government funds for alcohol-related research; and (4) the topic

of alcohol abuse may be more easily studied than other drugs, although there has been some attention given to the study of inhalants (Dworkin & Stephens, 1980; Rodriguez-Andrew, 1985; Rubio, 1980; Santos De Barona & Simpson, 1984) and heroin (Jimenez, 1980; Joseph, 1973).

Nevertheless, the literature strongly suggests that Hispanic adolescents who abuse generally abuse more than one drug at a time and can be classified as poly-drug users. Interestingly, the professional literature has not addressed the problem of crack among Hispanic adolescents (Kerr, 1988a, 1988b, 1988c). This may be the result of publication lag time since the problem of crack has only surfaced in the last few years and may be restricted to certain geographical areas of the country.

5. Survey settings: Sample populations appear to be evenly distributed between treatment settings (either inpatient or outpatient), schools (ranging from elementary school age youth to college students), and community surveys. Although community surveys have generally focused on housing projects, other scholars have surveyed entire communities (Gurin, 1986; Santos De Barona & Simpson, 1984; Stybel, Allen, & Lewis, 1976). The heavy emphasis on studying Hispanic adolescents in treatment and schools, as already noted, skews results and makes it difficult to generalize findings to those not in treatment or enrolled in schools.

6. Geographic locations: Almost all regions of the United States have received attention in the research literature on substance abuse among Hispanic adolescents, even if the Hispanic youth were only part of a broader sample (Humm-Delgado & Delgado, 1983). However, certain locations have been the setting for extensive amounts of research; particularly New York City, Texas, Miami, Puerto Rico, East Los Angeles, and New England.

7. Treatment approaches: Despite increasing concern about Hispanic adolescent substance abuse, relatively little is reported in the area of treatment. The importance of taking into consideration a client's cultural background has been included in the professional literature. However, this acceptance has not resulted in numerous publications on how this is to be accomplished (Delgado, 1988; Pattison, 1984). The literature on this topic stresses use of a variety of treatment

modalities (Delgado, 1989): (1) family focused whenever possible; (2) attention to individual needs and self-image; (3) use of group modality as a supplement to other approaches (Delgado & Humm-Delgado, 1983); (4) provision of a wide range of support services to meet the social and developmental needs of Hispanic adolescents (Delgado, 1989; Gilbert & Alcocer, 1988; Humm-Delgado & Delgado, 1983); and (5) attention to the impact of acculturation in the implementation of any form of intervention.

8. Acculturation and substance use: The role of acculturation as either a mediating or contributing factor in alcohol and other drug use has received considerable attention in the recent professional literature. However, at this point, there has been much speculation and little empirical data (Gilbert & Cervantes, 1986a). Language preference is probably one of the most frequently cited aspects of acculturation (Padilla, et al., 1977; Perez, et al., 1979), and has tremendous implications for the language fluency of the counselor assigned to a client. The Hispanic Health and Nutrition Examination Survey (HHANES) (1987) survey reported that higher levels of substance abuse were found for those respondents (age 12-44) who preferred to be interviewed in English. While language preferences were not provided by age categories, this finding is consistent with earlier research.

Clearly, the role of acculturation in alcohol and other drug abuse is vague because of the paucity of research studies, diversity of acculturation measures, and samples involving different subgroups. Nevertheless, counselors, planners, administrators, and researchers cannot ignore the potential influence of acculturation on service delivery to this population.

9. Evaluation instruments and research designs: Self-reports and self-administered questionnaires were the most frequently cited methods of gathering information. There were several modifications to this approach such as the use of peer interviewers (Bloom & Padilla, 1979; Padilla, et al., 1977; Perez, et al., 1979; Rodriguez-Andrew, 1985), and counselor observations and evaluations (Santos de Barona & Simpson, 1984). Several authors reported research designs that utilized follow-up evaluations as a central feature of the investigation. Only two studies have utilized secondary data analysis in their research (Puyo, 1980; Joseph, 1973). The absence of studies that control for a wide range of independent and intervening variables (Hispanic background being an important variable) makes evaluation impossible.

Emerging Characteristics of
High Risk Hispanic Youth

Our understanding of factors associated with the use of alcohol and other drugs among Hispanic youth is in the developmental stages. Comparable knowledge about etiological factors and childhood predictors associated with subsequent alcohol and other drug use among youth in the general population have not been examined among Hispanic youth (Hawkins, Lishner, Catalano, & Howard, 1986; Kumpfer & DeMarsh, 1986; Newcomb & Bentler, 1988b). While studies to date provide the foundation for more elaborate research, several emerging factors have been found to be associated with alcohol and other drug use specifically among Hispanic adolescents. More research is needed, however, in delineating whether there are specific (or a combination of) risk factors for all Hispanic groups or whether there are more salient factors to consider among specific groups such as Mexican Americans, Puerto Ricans, and Cubans.

Factors generally cluster into two broad categories: (1) family and (2) socioenvironmental. Each of these categories encompass several different dimensions. As with existing studies of risk factors, the literature on Hispanic adolescent substance abuse does not identify any one risk factor as being the cause of or exercising greater influence on subsequent alcohol and other drug abuse. Interestingly, the literature does not note the presence of several other risk factors commonly used in looking at adolescent substance abuse. The absence of these factors, however, may be attributed to the lack of research in this area rather than their deliberate omission from current investigations.

Family

Several studies noted that Hispanic youth have a higher likelihood of abusing drugs if parents or older siblings abuse alcohol and other substances (DiBartolomeo, 1980; Dworkin & Stephens, 1980; Estrada, Rabow & Watts, 1982). Family disintegration as a result of an absent father, frequent family disagreements, poor communication, and unclear expectations of parents were also prominently noted in the literature. The topic of religiosity (i.e., church attendance, importance of religion, and religious views associated with alcohol consumption) also was noted as being influential in determining use of alcohol and other drugs. However, findings from two studies were contradictory: Estrada, Rabow, & Watts, (1982) found religiosity to be associated with alcohol consumption for females and not males, while Guinn (1975) found alcohol consumption to be positively associated with church attendance—unfortunately, his study did not control for gender (Gilbert & Cervantes, 1986a).

Socioenvironmental

This category can be best divided into (1) the impact of poverty; (2) availability of alcohol and drugs; (3) schools; and (4) the influence of peers. Only a few authors noted the impact of poverty, as manifested by limited upward mobility opportunities, as a key risk factor in substance abuse. The availability of alcohol and other drugs within the community frequently was cited in the literature—in essence, these substances were prevalent, easily obtainable, and involved relatively minimal legal risk for the consumer. Another dimension to this issue has been raised by Dworkin and Stephens (1980) in their noting the importance of a prevailing coping style within a community as influencing risk-taking behavior involving drugs. Other authors raised the role of subcultures reinforcing drug use and abuse (Nuttall & Nuttall, 1981; Padilla, et al., 1977; Perez, et al., 1979). School performance has been cited as an important influence on Hispanic adolescent attitudes and behaviors towards alcohol and other drugs. Absenteeism, low educational achievement, and acting out behavior in the classroom often are associated with drug abuse. Finally, the impact of peer influence has received considerable attention and affirmation in the literature.

The professional literature does not identify, in any meaningful manner, suicide attempts, mental health problems, victimization by child abuse and neglect, and/or physical disability, as risk factors for alcohol and other drug abuse among Hispanic adolescents. Is it because these factors are not present in the Hispanic community? Or, are community-based agencies unwilling or unable to address these issues? Further research is needed to answer these questions.

Research, Treatment and
Prevention Recommendations

The recommendations that follow focus on research, treatment, and prevention, and are based upon a review of the literature, field research, and the provision of consultation-training in the field of substance abuse.

Research

There is a need for more studies in nontreatment, noncourt, and nonprison settings to determine accurate prevalence of alcohol and drug use. Further, researchers should experiment with innovative techniques such as those developed by Bloom and Padilla (1979) in which they used Hispanic adolescent peer interviewers in conducting their research.

Longitudinal studies are needed to obtain an in-depth understanding of changes in patterns of use over time; these would allow researchers to hypothesize about the impact of the social environment on substance abuse (e.g., drug availability, "fads," and regional shifts due to population changes). In addition, they would provide important information pertaining to substance abuse progression as well as the nature of alcohol and other drug use and abuse.

Researchers must clearly define the variables that enter into the dimensions of "Hispanic" or "minority." Failure to delineate these terms will seriously limit the generalizability of the findings.

Increased research activity is needed regarding various Hispanic subgroups and substances. Mexican Americans for example, have received a disproportionately low amount of research and relatively little is known about the impact on the community of "'new" drugs such as crack.

Research projects that endeavor to study the interplay of gender, age, and acculturation are lacking. The definition of acculturation used by researchers at the Spanish Guidance Center (Miami, Florida) is probably the most accepted in examining acculturation and substance abuse. However, more research is needed to examine whether this definition is applicable to other Hispanic groups. Szapocnik and Kurtines (1980) state that

According to this theoretical model, individual acculturation is a linear function of the amount of time a person has been exposed to the host culture, and the rate at which the acculturation process takes place is a function of the age and sex of the individual. Further, two aspects of the process of acculturation itself are a dimension of functioning and the process as it takes place with respect to internalized value orientations. (p. 141)

There is a need for research that examines the relationship between drug use/abuse and high risk factors for Hispanic youth and outlines what risk factors are more prominently associated with Hispanic substance abuse. More specifically, Hispanic subgroups need to be considered in exploring the extent and type of alcohol and other drug use that is reported by these groups.

Researchers should gather more specific information on environmental factors. Existing research indicates that Hispanic communities have higher numbers of liquor establishments and higher rates of crime—including alcohol-and other drug-related arrests (Gilbert & Cervantes, 1986a, 1986b). It appears that the role of the environment may be an important intervening variable in program outcome.

Data should be gathered on the characteristics and backgrounds of staff involved in providing prevention intervention services to Hispanic adolescents. Relatively little is known about who provides prevention activities to youth—particularly high risk youth.

Research studies need to obtain greater specificity in delineating characteristics of their target populations regarding their involvement with alcohol and other drugs. For example, gateway drug use was cited by several studies; however, the extent of this drug use was unknown. Youth who have a history of regular drug use are significantly different from youth who report having used "once or twice." The diversity of referral sources suggest that the target population reflects various levels of drug use ranging from experimental to regular use. Similarly, the objectives of intervention would vary based upon their level of involvement. Thus researchers must be specific about their target populations if national implications are to be derived from their experiences.

Treatment

It is imperative that treatment programs develop and implement culture-specific intervention approaches and techniques. For example, Delgado (1988) has developed a framework for a culture-specific intake that consists of the following aspects:

> Five principles should guide the development of an intake for Hispanic adolescents. First, every effort must be made to develop an understanding of the role alcohol and other drugs play in the adolescent's family . . . . Examining patterns and practices of alcohol and drug use provide a contextual framework from which to understand the client. . . . Second, does the adolescent identify him/herself as "Hispanic." The answer to this question may surprise an intake worker. . . . As noted by several researchers, classification into the term "Hispanic," or even "Cuban," "Puerto Rican," and so on, ignores major differences related to such factors as socio-economic status, legal status in the United States, degree of acculturation, and degree and extent of influence of Spanish, African and Indian backgrounds. . . . Third, it is necessary to determine language preference and much research has been reported on the importance of language assessment. . . . Fourth, what is the adolescent's social network? Information related to the constellation of an adolescent's social network will provide important information for the purposes of assessment and identify potential sources of support in the community. . . . Fifth, a determination must be made of what previous assistance has been used by the adolescent. This type of information should not be restricted to "formal" programs. . . . In addition, what natural support systems have been tapped in helping the adolescent and his/her family with the problem should be explored . . . (Delgado, 1988, pp. 62-63).

n short, the above example represents one aspect of a culture-pecific approach.

Treatment programs must endeavor to develop linkages with ther formal and informal (natural support systems) providers vithin the Hispanic community. Clearly, the socioenvironmental ssues associated with Hispanic substance abuse require a multi-aceted approach to intervention.

Program developers must be encouraged to use a variety of treatment modalities with special emphasis on use of family and groups in addition to the more traditional focused efforts.

Treatment approaches need to have greater specificity concerning the relationship between type of risk factor and substance abuse, and intervention designed to address this.

More information is needed on treatment outcomes. Research in this area is necessary because of the paucity of such projects in the field of substance abuse with Hispanic adolescents.

Prevention

Programs and funding sources should fund projects that support and interest Hispanic youth at an early age to remain in school. In addition, efforts must be undertaken to make schools more accountable to the community they serve.

Agencies must endeavor to collaborate with law enforcement and juvenile justice systems. The availability of drugs needs to be addressed at all levels of government. However, law enforcement agencies play a critical role in the process. Alternatives to the court system also must be explored in an effort to divert Hispanic youngsters into more therapeutic-educational programs.

Hispanic natural support systems should be utilized in prevention approaches; for example, religious organizations or the extended family can be educated to the realities of substance abuse in order to support adolescents in withstanding peer pressure to abuse alcohol and other drugs.

Funding sources should encourage the development of innovative outreach models that are effective in attracting and maintaining Hispanic youngsters in programs. A special emphasis on model development in this area can produce a wealth of material and data on how best to approach and attract Hispanic youngsters and their families.

Funding sources should fund special projects that seek to work with gangs in an effort to address the problem of substance abuse among members and potential members. Clearly, gangs are a force to be dealt with in any prevention effort addressing inner-city Hispanic youth.

For prevention to succeed, community support is essential. Funding sources can play a leadership role in helping to design and implement strategies at getting community support for drug prevention and intervention programs. This can be accomplished through special funding of such efforts that specifically address this aspect as part of programming and research, or as part of any demonstration project requiring funding.

There is a need to develop "innovative" community education campaigns that are not borrowed or modified from current Anglo efforts. This is particularly important since Anglo-oriented campaigns do not take into account the role of ethnicity/culture in the development and delivery of drug-related information.

References

Amsel, Z., Fishman, J. J., Rivkind, L., Kavaler, F., Krug, D., Cline, M., Brophy, F., & Conwell, D. (1971). The use of narcotics register for follow-up of a cohort of adolescent addicts. *International Journal of the Addictions, 6*(2), 225-239.

Bloom, D., & Padilla, A. (1979). A peer interviewer model in conducting surveys among Mexican American youth. *Journal of Community Psychology, 7,* 129-136.

Colon, W. (1987). The meaning of culturally appropriate treatment for the Hispanic adolescent—Panelist No. 2. In M. Singer, L. Davison, & F. Yalin (Eds.), *Conference proceedings: Alcohol use and abuse among Hispanic adolescents.* Hartford, CT: Hispanic Health Council.

Cruz, J. A. (1987). Prevention education for Hispanic adolescents—Panelist No. 2. In M. Singer, L. Davison, & F. Yalin (Eds.) *Conference proceedings: Alcohol use and abuse among Hispanic adolescents.* Hartford, CT: Hispanic Health Council.

Curtis, B., & Simpson, D. (1976). Demographic characteristics of groups classified by patterns of multiple drug abuse: A 1969-1971 sample. *International Journal of the Addictions, 11*(1), 161-173.

De Chello, P. (1987). Prevention education for Hispanic adolescents—Panelist No. 3. In M. Singer, L. Davison, & F. Yalin (Eds.), *Conference proceedings: Alcohol use and abuse among Hispanic adolescents.* Hartford, CT: Hispanic Health Council.

Delgado, M. (1988). Alcoholism treatment and Hispanic youth. *Journal of Drug Issues, 18*(1). 59-68.

Delgado, M. (1989). Treatment and prevention of alcoholism for Hispanics. In T. Watts & R. Wright, Jr. (Eds.). *Alcoholism in minority populations.* Springfield, IL: Charles C Thomas.

Delgado, D., & Humm-Delgado, M. (1983). Hispanic adolescents and substance abuse: Issues for the 1980's. In R. Isralowitz & M. Singer (Eds.), *Adolescent substance abuse: A guide to prevention and treatment.* New York: Haworth.

Del Valle, M. (1987). Prevention education for Hispanic adolescents—Panelist No. 1. In M. Singer, L. Davison and F. Yalin (Eds.), *Conference Proceedings: Alcohol Use and Abuse Among Hispanic Adolescents.* Hartford, CT: Hispanic Health Council.

DiBartolomeo, J. (1980). A descriptive study of the problem of drinking behavior among Spanish speaking youth of Puerto Rican heritage (Unpublished doctoral dissertation, University of Maryland).

Dworkin, A., & Stephens, R. (1980). Mexican American adolescent inhalant abuse: A proposed model. *Youth & Society, 11*(4), 493-506.

Estrada, A., Rabow, J., & Watts, R. (1982). Alcohol use among Hispanic adolescents: A preliminary report. *Hispanic Journal of Behavioral Sciences, 4*(3), 339-351.

Fitzpatrick, J. P. (1987). *Puerto Rican Americans*. Englewood Cliffs, NJ: Prentice-Hall.

Ford Foundation. (1984). *Hispanics: Challenges and Opportunities*. New York: Author.

Galan, F. (1988). Alcoholism prevention and Hispanic youth. *Journal of Drug Issues, 18*(1), 49-58.

Gilbert, M. (1987). Programmatic approaches to the alcohol related needs of Mexican Americans. In *Mexican Americans and alcohol*. Los Angeles: University of California at Los Angeles, Spanish Speaking Mental Health Research Center.

Gilbert, M., & Alcocer, A. M. (1988). Alcohol use and Hispanic youth: An overview. *Journal of Drug Issues, 18*(1), 33-48.

Gilbert, M., & Cervantes, R. (1986a). Patterns and practices of alcohol use among Mexican Americans: A comprehensive review. *Hispanic Journal of Behavioral Sciences, 8*(1), 1-60.

Gilbert, M., & Cervantes, R. (1986b). Alcohol services for Mexican Americans: A review of utilization patterns, treatment considerations and prevention activities. *Hispanic Journal of Behavioral Sciences, 8*(3), 191-223.

Guinn, R. (1975). Characteristics of drug use among Mexican-American students. *Journal of Drug Education, 5*(3), 235-241.

Gurin, G. (1986). Research issues: Drinking behavior, problems, and treatment among Mainland Puerto Ricans. *Research Bulletin Hispanic Research Center Fordham University, 9*(2), 1-7.

Hawkins, D., Lishner, D., Catalano, R., & Howard, M. (1986). Childhood predictors of adolescent substance abuse: Toward an empirically grounded theory. In S. Griswold-Ezekoye, K. Kumpfer, & W. Bukoski (Eds.), *Childhood and chemical abuse: Prevention and intervention*. New York: Haworth.

Hispanic Health and Nutrition Examination Survey (HHANES). (1987). Use of selected drugs among Hispanics: Mexican Americans, Puerto Ricans, Cuban Americans. Rockville, MD: U.S. Department of Health and Welfare.

Humm-Delgado, D., & Delgado, M. (1983). Assessing Hispanic mental health needs: Issues and recommendations. *Journal of Community Psychology, 11*(3), 363-375.

Jackson, N., Carlisi, J., Greenway, C. & Zalesnick, M. (1981). Age of initial drug experimentation among white and non-white ethnics. *International Journal of the Addictions, 16*(8), 1373-1386.

Jimenez, D. (1980). *A comparative analysis of the support system of white and Puerto Rican clients in drug treatment programs*. Saratoga, CA: Century Twenty-One Publishing.

Joseph, H. (1973). A probation department treats heroin addicts. *Federal Probation, 37*, 25-30.

Kerr, P. (1988a, May 2). Under 16, hooked on crack and no place to help them. *The New York Times*. p. B1, B4.

Kerr, P. (1988b, June 23). Addictions' hidden toll: Poor families in turmoil. *The New York Times*, p. A1, B4.

Kerr, P. (1988c, June 29). Syphilis surge and crack use raising fears on spread of AIDS. *The New York Times*, p. B1, B5.

Kumpfer, K., & DeMarsh, J. (1986). Family environmental and genetic influences on children's future chemical dependency. In S. Griswold-Ezekoye, K. Kumpfer, & W. Bukoski (Eds.), *Childhood and chemical abuse: Prevention and intervention.* New York: Haworth.

Mata, A. (1986). Alcohol use among rural South Texas youth. Austin: Texas Commission on Alcohol and Drug Abuse.

Morales, A. (1984). Substance abuse and Mexican American youth: An overview. *Journal of Drug Issues, 14*(3), 297-311.

Neff, J., Hoppe, S., & Perea, P. (1987). Acculturation and alcohol use: Drinking patterns and problems among Anglo and Mexican American male drinkers. *Hispanic Journal of Behavioral Sciences, 9*(2), 151-181.

Newcomb, M., & Bentler, P. (1988a). Substance use and ethnicity: Differential impact of peer and adult models. *The Journal of Psychology, 120*(1), 83-95.

Newcomb, M., & Bentler, P. (1988b). *Consequences of adolescent drug use.* Beverly Hills, CA: Sage.

Nuttall, R., & Nuttall, E. (1981). A longitudinal study predicting heroin and alcohol use among Puerto Ricans. In A. Schecter (Ed.), *Drug dependence and alcoholism volume 2: Social & behavior issues.* New York: Plenum.

National Commission on Secondary Schooling for Hispanics. (1984). *Hispanics and urban high school reform.* New York: Hispanic Policy Development Project.

Padilla, E., Padilla, A. M., Morales, A., Olmedo, E. L., & Ramirez, R. (1977). Inhalant, marijuana, and alcohol abuse among barrio children and adolescents. *International Journal of the Addictions, 14*(7), 945-964.

Page, J. (1980). The children of exile: Relationships between the acculturation process and drug use among Cuban youth. *Youth and Society, 11*(4), 431-447.

Pattison, E. (1984). Cultural level interventions in the arena of alcoholism. *Alcoholism: Clinical and Experimental Research, 8*(2), 160-164.

Perez, R., Padilla, A. M., Ramirez, A., Ramirez, R., & Rodriguez, M. (1979). Correlates and changes over time in drug and alcohol use within a barrio population. *American Journal of Community Psychology, 8*(6), 621-636.

Puyo, A. (1980). *Family headship and drug addiction among male Puerto Rican youth: An investigation of quality of family life.* Unpublished doctoral dissertation, Fordham University, New York.

Robles, R., Martinez, R., Moscoso, M. R. (1979). Drug use among public and private secondary school students in Puerto Rico. *International Journal of the Addictions, 14*(2), 243-256.

Robles, R., Martinez, R. E. & Moscoso, M. R. (1980). Predictors of adolescent drug behavior: The case of Puerto Rico. *Youth and Society, 6*(4), 415-430.

Rodriguez-Andrew, S. (1984). Los ninos: Intervention efforts with Mexican American families. *Focus on Family and Chemical Dependency, 7*(2), 8-29.

Rodriguez-Andrew, S. (1985). Inhalant abuse: An emerging problem among Mexican American adolescents. *Children Today, 14*(4), 23-25.

Rubio, G. (1980). CBO's helping inhalant abusers. *Agenda,* Sept-Oct., 9-11.

Santisteban, D., & Szapocnik, J. (1982). Substance abuse disorders among Hispanics: A focus on prevention. In R. Becerra, M. Harno, & J. Escobar (Eds.), *Mental health and Hispanic Americans: Clinical perspectives.* New York: Grune & Stratton.

Santos DeBarona, M., & Simpson, D. (1984). Inhalant users in drug abuse prevention programs. *American Journal of Drug and Alcohol Abuse, 10*(4), 503-518.

Singer, M. (1987). Indigenous treatment for alcoholism in the Hispanic community—Panelist No. 3. In M. Singer, L. Davison, & F. Yalin (Eds.), *Conference proceedings: Alcohol use and abuse among Hispanic adolescents.* Hartford, CT: Hispanic Health Council.

Stybel, L., Allen, P., & Lewis, F. (1976). Deliberate hydrocarbon inhalation among low socioeconomic adolescents not necessarily apprehended by the police. *International Journal of the Addictions, 11,* 345-361.

Szapocnik, J., & Kurtines, W. M. (1980). Acculturation, biculturalism and adjustment among Cuban Americans. In A. M. Padilla (Ed.), *Acculturation: Theory, models and some new findings.* Boulder, CO: Westview.

Szapocnik, J., Kurtines, W. M., Foote, F., Perez-Vidal, A., & Hervis, O. (1983). Conjoint versus one-person family therapy: Some evidence for the effectiveness of conducting family therapy through one person. *Journal of Consulting and Clinical Psychology, 51*(6), 889-899.

Szapocnik, J., Kurtines, W. M., Foote, F., Perez-Vidal, A., & Hervis, O. (1986). Conjoint versus one-person family therapy: Further evidence for the effectiveness of conducting family therapy through one person with drug-abusing adolescents. *Journal of Consulting and Clinical Psychology, 54*(3), 395-397.

Trotter, R. (1982). Ethnic and sexual patterns of alcohol use: Anglo and Mexican American college students. *Adolescence, 17*(66), 305-325.

Velez-Santori, C. (1981). Drug use among Puerto Rican youth: An exploration of generational status differences (Doctoral Dissertation, Columbia University).

Weyr, T. (1988). *Hispanic U.S.A.* New York: Harper & Row.

PART 5

Suicide

16

Suicidal Behavior Among Minority Youth in the United States

KAREN F. WYCHE

MARY JANE ROTHERAM-BORUS

Across ethnic groups, adolescent suicide has increased for the last 30 years, with parallel increases across all groups. Sex differences also remain consistent across ethnic groups: males complete suicide more frequently than females and females attempt suicide more frequently than males (May & Dizmang, 1974). While the rate of increase has been consistent across groups, the rates of completed and attempted suicides among adolescents vary substantially by ethnic group. American Indians die by suicide more frequently than white adolescents; black and Hispanic youths appear to complete suicide less often than white or American Indian youths (Gibbs, 1988; McIntosh, 1983-1984; Smith, Mercy, & Warren, 1985).

These rates are controversial and the factors associated with these differential rates are unclear. The goals of this chapter are (1) to describe ethnic differences observed in these rates, (2) to examine potential hypotheses that may lead one to question the validity of these rates, and (3) to outline the norms of the American Indian, black, and Hispanic culture that are hypothesized to influence the rates. The suicide-related cultural norms also impact the design of triage and therapeutic interventions with suicidal minority adolescents. Therefore, we will briefly discuss ways in which white therapists may acquire increased sensitivity to the norms of their minority patients' understanding of death, suicide, and the therapeutic process.

Incidence of Suicide Among Minority Youth

Suicidal behavior is a serious mental health problem for adolescents. It is second only to accidents and the leading cause of death (U.S. Department of Health and Human Services [USDHHS], 1985). Comparisons of adolescent suicide deaths for several years indicate that the rate has held fairly constant for ages 15-24 (Lewis, Johnson, Cohen, Garcia, & Velez, 1988). In 1980 the rate of suicide for all 15- to 24-year-olds was 12.3 per 100,000, and in 1978 the rate was 12.1 per 100,000. However, for ages 15-19 the rate increased from 3.6 per 100,000 in 1960 to 8.7 per 100,000 in 1982. This is contrasted to the suicide rates for the population as a whole that was 10.6 per 100,000 in 1960 and 12.2 per 100,000 in 1982 (Lewis et al., 1988). These overall rates mask considerable variability in rates by ethnic groups requiring a separate review for American Indian, black, and Hispanic youth.

American Indians

American Indians have the highest rate of completed suicide of any ethnic group in the United States (McIntosh, 1983-1984), even though the rate is decreasing. In 1980 the Indian Health Service reported a rate of 14.1 per 100,000 down from a rate of 26.6 per 100,000 in 1977 for the 28 reservation states (USDHHS, 1986). Alc hol abuse is a critical risk factor associated with suicidal behavior with 80% of American Indian suicide attempters also having alcohol abuse problems (Young, 1988). Age is also a risk factor. High rates of suicide are found primarily among young American Indians (late teen years to early 20s), the age group that makes up the largest proportion of the population (McIntosh, 1983-1984). Overall, the suicide rate among American Indians was two and one-half times greater than that of white youth from the same age group. (Manson, 1987). While it has been claimed that cluster suicides occur among American Indians (Manson, 1987), there are only a few specific examples reported (Gould, Wallenstein, & Davidson, 1989). Suicide rates differ by tribe (Shore, 1974; US-DHHS, 1986). Rates appear lower among the agricultural-based tribes of the Southwest and higher among the more migratory tribes in the Great Plains (Resnik & Dizmang, 1971). In 1980 the Navajo and the Chippewa had the lowest rates. The Shoshone-Bannock and Apache had rates that were 10 times the national average (USDHHS, 1986).

Black Americans

Suicide is the third leading cause of death among black youth age 15-24, after homicides and accidents (Gibbs, 1988). As is true for white youths, black male suicide deaths are more frequent in the 20-24 age range (18.5 per 100,000) than for ages 15-19 (8.2 per 100,000) (USDHHS, 1985). Overall, however, the suicide rate for youth age 15-24 tripled for black males and doubled for black females from 1960 to 1979 (Gibbs, 1988) with the highest rates in urban areas. For example, in New York City, the suicide rate among black males and females, age 15-30 is higher than among whites of the same age group (Hendin, 1987). This figure has held fairly constant for the last 70 years (Hendin, 1987).

Hispanic Americans

Few studies report suicide rates among Hispanic adolescents, and substantial discrepancies appear in the date that are reported. Recorded suicide rates for Mexican Americans have varied from 1.8 to 10.5 per 100,000 persons (Hope & Martin, 1986). Smith, Mercy, and Warren (1985) studied suicide in five Southwestern states (California, Colorado, Arizona, New Mexico, and Texas) where the majority of the Mexican American population resides. Mexican American rates were found to be approximately half that of Anglos. Those Hispanics who attempted and committed suicide were younger than the Anglo group, and the rate for Mexican American males was four times that of Mexican American females.

Explanations for Differential Suicide Rates

Several researchers have suggested that the apparent ethnic differences are artifacts of reporting procedures. Another explanation may be that the multiple and high stress experienced by minorities is expressed in different ways—as self-destructive behavior turned inward by American Indians and as self-destructive behavior turned outward by blacks and Hispanics. Individual differences in acculturation and enculturation, as well as differences in cultural norms also have been presented as potential explanations of the ethnic differences in suicidal behavior. We will briefly review these hypotheses.

Hypothesis 1: The Rates Are Not Different

Rather than reflecting true differences, ethnic differences may be created by the failure to consider geographic differences in urban versus rural settings or a failure to collect accurate statistics. Researchers also may have overlooked differences in drug overdoses, accidents, and provoked homicides as part of the suicide rates.

There are clear geographic differences for urban versus rural settings (Neiger & Hopkins, 1988). Most minorities in the United States are concentrated in urban, poor, inner-city neighborhoods; blacks in industrial cities and Hispanics in urban cities of the Southwest (Gibbs, 1988; Hendin, 1987; King, 1982). For example, suicide rates for blacks are higher in the northern and western parts of the United States; they are lower for southern blacks (Gibbs, 1988; Hendin, 1987; King, 1982). Little is known about American Indian suicide rates. It is estimated that 45% of all American Indians live in urban areas, 30% live on reservations, and the remainder move back and forth from the reservation to other areas (Young, 1988). However, the data on American Indian suicides comes primarily from reservation statistics (USDHHS, 1986).

Poor data gathering techniques also may explain some ethnic differences. For instance, the substantial discrepancies in the reported data on Hispanic populations (Hope & Martin, 1986) may be a product of grouping mortality data for Hispanics under rates for whites (USDHHS, 1985). Discrepancies in suicide rates among Mexican Americans can vary by study from 1.8 to 10.5 per 100,000 (Hope & Martin, 1986; Smith, Mercy, & Warren, 1985). As mentioned previously, mortality data for American Indians is reported for reservation, not urban, dwellers (USDHHS, 1986).

Some researchers have questioned whether the suicide rate for blacks is underestimated (Gibbs, 1988; Peck, 1983-1984). Peck (1983-1984) studied medical examiners' records of suicide victims and found nonwhite deaths to be less thoroughly investigated than white deaths. Concluding that a systematic racial and social class bias exists in the recording process, Peck argues that some black deaths that were recorded as accidental could be suicide.

Finally, Gibbs (1988) has argued that deaths that are classified as "unintentional and accidental" resulting from drug overdoses, automobile accidents, and adolescent-provoked homicides may, in fact, be disguised suicides. The 1985 mortality rate for death by homicide (per 100,000) for black male adolescents age 15-19, was 46.4 compared to 7.3 for white males; for youth age 20-24 the rate for black males was 86.2 compared to 14.8 for white males (USDHHS, 1985). A 1984 Center for Disease Control study in the Southwest reported a homicide rate of 39.3 per 100,000 for Hispanic men age 20-24. White men in the same age group had a rate of 11.4 (USDHHS, 1986).

Cultural attitudes can influence manipulation of self-destructive behavior. Black and Hispanic men tend to view suicide as a passive response to frustration and condone a more outwardly direct approach (Kalish & Reynolds, 1976). Dying is regarded as more honorable if it occurs in rage and aggression rather than in passive solitude. Provoking a fight and being killed as a result may be culturally more appropriate as an expression of suicidal intent, but will be reported as a homicide. Family attitudes also can create pressure to label a suicide death accidental or "undetermined," saving the surviving family from embarrassment or guilt (Gibbs, 1988).

Hypothesis 2: Minority Youth Experience Greater Stress than White American Youths

There is substantial evidence that minority youth experience greater stress than children of white Americans. Poverty, discrimination, unemployment, and fewer educational opportunities, as well as high fertility rates characterize American Indian, black, and Hispanic families in the United States. Moreover, an inverse relationship between socioeconomic status and psychological dysfunction is found consistently (Frederick, 1984; Neiger & Hopkins, 1988; Roberts, 1987; Whitlock, 1978). The stress hypothesis suggests that suicidal behavior is related to high levels of stress that can result in suicidal behavior. If this hypothesis is true then the expectation would be that all minority groups would have high suicide rates. However, the high rates of suicide among American Indians and the lower rates among blacks and Hispanics suggest variations in cultural adaptations to stress.

The stressors are multiple and have an interactive effect on the lives of these ethnic group members. One major stressor is poverty. In 1987, fewer than 11% of white children lived in families with incomes below the poverty level; 28% of Hispanic children and 33% of black children lived in families with incomes below the poverty level. (Current Population Reports, 1987). American Indian families earned on average $2,000 less than even black and Hispanic families (Yates, 1987). Unemployment is another stressor. Blacks and Hispanics also face limited options with respect to jobs, resulting in a high unemployment rate and unstable employment relative to whites (Current Population Reports, 1987). Often, those jobs that are available are accorded both low status and low pay. For example, blacks who have achieved a comparable level of education as whites receive less pay for the same job (Moore, 1982). High unemployment, particularly on reservations, is a major problem for American Indians (Young, 1988), as well as multiple health problems.

Success in school, one way to escape a culture of poverty (Ryan, 1981), is not characteristic of minority children in the United States. Hispanic and black students are overrepresented in the nation's special education classes (U.S. Department of Education, 1985). There is a 50% drop-out rate for black students (Moore, 1982) and for American Indian students (Yates, 1987). Lewis, Johnson, Cohen, Garcia, & Velez, (1988) identified a problem of low achievement in Hispanic students as has Berlin (1984) in American Indian students. Not only does low academic achievement have negative consequences for employment opportunities, but it also is identified with psychiatric problems (Lewis, Johnson, Cohen, Garcia, & Velez, 1988; Yates, 1987). Parenting styles of black and Hispanic parents reflect a different attitude than that of white parents (Powell, 1983). All parents want to protect their children from life's adversities, from pain, from ugliness. To do this, white children are taught that they have internal control over their lives, while black and Hispanic parents teach their children to expect adversity as a matter of course (Bowman & Howard, 1985; Escovar & Lazarus, 1982). They rear their children in communities where these stressors are a part of daily life and focus on preparing their children to survive. Minority children are taught to adapt to adversities over which they have little control. In the songs sung by slaves, in black and Hispanic literature, a historical attitude of "grit your teeth and bear it" is expressed (Kalish & Reynolds, 1976). Speaking only Spanish is an effective barrier to obtaining work that includes any interaction with the majority culture. Finally, of course, discrimination is present in the daily lives of any persons of color (Spencer, Brookins, & Allen, 1985).

Given that life is so much harder for minorities in the United States, should not the suicide rate be higher for American Indian, black, and Hispanic youth than for whites? Kalish and Reynolds (1976) have suggested that a cultural pattern toward expressing stress overtly, as violent behavior, is implied by high homicide rates. Among blacks and Hispanics aggressive responses to adversity are more acceptable than among American Indians. Multiple stressors may be more likely to threaten self-esteem and therefore provoke aggression (Axelson, 1985). The modeling of aggressive behaviors for black and Hispanic youth has been historical as well, since the mainstream culture has often turned aggression against minority groups. Being a victim of aggression either personally or vicariously because of one's minority group status may interact with culturally sanctioned ways of handling stress: the choice of suicide in the American Indian youth, or homicide, accidents, drug overdoses, and other self-destructive behaviors in black and Hispanic youth.

Hypothesis 3: Suicide Among Native Americans is Associated with Acculturation and Enculturation

Enculturation refers to the acquisition of the norms, values, attitudes, and behavior patterns of your own ethnic group. Acculturation refers to the acquisition of patterns of another's group. In the early 1930s, acculturative stress was presumed to occur among every minority group in the United States, since minorities needed to learn the norms of their own group, as well as that of the dominant group. Thus the term "Marginal Man" was used to refer to a minority person (Stonequist, 1935, 1964). Acculturation was associated with anxiety, stress, low self-esteem, insecurity, hostility, and defensiveness (Child, 1943; Goodman, 1964; Lewin, 1948; Mussen, 1953; Paz, 1961; Stevenson & Stewart, 1958). More recently, however, the concept of biculturalism or multicultural competence has become the goal in socializing nonwhite children in the United States. (Ramirez, 1977; Ramirez & Castaneda, 1974; Ramirez & Price-Williams, 1974). In this flexibility-synthesis model, children raised in two cultures are seen as demonstrating greater role flexibility in cognitive style, adaptability, and creativity.

The influence of acculturation can be seen among American Indians. Traditional tribes that are able to maintain their social customs have lower rates of suicide than nontraditional tribes (Berlin, 1984; Manson & Trimble, 1982; Spaulding, 1985-1986). Manson (1987) suggests that the relative stability among traditional tribes is due to the high degree of social integration and nonmigratory lifestyle. Traditional tribes maintain religious rituals, ceremonial roles, governmental structures, the clan and extended family. For youth in these traditional tribes, there is guidance from adolescence to adulthood (Hochkirchen & Jilek, 1985). Strong tribal traditions give the adolescent a feeling of security and a sense of belonging. The specific duties and obligations given to the adolescent through ceremonial rites of puberty provide needed direction and tie the adolescent to adults. Individuals from nontraditional tribes that were historically migratory, with a governance based on war chiefs and hunting activities, appear to be at higher risk for suicide (Manson, 1987). The forced movement to reservations and the forbidding by law of some ceremonial practices eroded the child rearing structure (Hochkirchen & Jilek, 1985; Manson, 1987).

For black and Hispanic youths there is substantial evidence from the developmental literature that some youth adopt a traditional orientation towards their group, others self-define as bicultural, and others adopt an out-group identification by identifying with the majority culture (Rotheram & Phinney, 1987). Some evidence suggests that biculturalism does not have a negative impact on adolescents' adjustment and self-esteem (Rotheram, 1989a). However, the setting in which identity development (the central task of adolescence) occurs determines the impact of adjustment (Erikson,

1968). For example, in schools and communities with high cross-ethnic tension, biculturalism appears to have a negative impact on depression, behavior problems, and achievement (Rotheram, in press). It would appear that children's ethnic identification and degree of enculturation and acculturation would be an important area for further investigation to help understand ethnic differences in the suicide rate. It is unclear whether these processes are related to suicide in blacks and Hispanics.

Hypothesis 4: There are Ethnic Differences that Prohibit Suicidal Behavior Among Blacks and Hispanics

The meaning one assigns to the events of daily life are shaped substantially by one's ethnic group (Forgas, 1979). Minority groups have different norms regarding: (1) the meaning of death and suicidal behavior; (2) the spiritual and environmental consequences for the family and the deceased as a function of the suicide; and (3) the degree of orientation to group and family. Rudestam (1987) reported that whites respond to suicidal behaviors primarily by avoidance of the parties involved, grief, and guilt. Kalish and Reynolds (1976) in their studies of ethnic attitude towards life and death found that blacks and Mexican Americans view suicide as a "crazy" act, a weakness, attention seeking, and an embarrassment to the family. Whites see suicide as a reaction to stress. Moreover, cultural beliefs regarding death and dying may relate to suicidal behavior. Blacks express the wish to live long lives and that pain and suffering are not reasons to die. Mexican Americans accept death as inevitable and there is a fatalistic expectation of violence and death associated with the tradition of machismo. American Indian tradition accepts death as a part of natural life without a concept of heaven or hell. The soul is seen as immortal (Axelson, 1985).

Religious beliefs may mediate suicidal behaviors and construct an ideology of life and death. Formal religion is important for both blacks and Hispanics. Blacks believe God's influence is direct and personal; pain and suffering can be endured because the Lord will provide help (Kalish & Reynolds, 1976). The church and religion become supports during times of crisis.

The teachings of the Roman Catholic faith influence Hispanics' view of life and death. The Catholic church teaches that suicide is a mortal sin and against the Fifth Commandment ("thou shall not kill"). A person who commits suicide probably will not be buried in the church because he or she has brought disgrace upon the family (Kalish & Reynolds, 1976). Religious Hispanic adolescents think suicide is contrary to church teachings and an evil act (Domino, 1981). For American Indians religion is an integral part of culture and promotes a philosophy of life that assumes all things are living (Axelson, 1985). A belief in the immortality of the soul provides no stigmatization of death. However, variability of suicide from tribe to tribe and the concomitant high alcohol abuse associated with completed suicides suggests that high suicide rates must be analyzed within a tribal context.

Are there ways that the family might insulate against suicide in black and Hispanic youth? black families have an extended family structure. Parents, aunts, uncles, grandparents, cousins, and siblings are counted on for support, financial aid, and help in crises. Because blacks believe problems should stay within the family network, family members, in addition to ministers in very religious families, are more likely to be sought out for help than professionals. The Hispanic family is tightly knit, extended, and male-dominated (Diaz-Guerrero, 1967). Family honor is stressed so that it is important to solve problems within the family and to avoid disclosing to outsiders. The extended family becomes a source of emotional and financial support. The collective sense of group responsibility and kinship in these families can serve as a buffer for suicidal behaviors in both black and Hispanic youth. Thus the social norms of each ethnic group serve to disinhibit suicide among American Indians and inhibit suicide among blacks and Hispanics.

Sociocultural Considerations and Treatment Issues

A minority adolescent's cultural values and norms guide behavior in interaction with peers, family, strangers, and those within and outside their own ethnic group. Not only will symptoms be expressed differently across cultural groups, but also the nature of the interaction between therapist and youth will vary as will the requirements for specific types of therapy. The assessment of depression and suicidal feelings and the establishment of a therapeutic relationship requires culturally specific knowledge.

Depression

A diagnosis of depression represents a major risk factor in the completion of teenage suicide (Neiger & Hopkins, 1988). Depression can be exhibited as low self-esteem, self-blame, self-criticism, and self-dislike. Cultural differences in the expression of depression exist. For example, instead of complaining of dysphoric mood, black adolescents might discuss multiple somatic complaints (Axelson, 1985; Adebimpe, 1982). American Indian youth can exhibit a reluctance to discuss depressive feelings since verbal expressions of feelings are not emphasized (Long, 1986). Feelings of depression can be expressed as anger, agitation, anxiety, hostility, or rage (Aguilera & Messick, 1978).

Communication Patterns

The therapist must discover why the adolescent is distressed, their motives for attempting suicide, and what is necessary to alleviate suicidal feelings. Decoding the minority adolescent's verbal and nonverbal communication patterns requires an understanding of culturally specific ways in which feelings are expressed. American Indian youth are taught that respect for one's elders is shown by diverting his or her gaze down when speaking or being spoken to and by never questioning adult authority (Richardson, 1981). Since silence is valued and verbal expressions of feelings are not emphasized, visual and nonverbal communication (such as in drawings) could be used to encourage expressiveness (Long, 1986).

Hispanic adolescents require the therapist to express friendliness and encouragement before they discuss problems (Acosta, Yamamota, Evans, & Skilbeck, 1983). They may avert their eyes as a sign of respect when being spoken to. Language barriers can block effective communication. An assessment should be made as to whether or not a bilingual therapist is needed. Adolescents may feel more comfortable in expressing suicidal thoughts and feelings if they are assigned a therapist of the same sex.

As with Hispanic adolescents, black youth can be reluctant to discuss personal problems and family relationships with outsiders. They can be verbal but not reveal personal problems (Axelson, 1985). Humor is important (Gibbs, 1988) and the ability to laugh at oneself or one's family is seen as a coping skill and should not be discouraged by therapists who may feel that jokes and lighthearted self-mockery are manifestations of denial or aggression turned inwards. Body language is used to communicate in specific ways. When black adolescents are talking they tend to look directly at the person to whom they are speaking. When listening, they tend to divert their gaze away from the person. There is also less physical distance when talking to people than is true for whites. For the black adolescent, distance may be interpreted as a lack of trust and therapeutic interest.

Establishing a Constructive Relationship

Establishing a constructive, therapeutic relationship is important. The need for help following a suicide attempt can be viewed as particularly threatening for black adolescents because they hold the cultural attitude that suicidal persons are mentally ill and mental health services are to be avoided. Hispanics and American Indians also avoid mental health services because of feelings that the services are culturally insensitive. Black and Hispanic youth have an expectation that their suicidal problems will be solved quickly. The relationship is strengthened by the therapist's understanding of these factors and the importance of explaining therapeutic goals.

Alcohol and Drug Abuse

Therapists need to assess the use of alcohol and drug abuse in suicidal attempts (Rotheram, 1987; Rotheram-Borus, 1989). An assessment is needed of peer group norms regarding consumption and types of alcohol and/or drug usage. Drugs can be used to self-medicate the adolescent against emotional pain. In small dosages alcohol and drugs can elevate mood so that depressive symptoms are masked (Adebimpe, 1982). High alcoholism rates among American Indians and drug usage among all minority youth become important assessment factors in examining their risk taking and suicidal behaviors.

Summary

This paper has focused on the serious problem of suicide among minority youth. While suicide rates for all youth have increased over the last 20 years, minority youth exhibit differing rates of suicide among ethnic groups. Americans Indians have the highest rates, with substantial variations across tribes, while black and Hispanic youth have lower rates. Reasons for these differences are not clear and various hypotheses for these differences were discussed. These hypotheses ranged from methods of data reporting that might underestimate Hispanic and black youths' rates of suicide, to cultural patterns in the expressions of stress, followed by ethnic norms and behaviors that might prohibit suicidal behaviors within cultural groups.

Treatment issues were discussed within a sociocultural framework. The focus was to examine the suicidal youth and his or her family in relation to cultural differences in the expression of depression, communication patterns, and the establishment of a treatment relationship. Better understanding of suicidal behaviors in minority youth and more effective therapeutic interventions should follow from research that acknowledges and clarifies the interaction of culture and behavior.

References

Acosta, F., Yamamoto, J., Evans, L., & Skilbeck, W. M. (1983). Preparing low-income Hispanic black, and white patients for psychotherapy: Evaluation of a new orientation program. *Journal of Consulting Clinical Psychology, 39,* 872-877.

Adebimpe, V. (1982). Psychiatric symptoms in black patients. In S. Turner & T. Jones (Eds.), *Behavior modification in black populations* (pp. 57-71). New York: Plenum.

Aquilera, D. C., & Messick, J. M. (1978). *Crisis intervention: Theory and methodology.* St. Louis: C. V. Mosby.

Axelson, J. A. (1985). *Counseling and development in a multicultural society.* Monterey, CA: Brooks/Cole.

Berlin, I. N. (1984). *Suicide among American Indian adolescents.* Available from the National Indian Law Library, 1506 Broadway, Boulder, CO 80302.

Bowman, P. J., & Howard, C. (1985). Race-related socialization, motivation and academic achievement: A study of black youths in three-generational families. *Journal of the American Academy of Child Psychiatry, 24,* 134-141.

Child, I. L. (1943). *Italian or American: The second generation in conflict.* New Haven, CT: Yale University Press.

Current population reports (1987). *Money, income and poverty status of families and persons. (Advanced data from the March 1987 current population series.* (P-60 No. 157). Washington, DC: U.S. Government Printing Office.

Diaz-Guerrero, R. (1967). The active and passive syndrome. *Revista Interamericana, 1,* 263-272.

Domino, G. (1981). Attitudes toward suicide among Mexican American and Anglo youth. *Hispanic Journal of Behavioral Sciences, 3,* 353-395.

Erikson, E. H. (1968). *Identity youth and crisis.* New York: Norton.

Escovar, P., & Lazarus, P. (1982). Cross-cultural child rearing practices: Implications for school psychologists. *School Psychology International, 3,* 143-148.

Forgas, J. (1979). *Social Episodes.* New York: Academic Press.

Frederick, C. J. (1984). Suicide in young minority group persons. In H. S. Sudak, A. B. Ford, & N. B. Rushforth (Eds.), *Suicide in the young* (pp. 31-43). London: John Wright-PSG.

Gibbs, J. T. (1988). Conceptual, methodological and sociocultural issues in black youth surveyed: Implications for assessment and early intervention. *Suicide & Life-Threatening Behavior, 18,* 73-89.

Goodman, M. E. (1964). *Race awareness in young children.* New York: Collier.

Gould, M., Wallenstein, S., & Davidson, L. (1989). Suicide clusters: A critical review. *Suicide and Life Threatening Behavior, 19,* 17-29.

Hendin, H. (1987). Youth suicide: A psychosocial perspective. *Suicide & Life-Threatening Behavior, 17*(2), 151-165.

Hochkirchen, B., & Jilek, W. (1985). Psychosocial dimensions of suicide and parasuicide in American Indians of the Pacific Northwest. *Journal of Operational Psychiatry, 16,* 24-28.

Hope, S. K., & Martin, H. W. (1986). Patterns of suicide among Mexican Americans and Anglos, 1960-1980. *Social Psychiatry, 21,* 83-88.

Kalish, R. A., & Reynolds, D. K. (1976). *Death and ethnicity.* Los Angeles: University of Southern California Press.

King, L. M. (1982). Suicide from a "black reality perspective." In B. Bass, G. Wyatt, & G. Powell (Eds.). *The Afro-American family: Assessment, treatment and research issues* (pp. 212-234). New York: Grune & Stratton.

Lewin, K. (1948). Self-hatred in Jews. In K. Lewin (Ed.), *Resolving social conflict.* New York: Harper & Row.

Lewis, S. A., Johnson, J., Cohen, P., Garcia, M., & Velez, C. N. (1988). Attempted suicide in youth: Its relationship to school achievement, educational goals, and socioeconomic status. *Journal of Abnormal Child Psychology, 16,* 459-471.

Long, K. A. (1986). Suicide intervention and prevention with Indian adolescent populations. *Issues in Mental Health Nursing, 8,* 247-253.

Manson, S. (1987). American Indians and Alaska natives. In P. Muehrer (Ed.), *Research perspectives on depression and suicide in minorities: Proceedings of a workshop sponsored by the National Institutes of Mental Health* (pp. 59-62). Bethesda, MD: U.S. Department of Health and Human Services.

Manson, S. M., & Trimble, J. E. (1982). American Indian and Alaska Native communities. In S. M. Manson (Ed.), *New direction in prevention among American Indian and Alaska native communities.* Portland, OR: Oregon Health Sciences University.

May, P. A., & Dizmang, L. H. (1974). Suicide and the American Indian. *Psychiatric Annals, 4,* 22-28.

McIntosh, J. L. (1983-1984). Suicide among Native Americans: Further tribal data and considerations. *Omega, 14*(3), 215-229.

Moore, T. (1982). Blacks: Rethinking service. In L. R. Snowden (Ed.), *Reaching the underserved* (Chap. 8). Beverly Hills, CA: Sage.

Mussen, P. (1953). Differences between the TAT responses of Negro and white boys. *Journal of Counseling Psychology, 17,* 373-376.

Neiger, B. L., & Hopkins, R. W. (1988). Adolescent suicide: Character traits of high-risk teenagers. *Adolescence, 23,* 469-475.

Paz, O. (1961). *The labyrinth of solitude.* New York: Grove.

Peck, D. (1983-84). Official documentation of the black suicide experience. *Omega, 14,* 21-31.

Powell, G. J. (1983). Coping with adversity: The psychological development of Afro-American children. In G. J. Powell (Ed.), *The psychological development of minority group children* (pp. 49-62). New York: Brunner-Mazel.

Ramirez, M. (1977). Reorganizing and understanding diversity: multiculturalism and Chicano movement in psychology. In J. Martinez (Ed.), *Chicano Psychology* (pp. 343-353). New York: Academic Press.

Ramirez, M., & Castaneda, A. (1974). *Cultural democracy, bicognitive development and education.* New York: Academic Press.

Ramirez, M., & Price-Williams, D. (1974). Cognitive styles of children of three ethnic groups in the United States. *Journal of Cross-Cultural Psychology, 5,* 212-219.

Resnik, H. L. P., & Dizmang, L. H. (1971). Observations on suicidal behavior among American Indians. *American Journal of Psychiatry, 127,* 882-887.

Richardson, E. H. (1981). Cultural and historical perspectives in counseling American Indians. In D. W. Sue (Ed.), *Counseling the culturally different: Theory and practice* (pp. 216-255). New York: John Wiley.

Roberts, R. E. (1987). The epidemiology of depression in minorities. In P. Meuhrer (Ed.), *Research perspectives on depression and suicide in minorities: Proceedings of a workshop sponsored by the National Institutes of Mental Health* (pp. 1-20). Bethesda, MD: U.S. Department of Health and Human Services.

Rotheram, M. J. (1987). Evaluation of imminent danger of suicide in children. *American Journal of Orthopsychiatry, 47*(1), 59-67.

Rotheram, M. J. (1989). Ethnic differences in adolescent's identity, status and associated behavior problems. *Journal of Adolescence, 12*(4), 361-374.

Rotheram, M. J. (in press). Adolescents' reference group choice, self-esteem and adjustment. *Journal of Personality and Social Psychology.*

Rotheram, M. J., & Phinney, J. S. (1987). Ethnic behavior patterns as an aspect of identity. In J. S. Phinney & M. J. Rotheram (Eds.), *Children's ethnic socialization: Pluralism and development* (pp. 201-218). London: Sage.

Rotheram-Borus, M. J. (1989). Evaluation of suicide risk among youth in community settings. *Suicide and Life Threatening Behaviors, 19*(1), 108-119.

Rudestam, K. F. (1987). Public perceptions of suicide services. In E. Dunne, J. McIntosh, & K. Dunne-Maxim, *Suicide and its aftermath* (pp. 31-45). New York: Norton.

Ryan, W. (1981). *Blaming the victims.* New York: Pantheon.

Shore, J. A. (1974). Psychiatric problems among American Indians. *Psychiatric Annals, 4,* 56-63.

Smith, J. C., Mercy, J. A., & Warren, C. W. (1985). Comparison of suicides among Anglos and Hispanics in jail southwestern states. *Suicide and Life-Threatening Behavior, 15,* 14-26.

Spaulding, J. M. (1985-1986). Recent suicide rates among ten Ojibwa bands of northwestern Ontario. *Omega, 16,* 347-353.

Spencer, M., Brookins, J., & Allen, W. R. (1985). *Beginnings: Social and affective development in black children.* Hillsdale, NJ: Lawrence Erlbaum.

Stevenson, H. W., & Stewart, E. C. (1958). A developmental study of racial awareness in young children. *Child Development, 29,* 399-409.

Stonequist, E. V. (1935). The problem of a marginal man. *American Journal of Sociology, 41,* 1-12.

Stonequist, E. V. (1964). The marginal man: A study in personal and cultural conflict. In E. Burgess & D. J. Bogue (Eds.), *Contributions to urban sociology* (pp. 35-48). Chicago: University of Chicago Press.

U.S. Department of Education (1985). *Seventh annual report to the Congress on the implementation of the Education of the Handicapped Act.* Washington, DC: U.S. Government Printing Office.

U.S. Department of Health and Human Services (1985). *Vital Statistics of the U.S.: Vol. II. Mortality.* Washington, DC: U.S. Government Printing Office.

U.S. Department of Health and Human Services (1986). *Report of secretary's task force on black and minority mental health: Vol. V. Homicide, suicide, and unintentional injuries.* Washington, DC: U.S. Government Printing Office.

Whitlock, G. (1978). *Understanding and coping with real life crises.* Belmont, CA: Wadsworth.

Yates, A. (1987). Current status and future directions of research on the American Indian child. *American Journal of Psychiatry, 144,* 1135-1142.

Young, T. J. (1988). Substance use and abuse among Native Americans. *Clinical Psychology Review, 8,* 125-138.

17

Suicide Among Black Adolescents and Young Adults: A Rising Problem

ESSIE MANUEL RUTLEDGE

Black suicide is a youth phenomenon, whereas among whites it is an older adult phenomenon. The suicide rate for black youth between the ages of 15-24 has more than doubled over the past 25 years, with most of the increase occurring within the 20-24 age group. Even though this precipitous increase arouses concern, the rate, relative to that of white youth, has remained rather stable and predictable. However, this is contrary to the prevailing belief that the suicide rate of black youth is converging on the white youth rate. In fact, the black youth rate seems to be leveling off (Gibbs, 1988). Then, why is there a concern about the black youth suicide rate when it is so much lower than the rate of white youth?

One immediate response to the question is that a concern for black suicide need not be justified relative to the white suicide rate. Second, the former must be considered in light of its impact on the black population. Suicide is the third leading cause of mortality in the 15-24 age group, and it has a disproportionate impact on the black population because it is a youthful population with a median age of 25.8 years. Furthermore, the total nonwhite population in the 18-24 age group is expected to increase to about 30% of the total

339

population in the year 2000 (Gibbs, 1988). If this prediction comes true, and if the suicide rate continues to increase at the present rate, it will significantly affect the black community and society at large. Davis (1979) states that because of the suicide rate the:

> Black community is being robbed of 30 to 40 years of useful manpower, earned wages, sources of reproduction, and a host of other contributions that young people make to society (p. 134).

Although the suicide rate for black youth has not yet reached an alarming level, its suggested impact is alarming. Furthermore, when the rate is considered together with other life-threatening behavior, it merits concern and examination. This is the same age group (15-24) that is victim of other forms of the new morbidity: life-threatening diseases or disabilities that are caused primarily by social rather than biological factors. Hence, black youth and especially black males are at serious risk because of the new morbidity, which includes suicide.

The purpose of this paper is to examine the suicidal trends of black youth age 15-24 and to provide explanations for various factors associated with suicide. The latter focuses mainly on macrosociological research with some attention to microsociology. Macrosociological research is the main choice of analysis because the data examined are aggregate trend data, and the focus is on those characteristics that might increase the probability of suicide within the black youth population. The microsociological research uses the individual as the unit of analysis; therefore, studies o: attempted suicides will be reviewed.

Macrosociological Analysis

Suicide Trends, 1960-1985

To provide a view of the pattern of black youth suicide, aggre gate population data from the United States bureau of the Census Statistical Abstracts (1986) for the period 1960-1985, are examined Table 17.1 presents suicide data by race, sex, and age (15-24). The data clearly show that the suicide rates for black youth are les than for white youth, and for this age group there is no evidence o

TABLE 17.1: Black and White Youth Suicide Rates for 15-24 Year Olds (Per 100,000 population)

15-24 Years	1960	1970	1975	1977	1978	1979	1980	1982	1984
Black Females	1.3	3.8	3.3	3.8	2.7	3.4	2.3	2.2	2.4
Black Males	4.1	10.5	12.9	13.3	13.4	14.4	12.3	11.0	11.2
White Females	2.3	4.2	4.9	5.5	5.0	5.1	4.6	4.5	4.7
White Males	8.6	13.9	19.6	22.9	20.8	21.0	21.4	21.2	22.0

SOURCE: United States Bureau of Census (1986), Statistical Abstracts of United States, 1986. Washington, DC.

a convergence of black and white rates. Moreover, it is obvious that suicide, in addition to being a black youth phenomenon, is a male phenomenon. Since 1960, the black male suicide rate has persisted in being three times greater than that of black females, except in 1970 when this ratio was slightly less. The greatest increase in the overall black rate occurred between 1960 and 1970 when it more than doubled for both females and males.

The suicide rate for black females almost tripled between 1960 and 1970, showing the greatest increase of any year between 1960-1980. Since 1970, the pattern has fluctuated, showing peaks and valleys. Between 1977 and 1978 and between 1979 and 1980, most variations in the suicide rates showed declines. During both periods, there was a 1.1 per 100,000 drop in the black female rate. But it appears that a leveling trend began in 1980, and the rate still was relatively stable in 1984.

For black males, too, the greatest increase in the suicide rate occurred between 1960 and 1970; it more than doubled and continued to rise until 1979, at which time the rate was greater than at any other time between 1960-1984. By 1980 the rate showed a decline of 2.1 per 100,000, the only decline since 1970. Hence, by 1982, it seems that a leveling trend began, showing the lowest rate since 1970, and this trend still was evident in 1984.

Further examination of the suicide data through disaggregation provides additional insight. Table 17.2 shows suicide rates for black females and males age 20-24. When examining these data and those data in Table 17.1, it becomes readily apparent that most of the increase in the overall suicide rate for black youth is ac-

**TABLE 17.2: Black Youth Suicide Rates By Age Sub-Groups
(per 100,000 population)**

Ages	1960	1970	1975	1980	1982	1985
15-19						
Black Females	1.1	2.9	1.5	1.6	1.5	1.5
Black Males	2.9	4.7	6.1	5.6	6.2	8.2
20-24						
Black Females	1.5	4.9	5.2	3.1	2.9	2.4
Black Males	5.8	18.7	21.1	20.0	16.0	18.5

Source: United States Bureau of Census (1986), Statistical Abstract of United States, 1986. Washington, DC.

counted for by the age 20-24 male group. Since 1960, the suicide rate for this group has more than doubled the rate for the 15-19 age group (8.2 versus 18.5). Additionally, in 1982 the suicide rate for the age 20-24 male group exceeds the overall suicide rate for black males in the 15-24 age group (16 versus 11). It is clear that suicide is more prevalent among black male youth than among black female youth. Yet, the pattern is similar to the black male pattern. Just as for black males, the rate for females is greater in the 20-24 age group than in the 15-19 age group. Furthermore, when examining the suicide rates for all years presented in Table 17.2 and those in Table 17.1, we find the difference between male and female suicide rates to be greater in the 20-24 age group than in the 15-19 age group.

Suicide rates for black youth are further exacerbated if we examine the unintentional accidental deaths, the "undetermined" deaths, and deaths from drug overdoses. Unintentional accidents include automobile accidents, drownings, and jumpings from tall buildings. Some of these accidents may be classified as disguised suicides. One researcher has intimated that many drug overdose deaths may be viewed as a form of suicide (Gibbs, 1988). These types of deaths most often lead to under-enumeration of black suicide rates. The factor most responsible for the under-enumeration of black suicide is the method used in committing suicide. Blacks tend to use methods of suicide that are least likely to be classified by medical examiners as "definite" suicides. This proba bly could result from the fact that suicide is a religious taboo in the black community. It is a sinful act. Indefinite suicides include jumpings and "other" methods—stabbings, jumps in front of subways or buses, carbon monoxide poisonings from car exhausts, and drownings. Warshauer and Monk (1978) found that suicide rates for males (age 18-24) increased 19.9% when all suicides were considered rather than only the "definite" suicides. For females of the same age group the increase was 96.4%. The corresponding rates were from 17.1% to 20.5% and 2.8% to 5.5% respectively. If the "unqualified" or indefinite suicides were combined with the definite suicides, it is believed that the black youth suicide rates would be much higher.

Sociocultural Variables Related to Suicide

Economic Status

Since suicide rates are aggregate population statistics, explanatory factors that are at the macro-level of analysis must be examined. This entails a review of such plausible explanations as economic stress, including unemployment and underemployment, and stress associated with urbanization, status integration, fatalistic suicide, and religiosity factors that impact the black population. The emphasis here is not on variables associated with suicide of the individual actor, but on factors that affect the black population as a whole—especially those characteristics that might increase the probability of suicide in the group, in this case black youth.

Unemployment has been a persistent problem for black youth. The unemployment rate in the 1970s and 1980s increased at a faster rate than ever before. It peaked in mid-1984 when it was 42.2%, the highest among all groups in the workforce (Pinkney, 1984). Black youth are three times as likely as white youth to be unemployed. Furthermore, a black youth who graduates from high school is more likely to be unemployed than a white youth who drops out of elementary school, and a black college graduate is as likely as a white high school dropout to be unemployed (Gibson, 1986). The pattern of black youth unemployment closely parallels the suicide rate. During the 1970s and 1980s, when the former was rising, a similar pattern prevailed for the latter. In other words, a positive relationship between unemployment and suicide exists.

Underemployment is another form of economic stress closely related to unemployment. It is not joblessness alone that increases the suicide potential. Other factors, such as being overeducated and underpaid for jobs performed, can have the same effect. Although hard data on such underemployment are difficult to find, one promising index has been found to be closely linked to suicide in the United States (Stack, 1987); it is relative cohort size (RCS). RCS is commonly measured as the ratio of young persons to older persons. In other words, it is simply a measure of the size of the youth cohort relative to that of the older cohort. This ratio is taken as a stress index for the younger cohort, because as the ratio increases more rigidity appears in the labor market for the young—greater competition for fewer jobs results in deteriorating economic positions, and this becomes associated with increases in suicidal behavior (Stack, 1987). Because there was a steady increase of the RCS between 1954 and 1978 and because the black population is youthful, the RCS helps to explain suicide as a youth phenomenon. On the basis of this index, we expect a deterioration of the economic position of black youth in the marketplace, while the labor market position for middle-aged blacks should improve.

Moreover, the RCS may interact with mass higher education to increase the suicide potential by raising students' aspirations for success (Stack, 1987). This may especially affect black youth whose aspirations often are blocked by racism and discrimination, factors that do not affect white youth. Hence, these conditions could further exacerbate the black youth suicide rate.

Urbanization

Urbanization and its concomitant indicators of urban decadence have disproportionately affected black youth. Many of these youth live in urban areas where they experience the urban stress that is associated with factors such as crime, poverty, and drug abuse. Hence, proponents of urban stress theory postulate that young blacks are overburdened by racism that is expressed in terms of various forms of urban stress. In response to the impact of stress, some young blacks are either socialized into violence or they select it in the form of suicide, including "victim-precipitated" and "revolutionary" suicide. The former is suicide arranged or demanded by the victim, while the latter is suicide motivated by a desire to change the system. Some researchers also include "fatalistic" suicide, which is a response to oppressive authority structures that are legitimized by racist, urban institutions (Davis, 1980). such as the criminal justice system. Some adolescents even perceive their parents as being oppressive.

Urban suicide rates provide support for the possible impact of urban stress on suicide. For example, studies of suicide in New York (Hendin, 1969) and Detroit (Stack, 1982) show the rates for urban youths to be higher than the rates in the general population. Such evidence suggests that stress factors associated with urban life may be a reason for the rate differential. Thus it seems reasonable to conclude that there is a link between youth suicide and urbanization as indicated by various forms of stress. Still other factors are associated with suicide.

Status integration, a suicide theory developed by Gibbs and Martin (1964), provides further understanding of suicide among young blacks, especially those of the middle class. The Civil Rights/Black Liberation Movement of the 1960s and the resultant rapid economic growth of young educated blacks are important factors in what Durkheim referred to as egoistic and anomic suicide. For those young blacks who are upwardly mobile and are moving toward the values and goals of whites, in hope of social acceptance, both types of suicide seem to apply. According to the former, suicide among young middle-class blacks is due to the discrepancy between their belief that they are totally integrated into the mainstream of American society, and the reality that there is a lack of such integration. However, they are forced to attempt to play a part—to act as though they are integrated into the white middle-class status system. Anomic suicide results from a failure of many blacks to adjust to social change. The sudden rise in social mobility of blacks gives rise to problems of adjustment and assimilation (Davis, 1980; Stack, 1987). Adjustment to a new life-style plus barriers to acceptance into middle class white America can lead to internal alienation that ultimately brings about self-destruction in the form of suicide.

The loosening or weakening of communal and family ties may be a consequence of status integration, especially for blacks who are under the illusion of widespread social acceptance and social opportunities. The very ties that traditionally provided a buffer against the impact of personal failures and frustrations no longer are used or available. Subsequently, alienation and anomie set in, and this also increases the likelihood of suicide.

Religiosity

Religiosity is another variable associated with suicide, and the relationship is negative. In cultures where people subscribe to a formal religion, it is generally believed that successful suicide is low, whereas it is higher when there is no formal religion (Bankston, Allen, & Cunningham, 1983; Hoelter, 1979; McAnarney, 1979; Stack, 1987). The behavior of black children who grow up where formal religious beliefs are taught may reflect the guidelines of the religion. Among blacks suicide is taboo. It contradicts religious values and beliefs about sin and forgiveness. Traditional black religion teaches that suicide is the one sin that is not forgiven. It also teaches that heavenly rewards will be given for earthly sufferings. Thus suicide is proscriptive behavior even for those not active in religious activities. Moreover, black religion is a source of social integration. However, when it fails to serve this function, negative consequences may follow.

When children reared in religious households become adolescents, they may choose to depart from their families' traditional beliefs and often are in transition between their own and their families' belief systems. Consequently, in times of stress these youth may find themselves isolated and without significant others who understand their dilemmas. This renders them vulnerable to isolation from caring persons, increasing their potential for suicide. Groups in transition experience more successful suicides than stable groups. Hence, perhaps for adolescents, the transition from a religious system to none is a more important variable than its mere presence or absence (McAnarney, 1979).

Microsociological Analysis

Analysis at this level focuses on the individual as the unit. The purpose is to try to understand what psychosocial factors are related to suicide. Data at the microsociological level are obtained from the interview or "psychological autopsy" (Stack, 1987). Case histories are conducted for committed suicides and interviews are conducted of attempted suicides. For black youths a paucity of research appears in the literature. However, some of the research on white adolescent suicides may provide some insight. There are several reasons to expect this: (1) as previously indicated black suicide is a youth phenomenon; (2) adolescence is a stage of life development that is similar in many ways for all youth; (3) blacks at this age (15-24) have obtained a level of education that most closely mirrors that of whites—possibly resulting in what some observers have suggested as the group most apt to take on aspects of a middle-class lifestyle, including a pattern of internalized aggression, such as suicide (Stack, 1982). Hence, a combination of literature pertaining to black youth suicide as well as some literature on white youth will be reviewed. Several factors considered applicable to the black sociocultural experience and germane to suicidal behavior will be discussed below: alienation, lack of positive identity, drug abuse, and family problems.

Feelings of alienation are stronger among suicidal than nonsuicidal groups (Corder, Shorr, & Corder, 1974; Kirk & Zucker, 1979). Alienation is a pervasive sense of self-estrangement, powerlessness, social isolation, meaningless, and normlessness. Research that tests alienation has shown or suggested that suicidal adolescents and young adults are differentiated by feelings of hopelessness, powerlessness, and social isolation. Because suicidal persons tend to display a lack of investment in their future, they are more likely than nonsuicidal persons to view their future with feelings of hopelessness and depression. These individuals are not able to articulate any future goals or plans. Powerlessness is another form of alienation that is characteristic of the affective state of some black people. For example, black males have greater negative involvement with police and courts than white males, leading to what Breed (1970) refers to as "authority suicide"; this reflects excessive social integration. Suicidal individuals, such as these, are subjected to the demands of both the black and white communities. They feel trapped because they are not able to control their lives. In other words, they have feelings of powerlessness. Still another form of alienation exhibited by those prone to suicide is social isolation. This feeling is likely to be experienced by individuals who wish to be or try to become assimilated into white America. This interest and or effort to assimilate has been suggested as an outcome of the Black Liberation Movement of the 1960s, which was a promise of equal opportunity and a better life for black people. Feelings of isolation are likely to develop in those individuals who try to assimilate to such an extent that they become isolated from the black community, yet they are rejected by the white community. They find themselves in a twilight zone. Put another way, such individuals are characterized by a lesser degree of group cohesiveness. This is most likely to happen to young adults who experience social mobility (Davis, 1980; Kirk & Zucker, 1979). Kirk and Zucker (1979) suggest that suicide attempters have greater alienation, and they lack a sense of positive identity.

A sense of positive identity has been examined in relationship to black consciousness. In other words, the less confusion and uncertainty one has about his or her identity as it related to blackness, the greater the degree of black consciousness. The 1960s was a period when black pride was popularized and germinated to develop a more positive identity. Consciousness of blackness makes one aware of what is and is not possible. Blacks who are not aware of this distinction are likely to be caught up in a marginal position, belonging neither to a black nor a white world. When this happens, individuals characterized by a lesser degree of black consciousness. Then it dovetails with a greater degree of alienation, leading to elevated feelings of isolation.

Another factor related to suicidal behavior is drug abuse, a serious social problem found among adolescents and young adults. The problem has reached "unsurpassed" proportions during the 1980s. Drug abusers are at high risk for suicide, because their rate of suicidal attempts is high and they are likely to be repeaters (Harris, Linn, & Hunter, 1979). Drug abuse has been cited by some researchers as a way to escape from intolerable conditions. When life's problems become too overwhelming, according to Shonfeld, adolescents escape by turning to alcohol, withdrawal, or suicide (cited in Davis, 1980). Adolescents who turn to drugs as a means of escape, often do not realize that drugs provide only temporary relief for their problems or that suicide offers permanent relief for what might have been a temporary problem.

Drugs often are used in suicide attempts. McKenry, Tishler, and Kelley (1983) found that, of 46 adolescents who attempted suicide, 39 used drugs in the attempt. In fact, 43% of the adolescent attempters had serious drug problems. The researchers also found that suicidal adolescents used significantly more drugs than the nonsuicidal ones. Furthermore, the parents of the attempters used significantly more drugs than the parents of the nonsuicidal group; and another finding was that drug abusers who had attempted suicide were much more likely to be depressed than abusers who had not attempted (Harris, Linn, & Hunter, 1979). Given the fact that an increasing number of black adolescents and young adults are drug abusers, especially since the advent of "crack," the prediction is that suicidal behavior will continue to rise among black youth.

Family problems form another category that puts adolescents at risk for suicide attempts. Many of these problems are related to the fact that the traditional nuclear family model is now being challenged in the 20th-century United States and that family ties may be loosening as well. A number of studies have reported a relationship between suicide and broken or disorganized families. For example, several studies have shown that attempted suicides come from broken families, mostly female-headed (Finch & Poznanski, cited in McAnarney, 1979). However, many of these studies are limited by the fact that they were without a control group, making it difficult to determine whether attempted suicide is more prevalent in female-headed families than in intact families.

McAnarney (1979) reported that several changes are taking place in the family that are resulting in the loss of the intact family. Whether this loss is by death, divorce, separation, or the family's changing status, it is an important variable in the lives of some adolescents who commit suicide. However, she suggests that most adolescents who have supportive families will pass through this stage of development without major problems. McAnarney is suggesting that a caring and supportive family is more important than an intact family. Another family problem that may lead to suicidal behavior is parent-child role reversal. This has been noted by Kreider and Motto (1974). The role reversal that they observed occurred in one-parent families, between mothers and a favorite child. The authors also suggest that a similar role reversal pattern could occur in mother-absent families. The role reversal pattern between mother and child occurred when there were significant unresolved and unsatisfied dependency needs that the parent tried to satisfy by interacting with the child. This led to various forms of hostility expressions in different children and in different circumstances.

Summary and Conclusion

This paper has focused on two sociological approaches in analyzing black adolescent and young adult suicide. First, the macrosociological level was applied in examining suicide rates for the 15-24 age group. This included an analysis of census data plus a review of independent variables that are in the macrosociological tradition. The variables reviewed were economic stress, urbanization, status integration, fatalistic suicide, and religiosity. Second, at the microsociological level attempted suicide studies were reviewed in order to examine the variables: alienation, lack of positive identity, drug abuse, and family problems. The variables examined at both levels of analysis have been found to be related to suicide theoretically and/or empirically.

Here suicide was viewed mainly as a social event that is a direct outgrowth of one's personal identity that relates to structural conditions and personal ties. In other words, suicide is a personal act, affected by the social relations and social conditions that help to form one's self-identity. This identity is affected by both intragroup and intergroup pressures.

The data analysis was intended mainly to show the rise in suicide rates among black adolescents and young adults from 1960-1985. This analysis provides some suggestions for future trends in suicide rates; however, these are tenuous. Hence, much more research is needed at both the macro- and micro-levels of analyses. Given the persistent pattern, suicide rates for black youth are likely to continue at a similar level that is relative to the level of white youth suicides. Yet, this does not negate the continual rise nor does it minimize a reason for concern.

A factor that is most likely to impact future suicide rates of black youth is their relational system. The strength of relational ties in the family and community is likely to affect any increase or decrease in future suicide rates. Even with continuing adversities in the larger society, strong relational ties could make a difference. Hence, suicidal intervention may be effective at the relational level.

References

Bankston, W. B., Allen, D., & Cunningham, D. S. (1983). Religion and suicide: A research note on sociology's "One Law." *Social Forces, 62*, 521-526.

Breed, W., (1970). The Negro and fatalistic suicide. *Pacific Sociological Review, 13*, 156-162.

Corder, B. F., Shorr, W., & Corder, R. (1974). A study of social and psychological characteristics of adolescent suicide attempters in an urban, disadvantaged area. *Adolescence, 9*, 1-6.

Davis, R. (1980). Suicide among young blacks: Trends and perspectives, *Phylon, 41*, 223-229.

Davis, R. (1979). Black suicide in the seventies: Current trends. *Suicide and Life-Threatening Behavior, 9*, 131-140.

Gibbs, J. T. (1988). The new morbidity: Homicide, suicide, accidents, and life threatening behaviors. In J. T. Gibbs (Ed.), *Young, black, and male in America: An endangered species* (pp. 258-293). Dover, MA: Auburn House.

Gibbs, J. P., & Martin, W. T. (1964). *Status integration and suicide: A sociological study.* Eugene: University of Oregon.

Gibson, R. C. (1986). Outlook for the black family. In A. Pifer & L. Bronte (Eds.), *Our aging society: Paradox and promise* (pp. 181-197). New York: Norton.

Harris, R., Linn, M., & Hunter, K. (1979). Suicide attempts among drug users, *Suicide and Life-Threatening Behavior, 9*, 25-32.

Hendin, H. (1969). *Black suicide.* New York: Basic Books.

Hoelter, J. W. (1979). Religiosity, fear of death and suicide acceptability. *Suicide and Life-Threatening Behavior, 9*, 163-172.

Kirk, A., & Zucker, R. (1979). Some sociopsychological factors in attempted suicide among urban black males. *Suicide and Life-Threatening Behavior, 9*, 76-86.

Kreider, D. G., & Motto, J. (1974). Parent-child role reversal and suicidal states in adolescence. *Adolescence, 9*, 365-370.

McAnarney, E. (1979). Adolescent and young adult suicide in the United States—a reflection of societal unrest. *Adolescence, 14*, 765-773.

McKenry, P. C., Tishler, C., & Kelley, C. (1983). The role of drugs in adolescent suicide attempts. *Suicide and Life-Threatening Behavior, 13*, 166-175.

Pinkney, A. (1984). *The myth of black progress.* New York: Cambridge University Press.

Stack S. (1982). Suicide in Detroit: 1975: Changes and continuities. *Suicide and Life-Threatening Behaviors, 12*, 67-83.

Stack, S. (1987). The sociological study of suicide: Methodological issues. *Suicide and Life-Threatening Behaviors, 17*, 133-150.

United States Bureau of the Census (1986). Statistical Abstract of the United States. Washington, DC: Author.

Warshauser, M., & Monk, M. (1978). Problems in suicide statistics for whites and blacks. *American Journal of Public Health, 68*, 383-388.

About the Authors

Pallassana R. Balgopal, D.S.W., is Professor of Social Work, Director of the Program for International and Cross-Cultural Social Welfare at the University of Illinois in Urbana-Champaign. He is a social work educator, researcher, and practitioner with over 30 years of teaching, curriculum development, research, consultation, and practice experience in clinical social work. He has published extensively in the areas of ethnic minority issues and social work, social group work, and occupational social work. In addition to numerous articles and book chapters, he has coauthored two books: *Groups in social work: An ecological perspective,* (1983) and *A three dimensional analysis of black leadership* (1978).

Ching-Fu Chang is Associate Professor of Sociology at Chung-Hsing University in Taipei, Taiwan. While obtaining his Ph.D. from the University of Illinois at Chicago, he worked as a Graduate Research Assistant at the Pacific/Asian American Mental Health Research Center. His area of specialization is demography, urban sociology, and research methodology.

John M. Chavez is Assistant Professor in the Department of Psychology, Occidental College. He received his M.A. and Ph.D. from Claremont Graduate School. His research interests include socialization practices and intellectual achievement in children, psychological factors related to immigration by Mexican immigrants, development of ethnic preferences in children, disciplinary practices, attitudes and perceptions of child abuse by Mexican Americans, effects of chronic illness in Mexican American families, and cultural aspects related to Seasonal Affective Disorders.

Larry E. Davis is Associate Professor at the George Warren Brown School of Social Work, Washington University. He served as a VISTA volunteer in New York City from 1969-1972 where he counseled youth in the areas of substance abuse, employment, and education. In 1984 he received a three-year National Institute of Mental Health training grant to prepare minority groupwork practitioners to work with youth. He recently coauthored a book which focuses on the effects of race, gender, and class on helping relationships. Currently he is conducting a research project, funded by the National Science Foundation, on interracial small group interaction and its consequences for black and white members' feelings of comfort and control.

Melvin Delgado is Professor of Social Work at Boston University School of Social Work, Boston, Massachusetts. His research interests focus on Hispanic natural support systems and their potential impact on adolescent substance abuse prevention efforts. He is currently studying what organizational factors influence the use or nonuse of natural support systems in Hispanic communities.

E. Daniel Edwards is Associate Professor, Graduate School of Social Work, University of Utah. He is a member of the Yurok Tribe, Weitchpec, California. He currently serves as Director of the American Indian Social Work Career Training Program and Director of Native American Ethnic Studies at the University of Utah. He is active in local, regional, and national organizations serving American Indian people, and has had experience working for the Bureau of Indian Affairs in Alaska, VISTA, The Western Region Indian Alcoholism Training Center, and foster care programs for Native American children.

Margie Egbert-Edwards is Professor of Social Work, Graduate School of Social Work, University of Utah. She has had experience working with American Indian people with the Bureau of Indian Affairs in Arizona; as director of a graduate social work training program at Intermountain Boarding School, in Brigham City, Utah; and with local and national organizations working with American Indian people. She was the codirector of the University of Utah's American Indian Social Work Career Training Program.

Marilyn Fernandez is Associate Director of Research with the Ounce of Prevention Fund in Chicago, a public/private partnership that focuses on children and families in high risk communities, where she is working on issues related to adolescent pregnancy and childbearing. Her other research interests include Asian American families, youth, and women; business entrepreneurship among Asian Americans; and sociology of Third World development. Publications in the area of Asian American studies include: *Intra-group differences in business participation: Three Asian immigrant groups* (1989), *Asian American households and strategies for family reunification,* (1987), and *Asian Indians in the United States: Economic, educational, and family profile from the 1980 census* (1986).

Edith M. Freeman is Professor at the University of Kansas School of Social Welfare. She teaches classes in clinical practice, community mental health practice, and school social work, and was awarded the Chancellor's Professorship for Excellence in Teaching in 1989. Her research has been in the areas of substance abuse, teenage pregnancy, and other topics related to families, children, and youth. She has published several books and numerous articles on these topics. Her most recent publication is a coauthored book on practice with black families, *Social work practice with black families: A culturally specific approach* (1990).

Jewelle Taylor Gibbs is Associate Professor at the School of Social Welfare at the University of California at Berkeley. She currently is a member of the Advisory Board of the National Center for Children in Poverty and has served on the Task Panel on Special Populations of President Carter's Commission on Mental Health and on the Board of Directors of the American Orthopsychiatric Association. She was the recipient of the 1987 McCormick Award from the American Association of Suicidology for her scholarly contributions to the study of minority suicide. She is the editor of *Young,* *black and male in America: An endangered species* (1988) and the coauthor of *Children of color: Psychological interventions with minority youth* (1989). She has also published numerous articles and chapters on the psychosocial problems of adolescents and minority mental health issues.

Nora S. Gustavsson is Assistant Professor at the School of Social Work, University of Illinois at Urbana. She received her M.S.W. from Hunter College, New York and her Ph.D. from the University of Southern California. Her areas of research include analyzing and developing services and policies for children, youth, and families with an emphasis on groups historically excluded from full participation in American society. She has an extensive background in providing direct services for at-risk populations.

Algea Harrison received her Ph.D. from the University of Michigan and is Professor of Psychology at Oakland University, Michigan. She has served as Visiting Professor of Psychology at the University of the Virgin Islands, University of California Los Angeles, and University of Zimbabwe. Her published papers and book chapters are concentrated on issues related to the development and socialization of African American women. She has served as reviewer for psychology journals, professional conferences, and governmental funding agencies. Her current research interest focuses on cross-cultural investigations of the development of interdependency and intradependency.

Amy Kohn is Director of Clinical Programs at Hawthorne Cedar Knolls Residential Treatment Center. She has worked in a variety of settings with adolescents for the past 12 years. Her doctoral dissertation research explored the mother-daughter relationship of pregnant teenagers. Her work was part of a larger study on the social networks of pregnant adolescents.

Sandra Y. Lewis holds a Psy.D. in Clinical Psychology from Rutgers University, Graduate School of Applied and Professional Psychology. She is in private practice and employed as a psychologist at the University of Medicine and Dentistry of New Jersey, Community Mental Health Center at Newark on the Child and Adolescent Unit of the Department of Psychiatry. She works predominantly with black children, adolescents, and their families in an inner-city setting. She services multiproblem families and is codeveloper of a parenting education and coping skills program for teen parents. Her interests include ethnic minority issues, program development and evaluation, and uses of metaphor in psychotherapy.

William T. Liu received his Ph.D. from Florida State University in Sociology, and completed his postdoctoral work at the University of Chicago and Yale University. His early work includes studies of families and teenagers in southeast Asia, and of kinship and fertility in the Philippines. For the past 15 years, his work has focused on mental health of Asian Americans and old age in China. He has taught at the University of Notre Dame and is currently Professor of Sociology and Director of the Pacific/Asian Research Center, University of Illinois at Chicago. He has published eight books and more than 100 papers and chapters in books.

Bruce T. Lochner is a doctoral candidate in Counseling Psychology at Texas Tech University. He completed his BA in Psychology at California State University, Long Beach, and he received his MA in Psychology at California State University, Los Angeles.

William Marsiglio is Assistant Professor of Sociology at the University of Florida. His theory and research interests include sexuality, fertility, parenthood, and primary relationship issues. He is specifically interested in males' relationship to the various aspects of the reproductive realm. His recent publications and current research plans address adolescent males' commitment to the social role of father and various aspects of adult fathers' relationships with their minor children. His articles have appeared in *Journal of Marriage and the Family, Family Planning Perspectives, Journal of Sex Research,* and *Journal of Adolescent Research.*

Brenda G. McGowan is Professor of Social Work at Columbia University where she teaches courses on clinical social work practice and family and children's services. She is the author or coauthor of four books as well as a number of articles related to practice and policy issues in the delivery of services for families and children at risk. Her most recent research involved an examination of "successful" community-based service programs in New York City. Earlier in her career, she spent six years working with teenage parents in Boston.

Rodolfo Murphy is a doctoral candidate in Social Psychology at the University of Florida. A native of Puerto Rico, he holds a MA in Psychology from California State University, Los Angeles, and received his BA in Psychology from Ohio State University.

Ura Jean Oyemade is Associate Professor of Human Development at Howard University in Washington, DC. Specializing in family and environmental factors relating to child development, she has conducted several major research projects including the Family Coping Styles and Adolescent Behavior Project, Head Start Parent Involvement, and Psychosocial Factors and the Outcome of Pregnancy. She is author of over 20 publications including a book on Project Head Start and the forthcoming proceedings of the conference, "Ecology of substance abuse: Toward primary prevention."

Jean S. Phinney is Professor of Psychology and Child Development at California State University, Los Angeles. She received her BA from Wellesley College and her Ph.D. from the University of California, Los Angeles. Her research focuses on the impact of ethnicity on development. Her publications include an edited volume, *Children's ethnic socialization*, and a major review of ethnic identity in adolescents and adults in *Psychological Bulletin*. She has published a number of empirical articles on ethnic identity and has received grant support from the National Institute of Mental Health.

Orlando Rodriguez is Professor of Sociology at Fordham University, Bronx, New York, and as of December 1990, Director of Fordham's Hispanic Research Center. He has participated in basic and applied research projects on the criminal justice experiences of minority inner-city youth, and on mental health issues relevant to Hispanic populations. Among his recent publications are *Hispanics and homicide in New York City, Hispanic mental health: A framework for research,* and *Hispanics and human services: Help-seeking in the inner city.*

Collette F. Roney received her BA degree in Psychology from Occidental College in 1989. Her research interests include cross-cultural studies of disciplinary practices, attitudes and perceptions of child abuse among Mexican Americans, and mental health problems affecting Mexican American adolescents as well as other multicultural issues. She is employed by Northern Virginia Family Service as the editor of a newsletter for low-income and refugee families.

Mary Jane Rotheram-Borus is Associate Professor of Clinical Psychology, Division of Child Psychiatry, Columbia University, College of Physicians and Surgeons, and Research Scientist at the New York State Psychiatric Institute. Her work has focused on adolescents who have engaged in multiple high risk, life-threatening behaviors. Over the past four years, she has monitored suicidal behaviors and high risk unprotected sex and drug use behaviors among youths in runaway shelters in New York City. She conducted a suicide and an AIDS intervention program to enhance staff's ability to evaluate and to reduce the incidence of these behaviors.

Essie Manuel Rutledge is Professor of Sociology, Western Illinois University and former Chair of the Department of Afro-American Studies. She received her Ph.D. from the University of Michigan and a certificate of aging from North Texas State University. She has conducted research in the areas of aging, quality of life, socialization/aspirations, marital and family relations, and race relations. She has published articles in books and journals on such topics as black women, black families, issues on gender and race, institutional racism, role knowledge, and socialization/aspirations.

John H. Scanzoni is Professor of Sociology at the University of Florida. His current theory and research interests focus on changes in patterns of relationships between women and men, including changes in sexual and economic behaviors--in both legal and non-legal settings. Past research has focused on such topics as gender issues, conflict and decision-making processes, women's labor force behaviors, fertility control, and public policies for families and primary relationships. He recently authored *The sexual bond:*

Rethinking families and close relationships with colleagues Karen Polonko, Jay Teachman, and Linda Thompson.

Arlene Rubin Stiffman is Assistant Professor at the George Warren Brown School of Social Work, Washington University. She has conducted programs for children of mentally ill parents, runaway youths, and youths at risk for suicide, drug abuse, and teen pregnancy. Her recent publications concern child abuse, runaway youths, teen pregnancy and parenting, suicide, and substance abuse. She has edited books on adolescent mental health issues; treatment methods; depression and suicide; and sexual behavior, pregnancy, and parenting. Currently she is conducting a national study, funded by the National Institute of Mental Health, on the effect of the AIDS epidemic on the risk behaviors of adolescents and young adults.

Cheryl L. Thompson is Assistant Professor of Child Clinical Psychology at Seton Hall University in South Orange, New Jersey. She is a graduate of the Adelphi University doctoral (Clinical Psychology) and postdoctoral (Psychotherapy and Psychoanalysis) programs. She has a long-standing interest in minority issues and a personal commitment to the articulation of these issues. She has been interested throughout her professional life in forensic assessment of antisocial adolescents.

Valora Washington is Professor of Education and Vice President at Antioch College in Yellow Springs, Ohio. With work focusing on issues of social policy and human diversity, she is the author of four books and over 40 journal articles. She and her colleague Ura Jean Oyemade have collaborated on several Head Start projects including research on parent involvement and drug abuse prevention.

Karen F. Wyche is Visiting Professor in Afro-American Studies at Brown University. She received her M.S.W. from the University of Maryland School of Social Work and her Ph.D. from the University of Missouri--Columbia in Clinical Psychology. Previously she taught at Hunter College, New York City and Stephen's College. Her research interests center on children's understandings of race, ethnicity, and gender, and mental health problems of minority populations.

Elena S. H. Yu is Professor of Epidemiology in the Graduate School of Public Health at San Diego State University, California. With the assistance of William T. Liu and Ching-Fu Chang, she contributed two chapters to Margaret Heckler's *Report of the Secretary's task force on black and minority health*, a landmark government publication documenting the paucity of accurate health data on nonwhite populations in the United States. Her area of specialty is ethnicity and health. She is currently doing research on aging and Alzheimer's disease across cultures.

Luis H. Zayas is Psychosocial Faculty Member of the Residency Program in Social Medicine, Department of Family Medicine, Montefiore Medical Center, the Bronx, New York. He is also on the faculty of psychiatry at the Albert Einstein College of Medicine and the faculty of psychology of Fordham University. He holds a MA in social work and a Ph.D. in psychology from Columbia University. Trained in psychoanalysis, his professional interests include child and adolescent development, adolescent and family therapy, and Hispanic family mental health.